THE GREEN CABINET

Pastoral Scene; an illustration to Virgil's *Georgics* III. Codex Romanus Vat. 3867, 5th century AD.

Photo: Courtesy Biblioteca Apostolica Vaticana

THE GREEN CABINET

Theocritus and the
European Pastoral Lyric

THOMAS G. ROSENMEYER

UNIVERSITY OF CALIFORNIA PRESS
Berkeley and Los Angeles, 1969

UNIVERSITY OF CALIFORNIA PRESS
BERKELEY AND LOS ANGELES, CALIFORNIA
UNIVERSITY OF CALIFORNIA PRESS, LTD.
LONDON, ENGLAND

COPYRIGHT © 1969, BY THE REGENTS OF THE UNIVERSITY OF CALIFORNIA
STANDARD BOOK NUMBER: 520-01381-6
LIBRARY OF CONGRESS CATALOG CARD NUMBER: 72-82376
PRINTED IN THE UNITED STATES OF AMERICA

For
Sophie Bennett, George Salomon, and Stanhope Joel
a token

Preface

The title of this book is a misnomer. Theocritus does not, as a rule, call his pleasance green, nor does he think of it as an enclosure. But "green cabinet" caught my eye when I read it in Spenser's "December," as "*vert cabinet*" had caught Spenser's eye when he found it in Marot's "Eglogue au Roy." It is the sort of phrase which is at home on a title page. And, with a bit of squeezing, it can be made to fit the *locus amoenus* of Greek pastoral poetry. In Spenser, as in Marot, the green cabinet is the habitat of Pan, to whom Colinet addresses his "rurall song." Theocritus, too, puts Pan in the center of his bucolic landscape; and the clarity with which the landscape is articulated suggests the limited confines of an interior.

The object of the study is twofold: to say something about the special qualities of Theocritus' pastoral poetry; and to find out to what extent these qualities are characteristic of the whole genre. There is something chimerical about discussing a genre rather than individual poems. Some will object that the book does not contain more analyses of Theocritean or Virgilian texts. The reply must be that the reading of a particular poem becomes more convincing once the tradition into which the critics fit it is better understood. The case of Theocritus is a warning example; working in a critical vacuum has produced few satisfactory interpretations. Hence I thought it more important, at this point, to ask a number of old-fashioned questions about the pastoral lyric as a whole, and to present some ideas about probabilities and expectations rather than about the finished products. Again, it may be felt that my account of the matter, with its conceptual pigeonholes, is too schematic, and that a more loose-jointed engagement would have been preferable. I would answer that the relative neglect of Theocritus has created a need for an orderly, systematic discussion, even if it means that some of the less tractable subtleties will not be captured this time around. I am fully aware of the disproportion between the lumbering logistics of the attack and the slender substance of much of the poetry, especially the Theocritean corpus. My hope is that if there is some gain in what I propose, the means whereby the gain was procured will soon be put out of mind.

Discussions of pastoral poetry that mention Theocritus usually cast him in the role of the founder, and that means the beginner. European pastoral is indebted to Virgil rather than to Theocritus; consequently, it is felt, there is no need to say much about the latter, except to suggest that he did things simply which later were done better, or at least more artfully. For a corrective, I suggest that we look on Theocritus as if he were a fellow worker, not a source. I shall argue that the issues and stimuli to which he responds are not so very different from those experienced by Milton or Spenser or Sannazaro, but that he responds in his own remarkably consistent way, and that his solutions deserve to be considered on a par with the seemingly more intricate solutions of the later pastoralists. In this I am not abjuring the historical perspective; it is impossible to make sense of Theocritus unless one pays some attention to the social and intellectual milieu that conditioned him. I do propose, however, to pass over the whole area of transmission and influence. Even if it can be shown securely that one poet learned from another this seems to me, at the present juncture, less crucial than the question how the two poets, given certain generic expectations, resolve their difficulties, and whose solution is the more attractive.

The book is divided into twelve chapters. The first is introductory, and touches briefly on points which will be developed at greater length in the subsequent discussion. Chapters Two and Eleven contain a large admixture of philological matters; in speculations about the origins of the genre, and the history of the concepts of Arcadia and Pan, it was impossible to avoid a thickening of texture. I console myself with the thought that Theocritus would not have objected to some degree of diversity. The order of topics which I have adopted makes for a number of duplications and overlaps. The animal simile, for instance, makes its appearance in Chapters Six and Twelve; the giving of seasonal gifts is taken up in Chapters Four and Seven. For the sake of completeness under each heading, I decided not to expunge such overlaps, though as a rule the full discussion is reserved for one slot only. Duplication crops up also in the snatches of poetry used for illustration. Repeatedly I refer to the same authors—besides Theocritus, chiefly Virgil, Milton, Sidney, Spenser, Drayton— and use the same texts to argue or exemplify a position. This is due not only to the severe limitations of my reading, but also to the fact that I have found some documents more useful than others in demonstrating what I consider to be important. Drayton, in particular, turned out to be the sort of poet whose genial and lucid exercises in the tradition made him eminently quotable for my purposes.

The magnitude of my debt to the great critics is obvious from the notes. At this point I should like to express my gratitude for how much I have learned from the writings of A. S. F. Gow, T. P. Harrison, J. A. Congleton, Mia I. Gerhardt, and Alice Hulubei. If it were not for their Herculean labors, my own small efforts at mopping up would have been unthinkable. The same is true of others, and especially of three critics whom I cite, more often than not only to register disagreement. Richard Reitzenstein, Renato Poggioli, and William Empson do not need my support; my departures from their positions are offered with all the respect that becomes a beneficiary of their lessons. I have learned much from Viktor Poeschl, who shared his knowledge and his good taste with me in conversations in Seattle and Heidelberg. I am further indebted to a number of friends, and students, in Seattle, Athens, and Berkeley, who patiently permitted me to try out some of my ideas on them; to Kendrick Pritchett and Alain Renoir for assistance beyond the call of friendship; to Charles Segal, Paul Alpers, and Philip Damon, who read the manuscript and suggested valuable changes; and to August Frugé and Martha Weir of the University of California Press, who did their prodding gently, and further improved the manuscript. For the errors and infelicities that remain I am, alas, responsible. Gilbert Lawall's *Theocritus' Coan Pastorals* (Boston 1967) came out after the bulk of my study was written. I recommend the book heartily. But its critical principles are entirely different from those employed in my book; I thought it better not to to enter into an argument with it.

Two fellowships, from the John Simon Guggenheim Memorial Foundation and from the University of California Humanities Research Committee, enabled me to take time out in the academic year 1967/68 to get the book written. I am deeply grateful for the help and the honor.

A few technicalities. The poems of Theocritus are cited by the edition of A. S. F. Gow (Oxford 1952). In the matter of authenticity, I generally fall back on the scholarly consensus; but I incline to the view that *Idyll* 8 is genuine, 9 is spurious, and 20 is so low in quality and significance as to make the question of authenticity unimportant. *Idyll*, capitalized and italicized, always designates a poem in the Theocritean corpus. The translations are my own unless stated to be otherwise. They are supposed to reproduce the sense and, if possible, the shape and feeling of the original. Hence they are not necessarily literal. But there is no attempt to make them into good poetry, or to conform to a particular theory of translation.

The dedication is to two men and a woman who, many years ago, went out of their way to help.

Contents

THE GREEN CABINET

I
Preliminaries

At the end of the first book of Plato's *Republic*, Socrates confesses to Thrasymachus that there has been something restless and greedy about his search. "For instead of finding out what justice is, I moved on to the next question and the one after that, asking whether justice is good or bad, or whether it is profitable." Discussions of the pastoral lyric often suffer from a similar lack of frugality. We are ready to assume that we are dealing with a pastoral whenever a poem shows an interest in the countryside, no matter whether the subject is cattle or olive groves, highland rocks or greensward; or whether the mood is lyrical or anthropological.[1] Even what I shall call the "Hesiodic" world, the arena of sweat and labor and farmers' almanacs, is often included in the general scope of what is understood by pastoral. The poets themselves, by certain willful or perhaps malicious titlings, have added to the lavishness. Tennyson's "Dora," a ballad in the spare biblical style without a trace of feeling for nature, prompted Wordsworth's admiration: "I have been endeavouring all my life to write a pastoral like your "Dora" and have not succeeded."[2]

It is important to listen to the poets. In all probability a tidy definition of what is pastoral about the pastoral tradition is beyond our reach. The tradition is extraordinarily rich and flexible. And yet, at first glance, definers may take courage from the presence of certain features which have always struck the critics of the genre, and prompted the charge that pastoral cramps originality. Dr. Johnson's notorious snort, "easy, vulgar, and therefore disgusting",[3] derives from his judgment that the genre is inherently imitative. It was, he felt, classical, and had changed little since the days of Theocritus and Virgil. The charge of imitativeness occurred early; Servius, writing in the fourth century AD, warned that any one writing pastorals must take special care that the eclogues do not resemble each other.[4] And a reader of Virgil's *Eclogues* is constantly made aware of Virgil's delight in the act of imitation. In the tenth *Eclogue*, to give a ready example, Gallus contemplates what might have been if he had been a pastoral poet: he would have loved Phyllis, or Amyntas—Amyntas is black, but so are violets and blueberries.[5] The reservation with which Gallus interrupts his reverie is an almost literal borrowing from Theocritus (*Idyll* 10.28). It has no apparent business in Gallus' speech, beyond the pleasure Virgil finds in acknowledging his debt to his predecessor, and in stressing the continuity of the tradition.[6]

Tradition, imitation, continuity of artistic purpose: these were the auspices under which the pastoral lyric was transmitted to the modern world. More than most literary forms its familiar patterns appealed to those who thought of the whole field of literature as compartmentalized, and who drew confidence from what they regarded a natural articulation of its parts. No wonder that Renaissance critics were surprised to find that Aristotle had not included the genre in his discussion. Antonio Sebastiano Minturno, one of their leaders, decided that Aristotle's omission could be accounted for on the assumption that Aristotle considered pastoral a subspecies of epic.[7] Aristotle would, of course, have had to be clairvoyant to include the pastoral in his treatment, seeing that the genre did no come into being until two generations after his death.[8] But even after the advent of Theocritus, Hellenistic and Roman critics appear to have made no room for a separate pastoral genre. Longinus, for instance, compares Homer favorably with Apollonius and Theocritus (*On the Sublime*, chapter 33).When, in speaking of Theocritus, he refers to his *Bucolica*, the term is parallel to the title of Apollonius' poem, *Argonautica*, hence not a genre designation. One is intrigued to note that, once again, Theocritus appears to be thought of as a writer of epic; and this is paralleled in Quintilian (10.1.55), though he describes the *musa rustica et pastoralis* as a special type of epic. We may assume that Proclus and other Byzantine scholars, as well as other medieval critics who failed to recognize a separate pastoral genre, were guided by this ancient classification of Theocritus and Virgil as writers of epic.[9] In imitation of Quintilian, Minturno divided epic verse into *heroici* (*summi*), *epici* (*mediocres*), and *bucolici* (*infimi*), though most of his immediate predecessors, presumably catching fire from the contemporary stirrings which were to lead to Tasso's *Aminta*, designated pastoral a *genus dramaticum*.[10] Another classification, which goes back to the first century AD and Manilius' *Astronomy* (2.39 ff.), counts Theocritus among the didactic poets, along with Homer and Hesiod.[11]

The scholars, it appears, found it rather difficult to identify the special characteristics of pastoral, more difficult, in fact, than Dr. Johnson's gibe would have led us to expect. We shall return to the pastoral as epic, which has much to be said in its favor. When the Renaissance finally came round to the view that pastoral was a genre in its own right, the identification was achieved at an unacceptable cost. The critics proceeded to argue for certain canons of theme, form, and mood which held out little hope for the inclusion of much of Theocritus or Virgil. This is especially true of the narrow definitions offered by J. C. Scaliger, with their stress on decorum and instruction.[12] Such exclusiveness was not destined to last. The quarrel between neo-classicists and the supporters of *le bon sens*—that is, in Britain, the quarrel between the camps of Rapin and Fontenelle—helped to relax the canon.[13]

In our day the pendulum may be said to have swung too

far in the opposite direction. William Empson's conception of the pastoral is so general that it accommodates an ample spectrum of experiences and styles.[14] The same latitude characterizes the treatment of pastoral in the essays of Renato Poggioli, the one modern critic whose pronouncements on the pastoral rival Empson's in influence.[15] The importance of the story of Ahab and Naboth in Poggioli's thinking indicates that he, like Empson, regards social criticism, whether overt or hidden, as an important element in the pastoral convention. Pastoral, on this assumption, is a kind of anatomy (cf. below, Chapter Ten). How uninformative the term "pastoral" has become, perhaps as a reaction to Renaissance constraints, is shown in the *Pastorals* of Graham Hough, a collection of poems which convey, above all, emptiness and horror.[16] A deliberate paradox, a transmogrification of a disavowed past? Verlaine and Stefan George likewise have pastorals which deviate sharply from the norm acknowledged in their own time. Social criticism, the moral thread followed by Empson and Poggioli, is Virgil's own contribution to the genre. His *Fourth Eclogue* has always stood out as an oddity within the collection of rustic scenes. Other idiosyncratic flashes light up the plain. Sannazaro's friend and mentor, Giovanni Pontano, has an eclogue, his sixth, in which a peasant mother tries to get her baby back to sleep. There is talk of ghosts, and bed-wetting, all in fine Latin, but not a trace of "pastoral" color.[17] And Mantuan's tenth *Eclogue*, on a schism in the Order of Carmelites, joins other manifestos of its time in perversely exploring contemporary issues under the cover of grazing sheep and worried swains.

Throughout the history of the genre, therefore, both critics and poets have on occasion permitted themselves a wide margin in their interpretation of what a pastoral is. A definition of the genre and its limits is likely to run counter to much accumulated experience. We are reminded of Coleridge's "Do not let us introduce an Act of Uniformity against poets."[18] Nevertheless it will be useful, if only for the establishing of first guidelines, to tabulate what earlier generations have found fit to include under the heading of the term. We need not indulge in the frenzy of division which mars some of the classifications of the Renaissance, particularly Scaliger's whose categories merrily scramble formal and substantive criteria: Quarrels, Rejoicings, Thanksgivings, Loves, Entreaties, Complaints, Love Songs, Monodies, Vows, Recitals of Happenings, Rustic Festivities, Encomia, Conversations, Dialogues between a Suitor and a Maiden, and so forth.[19] But we must recognize that this divisionary ardor, operating by the principle of "divide and conquer," is a critical response to the feeling that pastoral is full and expansionist.

The French *Eclogues of State*, headed by Ronsard's "Chant Pastoral,"[20] owed their thematic variety to the view that public as well as private matters could be taken up in pastoral form. But along with this pride in diversity went an important caveat. The apparatus, that is, the characters and the setting, were felt to be subject to restriction. Guillaume Colletet, for instance, a seventeenth-century successor of Scaliger, allows goatherds, shepherds, and cowherds; he disallows herders of pigs or horses, hunters, fishermen, laborers, and sailors.[21] The reasons Colletet gives for his exclusions are interesting, and bear on some of the matters which will be discussed in the body of this study. Pigs are dirty; horses are not essential to the economy; hunters are never still enough; fishermen may not talk; and laborers and sailors work too hard. The exclusions are, it appears, based on specific assumptions about the kind of people and activities that best represent the ethos to be associated with the pastoral. These assumptions may of course vary. Pope wishes to exclude Virgil's first *Eclogue* because its herdsmen are ex-soldiers; Chatterton's eclogues give soldiers a prominent place, as does Coleridge's "Fire, Famine, and Slaughter: A War Eclogue."[22] But these, along with the town eclogue (Swift), the native eclogue (Ramsay), and the exotic eclogue (Collins), are virtuoso attempts to conquer new territory. Their authors are conscious of the innovatory character of their undertakings. For our discussion they will prove to be of little use.

Before we continue with our survey of what the history of the pastoral has to offer, it may be appropriate to say something about terms. Each national tradition and each epoch tend to have their own uses. In sixteenth-century France, *églogues* (also called *bucoliques*), poems in the tradition of Theocritus and Virgil, must be distinguished from the more developed types, especially the *pastorale*, which is more or less identical with the *bergerie*. The latter has a larger set of characters, including nymphs and demigods, and makes room for music and dancing, but stops short of scenes and act divisions.[23] Elsewhere the lines are drawn differently, and later the term "eclogue" came to be of much wider significance. Formally, however, the term remained relatively stable; it continued to denote dialogue. The derivation of eclogue from the Greek *aix* (goat) can be traced back to Petrarch; there is some uncertainty about Petrarch's source.[24] Petrarch's conceit influenced the spelling of the French term, though there is no more emphasis on goats in the French *églogues* than there is on cattle in the Greek *boukolika* (from *boukolein*— herd cattle). The truth of the matter is that the terms bucolic, pastoral, eclogue, and others shift about so much that their usefulness as distinguishing labels has become questionable. The only term whose meaning has been narrow and consistent is *pastourelle*, which designates the colloquy of a knight with a peasant girl and her successful rebuttal of his advances. There is a forerunner of this form in the Theocritean corpus (*Idyll* 27) and some of the scenes in Longus' *Daphnis and Chloe* point in the same direction. But on the whole it is agreed that the *pastourelle* is a specifically medieval genre, and should not be linked too closely with the ancient pastoral.[25]

Perhaps the most remarkable deepening undergone by any of the terms is that of idyll. It started out as a completely un-charged word, meaning a specimen or species of poetry. It could be and was used to refer to any brief poem of whatever complexion.[26] But by the end of the eighteenth century, the reflections of Gessner and Herder[27] had promoted the term to high rank. Now the idyll was, in Herder's language, nothing but "the most delicate expression of the most highly refined passions and perceptions of those men who live together in smaller groups."[28] In this study I shall try to avoid using the term idyll, except to designate the poems in the Theocritean corpus, whether pastoral or not. Otherwise I employ it only when I have in mind the whole range of literature, both verse and prose, recommending the virtues of simplicity, strength, and happiness. This includes such diverse achievements as *La Nouvelle Héloise*, *Wilhelm Tell*, and parts of *Paradise Lost*. The pastoral lyric is only a small parish in that larger dominion.

There is another factor complicating matters. In antiquity the pastoral lyric is usually self-sufficient. Later its patterns and its moods become ingredients in other genres, especially drama and romance. Dio Chrysostom's *The Hunters of Euboea*[29] and Longus' *Daphnis and Chloe* provide our earliest hints of the new mixture. The pure pastoral lyric, on the order of Marlowe's "Passionate Shepherd to his Love," is rarely found among the more significant products of the European pastoral tradition. By comparison with the pastoral romance and pastoral drama, not to mention opera, the pastoral lyric is often the preserve of lesser poets, as if a serious poet could not properly concern himself with a type of literature that lacked complexity and weight. To compensate for this lack Thomas Purney, chaplain at Newgate Prison and one of the more interesting eighteenth-century critics of the pastoral, demanded that the pastoral have a plot and a certain length and a moral result. His insistence on what he calls the *implex fable*, corresponding roughly to Aristotle's complex plot, marks the impatience with which intelligent men regarded the slightness and the lack of Aristotelian virtues in the conventional pastoral lyric.[30]

This impatience, which is also at the root of Dr. Johnson's acerbity, has always been particularly pronounced in England. As a result of it, we may speak of two pastoral traditions in English literature. To quote E. K. Chambers:

On the one hand, there is a body of poetry, transparent, sensuous, melodious, dealing with all the fresh and simple elements of life, fond of the picture and the story, rejoicing in love and youth, in the morning and the spring; on the other, a more complex note, a deeper thrill of passion, an affection for the sombre, the obscure, the intricate, alike in rhythm and in thought, a verse frequent with reflections on birth and death, and their philosophies, a humor often cynical or pessimistic. . . . Donne and his fellows write pastorals, but the shepherd's smock sits awkwardly upon them. They twist the bucolic theme and imagery to the expression of alien emotions and alien ideas, . . . the hands are the hands of Esau, but the voice is the voice of Jacob." [31]

Much English criticism has, because of its attraction to complexity and ferment, encouraged the notion that the best pastoral is the least traditional. Chambers' first type is frequently referred to as merely decorative.[32] Dissatisfaction, even embarrassment, with the "thinness" of the Theocritean model has led to the conclusion that the value of a pastoral poem is proportionate to its distance from the ancient simplicities, and its convergence with the more complex structures of romance and drama. If a pastoral lyric cannot be used within the economy of a larger pattern, as in Sidney's *Arcadia* or a Shakespearean comedy, then it should itself exhibit some of the richer harmonies.[33]

The relation between pastoral and drama is of much interest (cf. also below, Chapter Seven). Allan Ramsay's drama *The Gentle Shepherd* (1724) grew from two eclogues, "Patie and Roger" (1721) and "Jenny and Meggie" (1723), which in expanded form came to constitute the first two scenes of the new play. The completed drama was realized from a potential residing in the pastoral poems. This is one way in which the early romantics came to terms with the pastoral tradition; there was in that tradition, they felt, a promise that they could carry further. Herder preferred Gessner to Fontenelle and Pope, and Theocritus to Gessner, because he thought the work of the Swiss, and especially of the Greek, more dramatic. Now it is undeniable that the pastoral lyric requires a sense of drama, even if there is no formal contest or confrontation between two characters. That is one of the reasons why Horace, Tibullus, and even Ovid are not lightly to be associated with the pastoral tradition. But it is important that the dramatic element in pastoral be distinguished from drama proper, the art of the theater. Pastoral does not make for a movement toward explosion or reconciliation, death or resolution, as tragedy and comedy do. If we take Theocritus as our norm, a pastoral lyric involves little action, no development, no dramatic peripety, and in fact only so much drama as is needed to show that men must love and hate to be men; which is to say that there are characters, and the natural friction between characters, but no plot.

There is another way of putting this. Let me, in anticipation of a later theme, distinguish between a Stoic and an Epicurean use of character. The Stoic, in his actions, seeks conformity with the natural patterns and tensions of his world. His behavior is founded on an insight into his standing within a larger whole. His conduct is, as it were, syllogistic; it answers to a continuous barrage of questions which he must ask himself as he goes along. That is why drama, and the autobiographical essay, are appropriate vehicles for Stoic thought. The Senecan character and the Elizabethan soliloquizer know that they are, in Epictetus' well-known phrase, players with an assigned role (*Enchiridion*, section 17). The Stoic strikes a pose because that pose is a token of his mission to fulfill his promise as a man.

The Epicurean, on the other hand, attempts to live a life determined by pleasure, and pleasure is unreflected. He is at his best, at his most enjoyably human, when he comes closest to the unposed simplicity of the animal, or, if the accent is on intellectual joy, when he achieves a simplicity that is analogous to the spontaneity of the animal. The herdsmen of Theocritus are, obviously, of the Epicurean rather than of the Stoic type. They rarely strike a pose; they never point beyond themselves. Their careers within the poetry are self-terminating; they do not invite us to meet them halfway on some common or uncommon ground of opinion. A Daphnis, in spite of his laments, is a part of the scenery; a Thyestes or an Oedipus—or, for that matter, a Colin Clout—tries to gauge his distance from the environment, or to grow into it.

The affinity between Theocritean pastoralism and Epicurean hedonism will continue to interest us in subsequent sections of this study. What matters here is the incommensurability of early pastoral, on the one hand, and dramatic tension, on the other. It follows that in a consideration of the classical forms of pastoral, the "pastoral" epigrams of Theocritus and the poets of the *Greek Anthology* should be disregarded. They exhibit the dramatic structure which Emil Staiger and others have analyzed.[34] They build to a climax, and a resolution, and they usually make a point. All this is quite the reverse of what is found in the pastoral idylls.[35] There are modern examples of pastoral poetry that show a kinship with the pastoral epigram. Mallarmé's "L'Après-midi d'un Faune" and Verlaine's *Fêtes galantes* are cases in point, the former exemplifying the dramatic structure and the intellectual brilliance, the latter exhibiting the mordancy and the minute compass of the epigram. Even some of the more traditional bucolics, such as Pope's fourth *Pastoral* ("Winter") and Ambrose Philips' fifth *Pastoral*, possess a degree of sophistication, a certain unquiet exoticism, that brings to mind the epigrammatic branch of the larger tradition of the idyll. But in the present study the pastoral epigram will be regarded as lying beyond the confines of the material in which we shall interest ourselves.

We conclude that drama plays only a very limited role in the pastoral of Chambers' first type. If we adopt the distinction proposed by Chambers and others, we must ask at what point a poem that contains pastoral elements ceases being a traditional or decorative pastoral. Once more, by a different route, we have returned to the principal issue: the nature of the pastoral; and once more the road appears to be blocked. It should not surprise anyone that the difficulties encountered in the criticism of any genre—the confluence and interdependence of romance, anatomy, apologue, and so forth—lie in wait also for the critic of the pastoral. The definition of a genre works by a process of abstraction. The vast majority of compositions must be triangulated from more than one fix. But pastoral has one advantage over the novel: it got its start in antiquity. If one looks for works that, given certain premises furnished by a succession of uneccentric critics, require a minimum of triangulation, the search leads us back into time, to pieces that stand at the beginning. Homer is likely to satisfy the demand for a test-case epic; Sophocles is looked to for supplying some of the important canons of tragedy; Heliodorus' *Ethiopian Tales* is generally accepted as the paradigm of romance. Just so it is easier to generate the criteria for an understanding of pastoral poetry from Theocritus rather than from Donne, and from Virgil rather than from Marino.

If we go to the ancient poems, and look first of all at their formal organization, the findings are disconcerting. Already in antiquity, long before the days of pastoral drama and its influence on the lyric, we meet with a number of different forms.[36] By one count, Virgil's *Eclogues* employ two modes of organization. The odd-numbered poems are dramatic dialogues; the even-numbered poems are narrated monologues. Servius, commenting on *Eclogue* 3.1, sees three modes: the dramatic, "in which the poet never speaks," the descriptive, "in which only the poet speaks," and a mixed mode, "as in the *Aeneid*." All of these, he says, are found in the *Eclogues*.[37] The division goes back to a remark of Plato's (*Republic*, Book 3.394B-C)[38] that is taken up again by Quintilian and develops into a favorite scheme for classifying literary material. Conceivably, therefore, the discovery of three modes in the *Eclogues* is no more appropriate to this particular genre than any rival count that may be proposed.

On another front, however, the formal properties of the ancient pastoral are wholly uniform. I am speaking of the versification. Theocritus' hexameters set the tone; Roman bucolic poetry, and medieval ecologues, not to mention the Renaissance Latin compositions studied by the late Leonard Grant,[39] all are written in dactylic hexameters. The hexameters are not exactly those which we know from epic verse. In fact, there is no one pastoral verse rhythm but a number of rhythms, depending on the nature of the piece. The famous "bucolic diaeresis," the frequent break between units of meaning after a trisyllabic fourth foot, appears in many of Theocritus' pastoral lines, but by no means in all of them. But these are subtleties of texture. The gross fact remains that pastoral lyric was at first composed in the same verse form as epic, and remained faithful to the pattern for over 1700 years.

More about the formal structure in later chapters. If the evidence of the meter is relatively straightforward, what about the mood? At first glance, as we have seen, no simple verdict seems possible. Spenser's pastorals are, following the hint of "E. K.," divided into three types: plaintive, recreative, and moral.[40] Similarly in the ancient pastoral the mood may run from mourning to reflection, from gentle courtesy to hot wrangling. The contest between Corydon and Thyrsis in Virgil's seventh *Eclogue* begins as a competition of two pastoral moods. Corydon's manner is lyrical, contemplative, positive; Thyrsis' is aggressive, negative, an example of what the ancients called *gephyrismos*— the scoffing and lampooning that went on along the path of religious processions.[41] In the course of the contest, the picture becomes more complicated as each contestant adopts the humor of his opponent. Similar changes of mood are found in Virgil's fifth *Eclogue*, and in the fifth *Idyll* of Theocritus, the spirit of which is, in large part, downright Aristophanic, tempered with flashes of humility. It is a rare pastoral in which a specific mood is carried through without some adjustment.

In spite of this variety, it is, I think, possible to differentiate the pastoral, and not only the ancient pastoral, from other kinds of poetry, and to define a unique pastoral mood which prevails when tempers clash, or when sadness jostles joy. The key word here is: detachment. About this I propose to speak at length in Chapter Three. Here I can only suggest that the pastoral of Theocritus and his successors tends to achieve its successes by showing rather than telling. It presents a bird's-eye view of characters in action rather than an intimate exploration of motives and impulses. Virgil stands somewhat apart from the norm, and so do many of the metaphysicals. In our day Frost's regionalism recovers the impersonality, the mental distance, that is the hallmark of Theocritus' vignettes.[42] John Crowe Ransom connects Milton's choice of the pastoral form for "Lycidas" with his "intention to be always anonymous as a poet."[43] It is probable that the pastoral was popular in the Renaissance because the rules of the genre permitted the poet to disregard, or virtually to refashion, his own feelings, and to disappear as a person behind the artifact of the poem.[44] This provides an additional reason why Horace's references to the country, and their echoes in later European literature, should not be counted examples of pastoral writing. They are part of his spiritual and aesthetic autobiography. Horace felt happy and comfortable on his farm, away from the city. The emphasis is on his own sensations, not on the responses of a small set of characters unrelated to himself. It does not matter that, as in *Epistles* 1.16, he can draw a rustic landscape better than anybody else in the Augustan age. On the contrary, this is further proof of the same non-pastoral perception; alone with his satisfactions and his genial ease, Horace can fix his eyes on the color and the contours of the setting. The pastoral lyric, as we shall see (Chapter Nine), eschews descriptions of nature.

Virgil is not Horace. But like Horace he refuses to go along with Theocritus' rigorous exclusion of the first person. His conception of the pastoral is closer to that of the confessional lyric, and of elegy. The dirge which in *Idyll* 1 is sung by Thyrsis, reappears in *Eclogue* 10, but this time sung, or rather recited, by the poet. Perhaps we ought to characterize Virgil's procedure as analogous to what happens in the *parabases* of Old Comedy, for the poet's speaking voice is heard chiefly in introductions and final paragraphs. There is a parallel to this in *Idyll* 7; but here the introduction and the epilogue are emphatically separated from the pastoral poem proper. *Eclogue* 7 shows the difference: Meliboeus, the shepherd poet who narrates the poem, is merely a bystander (the judge is Daphnis), yet we find out more about the witness and his thoughts than about the three actors. Nevertheless, in Virgil the confessional element remains minor, especially by comparison with what Boccaccio and his successors were to do with the form. I suspect that Poggioli's "pastoral of the self" is really the adaptation, and in effect the distortion, of pastoral toward confession and anatomy, purposes which are originally foreign to the mood of the pastoral.[45] Cervantes' Marcela, who, in Poggioli's opinion, paves the way for the pastoral of the self, is not a pastoral singer at all, but a tragic heroine who happens to choose the trappings of the pastoral life in order to make an impression on her fellows, while rejecting the advances of her lover.[46] She is the enemy of the pastoral ideal; she is the coy lady from the cup of Theocritus' *Idyll* 1.

I dwell on Poggioli's treatment because his essays are among the few really interesting modern discussions of the pastoral, but also because in their way they represent a typical trend. As his remarks on Marcela, on Shakespeare's Jaques, and on Rousseau and Goethe show, he looks at pastoral largely from the vantage point of one interested in the European scene during the sixteenth, seventeenth, and eighteenth centuries. When he coins the terms "pastoral of solitude," "pastoral of self," and the like, he appears to be committing himself to a teleological view: that pastoral started in a certain smallish way and developed to greater and greater heights, which were reached when the British and the Spanish poets created the pastoral of melancholy. Clearly, in Poggioli's mind, the poems of Donne and Marvell and the plays of Shakespeare and Goethe are more valuable and worthier of discussion than the rather bland structures which initiated the line.

A similar judgment is implied in the choices of William Empson. His speculations about the genre, like Poggioli's, are drawn from the most developed and the most differentiated products of the tradition. Like Poggioli also, Empson assumes that the pastoral must serve an openly moral purpose. With Scaliger and other Renaissance critics, Empson regards any literary piece, and especially the pastoral, as designed to impart instruction in a pleasurable form and to impel toward action. We can enjoy pastoral because it enables us to live, on our terms, with a nature we have abandoned; pastoral relieves our sense of loss without forcing us to give up our new gains as beneficiaries of the industrial age.[47] This comes remarkable close to an old theory of the origins of pastoral as therapy, a theory invented by the Peripatos to supply a history where none existed.[48] According to it, pastoral was designed as an instrument for salvation in a time of stress. Few ancient readers, one assumes, were fooled by this hypothesis. Plutarch's syllabus of reading matter for the young, *A Young Man's Guide to the Poets*, does not mention a single pastoral writer. Plutarch evidently did not believe that Theocritus would improve an adolescent mind or promote the integration of a youth in society.[49] True, moral purpose in Plutarch is something quite different from social adjustment in Empson; but the two meet on the common ground of improvement.

If we look at the Theocritean pastoral, we find that it is neither an instrument for action or reconciliation, nor the vehicle of a program, nor is it philosophical in the sense in which, say, the romantic lyric is. It does not body forth a view of the world, except by accident and implication. It presents a picture of human intercourse that has philosophical analogues, as we shall see. But it does not attempt to place man in his environment in conformity to a metaphysical or ideological scheme. This is to the advantage of the pastoral, for it escapes the need to confront what romantics discovered to be the chief difficulty, how man could be conceived both as a product of nature and as an autonomous being.

Poggioli's and Empson's contributions are on the whole unhelpful in what they have to say about the role of nature. The topic is difficult (more will be said about it below, in Chapter Nine); "nature" is one of those terms which mean different things to different men. In one branch of the pastoral, not the main branch by any means, there is an attempt to capture the earthy feel of the countryside. This is done, in part, by means of "vulgar" speech and national meters; Lorenzo de' Medici, Marot, and Spenser are representative of this tradition. This did not, however, make for a peasant poetry; and it is significant that the voices clamoring for a truly rural poetry in the late eighteenth century were hostile to the pastoral.[50] If the pastoral was ever designed to supply an experience of nature which reality was progressively cutting back, it could not have been doing a very good job. Dr. Johnson's objections were in part due to his regret that the pastoralists were not more adept at representing nature. Herder was more perceptive; he recognized that the landscape in post-Virgilian pastoral is a "geistiges Arkadien," a paradise of our hopes and wishes, a country that never was and never will be.[51] Herder's only error was to confine his evaluation to the poetry after Virgil. It is true of Virgil, and indeed of Theocritus.

Herder's comments on nature in the idyll continue to have great value. His main contention is that the type of setting chosen by the poet does not matter; any human action and any human environment may be turned to profit along idyllic lines. Perhaps, he suggests, the time is ripe for replacing the superannuated apparatus of herdsmen and flocks with the more familiar furniture of a bourgeois setting. As long as the group represented is small, and the setting simple, the peculiar emphases of the idyll may be realized against any background. Herder's proposal led to Schiller's call for a pastoral that does away with the sugary ideality of Gessner's heroes and replaces it with the innocence of an active and strenuous life.[52]

The difficulties of the word nature are apparent also in Dr. Johnson's usage. More often than not he means something close to the Greek *physis* rather than landscape, though a complete separation of the two does not seem possible: "Our descriptions may indeed differ from those of Virgil, as an English from an Italian summer, and, in some respects, as modern from ancient life; but as nature is in both countries nearly the same, and as poetry has to do rather with the passions of men, which are uniform, than their customs, which are changeable, the varieties, which time or place can furnish, will be inconsiderable."[53] This is not the place to sort out the small nuances which render the statement both suggestive and baffling. What Dr. Johnson appears to be saying is that the passions of men are logically prior, but what matters as the poetic reality is the rustic life. I doubt that he is recommending, as it has been said that Frost does, that "to make a picture of regional life true, in the deepest sense, one must not seek the unique traits of a place for their own sake, but must use these traits in such a way that they become symbols of what is universal."[54] Dr. Johnson is too level-headed, too discreet to regard the poetic language of the pastoral as a symbolic vehicle for universals. But his talk of nature shows a similar inclination; a pastoralist should be, not an excursionist or a slummer, but one for whom the country, a specific country, provides an appropriate frame for staging a way of life that is "natural," i.e., normative. There is nothing mysterious about the bond between the herdsman and his habitat; it is one of almost perfect ease.[55] Pastoral nature, as Dr. Johnson perceived, does not terrify; man does not fear or despise her. She gives pleasure, but only as a negative residue from the terrors for which Pan and the Nymphs stand in the savage hills of the real countryside.

ﻮ   ﻮ   ﻮ   ﻮ

Up to this point I have talked, digressively I fear, about some of the matters—drama, verse form, mood, nature, and much else—that have long been recognized as leading topics in any discussion of the pastoral. Much more needs to be said, both on these matters and on others yet to be mentioned. Meanwhile, however, I would like to address myself to one particular topic, already obliquely hinted at on several occasions, because it will give us a further chance of saying what pastoral is *not*. I have used the term "Hesiodic" to refer to a kind of writing that is, in its essence, hostile to the pastoral chant. For "Hesiodic" I might have said "rustic" or "agrarian" or even "Boeotian," but every single one of the alternatives has overtones that might prove misleading. It is better to settle for a word which recalls the ancestor of the tradition.

Calpurnius Siculus, Virgil's successor in the days of Nero, makes a clear distinction between Hesiodic and pastoral verse:

> I thought the forest gods had granted you
> Nothing but peasant songs, fit for fat ears.
> But the music you make with your matched pipes
> Flows sweet and liquid, dearer to me than nectar
> Lapped by swarms of Ovidian bees.[56]

The *rustica carmina* of which Calpurnius speaks need not be vulgar. Calpurnius' own fifth *Eclogue*, which is in imitation of Virgil's *Georgics* rather than his *Eclogues*, gains its ends as an artful peasant song.[57] The old Corycian farmer whom Virgil meets near Tarentum is neither Epicurean nor Stoic but an unphilosophical embodiment of Roman peasant virtue.[58] When Tibullus (2.3) distinguishes between the agricultural scene, filled with toil (61 : *dura seges*), and pre-agricultural primitivist utopia (68: *glans et aquae*), the distinction is also between two muscial strains: the rugged Hesiodic cadence, weighted down with the sweat and the rewards of the peasant's life (see especially Tibullus 2.1) and the lighter tune of the pastoral, which owes next to nothing to the experience of farmers and herdsmen alike. In all these versions, the Hesiodic note has a charm of its own; but it is not pastoral.

In its origins, with Hesiod and Aristophanes, the tradition is activist, critical, and realistic. Hesiod moralizes for the benefit of his brother Perses, not concealing the burden of the labor, yet recommending it as work dear in the eyes of the gods. He takes a downright proletarian pride in the fact that he must suffer, physically and spiritually, before he can achieve success. Aristophanes, in turn, makes scornful fun of those who do not work for a living and who do not have their feet solidly on the ground. The Hesiodic code of country living is one of discipline and foresight. The farmer does not live a random life of enjoyment and self-revelation. On the contrary, he plans and saves and reins himself in tightly for the sake of a future gain. The Hesiodic strain demands self-imposed regimentation. One of its prominent organizing techniques is the calendar or almanac, arranging the tasks of the farmer in accordance with the seasons and the environment. Calpurnius' fifth *Eclogue* is such a calendar, and Virgil's *Eclogue* 6 has structural affinities with this aspect of the tradition. The calendar is didactic, and indeed didactic poetry is one branch of Hesiodic homeliness, a fact that is borne out by the many seventeenth- and eighteenth-century works modelled on Virgil's *Georgics*.[59] The instruction is necessary, for without the expertise imparted, the harshness of the peasant's life would be overpowering.

By a twist well known in the history of social activism and sansculotte ethics, the Hesiodic tradition prizes difficulties and pain, while it has little but suspicion for beauty and elegance. *Ponos*, which is both labor and pain, is the keystone of the Hesiodic universe. I use the term *"ponos"* (*Works and Days* 91) rather than alternative terms for hardship and grief, of which there are many in Hesiod, in order to assimilate the wording of the discussion to the thinking current at the time when the pastoral came into being. I do not mean *ponos* in the sense in which Callimachus and his school use it, when they talk of the careful and self-denying labor that goes into the making of the good poem.[60] What I have in mind is the sense in which the philosophers, especially the Cynics, demanded that a good life furnish evidence of effort and suffering.[61] Epicureanism is the only Hellenistic school that turns against the notion of *ponos* as embodying a value;[62] and on the face of it, it would seem that pastoral also, with its glorification of leisure, could hardly countenance a substantial measure of *ponos*. It is often said that the pastoral vision is eminently untragic.[63] Generations of pastoral poets have supported this:

> How much (sayd he) more happie is the state,
> In which ye father here doe dwell at ease,
> Leading a life so free and fortunate,
> From all the tempests of these worldly seas,
> Which tosse the rest in daungerous disease;
> Where warres, and wreckes, and wicked enmitie
> Doe them afflict, which no man can appease,
> That certes I your happinesse enuie,
> And wish my lot were plast in such felicitie.[64]

The pastoral pleasance, as envisaged by many Renaissance poets, is unalloyed happiness. Even hunting and fishing are, as it were by sheer momentum, extensions of this happy life, not intrusions of another existence that has *ponos* built into it. But just as the "Shield of Achilles," one of Dr. Johnson's favorite analogues to the pastoral, introduces real warfare in the place of the stylized dueling of the epic, so the Theocritean pastoral also cannot do without intimations of a sterner and more hurtful life ostensibly excluded from the arbor. The cup in *Idyll* 1 registers scenes that serve notice of the anguish of life in the *polis*, grubbing for a livelihood, cruelty, and deception. This is the life for which *Eclogue* 4.31–36 provides a tune-up of sorts: "A few traces of the ancient sin will last." [65] Without these subtle reminders of a disavowed order, the pastoral becomes sweet and cloying.

But, in contrast to Hesiodic poetry, the pastoral has such reminders lightly edged in. They furnish muscle and tone; they do not attract our ideological attention. As Hugh Blair says of the pastoralist: "Distresses, indeed, and anxieties he may attribute to it; for it would be perfectly unnatural to suppose any condition of human life to be without them; but they must be of such a nature, as not to shock the fancy with anything particularly disgusting in the pastoral life." [66] Blair's way of putting this is squeamish; I would like to recognize an echo, though a violent one, of the ancient pastoral insinuation of *ponos* in some of the shocking things Marvell does: the killing of the bird by the mower's scythe, e.g., in the Mower episode of "Upon Appleton House" (393–400). [67] But when the intrusion of *ponos* becomes more than a minor counterpoint, as in Endelechius, who writes about a diseased herd, [68] it is difficult to imagine that we continue to be dealing with a pastoral poem. And, in fact, the *De mortibus boum* is a specimen of Hesiodic writing, in spite of the fact that the speakers are herdsmen. More typically, a poet realizes the desired *ponos* by means of a concrete but manageable enclave. A favorite device is a wound; the herdsman withdraws into solitude to inspect or talk about his wound. This is a motif which Theocritus anticipates in *Idyll* 4; note the characteristic delicacy with which is is handled:

So small a wound, and it throws a grown man! [69]

Generally speaking, the role of *ponos* in the pastoral is persistently minor. In the Hesiodic poem it is pervasive; *ponos* marks the man.

The heirs of Homer and of the ethics of the aristocratic world looked down on the farmers and their ways. In Theophrastus' *Characters*, rusticity is a fault.[70] Country life makes the man "selfish, sensual, gross, and hard-hearted," Coleridge finds (*Biographia Literaria*, chapter 17), in his discussion of the failure of Wordsworth to implement his theories in "Michael" and "Mad Mother." Wordsworth was foiled because he did not distinguish sufficiently between pastoral and Hesiodic. This failure shows up even worse in such a poem as John Clare's "The Rivals: A Pastoral," which mixes plebeian inelegance with refined affections in a mawkish fusion.[71] Gay's parodies, largely at the expense of Ambrose Philips, are aimed at the same kind of incongruity, often heralded by the use of "rustic" names within a polite setting. To an ear schooled in the gentle names of Theocritean and Virgilian herdsmen, there is little to choose between Philips' Cuddy and Hobbinol, and Gay's Cloddipole and Boobyclod.

Saint-Lambert solves the question posed by the conflict between pastoral and Hesiodic in a tastefully *ancien régime* fashion.[72] Poor peasants, he says, are unhappy, cheat, and lie, whereas rich peasants are happy and have manners; hence let us talk about the latter, and only rarely about the former. Greater poets do not make things so easy for themselves. Virgil certainly recognized the difference between the two traditions, but did not suppress one in favor of the other. The *Georgics* are almost entirely Hesiodic, though Book Two contains large stretches of pastoral interest; while the *Eclogues* are, for the most part, committed to a predominantly non-Hesiodic view of the country. But even if we discount such evidently non-Theocritean poems as *Eclogues* 4 and 6, it is the general feeling that Virgil's pastorals incorporate many details of the poet's own rustic, that is, non-pastoral, experience.[73]

The British pastoral tradition has a much greater admixture of the Hesiodic than, say, the French. In Jonson's *The Sad Shepherd*, for instance, the down-to-earth perspective of Robin Hood and his band gives short shrift to the pastoral utopia. Drayton's comparison of the lives of a woodsman, a fisherman, and a swain in the "Sixth Nimphall" of *The Muses Elizium* features work songs rather than bucolic performances.[74] On other occasions, the grimness and the absurdities of the Hesiodic world are emphasized in order to free the imagination for the perception of pastoral beauty and pastoral freedom. This is what Autolycus does for us in *The Winter's Tale*, creating room for what Florizel and Perdita have to offer.[75] The use of the Hesiodic strain as a deflector goes beyond the mere confrontation of Hesiodic and pastoral, and often has the effect of putting the pastoral in a humorous light. Of this, the chief ancient example is *Idyll* 10, the contest, or better the joint appearance, of peasant and swain.[76]

Mantuan showed his great virtuosity in deliberately mingling the pastoral and the Hesiodic, and producing charmingly incongruous effects. In his sixth *Eclogue*, the conversation is punctuated and interrupted by the performance of common chores in the stable, and in the eighth *Eclogue* there are several references to the castrating of hogs and sheep, not by way of marginal flourishes, but to complete the picture of what a countryman does in the course of carrying out his duties. The willingness to shock is obvious; though the achievement is impressive, one wonders whether the trick really comes off, whether, that is, the wholesale homogenization of the pastoral and Hesiodic is feasible. Theocritus also introduces certain farmyard touches into the pastoral tableau, but he is more restrained about it. In *Idyll* 8, for instance, the capping octave of an amoebean (63 ff.) consists of advice to wolf, dog, and sheep which is taken from the practical concerns of the ranch rather than from the spiritual reservoir of the pleasance. This is daring, but given the compass of the whole the topic is unobtrusive. Only in a few British "pastorals," notably in Marvell's Mower poems, do we find a successful, because highly personal, not to say perverse, mingling of the farmer's calendar with the chirping of crickets and noon-tide bliss.

Robin Hood's good sense, in *The Sad Shepherd*, was in the eighteenth century appropriated by those who wished to protest against the anemia of contemporary pastoral. Crabbe's lines

> Still in our lays fond Corydons complain,
> And shepherds' boys their amorous pains reveal,
> The only pains, alas! they never feel.

are representative.[77] Soon thereafter the British pastoral died a natural death, not to be resuscitated until it could be done on entirely new premises. The occasional exceptions to this—Arnold, Hardy—could not hide the fact of the demise, though it is useful to be reminded that the death of a genre is rarely total.

We have dealt with the Hesiodic element as one that does not mix easily with the pastoral; one, indeed, that is most usefully employed to offset the pastoral by way of contrast. But there is another side to this. From the beginning of its existence, Hesiodic poetry has counted among its features a mechanism which triggers bourgeois compromise rather than rustic truculence, which aims at relief, or sublimation, rather than peasant entrenchment. A reader of the *Works and Days*, the peasant manifesto, is impressed with the amount of space given over to proverbs and maxims, and whole chains of maxims. Like Hesiod, or the voice of the wronged churl in Hesiod's poem, Sancho Panza falls back on the pre-formulated wisdom of the tribe to secure his precarious foothold in a perplexing world. Now if we look at the pastoral of Cervantes' time and earlier we find that the proverb has an honorable place in it. Mantuan's eclogues bristle with adages and saws. Proverbs, and their aggressive relations, curses, have often served to anchor the pastoral dream in a more solid substratum.

The use of proverbs in Theocritus has been studied in detail.[78] Even Erasmus paid some attention to it when he stated: "Under the heading of 'proverb' we must consider also those familiar in pastoral poetry: those from impossibility, those from necessity, those from absurdity, those from similarity, and those from contrariety."[79] Of the types listed and documented by Erasmus, not all are of the same order as the maxims that we associate with the Hesiodic tradition. We must distinguish between the forceful statements which summarize the proposition at hand by bringing in a ready-made, unreflected phrase; and formulations which are specially devised for the occasion, and whose wit often betrays their analytic origin. The distinction is not always easy. But *impossibilia* and *absurda* tend to belong to the second category, and have little to do with the peasant wisdom of hard knocks and rote experience.[80]

There are other distinctions which may usefully be made, not between the kinds of maxims used, but between ways of using them. The sayings may be employed to add concreteness and zest to a sentiment that has already been expressed, or will be expressed, non-proverbially. On the other hand they may be introduced as substitutes or *allegoriai*, as sole carriers of the meaning. The latter, I dare say, is more appropriately called Hesiodic, since it involves the citation of proverbs as a way out of the supposed difficulty of articulating personal sentiments. Mantuan is especially fond of exhibiting characters who play hard to get (Silvanus in the fifth *Eclogue*), or who act the buffoon (Fortunatus in the first) by delivering themselves of Wellerisms. There is the further distinction between the safety-valve witticism of the underdog, and the prudential maxim of the sententious man of affairs.[81] Finally, the lack of immediate relevance of the thing said to the situation covered makes for a special brand of absurdity; this may be seen in the "Song of Capitulation," in *Mother Courage*, Act 4; or in "Sweeney Agonistes."

That all of these stratagems can be found in a great many pastoral poems, and that they make important contributions to such successes as are scored, is obvious. The ancient pastoral, once again, presents a special situation. In the total range of Greek literature the use of proverbs and maxims, both reflected and unreflected, proletarian and bourgeois, matching and mismatched, occurs most prominently in the mime. We are told by a reliable ancient critic that Sophron, the inventer and most admired composer of mimes, used proverbs in abundance.[82] The extant remains of his work confirm the ancient report. Theocritus' city mimes also, influenced as they are by the work of Sophron, feature a host of adages, by way of expostulation, remonstrance, resignation, or plain summation. They are usually cited in minimal form, often lacking verbs, to achieve the terseness which benefits their standing as epigrammatic markers. This kind of language appears to be associated with the artistic representation of simple people. It is significant that in New Comedy proverbial statements are as a rule put in the mouths of slaves.[83] We have reason to believe that the successors of Theocritus employed maxims even more freely than Theocritus himself.[84]

But what is true of Theocritus' *Idylls* 2, 14, and 15 need not be true of his pastorals. And in fact, in the pastoral poems the use of proverbs is severely limited to those situations where an admixture of the Hesiodic is desirable. The typical herdsman does not utter pieces of prudential wisdom or bits of unreflected lore. His feelings and actions are not those of a member of the tribe, or of a class, but of a free man, capable of responding in his own way to a world of his own making. Only where the herdsman moves into the vicinity of the fool, or of the city slicker, is the proverb brought into play. This happens, as one might expect, in the almost "Irish" *Idyll* 5, which is richly salted with patter, chiefly in the form of exclamations and curses. Now and then a maxim is cited to afford some consolation for the love-sick swain. In *Idyll* 4.41–43, for instance, Corydon, momentarily the straight man to Battus' short-lived melancholy, feeds him consolatory platitudes that would not deceive anyone, least of all a resilient shepherd. But these are infrequent occurrences. The pre-formulated saying, a verbal mechanism closely wedded to the Hesiodic manner, puts in only a few appearances in Theocritus' pastorals. In this respect, also, Theocritus seems to have been fully alert to the essential separateness of the Hesiodic and the pastoral demands.

I have dwelt on maxims and proverbs, and on Hesiodic poetry in the wider sense, because it is often taken for granted that they are part of the load which the pastoral tradition is fated to carry with it from the start. My point is that they are not. It seemed appropriate, as we are trying to clarify what is included in our understanding of the pastoral, to indicate where the possible confusions with other genres and other moods lurk. We can see our way more clearly if we free the discussion of the pastoral lyric of any obligation it might feel toward peasant poetry and didacticism. This does not get us much closer to a positive identification of the pastoral. But it enables us to concentrate our attack, and to avoid false trails.

One thing we can do is to tackle our task along historical lines, to show what Theocritus did and what he may have intended by so doing, and not doing something else. Let me repeat what I have said above, that the examples of romance and tragedy suggest that it is useful to seek guidelines by going to the earliest workers in the field. At the same time I propose that we look at Theocritus' work as if it were that of a fellow writer, a competitor, of the later pastoralists, rather than the source that it is. My treatment of the *Idylls* will be, I hope, comparative in this sense of a simulated synchronism. I shall look at Theocritus' choices and procedures in the belief that he picked them from a larger range of possibilities available to anyone who tries his hand at writing bucolic verse. The hard data of influence and transmission cannot be ruled out of court. But on the whole they have tended to work against Theocritus. The knowledge that he stands at the head of the line have put obstacles in the path of reading him fairly. It has created the presumption that he is simple, even crude, by comparison with his heirs. It is time, I think, to temper the justice of this backward glance with the equity of another view: that Theocritus is a great poet, and that the biological model has serious defects.

Homer showed his followers what an epic is. Can a similar claim be made for Theocritus and the pastoral? I realize that it is hazardous to enthrone a pastoral genre born fully equipped from the head of its creator. As a corrective of the developmental perspective, however, such a picture has its uses. I happen to believe that Theocritus' achievement—mature, subtle, tough— constitutes a standard that imposes considerable obligations. Dr. Johnson's slur on the imitativeness of the genre is, in part, a recognition of Theocritus' great authority. If in what follows I sometimes talk as if Theocritus were the only true pastoralist, the phrasing should be chalked up to my desire to modify the usual judgment that Theocritus is a forerunner rather than an implementer. The bias, if it is a bias, comes naturally to a Hellenist. Readers whose biases run along other grooves will no doubt make the necessary adjustments. It would be perverse to argue that Donne's pastorals, or Sannazaro's, or Sidney's, do not measure up to the Theocritean paradigm. On the other hand, and especially for my present purposes, I can see little wrong with the proposition that Theocritus did certain things superbly well, and that these things came to be accepted, in a general way, as pointing the orientation of the pastoral lyric.

One prior question needs to be raised: is it in fact correct to say that Theocritus was the first pastoralist, and if so, what were the influences that shaped his writing? A discussion of the origins of a genre which we are still in the process of defining may well, in the light of the Platonic figure with which I started the chapter, seem out of order. But in our present course of leisurely approximation we can, I should think, relax the logic, and step back into time.

2

Beginnings

Aristotle was the first to stress the difficulties that bedevil an inquiry into origins.[1] In the case of the pastoral, the inquiry has been confounded by a natural reluctance to accept the fact that there was no pastoral poetry prior to Theocritus. The Hellenistic age, it is widely assumed, did not produce any new literary genres, but merely witnessed the adaptation and occasionally the distortion of forms developed in the archaic and classical periods. Hence, so the reasoning runs, the pastoral must be an earlier creation also. In the seventeenth and eighteenth centuries, it was fashionable to go back to the earliest known shepherds and ascribe the invention of the genre to them. Rapin cites Jacob and Esau, Joseph, David, and Amos as early herdsmen who demonstrated the happiness of the bucolic life.[2] One century later, William Collins wrote a book of *Oriental Eclogues*; John Langhorne, who edited them in 1765, added a section of "Observations" in which he argued that the Greeks took the pastoral from the East and that Isaiah was a more significant pastoralist than Theocritus.[3]

The Orientalizing theory is very old. In Boccaccio's *Genealogia* (Book 14), the argument for the priority of the Greeks in poetry appears to be directed against a rival theory. Nor has the theory yet come to rest; voices are still heard to claim that the Song of Songs is the prototype of the pastoral and that it was the source from which the Greeks derived their bucolic poetry.[4] More commonly, however, speculations about the origins of pastoral disregard national boundaries and instead train their sights on levels of society or on the phases of human progress. Sannazaro, in the tenth prose of his *Arcadia*, traces the early history of pastoral as a series of personal achievements—from Pan to Theocritus to Virgil. But that is unusual; the Renaissance *fable convenue* is couched in anthropological terms. Scaliger's version is typical; he presents an account which can, in effect, be traced back via Isidore, Donatus, Suetonius, Varro, to the Epicureans, Dicaearchus, and Thucydides. It is roughly the same account that may still be read in Lucretius (Book 5), according to which early man, living his simple life, discovered music along with other basic constituents of culture, and sang pastoral songs before more developed types of music and poetry were invented. The account emphasizes the springtime of man—relatively happy, of few needs, possessing a sensitivity to match his vitality, and spontaneously uttering music and verse to express his native joys and ambitions.[5]

Another "primitivistic" theory, analogous to the theory of Golden Age origins, is more fashionable today. It asserts that pastoral was not invented at a particular time, but has always existed in a particular class of people. Each generation, we are told, has its peasants and herdsmen who sing the songs of the countryside. Andrew Lang impatiently brushes aside the sophisticated skepticism of Fontenelle,[6] and claims that Theocritus' songs "are all such as he might really have heard on the shores of Sicily," citing examples of modern Greek folk poetry to confirm his point.[7] Similarly Frank Kermode and Dimitrios Petropoulos, among others, look on Theocritus as a collector and imitator of folk material.[8]

The hypothesis of a Sicilian origin is seemingly strengthened by the prominence in the pastoral tradition of the hero Daphnis, a Sicilian cowherd who was said to have wooed a nymph and been punished by her for his subsequent desertion.[9] It used to be believed that Daphnis was, long before Theocritus, the hero of a pastoral folk tradition, and that he was the subject of herdsmen's songs. Today we are less sure about this. We are more ready to believe that the share of the lyric poet Stesichorus in the creation, or at least in the building up, of the legend of Daphnis was larger than that of the people.[10] Parallel traditions, notably the report that the pastoral was first sung by the Sicilian cowherd Diomos, carry even less conviction.[11] The Diomos legend is an invention of the comic dramatist Epicharmus to account, not for pastoral poetry, which Epicharmus did not know, but for a dance with flute accompaniment called the "cowherd dance."

The most commonly accepted anthropological reconstruction today singles out the Arcadians as the founders of the pastoral. Polybius, a hundred-odd years after Theocritus, reports (4.20) that the Arcadians engage in competitions; instead of listening to the performances of others, they challenge each other to singing contests. Elsewhere (Pausanias 8.5.7) we learn that Bukolion was the name of an ancient Arcadian prince. Some recent scholars are impressed with the importance of the Arcadian singing matches, if not for Theocritus, at least for Virgil.[12] Later in this study, in Chapter Eleven, I shall try to indicate some of the reasons, other than the ones favored by these scholars, why Arcadia came to be associated with the pastoral. The sad fact is that our information about ancient singing matches is unreliable, to say the least. It would be churlish to deny that the Sicilian countryside—and the Coan, and Arcadian, and Egyptian, for that matter—was alive with song. Some of the singing may have resembled this or that feature of Theocritean pastoral. But of singing contests organized by the herdsmen themselves for their own enjoyment, there is not the slightest hint in the early tradition.[13] Nor are the modern parallels helpful. The songs, amoebean and otherwise, of modern Greek herdsmen and rustics which Petropoulos and other field researchers have claimed for the pastoral genre consist mainly of boasting, invective, and repartee, along with some love poetry. It is true that name-calling is one of the ingredients in the developed bucolic tradition; but it is merely one of many, and certainly not the most significant.[14] It is better to disregard this possibility, at least until we have more information about the ancient practices. A dogmatism on the other side is equally hazardous; we simply do not know enough to be able to subscribe to Schwartz's ridicule of the picture of Theocritus "climbing up to the desolate mountain pastures of his island home, to find inspiration in the monotonous calls and whistles of the herdsmen; the raw desperadoes ... in the wilderness were not likely to furnish him with poetry."[15]

Not unlike this theory of popular origins is another, devised by the Peripatos to parallel Aristotle's reconstruction of the roots of drama.[16] This ritual hypothesis, which derives the invention of the pastoral from the worship of the goddess Artemis, is best studied in the ancient commentaries, particularly in an essay entitled "On the Invention of Bucolic Poetry."[17] There are three versions: (1) At the time the Persians were threatening Greece, the Spartans hid their young women. When Artemis Caryatis was to be honored, some country men sang in the place of the girls. The goddess liked it, and so the custom was continued. (2) When Orestes in his enforced travel came to Sicilian Tyndaris, he found the local population honoring Artemis with pastoral songs. (3) After a period of civic unrest, the Syracusans honored Artemis for bringing peace; farmers came to the city to sing, and loaves of decorated bread were offered for prizes.

The trouble with these tales is that they stipulate singing as a cult activity; and this explains nothing about early pastoral poetry, which is secular, recited rather than sung, and rarely encomiastic. If the pastoral does have ritual roots, we know nothing about the stages of transition from the situations pictured in the scholia to the finished product. The identity of the deity worshipped confirms our suspicion that the account is entirely hypothetical. Artemis is the goddess of the wild, of the feared range beyond the boundaries of the settled community. In this capacity she appears in many of the epigrams; she protects the traveller and invites his homage. The theorists chose her because they needed a divinity of the countryside, and Artemis appeared to be the logical contender. In fact, however, the pastoral pleasance is not a Petrarchan solitude, much less the terra incognita of James Fenimore Cooper. To the green cabinet Artemis is a complete stranger. The characterization of the worshippers of Artemis Caryatis as frenzied revellers removes the last shred of support from the ritual theory, or at least from this particular ritual theory.[18]

There is another which needs to be mentioned, if only because it has recently been revived by a respected Marxist scholar.[19] This is Reitzenstein's speculation[20] that *boukoliasdesthai*, Theocritus' word for the pastoral contest, refers to the activity of *boukoloi*, not real herdsmen, but members of a club of poets in Cos who regarded themselves as ritual celebrants and took the name of *boukoloi* because this was the name used by the initiates of Dionysus in some of his cults.[21] Reitzenstein even attempted to establish a connection between these *boukoloi* and the supposed Daphnis songs mentioned earlier, speculating that Daphnis was a *boukolos* of Artemis. Theocritus' *Idylls*, he thought, reflect the ceremonial performances that took place within the circle of Theocritus' Coan friends. Each idyll is, therefore, a kind of masquerade, with the poets—some of them well-known to the readers—parading under the names of herdsmen, and hiding profound intentions under the cloak of rusticity.

Few critics today still believe in Reitzenstein's complicated account, principally because the existence of ancient poetic *thiasoi*, groups of poets united in a common worship, is by no means assured, and also because the theory raises more problems than it was designed to settle.[22] Yet the Reitzenstein theory has one great advantage over rival theories in that it offers an explanation, however tortuous, for Theocritus' use of the term *boukoliasdesthai*. Already in the scholia the question is raised why the genre is called *boukolika* (cattle-herding songs), despite the fact that so many of the poems feature shepherds and goatherds rather than neatherds. One answer given by the scholiast, with characteristic insouciance, is that the name derives from the more important sector of the animal kingdom.[23] It has recently been proposed, more or less in the spirit of Reitzenstein, that *boukolikos* was originally a pejorative sobriquet used by Apollonius and the champions of epic to refer to the works of the Callimacheans, who opposed the writing of epic and favored the non-heroic in literature.[24] It is just possible that the derivation of *boukolikos* from *bous* (cattle) is just as spurious as Petrarch's derivation of eglogue from *aix* (goat). It is best to acknowledge that at this point we do not know why Theocritus' poems about herdsmen came to be called bucolics, or why Theocritus uses *boukoliasdesthai*.

On the larger front, also, the inquiry has been abortive. None of the theories constructed to explain the sudden appearance of Theocritus can be maintained; each of them faces overwhelming difficulties of evidence and logic. What, then, can be done to explain this remarkable phenomenon—the sudden creation of a new genre in the third century, long after the other genres had passed into the mainstream of Greek literature and the force creating new forms was supposedly spent? The principal editor of Theocritus in antiquity, Theon of Tarsus, is said to have argued for a kinship between pastoral and comedy. Thomas Warton, whose *De poesi bucolica Graecorum dissertatio* (1770) breaks new ground in the appreciation of the pastoral in spite of its academic flavor, suggested that the genre is in fact nothing new, but a descendant of Old Comedy. And a recent critic argues that comedy and pastoral both originate at the end of the sixth century BC.[25]

What these writers have in common is that they are willing to look for the roots of a literary form in other literary documents and traditions rather than in non-literary activities. It is certainly true that Old Comedy and satyr drama show many features that recur in Theocritus. Cratinus offers catalogues of flowers and herbs;[26] Eupolis has a comedy entitled *Goats*, which contains, among other things, a list of the foods that goats eat (frag. 14 Kock), all of them ubiquitous in Theocritus. Aristophanes' *Peace* (1140–1171) stages a rustic picnic, rougher than its pastoral cousins, but definitely akin. The comic institution of the *agon*, exemplified by the debate between the Just and the Unjust Postulate in the *Clouds*, is an instructive forerunner of bucolic contests. Euripides' *Cyclops* (41 ff.) contains a number of elements which we associate with Theocritus: the address to the goat, shooing it from one place to another; the references to simple pastoral activities, like milking and the suckling of kids; and finally the setting—the cave, the meadow, the spring, the breezes. Only at the end of the song is there a jarring note that returns us to the social realities of the satyr chorus, a dispirited reference to their servile status. In pastoral, as we shall see, the class system is almost completely exorcised.

Tragedy, likewise, provides some parallels, especially Euripides' *Antiope*. Amphion is a shepherd—philosopher—musician.[27] To be sure, he plays the lyre rather than the pipe, and the subject of his song is cosmogony, in the spirit of Hesiod and Virgil rather than Theocritus. What is more, Zethus, also, the representative of civic involvement, points to shepherding and other peasant activities as desirable, unlike the musings of his brother, which are not. But the theme of the contemplative, unbusinesslike shepherd is there, as it is in another fragmentary play of Euripides, his *Alexandros*, in which Paris apparently played a similar role.[28]

Drama is not the only kind of literature from which pastoral may have obtained its first impulses. In the Theocritean pastoral, there are two varieties of contest: the amoebean singing match, and the competition with full length songs. The former is

anticipated by the *skolia*, the "crooked songs" that were sung
back and forth at the symposium, and of which Athenaeus
(15.694C ff.) gives us a representative sampling. The latter variety
may be recognized in the contest advertised by Theognis:

> All right, Academus; you say: let's sing a song.
>   I say: the prize shall be
>   A pretty boy.
>   For this let's match our skills
>   And you'll find out that asses
>   Must bow to mules.[29]

The lines have a strikingly pastoral ring; the mockery is there, and
the cockiness, though perhaps less of the stylistic refinement that
spreads its special sheen over most of what Theocritus does.
Among the writers of *skolia* was Praxilla of Sicyon whom Anti-
pater of Thessalonica (*Anthol. Pal.* 9.26) puts in first place among
the poetesses.[30] Some of her work, only a small portion of which
has come down to us, shows the delight in nature and a certain
charming naiveté that are not found again until almost two
hundred years later when we come to Theocritus. And some of
the earliest choral poets, including Alcman, Stesichorus, and
Pindar, evidence similar formal and thematic antecedents.[31]

There are some poets and poetesses whom the tradition names
as having been instrumental in the creation of the pastoral.
According to Clearchus of Soloi, who delighted in gossip, the
lyric poetess Eriphanis used to pursue Menalcas up and down the
hillsides, with a desperate passion which made the beasts weep for
her; in the end she composed a song, the so-called *nomion* (pasture-
song), containing the words, or probably the refrain, "Large are
the oaks, Menalcas."[32] Since Clearchus is at best a contemporary
of Theocritus, this notice can hardly be said to demonstrate the
existence of a pastoral tradition prior to him. Actually Eriphanis
is probably a figure of legend, or perhaps a figure of fun invented by the irrepressible Clearchus to lampoon the new vogue
of shepherd-poets introduced by Theocritus.

More important, the same Clearchus mentions a dithyramb by a certain Lycophronides, in which a goatherd in love dedicates a rose, shoes, and hunting gear.[33] The last, he says, are no longer of use to him since he cannot think of anything but his girl. Wilamowitz thought that the dedication is to Artemis or Pan; and that Lycophronides may be identical with the sophist Lycophron mentioned by Aristotle.[34] The identification is uncertain, but there is nothing improbable about the notion of an early fourth-century dithyramb featuring a goatherd who combines the sexuality of a satyr with a post-Euripidean sentimentality. The lines do not, however, indicate anything more than a distant relationship with pastoral; above all, they are composed to be sung. We have already talked about the absence of cult and dedications from the Theocritean pastoral poem. For the same reason, the importance, in this connection, of the poetess Anyte of Tegea, famous for her epigrams about animals, should not be pressed.[35]

Two other names often mentioned in speculations about the origins of the pastoral are those of Sositheus and Hermesianax. According to the scholiast on Theocritus' *Idyll* 8, Sositheus, a member of the Alexandrian Pleiad, wrote about a contest between Daphnis and Menalcas, with Pan as judge. Menalcas was defeated, and the nymph Thaleia became Daphnis' bride. We know roughly what the contents of the drama were: the nymph had been stolen by the ruffian Lityerses, Daphnis tried to rescue her, was condemned to die, but was saved by Hercules in the nick of time.[36] How the contest fitted into the story we cannot say. But otherwise the implications are clear: the personae dramatis are demi-gods, and the action is one that has contacts with satyr drama. There is little here that could have influenced Theocritus more than, say, Euripides' *Cyclops*. Moreover, Sositheus may well have been a younger contemporary of Theocritus. As for Hermesianax, some critics believe that his elegiac poem "Leontion" contained material from the loves of herdsmen. One fragment, for instance, seems to be about Polyphemus looking at Galatea from afar.[37]

We also know, from the scholiast on Theocritus' *Idyll* 9, that Hermesianax wrote about the love of Menalcas for Euippe; Menalcas, disappointed in love, threw himself headlong from a rock. All this makes it likely that there existed, perhaps as early as in the fourth century BC, semi-operatic pieces in which actors dressed up as herdsmen performed skits and perhaps played on pipes. The plots were taken from the local legends, with some attempt to make the legends applicable to the personalities of the time, as in the case of Philoxenus, who adapted the tale of Polyphemus and Galatea to the intrigue of Dionysius II of Syracuse with his mistress.[38] But whether these skits, with their masquerades and their pathos, should be regarded as the first pastorals is highly questionable. For the most part the pastoral does not seem to rely on legend, local or otherwise, nor does it concern itself with living personages, but presents a scene that is virtually anonymous; it does not revel in intrigue and violence, but glances at little people in a setting of leisure and calm. The presence of herdsmen and their loves should not startle us; the theme is as old as Hesiod and Homer.

One final poet needs to be discussed; the claim that he is a forerunner of the pastoral is widely accepted. He is Philitas of Cos, a poet and critic, and, like Epicurus, a life-long invalid.[39] He is among the rare company of writers mentioned by name in Theocritus, and his extant remains show some interesting parallels with the *Idylls*, particularly a couplet in which there is talk of a fawn and the prick of a thorn and a loss of heart, a phrase which may well have influenced Theocritus (see *Idyll* 10.3–4).[40] But in spite of a preoccupation with nature and an expressed longing for release from suffering, there is nothing bucolic about the fragments we have.[41] The reason Philitas has been ranked with the pastoralists is because the teacher of Daphnis, in Longus' pastoral romance of a much later date, bears the name Philitas. It is usually held that this is Longus' way of acknowledging a debt to Philitas as the founder of the pastoral tradition. But it has been shown that this cannot have been Longus' intention; if his Philatas were the Coan returned, he would be piping in honor of Bittis, historically the object of his poetic addresses, rather than the Amaryllis who is his light of love in the novel.[42] In any case, the wording of Theocritus' reference to Philitas in *Idyll* 7 makes it probable that Philitas was *not*, in Theocritus' eyes, a bucolic poet.[43]

The many claims for poetic precedents for Theocritus' invention of the pastoral have, therefore, turned out to be, on the whole, delusory. That Theocritus learned from his predecessors is obvious; I for one believe firmly that he found more to interest him and to shape his poetic vision in the literature than in the folk traditions. All of the elements which he combined to construct a new kind of poetry were available in earlier achievements, but scattered and suspended in other compounds. As the lyric drew on the epic, and drama on both, so the Hellenistic pastoral was able to draw on all the earlier types of writing to bring about its special amalgam. And it was not only poetry that supplied many of the ingredients; prose also, particularly philosophical prose, was laid under contribution. This should not surprise us, in view of the debates in the *Clouds* and the *Antiope*. I should argue that the very earliest occurrence of a pastoral line is in Plato's *Phaedrus* (241D1):

Wolves love the lamb; so lovers crave their boy.[44]

If the Greek scans as a hexameter, which is made plausible by Socrates' subsequent remarks—"Haven't you noticed, my friend, that I have taken to intoning epic verse?"—and if it is in imitation of a contemporary statement about love, then we must be prepared for the possibility that there was, in the fourth century, some poetry that contained lines like Theocritus' *Idyll* 10, lines 30–31:

The goat pursues the clover, the wolf pursues the goat,
The crane pursues the plough; and I burn for you.

But even if the similarity of wording is an accident, and the
Platonic statement is the prose reflection of a pithy Attic remark
about the senselessness of lovers, there is much else in the *Phaedrus*,
particularly in the first half and near the end, that puts us in
mind of Theocritus: a heightened but economical sensitivity to
the surroundings, whether rural or not; a wavering between two
modes of experiencing the country, realistic and mythological
(the legend of Boreas and Orithyia); and of course the repeated
references to Pan and the Nymphs as emblems of a vitality that
cannot flourish in the ordinary pursuits of citizens.[45] There is
also Plato's fascination with herdsmen as the perpetuators of
civilization in times of stress.[46]

Socratic dialogue, or better, the disputations of the Sophists,
may have had their share in fertilizing the amoebean technique,
with its symmetries and mock symmetries, its formulations that
go beyond plottable argument, and its frequent semblance of
pleading a case at the bar. It would only be fitting if a poetic
form that in the Middle Ages came to be used for the sharpening
of theological *controversiae*, had itself developed from debates
which are the ancient equivalent of medieval casuistry. At a
very much later time Shaftesbury visualizes the moral (or moralists') dialogue modeled on pastoral poetry as well as Socratic
discourse. As they chat with one another, the friends free themselves of the trammels of society and recover a liberty, and a
detachment, that is prefigured in the world of Virgil's *Eclogues*.[47]

More immediately relevant than Socratic dialogue, and closer
in time to Theocritus, are the early Hellenistic schools of philosophy. The *hasychia*, the ease (*otium*) of which Simichidas
speaks (*Idyll* 7.126), is the same stillness and leisure that constitutes the central hope of Stoicism[48] and especially of Epicureanism. Here we touch on something which, I suspect, is more
important than all the poetic parallels we may be able to dredge up
from the far reaches of earlier writings. The new thing about
Theocritus is, if I may put it so crudely, an attitude, a way of

looking at man in his world, whereby Theocritus takes his place alongside certain prose writers of his day. In spite of the notorious hazards involved in such an attempt,[49] it should be possible to show that some of the suggestions, not to say ideas, implicit in the major pastoral *Idylls* are reminiscent of what is found in the utterances of the moral philosophers whose teachings ushered in the new culture of which Theocritus is a part. There is no need to ask, even if the evidence permitted it, whether there was a direct contact between the philosopher and the poet. The philosophical and literary policies of the Hellenistic rulers, who liked to assemble successful writers at their courts, make such contact a distinct possibility.[50] It is sufficient to observe that on many scores Epicurus and Theocritus seem to be talking the same language, despite the fact that one uses the privileged speech of philosophy, and the other the vernacular of poetry. Ettore Bignone, an expert in both Theocritus and Epicurus, did not choose, except in passing, to comment on what the two might have in common.[51] This should certainly put us on our guard. But in the case of Virgil's *Eclogues* there is general agreement that the poetry is full of Epicurean elements,[52] and it was largely on this basis that Tenney Frank called Virgil an outright Epicurean.[53] If it can be shown that it is the tradition of the pastoral, rather than Virgil or any other writer in particular, that is to be associated with Epicurus, Frank's biographical thrust would lose much of its force.

Let us be clear about this: Theocritus' relation to Epicurus is *not* comparable to, for example, that of Goethe to Spinoza, or Coleridge to Plotinus. Goethe and Coleridge are conscious of philosophizing, and they have an accurate awareness of the sources to which they are indebted. This is probably tied up with their notion of the poet as a creator rather than transmitter. As a creator, the poet needs to know the raw materials that go into his handiwork; he also prides himself on the diversity and sometimes the inaccessibility of the raw materials. But even so pure a transmitter-poet as Lucretius should not be considered in the same light: his commitment is to a single source, and he sees himself as a philosopher. Theocritus has no philosophy; he does not allow his own likes and dislikes and commitments to come through at all. It is the poem rather than the poet that conjures up the spirit of Epicurus. In the following chapters, I propose to take up some of the themes and ideas which seem to me to document this affinity. I also hope that the discussion will clarify what is meant by a pastoral that is Epicurean *malgré lui*, without the blessings of a school descent.

3
Simplicity

In his learned and elaborate listing of various conceptions of Nature, A. O. Lovejoy records, as the fifteenth type, self-expression without self-consciousness, freedom from premeditation or deliberate and reflective design, artlessness.[1] The example he gives is from Boileau, *Epître* 9. For a more recent example, we might go to Camus' *L'Etranger* and the qualities that Sartre has praised in it. Since Sartre's remarks seem to me extremely instructive for our discussion of the "artlessness" of the pastoral, I take leave to cite some of his observations in full.

Are we not dealing here with the analytic assumption that any reality is reducible to a sum total of elements? Now, though analysis may be the instrument of science, it is also the instrument of humor. If in describing a rugby match I write: "I saw adults in shorts fighting and throwing themselves on the ground in order to send a leather ball between a pair of wooden posts," I have summed up what I have *seen*, but I have intentionally missed its meaning. . . . [M. Camus] slyly eliminates all the significant links which are also part of the experience. That is what Hume did when he stated that he could find nothing in experience but isolated impressions. That is what the American neo-realists still do when they deny the existence of any but external relations between phenomena. . . . We are now in a better position to understand the form of his narrative. Each sentence is a present instant, but not an indecisive one that spreads like a stain to the following one.

The sentence is sharp, distinct, and self-contained. It is separated by a void from the following one. . . . The world is destroyed and reborn from sentence to sentence. . . . A nineteenth century naturalist would have written: "A bridge spanned the river;" M. Camus will have none of this anthropomorphism. He says: "Over the river was a bridge." This object thus immediately betrays its passiveness. It *is there* before us, plain and undifferentiated. . . . People used to say that Jules Renard would end by writing things like: "The hen lays." M. Camus and many other contemporary writers would write: "There is the hen and she lays." The reason is that they like things for their own sake and do not want to dilute them in the flux of duration. . . . The novelist prefers these short-lived little sparkles, each of which gives a bit of pleasure, to an organized narrative.[2]

For similar remarks, this time *à propos* Alain Robbe-Grillet, we may go to Roland Barthes.[3]

Several things here command attention, notably the emphasis on brief, disconnected sentences; the stress on things rather than the relations between them; the reluctance to project into them feelings and modes of existence that are analogous to human feelings and modes; and the perception of a world that is not continuous, but a series of discrete units, each to be savored for its own sake. The artlessness affected by the pastoralist has much in common with the novelist's attempt to capture the absurdity and the beauty of things by assuming a posture resembling naiveté. At the opposite end of the scale stands the romantic lyric, which seeks to reduce the total of experience to a singular truth or a single moment of passionate involvement. Such unifying romanticism is rare in antiquity; to find a convincing example one has to go to an out-of-the-way poet like Paulus Silentarius (*Anthol. Pal.* 5.283), whose Theano poem shows an almost strained effort to dovetail movements in time:

> Lovely Theano poured out melancholy tears
> All night long, as I held her close to me in bed.
> The evening star was rising to the firmament
> And she complained it was a messenger of dawn.

> Nothing proceeds as mortals wish; a full career
> In Love requires solid nights of Arctic gloom.[4]

The flow of time is compressed, to allow for a perfect condensa-
tion of feeling in a unique experience. This is rare enough in an
ancient poem; in pastoral the accent is on separation and dis-
persal, not on unity. In Theocritus and Virgil the net effect of the
structure, however complex, runs counter to Aristotle's recommendations. There is no single curve, no anticipation of a dramatic
development. Ring composition and other structural devices
designed to induce a sensation of unity by formal means are
absent in the pastoral, where symmetrization absorbs all structural
instincts.[5] One analogy that might throw some light on what
Theocritus does is that of the suite or a similar musical form of
successive units. *Idylls* 1 and 7 are the most ambitious achievements along these lines; but almost every Theocritean or
Virgilian pastoral is best analyzed as a loose combination of
independent elements. It is left to the listener to weld the parts
together in his imagination if he so wishes; the poet provides
few if any clues for such an act of consolidation.

Critics of the pastoral who hold up the ideals of unity and
harmony are, therefore, likely to miss one of the essentials of the
genre. Much recent criticism, including the valuable work
of Poeschl and Otis, is based on the axiom that the quality of a
pastoral lyric, or of a performance in a pastoral singing match,
is in proportion to its structural harmony.[6] George Crabbe,
two centuries ago, had a clear perception of what the pastoralists
were about, though his vestigial Aristotelianism has him cast a
jaundiced eye:

> They ask no thought, require no deep design,
> But swell the song, and liquify the line.[7]

The artlessness of the pastoral lyric is different from that of a
pastoral romance. In *Daphnis and Chloe*, as in its countless imitators, naiveté is a protection against danger and corruption.

The simplicity of the characters ensures their day-for-day well-being and their ultimate survival. The naiveté of the writing protects the pastoral experience against the profundities and the syntheses which the plot, like any plot, is always on the verge of triggering. The poem does not have a plot and is not exposed to these dangers. Consequently, the artlessness of the poem is not there for a reason, but exists of itself, which also means that it is harder to explain.

The grandest attempt in modern times to make sense of the pastoral along the lines of Aristotelian unities is that of Thomas Purney.[8] He uses Aristotelian terms, such as "the fable" and "the moral result," and complains that in the traditional pastoral the action is too simple: "Since all Poetry is an Imitation of the most Considerable, or the most Delightful Actions ... not any trifling Action can be sufficient to constitute the *Fable*" (1.2). Thus neoclassicism, in spite of its considerable flexibility, is in a less favored position to appreciate the pastoral than is the post-romanticism of a Verlaine or a Frost. To emphasize *mythos* is, in this genre, a fatal step. In Purney's defense it should be added that in the sequel of his treatise he has many fine things to say, particularly about the need for simplicity. But he does so at considerable expense to his commitments, wrestling with his premise that any good poem, to be really good, must embody the dramatic unities.

Nevertheless, some of the most persuasive arguments on behalf of artlessness were produced at the height of the neo-classical period. René Rapin, in his *Dissertatio*, stresses the three Graces that make up the character of the pastoral: simplicity, brevity, and neatness.[9] That is to say: simplicity of thought and expression, shortness of periods full of sense and spirit, and the delicacy of a most elegant, ravishing, and unaffected neatness. A little earlier, Gilles Boileau, in his *Avis à Monsieur Ménage sur son églogue intitulée Christine*, criticizes the poem on two grounds —its lack of simplicity and its excessive length.[10] And Pope argues in his "Discourse on Pastoral Poetry" that, "it is not sufficient that the sentences only be brief, the whole eclogue should be so too." One suspects that the neoclassical emphasis on the briefness of the poem is little more than an acknowledgment that the poems of the ancient pastoralists were, on the whole, short. The willful Purney argued that longer poems gave the poet a better chance to realize the necessities of his *implex fable*. Purney's reservations were anticipated by the practice of the Pléiade, who went in for mammoth eclogues and provoked Dr. Johnson's anguished sigh: "A pastoral of an hundred lines may be endured; but who will hear of sheep and goats, and myrtle bowers and purling rivulets, through five acts?"[11]

Simplicity can be equated with a variety of things. It can be clumsiness or lack of polish. The British proto-romantics— Ambrose Philips, Tickell, Purney—approved of Spenser's attempt, especially in the "September" eclogue, to imitate rustic language, or at least to produce a facsimile of it. As is well known, this was the major point of contention between Pope and Philips, and between Boileau and Ronsard.[12] The "studied barbarity" and "clownishness" of Allan Ramsay's lowland Scots put off many of his contemporaries. But the idea that simple thoughts required simple language, and hence rustic thoughts rustic language, continued to hold sway, particularly among the regional poets who emerged in the nineteenth century. J. P. Hebel's "Die Feldhueter," an unexpectedly successful pastoral lyric of that period, is written in the Alemannic dialect, perhaps because Hebel felt that it corresponded in some fashion to Theocritus' Doric. It was for a similar reason that Purney (4.3.2) regarded English as superior to Latin for writing pastoral because of the abundance of monosyllables; Greek, he thought, was better than Latin because of its wealth of particles —presumably particles make a language less abstract—and also because of the availability of dialect words. Still, Greek is "too sonorous for Pastoral;" and he illustrates this by citing three words for herdsman, all of them, he seems to feel, too elevated in sound: *agroikos, poimēn, boukolos*. He does not, however, go along with Spenser. His main objection is that Spenser's diction is not simple but harsh (4.1–2). Purney favors Old-Words, but he wants them tender. Also, he wants few consonants. Subsequently he muddies his waters when he expresses a preference for compound words, but only such as are barely different from their simple surroundings.

In spite of the characteristically erratic quality of this passage, Purney's argument *for* simplicity but *against* clumsiness and harshness would have won the hearty approval of Theocritus, and perhaps also of Virgil, though Virgil is not beyond using the occasional archaic word, especially in *Eclogue* 3.[13] Some of the other Alexandrians, notably Callimachus, made a special point of enriching poetic speech with a massive dose of archaisms and vulgarisms. But Theocritus chose to employ the "ordinary" language of cultured conversation, the same language that we know from Plato and Lysias except that the dialect is Doric. Theocritean herdsmen are not peasants, or even herdsmen in any realistic sense, but men, members of the city of letters—on vacation, to be sure, but not gone native. There is no reason why they should rid themselves of the advantages of acceptable speech.

The Doric dialect is not a function of their special status. Why Theocritus, in the pastorals, used Doric rather than one of the other dialects that he uses elsewhere in his poetry is not entirely certain. Part of the answer may be supplied by the accident of his birth in Dorian Syracuse, and his sojourn in Dorian Cos. I would be inclined to attach a greater importance to his obvious indebtedness to archaic choral poetry;[14] his Doric is akin to the artificial idiom of Alcman and Stesichorus, rather than to the living speech of Syracuse.[15] Perhaps Attic, then the standard literary language, was for him so heavily invested with the trappings of city culture that he felt he could no longer use it for his purposes, much as it must have pained him to give up the vehicle of Socrates and Aristophanes. Like his landscape, his language was to be liberating, unpreempted; and so he chose a stylized version of Dorian. Theocritus knew better than to fall into the trap of Wordsworth, who thought that the "real language of men" is best for poetry, and who needed Coleridge to point out to him the equivocation in "real" and "ordinary."[16] Frost's pastoral diction furnishes an ironic parallel; it is colloquial but not provincial or rustic or dialectal. His poems do, however, show a certain folksiness, a tobacco-chewing drawl, that sets them apart from the elegance of Theocritus' surfaces, and in a sense renders them *more* dialectal. Theocritus' speech, in spite of its clean-cut simplicity, is his own creation, much as Milton's language in "Lycidas" was his own.[17] The diction is personal, but wholly devoid of difficulty. No special dictionary is needed for Theocritus, as there is for Ambrose Philips and Robert Burns.

The ancient critics do not often comment on Theocritus' style, but where they do, they tend to classify it as *humilis* or *aphelēs*.[18] That is to say, the ancient judgments lie between the poles of "unpretentious" and "clear." The most useful estimate of the plain style is given in Demetrius' *On Style*. Its recommendations provide, in some ways, the best introduction to Theocritus' use of language, in spite of the fact that they are designed to aid the composition of prose oratory rather than poetry. Demetrius emphasizes the need for short clauses with clearly felt, unprotracted endings (par. 204); he recommends the avoidance of unusual words and pointed rhythmic effects (221); he presses for concreteness and a full presentation of details (209).[19] He further warns against internal hiatus of long vowels (207—the warning is tacitly cancelled in 219), and anything else that might induce the effects of drama and tension rather than lucidity (192). All of this reads like a body of recommendations drawn from some of Theocritus' most characteristic poetry; it comes almost as a shock to realize that Demetrius does not consider Theocritus worthy of quotation.[20] Longinus, as might be expected, also leaves Theocritus out of the picture, since Longinus' work has the avowed purpose of reaffirming the status of "fine writing" —*hypsos*—against the champions of the plain style. Theocritus would have found Longinus' approach overly romantic, lacking in a sense of humor and in a knowledge of the kinds of decisions a poet has to make.

In the later nineteenth century, after the experiment of Wordsworth had run its course, there was a feeling that Theocritus was to be preferred to Virgil because of the elegance of his plain style. As Leigh Hunt puts it: in Virgil this elegant simplicity "became a rhetorical mistake, an artificial flower stuck in the ground. In Theocritus it was the growth of the soil; myrtle and almond springing by the wayside."[21] Hunt gives examples, from his own experience, of simple people using elegant and witty language "when sensibility gives them the power of expression, and animal spirits the courage to use it." The Wordsworthian echo outlives the Wordsworthian value judgment.

Coleridge was not fooled by such fancies, and his remarks may serve as an introduction to our next subject, that of syntax. Coleridge writes that

the rustic, from the more imperfect development of his faculties and from the lower state of their cultivation, aims almost solely to convey insulated facts, either those of his scanty experience or his traditional belief; while the educated man chiefly seeks to discover and express those connections of things . . . from which some more or less general law is deducible.[22]

This is part of his argument against Wordsworth, but the argument also turns against Coleridge himself; for pastoral is *not* a chain of links leading to a conclusion. Coleridge's poetic principles put him on the side of the educated man and the deducing of general laws. It is a measure of the distance between Coleridge's view of poetry and Theocritus' practice that Theocritus gives us the paratactic units of experience which Coleridge chalks up to rusticity, but which have just as much in common with the epic.[23] Like the epic, the pastoral refuses to prescribe a hierarchy of values; each unit of the pastoral world is savored as independently important. The universal democracy of pastoral beings is reflected in the disjunctive patterns of pastoral speech.

Here again, Frost comes close to the pastoral paradigm. Frost's construction is loose and informal; he has few strong connectives; there is a wordiness that makes for economy because it bypasses logical sutures. The texture of the speech is casual, and in this the grammar mirrors a larger looseness. "In Pastoral, the serious and the humorous, the important and the humble commonplace are not opposites," but continuous, or rather serial.[24] The same commentator goes on to explain that, "the casualness on the part of the speaker is really the means of implying more serious things." This may be true of Frost, though I suspect that Frost himself would pour cold water on intimations of profundity in his pastorals. "It is a wild tune," he writes in "The Figure a Poem Makes," "it is a poem. Our problem then is, as modern abstractionists, to have the wildness pure; to be wild with nothing to be wild about. We bring up as aberrationists, giving way to undirected associations and kicking ourselves from one chance suggestion to another in all directions as of a hot afternoon in the life of a grasshopper." To have the wildness pure, and yet to make a poem out of it: that is the problem of the Theocritean pastoralist. The pastoral lyric transcribes life in its discreteness. And this is what comes out in the syntax also.

Rapin explains, in his *Dissertatio*, what he means by brevity as a characteristic of pastoral. In many of the poems of Theocritus and Virgil, he says, the "periods . . . have no conjunctions to connect them;" and there should be "many stops and breakings off," else the pastorals cannot please.[25] On this score of internal asyntaxis, he feels that the Italians are deficient; their wit and their grandiloquence make them incapable of observing the disconnective decorum of the pastoral tradition. Strangely enough, Rapin thinks that Virgil does better in this than Theocritus: "Virgil is neither so continued nor so long as Theocritus." But probably this means nothing more than what Scaliger has to say on the matter: Theocritus is everywhere relaxed and extended; Virgil is economical, concise, polished, smooth, compact.[26] Here again, Theocritus' speech is characterized as casual, unperiodic, loose-jointed. These are the qualities demanded by the freedom and the simplicity of the genre.[27]

This brings us to a third way of understanding simplicity, in addition to plain diction and loose syntax: simplicity as lack of insight, deficiency in logic, naiveté. The artlessness of which Lovejoy speaks, and Coleridge's "imperfect development of faculties," is in Theocritus a very special sort of freedom, akin to the freedom from the ballast of civilization recommended by Epicurus. Cicero's Torquatus, in the apologia for Epicureanism that fills most of the first book of De finibus, exclaims on the accessibility, simplicity, and immediacy of the path pioneered by Epicurus.[28] Epicurus' advice to Pythocles to forsake all culture and overrefinement, and the general Epicurean principle that the life of politics and the public calendar is a prison house, point straight to the Hellenistic figures who embody a simplicity far removed from the turmoil of the city: Callimachus' Hecale, Eratosthenes' Erigone, and in the end Ovid's Philemon and Baucis.[29] Delight in nature requires little sophistication. Since the Epicurean sage—or, for that matter, the pastoral character—does not live in fear, he does not need the defense mechanisms of *paideia*.

Thus revulsion against the burden of the city leads to primitivism. Athenaeus (12.536E) tells a story about Ptolemy Philadelphus looking out of his palace window and envying the simple fellahin he could see from there.[30] There are varieties of primitivism; the type evinced by Epicurus (and, if I am right, Theocritus) should not be regarded in the same light as the brute animal primitivism of the Cynics, though the latter is not uncongenial to at least one Epicurean, Lucretius. According to Epicurus,

autarkeia, the principle of animal self-sufficiency and self-satis-
faction, must be practiced with moderation.[31] The emphasis on
friendship safeguards the Epicurean against surrendering the communal instinct altogether. But, it is felt, friendship flourishes
more securely in the absence of those elements in the culture that
make for affectation and anxiety.

In his Preface to *Sylvae* (1685) Dryden complains that Virgil's
shepherds are too well read in the philosophy of Epicurus and
Plato, but Theocritus and Tasso have taken theirs from cottages
and plains. He is wrong on both counts, since Virgil's herdsmen
are not as a rule learned, and Theocritus' herdsmen have little to
do with Hesiod and his cottage. But the instinct that prompted the
complaint and the praise is sound. The pastoral character must be
limited in insight precisely because he is free and need not ferret
out mysteries or solve problems. When, *à propos* of an edition of
Spenser in 1810, John Aikin objected to Spenser's learning, he is
on firmer ground.[32] One imagines he preferred Michael Drayton,
who, in his "To The Reader of his Pastorals" (1619), proposes to
leave allegory and high matters to others.

The naiveté of the pastoral herdsmen is not the same as the
naiveté celebrated by the Pléiade, which is not without grandeur,
or as *das Naive* of Schiller, which is a variety of spontaneity.[33]
Unlike these conceptions, which do not involve any sense of
limitation, the pastoral naiveté borders on childishness and even
silliness. Callimachus is especially adept at portraying an immature,
harmlessly unfocused mentality entrusted with the task of telling impossible tales. The Hellenistic age witnessed an increased
interest in children and their artless gestures. Some of the most
charming and convincing moments in Alexandrian poetry and
painting come about when the elusive world of action is har-
dened into miniature by allowing children to be in apparent
control.[34] Prior to this period, only Aeschylus shows a similar
understanding of infantile simplicity; note the portrayal of Perseus
in his satyr play, *The Netfishers*.

Theocritus does not actually have children among his *personae*. The slaves of *Idyll* 8 are conceived as teen-agers rather than children, in spite of the reference to the stern parents (line 15). *Idyll* 19 is spurious. But Theocritus' reduction of complex experiences by means of a concentration upon youthful inexperience is of the same sort. Youth, rather than maturity or old age, is in control; vigor, not wisdom, is the norm. And the patterns of expression are often curiously like the simple phrases of children's songs and games. In the eyes of the Hesiodic farmer of *Idyll* 10, lines 56–58, this is exactly what they are. It is as if the pastoral singer had taken Plato's Callicles or Euripides' Zethus at his word, and decided that art was indeed a children's game, and that only a children's game was true art, free of the compulsions and compressions of a civic existence.

When Bucaeus, the pastoral lover of *Idyll* 10, imagines himself coming into a fortune, he conceives his life with his beloved Bombyca as a model of playful innocence:

> We would be golden, you and I, trophies of Venus,
> You with your double pipe, an apple, or a rose,
> I in my new suit, and sandals for both feet.[35]

A lover who plans to use the wealth of Croesus to buy himself a suit of clothes and a pair of shoes, one for each foot, reminds us of a street urchin playing games. Compare the ingenuousness of the distributive arrangement in Virgil's *Eclogue* 4, lines 55–57 (I give the Latin; translation obscures the point at issue):

> Non me carminibus vincat nec Thracius Orpheus,
> nec Linus, huic mater quamvis atque huic pater adsit,
> Orphei Calliopea, Lino formosus Apollo.[36]

Or the guileless parenthesis of "Lycidas," line 111:

> The Golden opes, the Iron shuts amain.[37]

For another example of pastoral naiveté we may go to Praxilla, a poetess briefly mentioned as one of the possible predecessors of the pastoralists. We have a fragment from a Hymn to Adonis (frag. 1) in which Adonis is asked what he most hated to leave behind when he died. His answer:

> The finest thing I leave behind is the light of the sun;
> Next come the bright stars, and the face of the moon;
> And after that—ripe figs, and apples, and pears.[38]

Antiquity recognized the special humor of counting heavenly bodies and fruits within the same system of values, and spoke of a person of slow wits as one more foolish than the Adonis of Praxilla. This tradition of childlike simplicity in the pastoral may have persuaded Empson to classify the Alice books as pastoral: "The formula is now 'child-become-judge,' and if Dodgson identifies himself with the child so does the writer of the primary sort of pastoral with his magnified version of the swain."[39] And yet, as already stated, Theocritus does not include children, deliberately one assumes because, as a recent theatrical production of *Peanuts* has shown, the humorous effect of ingenuousness is more powerful if the voices are those of young adults.

The pastoral herdsmen, we conclude, are, if not children, at least protected by the same patterns that make the child's world familiar and pleasurable. The shepherd's range of understanding and reasoning is limited, but the limitation has its advantages; for, as Coleridge reminds us in spite of himself, the herdsman discovers all manner of realities, including some not commonly recognized, though he fails to become fully aware of their connection, or of the inferences that may be drawn from them. He is not a thinker, much less a logician, or an oxymorist, but a perceiver of concrete sensations and beautiful things.[40] There is humor in the limitation; here as elsewhere, Theocritus' handling of the pastoral business is often also an act of deprecation and of parody.[41] But, more importantly, there is strength and cheerfulness.

Theocritus has no older herdsmen, which should have been a sufficient warning signal that he is not copying the conditions of the farming and ranching life. For the age desired in real herdsmen we turn to Varro who describes the type of herdsman wanted for each flock.[42] He concludes: neither old men nor mere boys can easily endure the hardships of the trail and the steepness and roughness of the mountains. Thus, the best herdsmen are men in their prime. The youthful age of the Theocritean characters has more to do with the situation described by Aristotle: the young practice kindness because of their natural humanity, while the old do so from weakness and self-protection.[43] Soon after Theocritus, however, mature and old men invade the pleasance. In Bion's "The Bird Catcher" (frag. 13) the catcher is too young to recognize Love, and has to be tutored by an older man.[44] Virgil's first *Eclogue* features an older man; perhaps it is significant that Tityrus has given up the pure pastoral life for something more complex, compounding *otium* with admiration for God and City. The pseudo-virgilian "Culex" also has an old herdsman who, like Bion's instructor, makes it his business to teach. One might compare Milon in Theocritus' *Idyll* 10; but his age is not specified, and though extremely narrow in his reactions, he is *not* a herdsman but a farmer. In later pastoral the theme of youth versus maturity and old age become an accepted *topos*. In Spenser's "Februarie," Old Age is under attack, through the instrument of the tale of the Oak and the Briar. In *Eglog* 7 of Drayton's *Idea, The Shepheards Garland*, old Borrill's surly verses are spelled by young Batte's foolish stanzas in praise of love. Throughout this collection of Drayton's, the main figure is more likely than not an older, disenchanted man who advises a lusty youth to go slow. Finally, in Wordsworth's "Michael," all virtue is on the side of the old; not only the father and the mother, even the housewife's lamp is aged. This is not the scheme of the pastoral, but that of the georgic; and it is wrong to take the Philemon and Baucis episode in *Faust* II as a pastoral scene, *pace* Poggioli, who attempts to show that what he calls the "pastoral of innocence" makes for idylls of Old Age rather than of Youth.[45] That Philemon and Baucis belong in the Hesiodic tradition is shown also by the final pages of Saint-Lambert's *Saisons*. In the Theocritean pastoral, the old man is best suited to the role of a marginal character: a listener, or a former pastoral hero, or an umpire, but not a central figure:

> And old Damoetas lov'd to hear our song.

To return to the larger subject of pastoral naiveté: a glance at *Eclogue* 3, line 40, may help to show that Virgil's objectives are slightly different from those of Theocritus. Menalcas tries, vainly, to remember the name of an astronomer. This is the technique of the artist who lets his readers know that his characters are untutored, or badly tutored. Virgil is, as it were, in agreement with the rules of decorum pronounced by the neoclassicists: a herdsman should not be able to talk about matters which are beyond his ken. Or, to speak more precisely, Virgil has his character strain against the rule, but at the last minute pulls back, and by this jolt reminds the reader of the existence of the rule more effectively than if he had never broached the possibility of the herdsman facing up to his test. Theocritus chooses not to remind us of the rule; he follows it from the start, and thereby allows us not to be conscious of it. He does not interpose his own perspective; his herdsmen never search for words. They know all that they need to know—and that, on occasion, includes book learning such as mythology. We accept the fact that a Daphnis knows his Homeric heroes; we are ready to assume that he knows their names from public recitals or primary schooling rather than, as a sober second thought must admit, from the mythological handbooks. What he knows, he expresses fully. Perhaps the difference can best be formulated in the following way: Virgil's herdsmen can be reflective to the extent of bringing up perceptibly against the limits of their capacity; Theocritus' herdsmen raise only such questions as they can answer.

Thomas Purney, in one of his moments of insight, praises Ovid for the first two lines of his treatment of Proserpina dropping her flowers, and condemns him for the following lines: "If he he had stopt with the second line he had put himself, as 'twere, in the place of a Shepherd, and spoke of the Misfortune as if it came from his Heart. . . . But in the two last lines he takes upon him the Author, is grave and reflecting. . . ."[46] Purney criticizes Ovid for investing his characters with mental efforts that do not go on all fours with the ethos of the poem. The teasing of Virgil's Menalcas, who labors to recollect a piece of learning, is similarly corruptive. It transforms the modality of the tradition, and starts the pastoral off on a track which was to lead to Boccaccio and Donne. It is perfectly proper for Horace (*Satires* 1.10.44–45) to remark of Virgil's pastoral that it is *molle et facetum*; I suspect *facetum* refers to the latent relations and significances upon which the Virgilian herdsmen seem about to stumble much of the time. Nor is it mistaken for modern critics to regard Virgil's shepherd as a kind of wise fool, though there is a danger that this romantic concept is taken too far.[47]

The real distinction between Theocritus and Virgil, a distinction that underlies many of the things we have been talking about, has something to do with the difference between epic and lyric. One way of testing this is to note the divergences between Theocritus' *Idyll* 11, "Polyphemus," and Virgil's *Eclogue* 2, "Corydon," which the poet clearly wanted to be read as a re-working of "Polyphemus."[48] Polyphemus' song is a neatly articulated series of entreaties, reminiscences, reproaches, and boasts. Each of these forms a separate paragraph, insulated from what comes before and what comes after. Each thought is fully and palpably expressed, without the reservations or assimilations that a larger plan might necessitate. The series is discontinuous, a fine example of what Frost calls "giving way to undirected associations . . . as of a hot afternoon in the life of a grasshopper." The order of ideas is not unnatural; but it is not inconceivable that a different ordering might have done equally well. As Polyphemus slips—or, rather, skips—from his memory of the first meeting with Galatea, to the ugliness of his face, to the mountains of cheese he owns, to the loveliness of his habitat, to his remarkable wish dreams—he wants to be even uglier, a sort of fish, so he can swim to his girl—we witness an art that delights in limitation: the limited understanding, the self-contained thought set off against the next thought, the narrow sensibility that shies away from excesses and fixations.

Virgil's Corydon does not kick himself from one chance suggestion to another in all directions. The pastoral facade of discontinuity is there, but it is only a facade. Behind it the impulses are synthetic and sustained. The lover longs for death, but into his contemplation of despair the colorful life of the senses insinuates itself. The images of Thestylis pounding and tossing her rustic salad, and of the cicada shrilling in the burning sun, jostle his query, "Do you, then, force me to die?" and with it produce a new, unified texture in which life and death are held in a lyric tension. The gifts are not, as in "Polyphemus," offered abruptly and with abandon; the singer moves into this section gently, almost insensibly, via a reminder of Pan's invention of the pipes. At first, that is, the pipe is mentioned as a means of companionship, enabling Corydon and his beloved to hold their concert in imitation of Pan; only secondarily does it become clear that the pipe is the first in a series of gifts. Throughout, the poem brings together dream with reality, light and fire with darkness and shade, love with work, in a pattern that moves through contrasts into a larger harmony. The "incoherent strains" announced at the beginning of the poem[49] emerge as the nicely calculated elements which dovetail into a lyric whole. Virgil's pastorals already exhibit the qualities that were to distinguish the writing of the *Aeneid*, the lyricism which combines disparate segments into charged aggregates and in the process uncovers deeper levels of sympathy. One of the results is that Virgilian man is less concretely isolated, less securely limited in his animal strength than the Theocritean shepherd; the harmonizing force of

Virgil's vision rescues Corydon from his niche and makes him into a sufferer. The speech continues to be that of the traditional herdsman whose simplicity is his strength. But the sensibility is that of a larger, more integrated world.

Theocritus, faithful to the demands of naiveté, avoids syntheses, and rewards us with a world savored as discrete units. His herdsmen respond to memories and pleasures and pains, but do not attempt to mold them into larger perceptions, and thus do not surrender a shred of their singularity. Note the curious sequence in *Idyll* 6, lines 15–19: Daphnis, purportedly addressing the Cyclops, develops these thoughts, in this order: (1) Galatea makes fun of you; (2) in summer her hair is dry; (3) she alternately pursues and avoids you; (4) she plays a desperate game; (5) in love all is fair. The procedure is akin to that of the epic rather than the lyric, according to the terms stipulated by Emil Staiger.[50] This is one more vindication of the usefulness of the ancient discussions which classified the pastoral under the heading of epic. It ratifies Theocritus' instinct in choosing epic verse, rather than Anacreontics or Aristophanic meters, to express his kind of lyricism, the pastoral vision of paratactic beauties and joys. The verse structure is designed to block the centripetal energies of the lyric. That Virgil chose to by-pass the safeguard, and to open the epic edifice to the full lyric impulse, is proof of his great originality and of his special standing in the repertory of ancient pastoral.

Finally, a few remarks about "anonymity." In a now notorious essay, originally published in 1933, John Crowe Ransom called "Lycidas" "A Poem Nearly Anonymous."[51] He argued that it was one of the features of the poem that it seemed to be devoid of the personal lyricism which one might expect from a poem written ostensibly to voice one person's grief over the death of another. "Lycidas" depersonalizes grief; and in a way that is the secret of its consolatory power. Ransom chooses to say nothing about the possible links between this technique of anonymity and the pastoral tradition as such. It must be admitted that the Renaissance pastoral, with its heavy admixture of devices borrowed from other genres, had done much to efface earlier moves in this direction. But in this respect "Lycidas" is squarely in the succession of Theocritus. Unlike the "subjective," "confessional" lyricism of the archaic poets, the mood of the Theocritean pastoral is public; the authorial reticence is comparable to what we find in drama and epic, and, more appropriately perhaps, in philosophy. What such a poem as *Idyll* 7 gives us is personal sentiment without personal reference, via the neutral agency of the third person. We may wish to identify the narrator with Theocritus himself; but the author wards off the identification, or rather plays cat and mouse with it by interposing the name Simichidas, which is not a *Schluesselname*, but a device to bar the ego. The paratactic naiveté sees to it that the lyricism, such as it is, does not turn private or ego-centered. Virgil's nameless poet (*Eclogue* 10.70) and Milton's "uncouth swain" permit a fleeting appearance of the author. Theocritus rules out even this much; when he does refer to himself, in the epistolary introduction of *Idylls* 11 and 13, it is not in the guise of a herdsman. Theocritus' pastoral locates the source of pleasure and vitality not within the man, as the archaic lyric had done, but in external stimuli and in the relations between men, and between all animate creatures including the brooks and the pines. The lyricism is distributive, disengaged, "cool." Theocritus refers to himself in the third person, and under another name; and though the herdsmen in their songs and conversations use the first person "I," our imagination is conditioned to convert the "I's" into "he's" and "she's," and to add the information given in the speeches and performances to the random picture of animate beings inspected and overheard. The purpose of this expunging of the ego is to avoid the potential grossness of the earlier lyric, and also its didacticism. With a great artist like Theocritus, the coolness does not degenerate into frigidity; its simplicity and its humor save it from that. Other pastoral writers are less skillful.

Nevertheless, the anonymity of the Theocritean pastoral continued to be one of the characteristic features of the genre, in spite of the many deviations from the norm. The amused detachment of Drayton's *The Muses Elizium* is a persuasive witness. One reason why the pastoral appealed to the neoclassicists, and did not sit well with the romantics, is this quality of "public" lyricism. The pastoral puts obstacles in the way of the romantic ego delivering itself of its passionate convictions. It defies empathy, and calls for detached admiration. Our present age, with its taste for a non-sentimental and non-sermonizing poetry, has once more taken kindly to it. To demonstrate the lasting power of pastoral impersonality, I would like to end with some remarks of Kermode about Yeats' pastoral elegy for Robert Gregory.[52] Yeats saw in the pastoral form

a device for ensuring an aristocratic distance between the poet and his subject, a possibility of achieving an interesting stoic [I would have said Epicurean] coldness, as of carved flames. The best he could hope to achieve in the pastoral elegy would be this monumental apathy. . . . But where Spenser could not escape frigidity, and Milton . . . could not escape the charge of it, Yeats could not succeed.

The reasons for the failure alleged by Kermode are connected with the "system" which Yeats was then working out for himself. But the example of Theocritus suggests that Kermode is incautious in equating pastoral detachment with coldness or apathy. "Lycidas," like *Idyll* 1, shows us that the pastoral elegy is not calculated to provoke grief, but to assuage it, with the reminder that the self (both the victim's and the mourner's) is only one of many, and that tangible beauty counts for more than spiritual pain. Yeats' poem is not one of his best, but this has nothing whatever to do with the choice of the pastoral form. The detached perspective of the pastoral lyric, crisp, clear, distributive, is one the most subtle corollaries of Theocritean simplicity.

4
Otium

One of the Epicurean mottos runs as follows: "It is better to lie on the naked ground and be at ease, than to have a golden couch and a rich table and be worried."[1] "To be at ease": the Greek is *tharrein*, which is variously translated "to be of good cheer," or "to be without fear," depending on whether the context emphasizes the absence of worry or the presence of a feeling of comfort. Lack of fear and a sense of well-being: the two are interdependent. The most striking demonstration of their correlation is given by Virgil toward the end of the second book of the *Georgics* (lines 458 ff.). The passage is too long to quote; I hope I will be forgiven if I summarize. Virgil starts with a curiously un-Hesiodic description of life in the country. Farmers are fortunate, if only they knew it. They live far from the noise of battle; the earth produces for them on her own accord. They may not live in luxury, but in carefree tranquillity (*secura quies*); they do not know deception; they are wealthy in many things, such as leisure, caves, fresh-water lakes, cool Tempe, the lowing of cattle, sleep under a tree, groves, clearings for beasts, a hardy young manhood, gods worshiped and parents honored. Then Virgil begins a new paragraph: I hope, he says, the Muses will accept me and instruct me in astronomy, the causes of earthquakes and tides, and the reasons for the variations of the seasons. But if my advancement in that field is blocked by my own lack of talent, then may I find pleasure in the country and in cool rivers and brooks and woods. Another new paragraph: happy is he who first determined the causes of things (i.e., most probably, Epicurus), who expelled fear and the preoccupation with death. Fortunate also he who knows the country gods, Pan, Silvanus, the Nymphs. He is indifferent to the life of the state, the turmoil of history; he is indifferent to commiseration or envy. He is maintained by the earth and her fruits, and has no dealings with the instruments of war and politics.

To begin with, Virgil pictures the life in the country and the life of scientific endeavour as alternatives. But as the encomium continues, it becomes clear that, poetically speaking at least, the two lives reinforce each other. Science removes anxiety, and only a man without fears can achieve the calm and the happiness that can no longer be found in the city. The last paragraph, with its rejection of commiseration, has a touch of Stoicism about it. But the bulk of the passage is orthodox Epicureanism. This is the more striking as the rest of the second book is by no means devoted to a praise of leisure. The craft of arboriculture, which accounts for most the book, involves its own hardships and its own anxieties. But the life described in our passage is not that of the farmer but that of the pastoral man. The two things, Virgil suggests, that will help us to achieve the stability of mind which makes for happiness are, first, a thorough understanding of the workings of the universe; and, second, a life of simple good fellowship, with a company of like-minded and unambitious friends. The former neutralizes the fear of the gods; the latter removes the fear of tyranny and enslavement. As Epicurus says in his *Letter to Pythocles*: The chief objective in learning the science of the *meteōra*, of physical phenomena, as in all else, is the achievement of *ataraxia*, imperturbability, and self-confidence.[2] The correlation between the study of astronomy and the enjoyment of a country life is, therefore, an Epicurean *topos*; it is that, I suspect, also in Virgil's *Eclogue* 6 where the trapped Silenus, forcibly becalmed by his friends and singing in the shade of a secluded grotto, starts his song about the misuse of human talents with an extended cosmology couched in Epicurean meteorological terms.

But the main thing is the calmness, the tranquillity of the spirit. In Theocritus' seventh *Idyll*, the goatherd poet Lycidas addresses Simichidas as follows:

> Simichidas, where are you going at this noon hour
> When even the lizard sleeps on his wall of rock
> And the larks, the tomb birds, do not fly abroad?[3]

Lycidas is surprised that Simichidas is afoot, and he may well be, for in the typical pastoral landscape people are ordinarily at rest, standing, more often sitting or reclining. The time is usually the noon hour, when the sun burns too fiercely for comfort, when the whole nature enters into a state of suspension, and all flux, or almost all, is put to rest. It is then that nature does for the herdsman what Virgil's Silenus has done for him by his friends; it forces him into a condition of *hasychia*, or *otium*, to use the Latin equivalent.[4] *Otium* is a keyword in the discussion of the pastoral. Its frequency in Latin pastoral texts is remarkable, especially if compared with the rarity of *hasychia* and *hasychos* in Theocritus. The latter is due to Theocritus' refusal to use abstractions, to talk theoretically about what is concretely dramatized in the poems, which would permit his herdsmen an awareness of the implications of their lives. Only at the end of *Idyll* 7 is *hasychia* prominently mentioned, at a moment when the narrator takes matters into his own hands and describes the near take-over of nature at the Coan picnic.

Otium, as has recently been made plausible, is originally a military term, meaning something like the American "liberty," a soldier's leave from duty.[5] Duty, in the early texts, is often *negotium*. *Otium*, then, is vacation, freedom, escape from pressing

business, particularly a business with overtones of death. Within
the pastoral, *otium* is two things; it is the condition under which
the herdsmen operate, the social and psychological characteristics
of their world; but it is also a function of the ethos of the poem,
the idea which the poem is expected to communicate over and
beyond the dramatic realities within it. Precisely what this
means will have to emerge later. For the present, it is important
to recognize that the *otium* of pastoral poetry is not, as is sometimes averred, an escapist mechanism, motivated by a generally
pessimistic view about the real world. Pastoral is, for instance,
sometimes compared with the landscape painting which flourished
in seventeenth-century Holland. Kenneth Clark says in his
illuminating book on landscape painting: "We may . . . count
landscape painting as a symptom of quietism. After the pande-
monium of religious war and the hurly-burly of, shall we say,
Ben Jonson's plays, man needed an interval of calm."[6] This
is roughly the view which Poggioli has of the pastoral: pastoral,
as a fruit of Hellenistic retrenchment, is premised on retreat,
on wish dream, on *Platzangst*.[7] In a sense all literature is a retreat
from action. But to put pastoral on the same level as Timon's
scheme to live by himself in a garden in order to avoid human
intercourse is a risky business.[8] To be sure, during the Hellenistic
age, particularly in the early decades of it during and immediately
after the wars of the Successors, quietism and escapism were
common enough. The Cynic preachers, as well as the Epicureans
and poets like Posidippus, recommended "retirement into conversation with oneself," and suggested that this best be done
away from the madding crowd, in the country or the garden.[9]
Menander's *Dyskolos*, the embittered man who seeks solitude in
the country, has recently become the leading ancient exemplar
of this flight from civic reality.

Another celebrated theme of this kind is the rustic picnic, the
coming together of like-minded recusants for the sake of eating
and drinking in the country. Of this Theocritus has one example,

in the last section of *Idyll* 7; in Roman poetry it comes to be very common.[10] We may compare the open-air party in Renaissance painting, and then again in nineteenth-century France; in Giorgione and Bellini and in Corot. This theme has in it less of the flight from reality and more of the joy of living. It is much closer to what the pastoral has to offer, though in fact, with its crowded company, its distant *veduta* of buildings, and its occasional mythological superstructure, it does not make as clean a break with the world of the court and the academy as the pastoral demands. Neither the hermit's cell nor the picnic provide full scope for the *otium*, for the cancellation of disturbance and hardship and change to which the pastoral aspires.[11]

One Renaissance pastoral, Thomas Lodge's "The Shepheards Sorrow, Being Disdained in Love" (1593), enters a forceful protest against the world's changeability:

> Rob the Spheare of lines united,
>   Make a suddaine voide in nature:
> Force the day to be benighted,
>   Reave the cause of time and creature,
> Ere the world will cease to varie.[12]

Because the poem is a pastoral, the protest is reinforced with *adynata*, challenges from impossibility. The same protest against variety, underscored by Spenser's Platonism, is found in the *Mutabilitie Cantos* added to the *Fairie Queene* in the 1609 edition, and featuring Nature's decision against the Titaness, Mutabilitie.[13] The polemical nature of this, as of many Renaissance arguments against *kinēsis*, is obvious. The case of Theocritus is different. For him the Platonic depreciation of flux is less relevant than the Epicurean notion of *hēdonē katastēmatikē* (tranquil joy). Epicurus recognized the difficulty of positing *stasis* in a world in which nothing stands still. His use of the word *galēnē* (calm of the storm) and its derivatives shows his awareness of the marginal swirl, which no philosophy can throw out entirely.

The Epicurean invocation of calm is assisted by the axiom that there is, objectively speaking, no time. The present is all; memories and hopes are insubstantial; time relations are merely secondary functions of body and place.[14] Thus the Epicurean sage assures himself that there is nothing to fear. But unlike the Stoic saint, who takes the same premise as his cue for cancelling all effects and all emotional ties between men, the Epicurean sage is not dispassionate.[15] Tranquillity, not coldness, is the Epicurean goal. Epicurus' call for *otium* makes room for friendship and gratitude and compassion, feelings that take the sting of paralysis out of the calm of the bower. Between the *otium* of the Epicurean and the *otium* of the herdsman there is only one significant difference; the *otium* of the pastoral, as envisaged by Theocritus, is not argumentative but casual. Its *stasis* is, as we have said, not just a function of the setting but also a quality of the poem itself.

The concept of *hasychia* comes in quite early in Greek literature. In Pindar, its associations are aristocratic; *hasychia* is the quiet refinement of the chosen few. It can be exercised, in fact *must* be exercised along with the activities of the responsible citizen. Its opposite is, not life in the city, but life in a democracy. Similarly the *otium* advocated by Euripides' Amphion is of a different order:

> The man who leads a quiet life is a safe friend
> To his friends, and best for the city . . .
> . . . I have no truck with the mighty daring
> Of sailors or of heads of state.[16]

Here, in spite of the opposition to the turbulence of political life, the chief criterion continues to be the usefulness to the city. Amphion's comments are very much in the tradition of Xenophanes' protest against the veneration of athletes and soldiers. Wisdom, Xenophanes holds, has as much to contribute to the welfare of society as the exertions of those who labor with their bodies.[17]

This kind of *otium*, which does not shut itself off from the affairs of the city but offers certain advantages to her, is regularly found as an object of praise and nostalgia in Augustan poetry. The temper of the Augustan restoration would have frowned on any interpretation of *otium* that completely disregarded the welfare of the commonwealth and of the citizen. Hence the stalwart, and quite unpastoral, quality of *otium* advocated by Horace, in what is perhaps the most famous ancient poem about *otium*, *Ode* 16 of Book 2.[18] Similarly when Ovid and Tibullus speak of taking a vacation in the country or in the garden, the minor sacrifices to be made to the garden divinities remind us that this kind of *otium* is an extension of the *negotium* beyond it, a busman's holiday.

Another form of *otium*, again not quite the one featured in Theocritus, is recommended by Borrill, an old man, against the frolic advocated by the younger Batte, in the seventh *Eglog* of Drayton's *Idea*. At the end of the eclogue, Batte come round and accepts the peaceful resignation supported by the old man. Theocritus' *otium*, on the contrary, is *not* the abolition of energy, not withdrawal and curtailment, but a fullness in its own right. Schiller has a fine perception of what the pastoral *otium*, at its best, is, and what it is not.

It is determined by the fact that the opposition between reality and ideal, which had supplied satire and elegy with material, is entirely abolished, and with it also the conflict between the passions. The prevailing character of this kind of poetry is calm, the calm of perfection, not the calm of idleness; a calm which derives from the equilibrium of forces, not from their paralysis, from fullness, not from a vacuum. . . . But precisely because all resistance is gone, it becomes very much more difficult . . . to generate the movement, without which poetry cannot be effective at all.[19]

Schiller has caught the special qualities, but also the special difficulties of the Theocritean *otium*: the difficulty, above all, of giving shape to a tranquillity which is not anemic and cold, a calm which allows for liveliness and play. This is a difficulty that has philosophical dimensions. The cancellation of *kinēsis* that we find in Platonism makes either for the mortification of the ascetic or for the drug-culture of the hedonist. Neither solution will do; the hard primitivism of the Cynic is just as useless to the pastoral as the soft primitivism of the Aristippean or the flower children. The recluse who isolates himself in the wilderness and practices a hermetic existence, rarely enough described in ancient pagan letters, is certainly unwelcome in the bucolic pleasance.[20] Conversely, the orgies of a Cockaigne are not conducive to the pastoral vision.

Fontenelle saw the solution of the pastoral puzzle in an elegant combination of idleness and love. Men do not "relish a state of absolute Laziness. . . . No, they must have some motion, some agitation, but it must be such a motion and agitation as may be reconcil'd, if possible, to the kind of Laziness that possesses 'em, and this is most happily to be found in Love."[21] Idleness is important, or at least the absence of labor. In Greek, the ideas of absence of labor and absence of trouble happen to be very closely allied. The peasant ideal includes some activities, such as harvesting, which gladden the farmer's heart. But even the most puritanical tiller of the soil would be inclined to dispense with the chores that break his back and kill his spirit. Thus Hesiod, in speaking of the Golden Age, remarks that the farmers brought in their fruits *hēsychoi*, without toil and with peace of mind.[22] The ancient document in which we find the most ambitious attempt to formulate the function of peace of mind in a healthy life is Plutarch's essay, *De tranquillitate animi* (see also Seneca's essay of the same name). In spite of the eclectic nature of the work, it has been plausibly argued that its main springs are Epicurean. Plutarch's own argument is of course largely anti-Epicurean. That is to say, even a man who regarded Epicureanism as a corrupting philosophy could not but go back to Epicurean formulations when he wanted to define the dimensions of *otium*.

For the Stoic, *otium* can easily become a vicious condition, particularly to an active mind; and, the Stoic thinks, all minds are more or less active.[23] The Stoic king is a planner, a programmer, a protester against the present; in short, he stands in the tradition of Hesiod. The Epicurean, like the herdsman, is wrapped up in the present, a natural enjoyer of *otium* rather than an analyzer of it. *Tranquillitas animi* is the Latin translation of the Greek term *euthymia*, a term first brought into currency by Democritus (B3 Diels): "A man who wants to enjoy *euthymia* must not engage in many activities, either in private or in public." Especially in public; both Plutarch and Seneca strive to come to grips with the difficulty of reconciling the demands of peace of mind with the Stoic call for public service. Plutarch takes issue with Democritus; it is illuminating to see how he begins by finding that abstinence from public affairs does not necessarily produce tranquillity; but then, as the essay continues, its attacks are, in part, directed against the life of the public man. The predictable conclusion is that the philosophic life is best. Seneca, in his *De otio*, takes his seat even more solidly on the fence. The fragmentary essay is an uninspired, vacillating venture to allow some measure of *otium* for a follower of Stoic doctrine. The distance of this from the unembarrassed Epicurean stress on *otium* is enormous. It is an indication of the complexity of the *otium* ideal in Sidney's *Arcadia* that it features both the Epicurean-pastoral delight in its pleasures, and the Stoic doubts concerning its feasibility in a sinful world.

Leisure is not, of course, more typically at home in the country than in the city. Xenophon's *Oeconomicus*, a jovial gentleman farmer's almanac, actually contrasts leisure and the good life (20.16–19), and compares the slothful worker with a hobo who, instead of marching steadily toward his goal, eases up in his soul, rests a while at springs and in the shade, admires the view, and chases soft breezes. Xenophon's idle wayfarer looks remarkably like the inhabitant of the pastoral pleasance, except that Xeno-

phon cannot get himself to think of the type as anything but
restless and erratic. But all that Theocritus needed to do was to
take Xenophon's hobo, aimless and playful as he was, strip him of
his *Wanderlust*, put a herdsman's weeds on him, polish the hobo's
natural elegance of speech—and there stood a Comatas, ready for
use.

It is somewhat surprising that the condition of *otium*, of
leisure without hardship, was associated with the shepherd's
life, for the loneliness of the shepherd, his exposure to the vicissi-
tudes of fierce weather and fiercer beasts, hardly make him the
logical choice for a *locus amoenus*.[24] Perhaps the choice has something to do with the anthropological fiction, instanced by Plato
in the *Laws*, that after each of the periodic destructions that
separate one Great Year from the next, the beginnings of the new
life and the new civilization are first experienced on the pastoral
level.[25] The herdsmen are without knowledge of the stratagems
of civilization, especially of the tricks used by people in the cities
toward one another for the furthering of their power. The few
men who are left behind at each destruction herd their meager
flocks, but they have no metallurgy and little lumbering, so there
is no traffic between groups. The result is peace and good will.

But this is not the whole story. The ancient scholar most
often associated with the view that the pastoral life came early
in the history of culture is a student of Aristotle, Dicaearchus of
Messene. Dicaearchus traced the history of civilized man in three
stages.[26] During the golden age men lived with the gods; they
killed nothing animate; the growth of food plants was automatic
(it had to be, because the men of the first age had no skills).
This was responsible for their having leisure, for living without
toil or anxiety and without disease because they did not surfeit
their bodies. They knew no wars or social unrest, for there were
no rewards worth fighting for. Their life was full of ease, health,
peace, friendship. Later less happy generations came to regard
this stage as utopian. The second stage was the *nomadikos bios*,

the life on the range. Men acquired property and handled animals, distinguishing between the harmless and the harmful, taming the first and attacking the latter. Then also war entered the picture, with competition for ownership, ambition, challenges, and protective measures. This led into the third stage, the life of the settled farmer.

It is clear from this rapid summary of the most important ancient extension of Hesiod's system of generations, that the *nomadikos bios* is not at all the stage with which we would want to associate the Theocritean herdsmen. Theocritus avoids references to the pastoral dependence on meat and hunting for food, and rather emphasizes *otium* and self-sufficiency, the features of Dicaearchus' first age. It appears, therefore, that Theocritus decided not to go by the anthropology of his day but to adopt the literary associations of the shepherd's life. These may be traced all the way back to Homer, especially in the passage of the "Shield of Achilles" (*Iliad* 18.525–526) which Dr. Johnson chose as a motto for his *Rambler* essay, No. 36; in Pope's translation:

> Piping on their reeds the shepherds go
> Nor fear an ambush, nor suspect a foe.

Johnson knew very well that these very herdsmen are about to be killed by the enemy; perhaps his choice of the lines is an ironic commentary on the viability of a genre he holds in little respect. Still, he emphasizes the "peace, and leisure, and innocence" of the pastoral bower. We should recall that the popularity of Paris, and of the Judgment of Paris, in the Renaissance had something to do with the fact that Paris was a shepherd on Ida. Because of this, his judgment, though hardly acute, could be relied upon to function without guile, without the vices of what the Renaissance feared as "the aspiring mind."[27]

Whatever the origins of the choice, then, the herdsman came to be the archetypal representative of *otium*. But not just any herdsman, and not under just any conditions. The shepherd and the goatherd were, on the whole, preferred to the neatherd, in spite of the Sicilian legend of the neatherd Daphnis, because it was felt that their herding involved a larger share of the required *otium*. And the time of day chosen as the hour when *otium* could best be realized is noon. When Virgil has Menalcas praise Mopsus' singing by employing a comparison,

> Your singing is like sleep for the tired in the grass,
> Like quenching thirst from a dancing river in the heat,[28]

there is humor in the similes, because the terms point to the noon hour, which is the setting of the song in the first place. At noon, the heat becomes unbearable and shade becomes a necessity of life; the intersection of morning and evening is a kind of death, which paralyzes nature and imperils its resurgence. At such a moment only a limited range of activities is permitted;

> It is not proper, shepherd, to play the pipe
> At noon, for fear of Pan. He is resting now,
> Exhausted from the hunt. He is fiery,
> And acrid choler rises from his nostril.[29]

Contrast this scene with Calpurnius' grove, silent in the presence of Nero (*Eclogue* 4.97 ff.). In the later pastoral, the noon suspension is equated with a Dionysiac fullness; the epiphany of the god-emperor, with the attendant *plerosis* of the natural world, takes the place of a nature temporarily stilled to make room for the plain song of natural man. Calpurnius' herdsmen are worshippers humbling themselves before their master, in the sight of a nature whose lushness testifies to the magic properties of the master. Theocritus' herdsmen are free men (in spite of their servile status; see below, Chapter Five) attempting to express what is in their hearts, at an hour when nature least interferes with their freedom. Yet the awareness of the anger of Pan is there; not the self-abasement before a divine master, but the knowledge that the noon hour is a short-lived thing; beyond it there are motions and passions that engulf *otium*, and never cease to threaten the balance.

         ᶿ   ᶿ   ᶿ   ᶿ

Fontenelle, it will be recalled, has a special theory that pastoral is the product of a marriage between idleness and love. Leisure is necessary to empower the life of the spirit; to prevent leisure from sliding into sloth, love is summoned to the rescue. Love furnishes *otium* with the required minimum of tension and motor activity and, perhaps, passion. It is correct to say that much pastoral, especially beginning with the Renaissance, concerns itself with love, notably with plaintive love,

Wearying Echo with one changeless word.[30]

If we may trust Mnasalcas of Sicyon (the author of *Anthol. Pal.* 9.324) bucolic poetry was thought even in antiquity to address itself to erotic themes.[31] The poem is an appeal to Syrinx: why have you come to join Aphrodite, the Foam-born, instead of staying in your hills and valleys? Here is an author who thinks that what he calls the country Muse (*agria Mousa*) was developing an unseemly interest in amorous pursuits. The point, built as it is on the sight of a shepherd's pipe dedicated in a temple of Aphrodite, is made cleverly and amusingly. But I like to think that the poet was seriously concerned about a tendency which, he feared, might work against the desired mood of simplicity. For, as Fontenelle himself stresses, love plays a distinctly secondary role: idleness is primary, love bails it out. On the whole, the pastoral tradition bears out this ranking. In the vast majority of amatory eclogues, love is a pallid thing of perfunctory kisses and hesitant remonstrances, a thing neither of the flesh nor of the spirit, but a cheat.

Critics like Poggioli have been very harsh in their judgment of the writers' motives. "The pastoral longing is but the wishful dream of . . . an erotic bliss made absolute by its own irresponsibility. This, rather than a sense of decency, is the very reason why

the pastoral often limits the sexual embrace to mere kissing, so
as to escape the danger of parenthood, and the nuisance of birth
control."[32] In the end, the pastoral poet bares "the emptiness,
rather than the fullness, of a frustrated heart." That is to say,
the pastoral aims at expressing the spiritual potential of man,
but usually, willy-nilly, manages only to show up his spiritual
deficiencies. This, I think, is a false inference from an inadequate
premise; it follows from the expectation that only a poetry that
calls a spade a spade is to be taken seriously. But to continue with
our critic's complaints: the special fault of pastoral is that it
lacks an awareness of passion; Rousseau tried to channel passion
back into the pastoral spectrum, but now in the form of narcis-
sism.[33] It could be argued that passion in the pastoral, especially
on the part of the lover chanting his love, always hovers on the
borderline of the narcissistic. By the same token, the consummation of love is an element that would be hard to fit into the pastoral frame. Marvell's "Clorinda and Damon" constitutes one
Renaissance poet's avowal that love needs to be sublimated and
de-natured if it is to be acceptable to Pan:

> Damon   These once had been enticing things,
>   Clorinda, pastures, caves, and springs.
> Clorinda   And what late change?
> Damon   The other day
>   Pan met me.

Whether Pan is, in this instance, a cover name for Christ or not,
the symbolism is more broadly valid than might be suspected
from Marvell's particular intent.

Fontenelle's second-ranking of love in pastoral looks perverse
if we think of the central position that love holds in so much
Renaissance pastoral. But it does seem to make sense for Theocritus. Love's volatile nature is at cross purposes with the im-
mobilizing instinct, with the original impulses that embrace the
noon peace. Its power is reduced by virtue of the focus on relaxation, on freedom and *otium* or the possibility of it. Matched

against the goal of *otium*, love, in spite of the appeal of its genuine-
ness and spontaneity, must always have an air of the preliminary
or the faintly ludicrous about it. Hence the mocking quality of
love in Theocritus. A Polyphemus and a Satyriskos display a
passion and a devotion which beg not to be taken seriously. Their
claims are undercut either through the agency of an incredulous
bystander or by a note of disbelief sounded in the songs or
speeches themselves. I do not mean to suggest that the Theocritean lovers play games or over-dramatize their sufferings. It is
rather that we are made to sense their naiveté more directly than
their sufferings. There is a disproportion between the note of
frustration or pain uttered and the innocence radiated by their
persons. We cannot quite believe that the snub-nosed goatherd
is close to committing suicide when he exclaims:

> First I'll take off my shirt, and then jump down
> Into the sea where Olpis does his fishing;
> And if I die, that is your sweet desire.[34]

Similarly the rude farmer of *Idyll* 10 cannot take Bucaeus at his
word, not, as one might think, because he pities and protects
him, but rather because he feels that the man is uttering sentiments which are hardly authenticated by anything he has done
or felt in the past.

Even where there is no humor, as in these disproportions
between claim and substance, passionate love is rarely the dominant issue. Characteristically, the great preoccupation with pure
love and chastity, which comes to be so important in the pastoral
drama of the Renaissance, does not exist in Theocritus or, for
that matter, in Virgil.[35] Daphnis' refusal to love, in *Idyll* 1, has
little in common with the similar refusal of Fletcher's Daphnis
in *The Faithful Shepherdess* (1.3):

> Let other men
> Set up their bloods to sale, mine shall be ever
> Faire as the soul it carries, and unchaste never.

Theocritus' Daphnis does not know the concept of chastity. His refusal to love is not a matter of spiritual sacrifice or commitment, but an assertion of his freedom against what he regards as an illicit compulsion. He does not consider love wrong; he wishes to choose his love, of the kind and in the manner that he elects. It would, of course, be going too far to deny that Theocritus' hero does in some fashion anticipate the distinction, pervasive in pastoral drama, between the good—i.e., non-carnal—hero and the bad, aggressive, satyr villain.

Theocritus is not one of those poets who value love as an ennobling or purifying passion. Love, in the *Idylls*, does not make for a purer vision or an enlarged understanding. On the contrary, it appears to serve as a hindrance to the understanding. In Spenser's "December," unhappy love changes the shepherd's vision radically:

> where the chaunting birds luld me asleepe,
> The ghastlie owle her grievous ynne doth keepe.

No such violent changes of perspective are contemplated in the less labile world of Theocritus. It is as if the herdsmen were assured that love is at its best ranked on the same level as other natural occupations, eating and drinking, and the delights found in them. True, the tradition puts love on a higher pedestal, and constructs an elaborate mythology to account for its mysteries. In Theocritus, the mythology is held up to ridicule by the dying Daphnis (*Idyll* 1.105):

> Remember Cypris, how the cowherd — —?

The aposiopesis deflates the standing of Aphrodite as a member of the mythological establishment. Likewise, when the barred lover of *Idyll* 3 conjectures (15–17) that Love was suckled by a lioness, the avowal of the *saevus amor* theme is little more than a half-hearted gesture. The effect is decorative at best, but more probably incongruous.

Of Theocritus' many devices for the neutralization of the claims of the romantic passion, the favorite device is to pit sex against merely being in love. The Cyclops reminds himself, at a point when his passion has run the course of its foolishness, that there are other cows to milk (*Idyll* 11.75), a really brutal phrase, which in our day has been used by a famous movie star when asked why he would not marry. In the notorious *Idyll* 5, the agon degenerates into mutual reminders of animal sex. The celestial visitors in *Idyll* 1 try to convince Daphnis that he is making too much of what is after all a very simple thing, and admonish him to follow the course of nature. Priapus and Aphrodite are good Epicureans; they recommend *aphrodisia* in the place of *erōs*, light-hearted sex instead of troubled passion. Epicurus' definition of love makes it clear why it is to be spurned: *erōs* is a tense straining, coupled with frenzy and distress, for sexual satisfaction.[36] Elsewhere, in the *Life of Epicurus* (118), it is said that the wise man does not fall in love, and that love is not god-sent. Lucretius, in the fourth book of the *De rerum natura*, furnishes the *locus classicus* of the Epicurean condemnation of love. The Epicurean sage is not dispassionate; as we remarked before, his acceptance of pity and friendship prove that he is not. But love is quite another thing; it is rejected because of what it does to the senses, to the sensibilities, and to the judgment. It frenzies the lover, as the cow-fly frenzied Io; and it blinds him to the realities of his position and commitments. Lucretius formulates this in a couplet which seems to me almost literally borrowed from the tenth *Idyll* of Theocritus:

> If she's a chocolate color, he calls her honey-brown;
> Is she a stinking slattern, he finds her "genuine;"
> Frost-eyed? he calls "Minerva!"; scrawny? he says "gazelle."[37]

Epicureanism, then, condemns the grand passion because it shackles and blinds the lover. On the other hand it condones, but only just condones, a sexual union which liberates and cleanses, even if the sex has to be bought.[38] Sex does not deprive its practitioner of his peace of mind, at least not for long; nor does sex make for delusions. Horace, in his Epicurean mood, advances a similar recommendation, if that is not too strong a word, of *parabilis Venus facilisque*.[39] Note, however, that it is not Daphnis, but Priapus and Aphrodite who are the spokesmen for this attitude in *Idyll* 1. Theocritus is a poet, not a philosopher. His subtle manipulation of the ambivalences of love is not the same as Epicurus' hard-headed rejection of *erōs*. Nevertheless there are some intriguing points of contact, under the general heading of *kinēsis* versus *stasis*. Epicureanism, as it were, forms the boundary that separates two important strands in the pastoral texture. Where passion and pain are neutralized via parody, as in *Idyll* 3, or via embalmment, as in the sculptured image of the lovers on the cup of *Idyll* 1, Epicurus' caveats are accepted. Where they break through the fetters of courtesy and stability, as in the stormy declarations of *Idylls* 1, 2, 7, and (in a different manner) 10, Epicurus is rejected. The parody need not mean a negation of the value of passion, but only an amused recognition of its inevitability; then also Epicurus is left behind. In any case, the special qualities of the pastoral mode, its lack of a sustained curve and its cool impersonality, severely limit the scope of passionate *erōs* within the pleasance.

As a poet, Theocritus does not condemn; at the worst he makes fun of the indignities and the awkwardnesses heaped upon the frustrated lover. Most of the touches used, such as the notorious sleeplessness of the unhappy wooer (*Idyll* 10.10), are not original with him. The important thing is that Theocritus succeeds in having us smile at the spectacle of a man in love, and that he can put words and songs into the mouths of lovers that betray their own limitations, or rather the limitations that the genre imposes on their feelings. Contrast the Petrarchan *canzone*, and its celebration of unrequited love, fully articulated in a world emptied of all else. At first blush, it might seem that when Virgil places an unhappy lover in the resonant locale of woods and mountains, he is doing something very similar. But a close look at the second *Eclogue*—the same is true of Nemesianus' *Eclogue* 2—shows that the genre, through its associations with innocence and strength, helps us to view the love as a momentary aberration. If there is a natural state for men, it is one of quiet happiness. When the ripples of passion, designed to enliven *otium*, end up by disturbing it, they cannot fail to impress us as bizarre and unnatural. Only in the tenth *Eclogue* does Virgil dramatize a love that asks to be taken seriously. But the poem is, after all, Virgil's leave-taking from the pastoral. Even so, a second look at this poem also shows that the incongruity of the elegist taking on the mask of the pastoralist makes, if not for humor, at least for some very peculiar obliquities. The dislocations and cross-overs are such that the listener's sympathies are deflected from coming to rest on the hero's passion.[40]

Some of the most familiar pastoral poems of the later European tradition are *about* love. That is to say, they present the advantages and disadvantages of love, in the form of herdsmen engaging in a debate. Such is Drayton's seventh *Eglog*, and countless other poems that have swains in alternating stanzas exploring the nature of love. It is hard to distinguish neatly between a poem which shows a hero manifesting his frustrations in love by arguing with himself; and, on the other hand, a poem that presents the same issue in a more abstract fashion. The latter is, however, foreign to the pastoral vision of Theocritus. The true herdsman is too much given to responses of the moment to be able to carry a sustained argument and score cumulative points. Yet some successes with this scheme show a clear recognition of what is fitting for pastoral characters. A good example is the anonymous "The Shepherd's Description of Love."[41] Meliboeus asks Faustus what Love is, and Faustus answers with several stanzas, each exploiting the rhyme proposed in the pertinent question. Throughout there is an emphasis on the double nature of love: happy and unhappy; "It is December mat'ched with May." The rhymes indicate a continuity of sorts; the sentiments are arrayed in sequential order, each line representing a self-contained, epigrammatic thought. The combination of continuity and discontinuity produces the special charm that we expect of the pastoral and allows us to absorb the sentiments *as if* they formed an argument. If Theocritus had recognized rhyme, he would have approved of this solution.

The circumscribed status of love in the pastoral is borne out also by its close connection with music. The Muses, says Bion (frag. 9), inspire only him whose heart is tossed by Love; only when I sing of Lycidas does my song come off. Theocritus' Cyclops starts singing *because* he is in love; in the end the song helps him to divest himself of that same love. It is a fair presumption that the fiction of love as a source of inspiration helps Theocritus to make more plausible the notion of the herdsman-singer. This is, in effect, the old Platonic view (*Symposium* 212B3) that *erōs* supplies a fuel, of suprapersonal origin, to help man in his efforts to make music, whether the music is philosophy, as in Plato, or singing and piping, as it is in the pastoral. For an audience more familiar with the rude herdsmen of the Greek hill country than with the pastoral hero, the musical gifts of the shepherd may have been a little difficult to swallow. Here the notion of *erōs* permits Theocritus to define a new species of literary persona, one quite close to the partners in Socratic conversations, at least in the sense that he is privileged to utter impressive remarks without being fully aware of what got him there. Conversely, the empirical fact that herdsmen were known to amuse themselves on pipes helped to make them more convincing as lovers. Their musical gifts invest them with a charter which confirms their role as suitors—always granting Theocritus' ironical perspective on their love. A similar mechanism is still observable in Sidney:

> Seely shepheards are not witting
> What in art of Love is fitting.[42]

This question, whether Love is possible among herdsmen, whether it does not require an art that is not accessible to their rude ways, is sufficiently answered in the poem itself by the shepherds' obvious refinement in music and song. The question is never raised by Theocritus; it is not part of his view of what we should expect of a pastoral, to raise questions of competence. His shepherds sing and they hold out the prospect of love in virtue of the ukase which has prompted a poetry about herdsmen-singers and swain lovers. But whereas the song is always felt to be soul-satisfying, and indeed almost compulsive in its inevitability, the love is, in the subtle ways I have tried to trace, offered up to question. Unlike song, love is not successful; and because it is not successful—or, perhaps better: the way in which it is shown not to be successful—it may be said to be lacking in conviction. Love, in Theocritus, is the animating force that enlivens *otium*, without however spelling the end of *otium*. If the love were successful, either spiritually or physically, it would establish itself as a higher value than *hasychia*. If it were profoundly unhappy, it would disrupt the equilibrium without which *otium* cannot flourish. And so love is, in its various manifestations, held in a state of suspension, which relieves *otium* without undoing its benefits.

To sum up, the naturalness of love emerges in two ways. On the one hand, all pastoral characters are potential lovers and are quick to refer to their beloveds in a manner indicating that love is a normal part of their lives. On the other hand, sex, in its cruder forms, is allowed to color the context marginally, without reducing the pastoral bower to the conditions of a stable.[43] The naturalness of love is tempered by its lack of consummation; the herdsman either refuses love, or he loves without success. Only in this way can the poet control passion within the boundaries that it needs to observe so as not to dispel the mood of the noon peace.

❧ ❧ ❧ ❧

Theocritus' *otium* is not the somnolent indulgence of one who acknowledges the *pax Romana*,[44] but the vital experience of a moment which it is known will be brief, but which is so fully entertained that the future and the past are largely shut out. The emphasis is on the right moment, on the proper season, not on a habit or a lasting order. We must distinguish this concentration upon the moment from the *carpe diem* ethos that is so common in British pastoral. The Theocritean herdsman is not aware of time as fleeting; he merely proceeds with a special kind of unselfconscious urgency. Nor is the Theocritean noon hour held up as a mean. Bion, to be sure, stresses a mixture, an equilibrium produced by opposing forces, in preferring spring to summer and winter and fall (frag. 2). Theocritus does not even consider other seasons. The only poem of Theocritus that explicitly distinguishes between seasons and temporal perspectives is *Idyll* 7, a poem featuring townsmen rather than herdsmen, perambulation rather than a séance, and in a number of ways blinking at the limits observed in the shorter poems. The meeting and the festival are said to be taking place in mid-summer; the events are reported in the narrative past. The song of Lycidas begins with a reference to the late fall and winter, i.e., the future (lines 53–54), and this continues to be the temporal setting for the song of Tityrus, which itself cites legends of the past and ends on a terminal link with the present (from the larger vantage point, the future) (86). The song of Simichidas operates with the present and the wished-for future. Finally we revert to the summer-present of the frame, reported once more in the narrative past, and close with references to the legendary past (149 ff.) and the wished-for future (156–157). Clearly the poem swarms with a multiplicity of temporal relations; they take us a considerable distance from the noon-fixation maintained elsewhere. It is as if the Hesiodic calendar, the planner's division into seasons, asserted itself over the pastoral *otium*.

The same is true in several of Virgil's *Eclogues*, particularly in

the two poems most vigorously removed from the center of the
pastoral tradition, the "Messianic" fourth, and the concluding
tenth, whose artistic plan, the encampment of the elegiac poet
in a pastoral setting, naturally triggers a temporal friction.[45] In
the later European tradition, the Hesiodic calendar comes into
its own to the same degree that the autobiographical element
takes possession of the field. Poets adopt the fashion of talking
about their own lives under the guise of seasonal sequences. In
the end, collections of eclogues come to be organized by the
months or seasons of the year. Most notably this is done by
Spenser, who in "December" has Colin compare his life to a
year with four seasons.

It is, I think, important to see how little there is of all this
in Theocritus. Beside *Idyll* 7, which records a process of conversion and investiture, and *Idyll* 27, a (post-Theocritean) pastourelle which must contain the *topos* "love before you get old and
lose your looks," only the Cyclops of *Idyll* 11 anticipates the
sense of time in Perdita's remarks about the proper season for
certain flowers.[46] He can do this because he is not a natural
herdsman, but a budding, still very immature man of business
who play-acts at being a pastoral hero. There is a touch of
Callimachean realism about the one-eyed suitor; note his preoccupation with his looks, his resentment toward his mother,[47]
his boasting of his wealth, his offer of gifts worthy of the hot-
house atmosphere of the Ptolemaic court, and the atrocious
extravagance of his wish: If only my mother had born me with
gills! This portrait of the god-fearing, properly brought up
scion of a good family, whose unfortunate disability is dis-
closed in hints rather than explicitly, does not fit smoothly
into the pastoral frame.[48] The truth is that he cannot shrug off
his Homeric descent. A character with a literary past, he is the
victim of his own historicity; it ties him down in ways which
disqualify him from full partnership in the idyllic company.
It is indicative of the later dissatisfaction with the "pure" bucolic

that the Cyclops should have become one of the most imitated
models of European pastoral poetry.[49] The Cyclops' sly comment
about the seasonal incommensurability of narcissus and poppy
(lines 56–59) should not, therefore, surprise us; it demonstrates
that he is only partially at home in the green cabinet. Herrick's

> I sing of Brooks, of Blossoms, Birds, and Bowers,
> Of April, May, of June, and July Flowers

is not the kind of statement Theocritus would, as a rule, put in the
mouth of a herdsman.

What he does is to bear down hard on the time during which,
he implies, *otium* is most conductive to song; during which, in
Fontenelle's scheme, idleness and energy mix best. *Idyll* 6
furnishes a case in point. In this gentle genre piece, we observe
Polyphemus—a thoroughly different Polyphemus from the
brash upstart of *Idyll* 11—with his dog at the sea shore, at a
moment when he has ceased from pursuing Galatea. There are
intimations that she is now pursuing him. But the dramatic
technique of the poem—an address by one herdsman to the
imaginary Polyphemus, and an answer by another herdsman
in the role of Polyphemus—facilitates the detachment with
which we witness the temporary lull in the Cyclops' affairs.
From the whole range of the legendary tale, a particular moment
is chosen; it is a moment of inaction, of relaxation, but also of
suspense. The procedure is similar to what happens in many
epyllia; but the moment is chosen for its stillness, its balanced
simplicity, and not, as in the typical epyllion, for the refracted
light it sheds on the old legend.

That this pastoral moment is usually the noon hour is due to
an old literary, and perhaps also non-literary, tradition that came
to be stressed particularly by the Alexandrian writers.[50] Hesiod's
vision of the Muses occurred during the noon hour, if we may
take it that the adjective *ennychiai*, literally "shrouded in night,"
is not a temporal clue but a reference to the invisibility of the

Muses. This is the way Asclepiades (*Anthol. Pal.* 9.64.1–2) understood it. Plato's *Phaedrus* is our best early evidence for the special
character of the noon hour as a time for exaltation and discovery
of the self. After the Alexandrian period, the tradition remained
alive. In the *Culex* (lines 101 ff.), the noon period is set aside as an
hour of rest and inspiration. In Apuleius' *Metamorphoses*, the
reed that advises Psyche has a speech about noon (6.12) that
advertises certain profits to be derived from the coincidence of
fierce heat and refreshing shade. For a Christian version of the
theme, there is Petrarch's *De vita solitaria* (1.2.5): "The retired
man . . . does nothing hurriedly [at noon], but noting the passage
of time in its flight and longing to be where there is life without
flow of time or fear of death, he turns once more to his devotions,
praying not only for the light of a single day but for the clear evening of his whole existence and the glory of a never-setting life."

A number of passages document the belief that supernatural
beings are most likely to be encountered during the noon hour.[51]
These passages stretch from the *Odyssey* (4.400 and 450) to Lucian
(*Philopseudes* 22). The same belief is also found in the Judaeo-
Christian orbit: Genesis 18.1, Acts 22.6. Whether the *frisson*
provoked by the encounter with the god is to be read also into
some of the Hellenistic passages relating noon-hour experiences
is a moot question.[52] In the pastoral uses of the motif, notably
the vision of Pan in Theocritus' *Idyll* 1 (15 ff.), it would be wrong
to read more than a slight tremor into the equanimity of the
herdsman. He is not afraid of Pan, much less mysteriously
touched. Theocritus merely uses the ancient motif, not without
humor, to indicate that even this almost perfect stillness has a
core of suspended energy to be reckoned with, and that the
herdsmen-poets must be careful to do the right thing by the
opportunity given to them.

The noon-day cancellation of *kinēsis* will, if the poet wishes,
turn into a full-fledged cancellation of life. Then the quasi-death
becomes a true death, and the pastoral ripens into a dirge. An-

tiquity was comparatively reluctant to avail itself of this extension
of the notion of paralysis into the notion of extinction. But
beginning in the Middle Ages the pastoral elegy, as it came to be
known, gained an extraordinary vogue. Neither the Daphnis
hymn of *Idyll* 1 nor its imitations in Virgil are, properly speaking,
dirges; they stage a man's dying, and do not praise him as
dead.[53] The encomium of the dead comes later; it must be
regarded as yet another deviation from the original course of the
pastoral lyric, not only because the extended celebration of one
man flies in the face of the genre's democratic tenor, but also
because the insistence on death runs counter to the pastoral
embrace of life here and now, without eschatological alibis.
This accounts for the special charm of Perdita's jesting when she
talks of showering spring flowers over Florizel:

> like a bank for love to lie and play on.
> Not like a corse; or if—not to be buried,
> But quick, and in mine arms.

She binds death, *otium*, and love together into a posy of pastoral
attractions that makes nonsense of the threat of death. This is
only one of several ways in which Perdita dares to loosen and
dissolve complexes of meaning which, by the time of Shakespeare, had become standard in the pastoral. Her humor is liberating and points the way back to the greater simplicities of the
earlier vision. The vision is no longer immediately available to
Shakespeare except as the flash of a joke.

Theocritus' *otium* is never dead. Its latent excitement is not at
all unlike the restlessness that tenses the shade in Mallarmé's
"Après-midi":

> Couple, adieu; je vais voir l'ombre que tu devins.

The formulation is Ovidian. But the shade is in a different mode;
it is a key for dreaming, for somnolence, but also for remembered
and projected sexual excitement. True, Mallarmé's poem is in
the tradition of the *Anthology*; its wit, its special frustrations, its

central excitement and final resolution, and its rather cerebral argument, all take it out of the running for a position in the tradition I am trying to sketch. So do its symbolist syntheses, its abstractions, its air of being only half-awake. But on the score of building energy and tension into a noon-hour shade, the parallel between the two poets stands. Note, for instance, the function of the cup in *Idyll* 1. Its panels exhibit typical scenes of the non-pastoral world of competition and worry; the coy mistress with her unlucky suitors, the aged fisherman with his bulging muscles, the boy who is trying to trap a cricket while foxes raid his knapsack: cold love, hard work, plotting, deceitfulness. What matters about these echoes of the world beyond the pleasance is that they are stilled, frozen into sculptured beauty, hemmed in by the ivy frame that winds around the lip of the cup.[54] Within the poem, their life force is minimal. Their stillness is comparable to the stillness of the noon hour. But like the noon hour, they are charged with reminders of friction.

For contrast, it may be useful to glance at Keats' "Ode on a Grecian Urn" (stanza 5.4–5):

> Thou, silent form, dost tease us out of thought
> As doth eternity: Cold Pastoral!

As we learn in stanza two, the images on the urn are conceived of as checks on the life force, as mummification rather than temporary stoppage, which is all that Theocritus' panels mean to suggest. Elsewhere also Keats works with the pastoral convention of *otium*:

> Ripe was the drowsy hour;
> The blissful cloud of summer indolence
> Benumb'd my eyes; my pulse grew less and less;
> Pain had no sting, and pleasure's wreath no flower:
> Oh, why did ye not melt, and leave my sense
> Unhaunted quite of all but—nothingness?[55]

The pastoral expectation is distorted by the special demands of the poem, which call for an ideal emptiness rather than peace. But it is generally true of Keats' neoclassicism that it welcomes *stasis* in the panels of human action, and dismisses the elements of joy and bustle that animate the pastoral *otium*. Marvell's

> Annihilating all that's made
> To a green thought in a green shade

is more hospitable to the tough exertions of a mind intent on happiness. But it too steers the movement to a conclusion in which all motion, even the most marginal, is suspended.

Theocritus' *hasychia*, the fixity which endorses the pulse of life, comes through also in the manner of his writing. It is useful to remember that Theocritus is one of the first practitioners of sustained *Tonmalerei* for achieving a poetic texture. The liquidities prominent in Virgil's *Eclogues*, and in Horace's second *Epode*, were made possible by a scrupulous care for the relation between meaning and sound, which did not come into its own until the beginnings of the Hellenistic age.[56] The sibilants and surds of the programmatic first lines of *Idyll* 1 may well, as the ancient scholiast thought, involve a touch of onomatopoeia. More important than the sound patterns, perhaps, are the mechanics of the meter. We have suggested possible reasons why Theocritus chose the epic hexameter, or rather a less sonorous adaptation of it, for his purposes. We should now add that of all the meters available to him, the hexameter is best suited to buttress the fixity of the pastoral *otium*, certainly more so than either the irregular lyric meters or the nervous trochaic or the colloquial iambic. Theocritus' special handling of the measure adds to the effect of stability and composure. Lines are rarely broken up between two speakers or singers;[57] on the other hand the bucolic diaeresis, which divides the period into independent cola, helps to stem and articulate the regular flow of the hexameter. The rhythmic effect is one of small, independent units, quietly steady within themselves, and relatively detached from their neighbors.

The convention that pastoral should be written in hexameters was remarkably long-lived; it lasted till the Renaissance and beyond. Sannazaro was the first to draw on a variety of lyric forms. In this he was followed by the Pléiade, who in turn influenced Spenser. Actually even Marot and other predecessors of the Pléiade had gone to folk meters in their vernacular adaptations of the pastoral model. The complex pastorals ushered in by the Renaissance poets called for complex structures, metrical and otherwise. A typical example is that of Drayton's *Eglog* 7 of *Idea*. Borrill, the old man, shapes his song against love on a model that has analogies with the Virgilian pastoral hexameter: tight, largely spondaic-trochaic dimeters, compressed syntax, extravagant "metaphysical" combinations. Batte, on the other hand, the youthful eulogizer of love, uses lyric stanzas, airy, simple, almost foolish, with iambic dimeters accounting for the bulk of his metrical structure.

Milton's "Lycidas" represents a retrogression from the metrical ambitions of other pastoralists. When at the end of the poem Milton speaks of his "Dorick lay," it is probably the freedom of his verse, its colloquial quality, that he has in mind, though it has been shown that the verse is dependent on a variety of Italian models.[58] Pope, and other neoclassicists, objected to the ambitious versification employed by Spenser and his school: "He has employ'd the Lyric measure, which is contrary to the practice of the old Poets. His Stanza is not still the same, nor always well chosen."[59] Behind Pope's objection, as behind Rapin's insistence on a form of the "Heroick Measure, but not so strong and sounding as in Epicks," lies the conviction that the variety and changeability of lyric meters made them too fussy for what the pastoral needed, and that the pastoral *otium* could find better shape through the medium of a regular, firmly paced meter.

In this light it is not surprising that the sestina and the double
sestina should have become so popular with pastoral writers,
beginning with Sannazaro. Sidney's double sestina, which
begins "You Gote-heard Gods," with its recurring word patterns
and its obsessively repetitive verse, pushes the bucolic trend
toward fixity to the extreme of its possibilities. David Kalstone's
perceptive analysis of these matters leads to the conclusion:
"What Empson terms 'flatness' results from Sidney's low-
keyed vocabulary, his use of monosyllables, and his reliance on
rhythm, grammar, and devices of repetition. . . . As if the double
sestina did not have enough of its own built-in repetitions,
Sidney introduces further repeating schemes . . . anaphora and
the rigidly parallel stanzas—not demanded by the form." [60]

In spite of the seeming difference in verse structure, the same
tendencies are observable also in Theocritus. With greater or
smaller variations, depending on whether the poetic language
is hymnodic — as in *Idyll* 1,64–142 — or colloquial, the steady
pace of the hexameter is further slowed by refrains and anaphora
and other kinds of blocking maneuvers. Refrain, in particular,
has the function of reemphasizing the point of origin; the beginning, the source, reaches out to form a frame, much like the
ivy whose tendrils surround the panels on the cup. The bower
reveals itself as the beginning and the end; development is
specious, and demonstrated to be so. That is not to say that all
the refrains in pastoral have this function. But wherever the
refrains are prominent, the idea of going back to the beginning,
of periodically re-anchoring the imagination in a fundamental
motif, is present. Note particularly that a refrain may stand in
mid-sentence and break the sentence up into discrete units.

Wilamowitz thought that it was a mistake to speak of refrains
because there are no regular stanzas. [61] He preferred to think of
the repeated lines as, so the speak, musical doodles, put in by the
performers wherever they are thought to pause for breath. It is
true that the units separated by the refrains may vary from three

or even two to five or six lines. But this variation does not alter
the fact that the typical pastoral song is built up of comparatively short, discontinuous units; and I for one see no objection
to calling these units stanzas. This stanzaic pattern permits us to
speak of the pastoral "lyric." There are rough parallels in the
Homeric epic and in Hesiod; some recent critics have gone
rather far in wishing to read a stanzaic structure into the *Theog-
ony*.[62] But I think that in the Theocritean and Virgilian pastoral
this structural feature is more pervasive, and more pronounced,
than in other kinds of hexameter poetry. The refrains serve to
underscore the pattern of discontinuity.

Another stratagem of the same order, designed to block development and flux, is bucolic symmetry, the arrangement
whereby the second performer uses the paradigm supplied by the
first performer to make up his contribution.[63] Such symmetry
blocks progress as surely as mere repetition would, and admits only
the minor adjustments that lend animation to what otherwise
would be complete *stasis*. The first few lines of *Idyll* 1 will show
what is involved.

> *Thyrsis*   Sweet are the whispers, goatherd, of the song
>   Sung by the brook-fed pine; and sweet the warbling
>   Of your pipe. After Pan, the prize is yours:
>   If he prefers the buck, you'll have the goat;
>   If he selects the goat, your prize will be
>   The kid; and kid tastes good, until you milk it.
> *Goatherd*   Much sweeter, shepherd, is your singing than
>   The hum of the brook cascading down the rocks.
>   So if the Muses please to take the ewe,
>   You'll have the fatted lamb; and if they take
>   The lamb, your consolation is—the ewe.[64]

On the face of it, the symmetry of the two statements seems to be
virtually complete. The goatherd seems to be doing little else
than exhausting the impulses supplied by the shepherd. The surface effect is a draw, a standstill; and this is certainly what Theo-

critus desired at this point. But a closer look reveals those subtle
deflections and surprises that save the symmetry from the charge
of dull rigidity. For one thing, while both men are complimentary, the goatherd is more so, for he finds his friend's music
sweeter than, instead of as sweet as (the shepherd's terms), the
natural element. For another, the shepherd's alternatives are in
descending order; whichever prize Pan chooses for himself, the
goatherd will receive a lesser one. The goatherd is, again, more
complimentary: his friend will receive whatever the Muses do not
choose to have, even if this means that the Muses will receive
the lesser gift. In this case, therefore, the alternative prizes are
arranged in circular not in descending order. The goatherd, it
appears, is an expert in one-upmanship; he can top any compliment his friend proposes. Still, the gain for what follows is
infinitesimal. At the conclusion of the exchange, a fresh start is
needed. As it turns out, the fresh start is not so very fresh after
all; within the pastoral all new starts are also variations upon the
theme voiced at the outset. Thus the mechanics of the poem
contribute to the sense of standing still.

The passage just cited exhibits a massive accumulation of
anaphora. The frequency of anaphora and other types of repetition in pastoral poetry has not escaped the critics.[65] Like the
refrain, anaphora can be used for a variety of effect. One species
may be called the "nervous" anaphora. Its use is especially
familiar from Senecan drama, where repetition is employed to
reinforce the air of restlessness and disorientation:

> I find no peace
> Unless the universe joins me in my ruin;
> Unless the world splinters and breaks.[66]

Empson has a fine paragraph on repetition in Marlowe's *Tamburlane*, in which he argues that

Tamburlane can only use the same words again and again, because
his mind is glutted with astonishment at them. . . . the heroic soul
has extreme simplicity and unbounded appetite, so that after however

great an expression of his desire for glory, after one subordinate clause has opened out of another, with unalterable energy, it can still roar at the close with the same directness as in the opening line.[67]

Here repetition is used to exhibit a mentality that is, as it were, muscle-bound with admiration of itself. Or is Tamburlane's mind, "glutted with astonishment" at words, really Empson's in heroic disguise?

There are moments in the pastoral also when the aggressive spirit refuses to be calmed, and the considerable energies poised at the margin of the bower make themselves felt. It is not surprising that we should not always be sure whether anaphora, or refrains, are in support of *otium* or whether they exemplify the nervous jingle. In the large majority of pastoral poems, however, anaphora is not a statement about the condition of a soul so much as about the world within which a band of souls have joined forces to relax. Like the rhyme scheme of the sestina, anaphora functions as what Leslie Fiedler has called "a kind of cold mathematics."[68] But unlike the mathematics of the sestina, which often issues in obsession and hysteria, pastoral anaphora usually calms and soothes, perhaps because it is conceived musically and not, as in our famous sestine, forensically. The musical repeats and doublets help to secure the *otium*. With each anaphora, *kinēsis* is arrested, continuity blocked, progression cut off. As a result, the herdsmen rest more solidly than ever in a pleasance in which only the present counts; a suitable setting for a minuscule life fully lived, without regard for vistas and relations that extend beyond the exclusive bower. The noon peace is an imperious master; it brooks no rivals. *Hasychia* is all.

5
Freedom

Liberty, Epicurus says, is one of the essential foundations of the dignity of man. Slaves cannot develop their human
potential. Or rather, men who happen to be slaves by the vagaries
of fortune may show in their lives that they are actually, in the
philosophical sense, free. In this all Hellenistic philosophies
concurred; the social status of a man is less significant than the
quality of his character and of his conduct. Whether king or
slave, it is up to the individual to prove that he is a human being
whose choices are not limited except by what is beyond his control.

In spite of these noble sentiments, however, a realistic appraisal
of the facts had to conclude that life in the country, in the Hellenistic and particularly in the Roman age, was likely to mean
servitude rather than liberty. Tibullus grimly contemplates the
tasks, that is, the ordeals he would gladly perform to be near his
girl in the country. A town dweller, he takes it for granted that
freedom can be found only in the city, and not on the *latifundia*
of the Italian countryside (2.3.5–13; 79–80). Similar avowals
are found in other writers, both Latin and Greek; they accept the
Hesiodic principle that the fields and the ranches are the seat of
hardship and constraint.

In the face of this resigned attitude, the pastoral issues its
challenge with the declaration that freedom is possible *only*

in the country. The challenge succeeded; the pastoral fiction
became so powerful that on occasion even those who thought
they were talking about the real country fell under its spell.
When Themistius (*Oration* 1, pp. 10–11, Dindorf) takes up the
question of what happens to a bad cowherd who does not take
care of his cattle, he remarks: his herd perishes, and the man
himself will become a hireling, a porter, perhaps, or a charcoal-
man. He answers as if the natural condition of the cowherd in his
world were not that of a hired hand. His confusion, if we may
call it that, is one that might have been expected. For in talking
about herdsmen and herds, Themistius insensibly slips into
applying a grand trope, the metaphor of the herdsman that is
found from Homer to Plato and beyond. It characterizes the
relation between ruler and ruled as one in which the ruler looks
after his people in the manner of a shepherd or neatherd. The
implications of the metaphor are open to argument; Thrasymachus and Callicles, Socrates' partners, argue strongly for
the position that, like a herdsman, a ruler must look after his
own advantage in order to be successful. Socrates, on the
other hand, claims that a true herdsman has only the welfare
of his flock at heart. His logical distinction between the herdsman as curator and the herdsman as businessman is not convincing (*Republic*, Book 1). Callicles and Thrasymachus have
tradition on their side; a herdsman, in the sense conveyed
by the trope, is not responsible to anyone but himself. Certainly Homer's "shepherd of the people" is master of his own
fate, and not much interested in bettering the conditions of his
subjects.

The herdsman of literature, then, is thought of as free. But is he
an owner of his flocks? In the prologue to *The Faithful Shepherdess* (p. 18 Bullen), John Fletcher answers the people who were
disappointed with the refinement of the characters in the play:
"You are to remember shepherds to be such as all the ancient
poets, and modern of understanding, have received them;

that is, the owners of flocks, and not hirelings." Likewise Spenser, in the "December" eclogue (line 11) refers to shepherds as "maisters" of the flock. This, according to "E.K.," is in imitation of Virgil's

> Pan looks after the sheep and the masters of the sheep,

though one may wonder whether "master" (*magister*) is much more than curator in this context.[1] But there is a difference between the social status of the Virgilian *pastor* and that of the Theocritean *poimēn*. Virgil's herdsmen are, for the most part, characterized as small owners and entrepreneurs; those of Theocritus tend more to be employees, but employees of a very special sort.[2] Fletcher's argument was that only free owners of flocks could be expected to show the refinement and experience which are voiced in a good pastoral. His instinct that the hired hands with whom he is familiar will not do is right; but his purely sociological determination is too narrow. Virgil's herdsmen are free; but their approximation to the status of small land owners means that they worry about the title to their property and doubt whether the farmstead will furnish enough to eat. This has the potential effect of depriving them of the very quality which Fletcher's insistence on free enterprise was designed to procure. The herdsmen of Theocritus have no such worries. Though their social status may be that of slaves, their conduct, as a rule, belies their standing. We shall return to this directly.

The position against which Fletcher was arguing is represented by Shakespeare's Corin, in *As You Like It*. He does not own his flocks; both he and the herd obey their master. The result is unpastoral. As a matter of fact, however, it is not so much the precise status of the herdsman as the handling of the principle of ownership as such that inhibits a full deployment of the pastoral vision. Don Quixote, a Rousseau before his time, announces to the shepherds that our troubles began when "mine" and "yours" were introduced into the vocabulary. In Chapter Six I shall argue that the herdsman must not be thought of as owning his flock to the extent of having the authority to dispose of the animals as food. But if the herdsman does not own his animals, who does? In *Idyll* 5, Theocritus is more explicit than elsewhere about the servile status of his characters, and about the motif of ownership. Comatas boasts that the sheep of Lacon belong to Thurian Sibyrtas, and that his own goats are the property of Eumaras of Sybaris. Apparently he hopes to win favor from the judge by referring to the respective owners; one is left to conjecture that Eumaras is the more powerful man. Lacon, on the other hand, is embarrassed by the disclosure that the animals are not his own:

> Did anyone question, damn you!, whose they are?
> You talk and talk. . . .

In fact Lacon is a bit of a snob; his use of the metronymic (line 15) is a pathetic substitute for the name of the father he has never known. Each man accuses the other of being a thief. There is, then, no doubt that they are non-owners, and are owned themselves. Yet they wager animals without compunction and quarrel over imaginary stakes. Lacon's protest leaves the whole question of title under a cloud. The matter of ownership and control has been sufficiently muddied to diminish its importance vis-à-vis the judge, a man from the city, and that means, vis-à-vis the listener. In this least musical and least idyllic of idylls, Theocritus accepts ownership as a fact of life; but as he draws the phenomenon out into the open, he blunts its edge by the contradictions he allows to stand.

In *Idyll* 4 the issue of ownership is handled with similar finesse. The cowherd who has gone to Olympia is, it appears, in control of the stock; he has taken twenty sheep with him as his rations. But more than being an owner (a fact that is not overtly stated) he is also a wrestler and a glutton (both of these *are* stated), penchants which have drawn him elsewhere, leaving the animals and his pipe in the charge of Corydon. The poem gets much of its charm from the elaborate arrangements made for the absence of a man who is a buffoon, a friend, and an enthusiast, contrasting with the speaker, whose lack of spirit is the more vividly felt. Again, therefore, ownership appears to be less crucial in this tissue of personal relations than the contrasting of two characters, and the assertion that the character on the scene is substituting for someone else. His own social status is hardly touched on.

The Cyclops in *Idyll* 11 is an owner, to be sure; an owner with a vengeance, one might say. He herds a thousand cattle, and even manages to drink their milk. What is more, he raises fawns and bear cubs, to present them as gifts to Galatea. He is the exception that confirms the rule; for, as we saw above, the Cyclops does not fully understand what it means to be a pastoral herdsman. He prides himself on his pastoral empire, but at heart he is a clown, a *nouveau riche* exhibitionist rather than a gentle swain. The pelt of the herdsman sits awkwardly on his brawny shoulders. The pride in wealth that distinguishes him comes to be fairly common in later pastoral; Calpurnius' *Eclogue* 3 is an example. In Theocritus this kind of boasting is quite rare, and is brought in for the purposes of humor. The Cyclops looks upon his animals with the calculating eye of a breeder for profit, precisely as his prototype in the *Odyssey*, and indeed most characters in the *Odyssey*, had done. Eumaeus values his animals as a commodity to be administered for the greatest gain; flocks and herds are strictly for food, and not for companionship, except *in extremis*, as when the Homeric Cyclops cajoles the ram carrying Odysseus. It is important to recognize that the relation between herdsman and herd in pastoral is entirely different from that found in other genres, including tragedy, philosophy, and rhetoric. The pastoral herdsman does not look upon his flock as chattel, and instruments of profit, but as associates in pleasure and happiness

Instead of bookkeeping, camaraderie; instead of insensibility, the solidarity of the senses.

Ovid catches a glimpse of the freedom that reigns in the pastoral bower then he says of his Philemon and Baucis:

> No point in asking for the master, for the servant;
> *They* are the house, *they* give the orders and obey them.[3]

"House," *domus*, is the one non-pastoral touch here. The house, with its overtones of domestic economy and family organization, takes us back to the Homeric heroes and their self-sufficiency.[4] But the freedom, the impossibility of distinguishing between masters and slaves, is the proper pastoral note. Even Calpurnius, with his glorification of the emperor, knew this. His fourth *Eclogue* develops a picture of the emperor being worshipped by nature, which is also a picture of peace and freedom. And when, in his third *Eclogue*, the herdsman offers his hands to be bound, the posture is an indirect affirmation of freedom as the normal condition. Later, especially after pastoral and *pastourelle* had pooled their resources, this makes for a peculiar consequence, which may be observed in Spenser: since the herdsman must be free, the best herdsman is a courtier who has freely chosen to be a herdsman, or to mingle with herdsmen. In Theocritus and Virgil, courtesy is one of the natural virtues of every herdsman; in the medieval and post-medieval tradition, courtesy contracts its scope, and becomes the special privilege of a few. As its name in English shows, it comes to be based on an awareness of hierarchy. In Spenser's pastoral, and in Shakespeare's use of the motifs, the characters know where they belong in the social and moral class structure. This is, at bottom, a betrayal of one of the original incentives of the bucolic tradition.

> For a man by nothing is so well bewrayd
> As by his manners, in which plaine is showne
> Of what degree and what race he is growne.[5]

The sentiment is perfectly intelligible within a Greek setting; it might have come straight out of Plato or Aristophanes. But the pastoralists, above all Theocritus, would reject it as destructive of the *otium* of the pleasance, which does not admit class distinctions or pride of race.

But here we have to be careful. The democracy of the green cabinet differs considerably from the democracy of the romantic forest, especially as formulated by Walt Whitman, in which even the least significant elements have equal rights, and all values are thereby homogenized or thrown over.[6] There are differentiations of human worth in the pastoral; the straining figures represented on the cup of *Idyll* 1, or for that matter the bucking goats and errant kids, do not possess the same credentials as the singing herdsman or the chirping cicada. The pastoral does not level or merge or subsume; one of its virtues is the clarity of its vision. True to the paratactic mode of its psychology and its formal organization, it keeps its grouping of the animate beings in the bower sharply articulated. Each creature contributes its own special powers. In the romantic conception, on the other hand, the soothing grove tends to cancel human association. Man is called upon to deny his friends so that he can experience what nature has in store for him:

> Alas! thine is the bankruptcy,
> Blessed Nature so to see.
> Come, lay thee in my soothing shade,
> And heal the hurts which sin has made.
> I see thee in the crowd alone;
> I will be thy companion.
> Quit thy friends, as the dead in doom,
> And build to them a final tomb.

The speaker is the pine tree, in Emerson's "Woodnotes." His message is one of surrender, of devotion and salvation via abnegation. According to this view, which is ultimately Stoic in origin, man can be free only if he gives up his dependence on other beings.

Not so in the pastoral, which is Epicurean by persuasion. The proper freedom is possible only if it is enjoyed in a circle of friends; true friendship, in turn, is enjoyable only if it is attended by liberty.

> Come now, we share the walk, we share the morning;
> Strike up the pastoral song; one will support the other.[7]

Companionship, pastoral song, mutual benefit; these are the conditions upon which pastoral freedom is based, freedom both as a condition and as an awareness. As Epicurus recommended it, and as his philosophical and literary successors continued to emphasize,[8] genuine inner freedom can be documented only in the manner of one's conduct toward one's associates. It requires the limiting provisions imposed by human fellowship to show its mettle. The three chief vices, according to Epicurus, were hatred, envy, and contempt (Diogenes Laertius 10.117). The Epicureans have been called a true Society of Friends.[9] Intimacy without deference, amiability, courtesy, and fellow feeling rather than cultivation of the self: these formed the premises on which living in the Garden was founded. The Cynic preachers taught that a man's virtue was dependent on his ability to live a life of his own, without assistance from others. The Peripatetics held that a man can be self-sufficient only within the setting, and with the help, of a community; this was contested by the Cynics, who insisted that *autarkeia* was accessible to the individual man, and to him only. Menander's *Dyskolos*, which shows the shortcomings of the Cynic philosophy, suggests that the issue of self-sufficiency was being widely discussed at the time.[10] In the quarrel between Peripatetics and Cynics, the Epicureans would have aligned themselves on the side of the former, save that not a political community but association with friends was needed for the achievement of happiness and *ataraxia*, imperturbability.

Typically, the Epicurean does not write treatises but letters; between friends the proper channel of communication is the informal, free exchange of views that a correspondence permits, rather than *ex cathedra* lecturing.[11] It is significant that Epicurus was the first philosopher to use the medium of the epistle to formulate his position. His successors include Horace, in his *Epistles*. It is worth mentioning, also, that several of Theocritus' most successful poems are designed as letters to a friend. But since Theocritus keeps authorial statement and pastoral poem strictly separate, the significance of his epistolary openings should not be exaggerated. In later pastoral, and especially in pastoral romance, epistolary exchanges between lovers are not uncommon. There are obvious formal similarities between such exchanges and pastoral contests; the daring symmetries of the singing match are equaled only in the fiendishly constructed correspondences of the erotic novel, from *Clarissa* to *Les Liaisons Dangereuses*.

In the Epicurean circle of friends, as in the Socratic group, writing is a pis aller, for the company is likely to be small, much smaller even than one of Menander's intimate sets.[12] Living speech is the commensurate vehicle for the bonds of friendship prized in the Garden. The same is true of the pastoral fellowship; it is neither too big—its size varies from two to six or seven— nor does it isolate a man into solipsistic contemplation. The pastoral idylls that feature a herdsman singing to himself usually include a number of listeners; or again there is enough group experience built into the content of his song to satisfy us that he is indeed concerned with other people. In fact it is the solo arias, rather than the contests, that show us singers most forgetful of their own prerogatives, and most intent on sharing their lot with someone else, through love. At this point, as we have seen, Theocritus and Virgil part company with Epicurus, who favors sex but eschews the passion of love. But the Epicurean tenet that happiness is achieved only in association with others continues to hold.

Of all the literary genres available then or now, the pastoral is best qualified to record the spirit of intimacy which rules in the Epicurean circle. Even the rhetoric of "Where were ye, Nymphs...?" is an apostrophe which confirms the bond that has been temporarily interrupted. The most characteristic pastoral technique in this respect is the use of names without introduction. Contrary to the epic, which underscores the introduction of its characters by means of patronymics and references to the land of birth, pastoral ingenuously scatters names about, on the presumption that everybody—and that includes the listener as well as the narrator and his characters—surely knows who these people are. "And old Damoetas lov'd to hear our song" is not only an appeal to the erudition of the reader, whom Milton expects to be steeped in the prosopography of the bucolic tradition; it is, more importantly, a continuation of the convention that, within the pastoral world, introductions are odious. There are anticipations of this, prior to Theocritus; when the girls in Alcman's *Maiden-Songs* sing about each other, or when Aristophanes' comic heroes lampoon citizens in high places, the method and the spirit are comparable. But Alcman's and Aristophanes' humor is at the expense of characters who are known to the members of the society that furnishes the listeners; the pastoral characters are merely pretended to be known.[13] The fiction operates with the willingness, on the part of the listener, to accept whatever names are brought in. Thus Chromis from Libya and the ferryman from Calydna (*Idyll* 1.24,57) corroborate the impression of intimacy, precisely because we must adapt ourselves to the stipulation that they are old acquaintances. From this convention, Virgil chooses to stray. In the *Aeneid*, Book 7, he offends against epic decorum by introducing a nameless mother; an equally anonymous mother in *Eclogue* 5 offends against the pastoral canon. Namelessness introduces a puzzle, and teases the listener into a mood of inquiry which defies the pastoral principles of clarity and open association.

I return to the issue of freedom, of which friendship and intimacy are vital corollaries. It would be a mistake to think that the freedom of the herdsman must be voiced within the poem as a boast, or demand, or even as a flat statement of fact. The pastoral, as we have seen already, and as we shall argue in greater detail below (Chapter Ten), is not a species of anatomy; it is not argumentative, it does not tell, but merely shows. The herdsmen are free; they do not need to talk about their freedom. This abstraction, "freedom," is just as inappropriate to their natively direct speech as are other abstractions, such as justice [14] or courtesy. [15] Poggioli says that the idea of justice has always played an important role in the pastoral dream, and cites the story of Naboth and his Vineyard in the Old Testament. [16] The choice of the example refutes the proposition. The tale of Naboth is, at best, a Hesiodic legend, illustrating the hubris of the princes of the world toward the poor. Many of the items in the tale—the motif of ownership, the emphasis on the miscarriage of justice, the class struggle, and the moralizing—disqualify the tale from being a specimen of pastoral. Above all, the action does not take place in the green cabinet, the secluded locus of the pastoral, but in the world of power and politics. The Biblical author shares the sentiments of Euripides to which I alluded earlier (above, Chapter Four). Amphion's

> The man who leads a quiet life is a safe friend
> To his friends, and best for the city. . . .

takes its criteria of judgment from the city, hence breaches the boundaries of the *locus amoenus*. Because pastoral sets up its own universe, which has no overt points of contact with the universe analyzed by anatomy and the confessional lyric, it is invulnerable to attack. The freedom of the pastoral swain is not functionally related to the political and the social freedoms that have formed the center of speculation in the past several centuries. Poggioli thinks that "the modern world destroyed the conventional and

traditional pastoral through four cultural trends . . . the humanitarian outlook, the idea of material progress, the scientific
spirit, and artistic realism."[17] Poggioli's error is the assumption
that pastoral offers an explicit and exploitable moral, and that it is
therefore susceptible to attack from a divergent moral. In reality,
the freedom of the herdsman is incorruptible; sealed in the bower,
the object of example rather than argument, it survives and
flourishes, and is capable of assimilating a variety of moral and
social choices. Its own ethical stance is unmistakable, and, as I
have tried to show, bears a resemblance to that of the Garden.
But the herdsman would be the last person in the world to wish
to persuade others of the correctness of his commitments. Indeed,
as far as we know he is not aware of having commitments; his
freedom is a gift of the natural world in which he moves; alternatives are unthinkable. The pastoral is like the herdsman; it
raises no doubts and asks no questions. Its simplicity is its defense,
or rather it would be, if it needed one.

᪥   ᪥   ᪥   ᪥

We come now to a matter which at first blush appears to cast
considerable doubt on the axiom of pastoral freedom and equality.
It is best, once more, to begin with a glance at the Epicurean
analogue. The democracy of the Epicurean circle of friends is
limited in one important way. The master himself, we are told,
wished to be regarded as a man-turned-god, or god-in-man—a
Gottmensch, to use the term invented to make sense of the Hellenistic phenomenon of a prince receiving divine honors.[18] Epicurus
inserted a clause in his last will and testament which set up a
fund for monthly ritual banquets in his honor.[19] The deification
of Epicurus is a consequence of the Epicurean tenet that spiritually,
though not atomically, the sage and the god are one. The man
who has achieved joy is an equal of the gods. He is equal and
separate, for the gods have no moral communication with men;
that would imperil their perfection. They can be intellected,

but that is all. Gods are happy only if they are at rest; hence they do not run the universe.[20]

There is much here that reminds us of the standing of the gods in the Homeric universe, in spite of the ostensible communication between gods and men stipulated by the divine apparatus. As one scholar has put it: the Epicurean gods are a further development of the blessed Homeric gods, but with the addition of a touch of Aristotle. They do not participate in human affairs, but men are affected by them through the love they, men, feel for them.[21] Certainly there is no communication via prophecy; Epicurus unambiguously condemns *mantikē* as having no basis in being. He is willing to swear by the popular gods, and to rejoice with them on religious occasions;[22] but he rejects sacrifices and supplications and the whole machinery of fear and tension that is traditionally associated with divine privilege. Like the Homeric hero, the Epicurean sage knows that in his venture to shape his life and his well being, he must go it alone. And precisely as the Homeric hero, relying upon his own strength, achieves an air of godhood, so the Epicurean wise man, through the wisdom that defines a god, appears to his less perfect fellow men a god-on-earth. Gestures of respect and admiration, customarily performed in honor of the gods, should be reserved for men; for there we can know for sure whether the homage is merited or not.

Scholars, especially English-speaking scholars, have always been a little embarrassed by an excerpt from a letter written by Epicurus to his disciple Colotes and reported by Plutarch.[23] There is nothing embarrassing about the feeling expressed, once we understand that the Epicurean world is a world without gods, without ritual, without eschatology, and therefore in need of a new orientation for what is after all a basic human requirement: the urge to make obeisance.

In your feeling of reverence for what I was then saying you were seized with an unaccountable desire to embrace me and to clasp my knees and show me all the signs of homage paid by men in supplications and prayers to others. So you made me return all these proofs of veneration and respect to you. Go on your way as an immortal, and think of us too as immortals.[24]

These sentiments, far from being blasphemous, point up the urgency with which Epicurus puts man in the position vacated by god. They also serve to tell us how the comrades of the Garden felt about the master.

This is where we reach our difficulty. On the one hand, the Epicurean friends are peers whose happiness depends on their respect for each others' rights and feelings. On the other, the remoteness of the gods needs to be compensated for by the living divinity of the wise man who exacts admiration and a worship that exceeds fellow feeling. The same friction is found in the pastoral, especially in the pastoral lament of which our first and, if I may be allowed to say so, subtlest example is the song of Thyrsis in Theocritus' *Idyll* 1. Daphnis towers larger than the rest; herdsmen, animals, even gods, are shown visiting him and failing to measure up to his greatness. The mise-en-scène is iconographically identical with that of the hero or savior receiving the homage of his followers. The visitation scene became a stock theme in later pastoral laments; the *divus homo* is paid his last rites, complete with tears and chaplets of flowers. Virgil's Daphnis and Gallus, Marot's Loyse, Milton's Lycidas, all exhibit a stature larger than life, out of proportion with the other beings who populate the stage. It would seem as if their elevated position undid the spirit of freedom and equality which has emerged as a desideratum of the pastoral pleasance.

Here again, however, Theocritus' mastery is complete. Loyse has her disciples; Gallus has a rival; but Theocritus' Daphnis—and this is essentially true of Virgil's Daphnis also—stands alone, as pastoral man writ large. Thyrsis' sights are trained so fully on Daphnis that the other players on the scene are given short shrift. Daphnis defies the gods and calls upon nature to reverse its course, in consonance with his own upheaval. Here human vigor borders on hubris, and *otium* is momentarily shattered by pretension. But the larger effect is, I suggest, one of concentration rather than overturning. The freedom of the herdsman is distilled in an energetic image of the herdsman-saint who protests his independence (in love) and rebuts the restraints imposed by external authority. There is pathos in the fiction and some humor; there is also the risk that goes with compressing the disjunct world of the bower into this charged image, almost an emblem, but not quite, of pastoral liberty. Pleasure and *otium* are slighted so that freedom may ring out. Characteristically, Theocritus attempts this venture only once, and that in a poem which should be regarded as an overture or a manifesto. Comatas in *Idyll* 7 is a more mysterious figure, but also less violent; his *Gottmenschentum* is less exclusive of human company, more accessible to beasts, and defiant of tyrants rather than of gods. Still, intimacy, that most precious commodity of pastoral *otium*, is difficult to achieve when the heroic herdsman occupies the center of the stage. Hence the unsettled climate of those poems, as Virgil's *Eclogues* 1 and 10, in which the circle of friends is subordinated or abandoned for the sake of an emphasis on the central hero.

It is, therefore, somewhat surprising that the pastoral lament became, in the European tradition, the most viable of the various applications of the pastoral form.[25] In the pastoral lament, the noontime peace is understood to have become a more lasting kind of peace; depending on the interpretation put on it, it is either a tragic extinction of life, or the glorious achievement of immortality. The two are often combined. In either case the special conditions of the bower have the effect of muting the pathos and the glory; the pasture envelops poignancy with gentleness, and soft-pedals triumph. This, at least, is the way the poets attuned to the possibilities of the genre proceed. Others push the grief and the hosannahs close to the timbre customary in heroic poetry or in drama and thus forfeit the special powers of pastoral to furnish a comment on death.

When Sannazaro initiated the Renaissance vogue of the pastoral lament, he abandoned all caution. The impression one receives from reading the *Arcadia* today is that, for Sannazaro, the pastoral lyric is essentially lament and little else.[26]He appears to regard the shepherd's pipe as the instrument for sad occasions. The cardinal occasion is the loss of a dear one, either lover or friend. This is a very old use of pastoral patterns; in the hands of a minor poet, the narrowness of the bucolic vision can become extremely restrictive, especially in this branch. Some of the Hellenistic laments for pet animals, cicadas, or locusts or birds,[27] exhibit a nervous dalliance that defies the native demands of *otium*. The successful combination of "metaphysical" conceits with pastoral simplicity had to wait another eighteen or nineteen hundred years. Nor does cepotaphic verse, lines supposedly inscribed over garden burials,[28] furnish a satisfactory outlet for what the genre has to offer, in spite of the linking of Death and the garden. The scope is too small, the manner too playful, and the self-consciousness too evident. In reading some of these poems, one is reminded of Dr. Johnson's comment on Congreve's pastoral elegies: when the author "has yelled out many syllables of senseless dolor, he dismisses his reader with senseless consolation."[29]

The grand tradition of the pastoral lament, from Theocritus' "Daphnis" via Virgil's "Daphnis" and Marot, Spenser and Sidney to Milton's "Lycidas" and Pope's fourth *Pastoral*, offers two leading avenues for the expression of feeling.[30] Either nature is shown to be dying with the man or woman lamented, in which case the emphasis is on the mortificatory side of *otium*. An example is Nicolas Breton's "A Sweete Pastoral," Number 23 in *England's Helicon* (ed. Rollins). Or else nature is said to be exercising a refreshing and consoling power, in which case the accent is on the restorative character of *otium*. Spenser's "November" is a case in point. But whether restorative or deletory, there is much attention to the integration of man into a larger universe of animal and vegetable life, of which the immediate scene, the bower, is for once a more transparent agent than in some of the other varieties of pastoral.

The poetic tendency to draw nature into the complex of the passion at the moment of grief, and thereby to achieve a degree of equalization, is found everywhere in the world. In a Chinook legend, "the mournful bear woman, grieving for her infant who has just died, expresses her feeling about the child. She redirects her intense grief into anger at the ripe, edible, and tempting salmon-berries which are falling on her and which, she supposes in her depression, are dropping deliberately on her. She sings over and over:

> Keep away! salmonberries!
> My child is dead! salmonberries."[31]

Here we have a re-channeling of grief into a comment on nature, and a projection of human passions into the behavior of the vegetable world. This is the way of the American Indian lament, in which no clear distinction is made between the various forms of animate life; man and salmonberries are dimly felt to subsist on the same level. In the Western pastoral lament, the differentiation between man and nature is usually firmer. It is precisely because man is regarded as essentially different from his surroundings that the grief can be assuaged by closing the gap between the two.

The cushioning force of the larger scene can be activated by stressing the sheer geographical extent of the world. The bower is transcended, exotic landscapes are brought in in the form of catalogues or even learned quotations, and the vast world opens up before us to enhance the fiction that the grief cannot be contained, but also to point up the wealth of consolatory energies available to blunt the death agony.

> Swans of the Strymon, cry woe and chant laments
> . . . .
> Tell the young women in Thrace, tell all the maids
> In Macedon: the Dorian Orpheus is dead!
> . . . .
> The famous cities, Bion, all the towns grieve for you.

And the poet proceeds to name them: Ascra, Boeotia, Lesbos,
Teos, Paros, Mitylene....[32] The names of mountains and
rivers and far-away landmarks are chosen with an eye to their
mythological or ethnographic or, as in the present case, their
artistic associations. Or again, for their sheer beauty of sound.
Lycidas' forecast of Tityrus' lament for the dying Daphnis is
worth citing:

> How the mountains grieved, and the oaks sang their dirge,
> The trees which grow on the banks of the Himeras,
> When he melted as snow would from towering Haemus
> Or Athos or Rhodope or the furthest Caucasus.[33]

As usual, Theocritus' learning is not pedantic; the excitement is
not unlike that which is sparked by the catalogues of places
visited by Dionysiac revellers.[34] To guard against the possibility
of the appearance of pedantry, Virgil was said to have deliberately placed in the mouths of his herdsmen geographical statements that are false or confusing. The main example cited by
Servius is *Eclogue* 2, line 24: Virgil locates Aracinthus in Attica
rather than in Thebes, where it belongs.[35] According to Servius,
Theocritus uses the same ingenious technique. Whether there is
truth in the allegation or not—the evidence is at best doubtful—
the fact remains that cumulative geography in the pastoral per-
forms a variety of functions. The catalogues have a Hesiodic
ring; but the force of this is weakened by a certain naiveté of
application. A catalogue that is colorful and sonorous rather
than informative cannot be taken very seriously as catalogue.

Only rarely do such lists have an explicitly symbolic value.
The melting of the snow on Caucasus and Haemus, though in
sympathy with Daphnis' own melting, is not as important as the
widening of the horizon as such, and the balm offered by the
unfolding of a larger world. The address to the Nymphs at the
beginning of Thyrsis' song, and their association with Peneius
and Pindus and Anapus and Etna and Acis, bring in the resonance
of all the wild places of the world to magnify and eventually

to assuage the grief for the central hero. It has been suggested that the Greek names in Virgil have a special, because foreign-sounding, sonorousness which makes them doubly suitable as beautifiers and palliators.[36] The suggestion is valuable, but should not be exaggerated. In Virgil's day, Italy and Greece are not strangers to one another. In any case, I suspect that beauty of sound counts for less in this regard than the perception of a vast world coming to the rescue. The two geographical catalogues in *Eclogue* 10 (55–60 and 65–68) mark the peak of the convention. Gallus lists the lands where his fevered imagination has him living a silvan life, and follows this up with a list of the lands which, though remote and inaccessible, will not provide shelter from the onrush of Love. Ostensibly, therefore, the distant places are conceived as havens for escape and seclusion. Beyond this, however, their echoes provide the enlargement and the cushioning which the beatification of the dying hero requires.

Later pastoral retains and further develops the convention, but with a difference. Alamanni mixes the realities of his own day with the classical *topoi*. Pope similarly mingles English names, above all that of the Thames, with the Greek. The incongruity is exploited most successfully in Milton's "Lycidas" (154–164):

> Ay me! Whilst thee the shores, and sounding Seas
> Wash far away, where ere thy bones are hurld,
> Whether beyond the stormy *Hebrides*,
> Where thou perhaps under the whelming tide
> Visit'st the bottom of the monstrous world;
> Or whether thou to our moist vows deny'd,
> Sleep'st by the fable of *Bellerus* old,
> Where the great vision of the guarded Mount
> Looks toward *Namancos* and *Bayona's* hold;
> Look homeward Angel now, and melt with ruth,
> And, O ye *Dolphins*, waft the haples youth.

Regionalism joins hands with the old cosmic enlargement, snatches of classical verse with flashes of private experience, to touch the old sonorities with a note of humbleness, or better, of (Christian) humility.

Christianity is responsible also for another extension of the ancient pattern. This shows the dead man enjoying the energizing breath of nature in the form of a new life after death, in paradise. There is a tendency in modern criticism to suggest that by his apotheosis of King, Milton "breaks the pattern of both the funeral elegy and the pastoral of friendship," and that he comes to reject the pagan pastoral in favor of an entirely novel and irreconcilable Christian version.[37] According to this view, Milton could not accept the fatalism of the pastoral lament; his Christianity dictated another kind of dirge that brought his poetic instincts into conflict with the old pastoral procedure. Though the ancients thought they could accommodate even death in the *locus amoenus*, the experiment had failed, and the Christian paradise needed to be substituted for a temporal setting which had proved inadequate.

Now it is perfectly true that "Lycidas" embodies many tensions and fruitful contradictions that go far beyond the comparatively simple frictions of the old order. But on this particular score—the transcendence of the temporal scale and the apotheosis of the central herdsman—Milton's solution is not so very far removed from what may be found in the ancient tradition. Virgil's "Daphnis" locates the dead herdsman in a new and lasting bower, one that mirrors the bower below and adds further glamor to it. It is wrong, even in Milton, to suppose that the heavenly pleasance cancels out or debases the attractions of the terrestrial *locus amoenus*. In spite of some sharp talk about ugliness and corruption, the poem as a whole conveys a sensation of well being; the world below continues to be thought of as welcoming the efforts of King and his friends. The extension of the horizon to include a vista of Paradise does roughly the same duty as the interludes on Olympus in the ancient epic: they do not overturn; they add and reinforce. Lycidas translated into Heaven clinches the pastoral promise of freedom and *otium*; the manner differs from the ancient manner only in the degree of its eschatological fervor, not in the nature of the program.

Still there is something risky about showing the beloved dead irrevocably removed from the embraces of the mourner. The older form of the consolation simply balances the momentary loss of the beloved with a heightened awareness of the beauty and the pulse of nature. This may well present the subtler option because the commitment of the poet, whether religious or iconographic, is less in evidence. Of the several subspecies of pastoral, the pastoral lament is generally held to exhibit the largest number of fixed conventions;[38] and Theocritus is credited with having invented most of them. But his one venture in the form, the Song of Thyrsis, is significantly unconventional; it shows the victim not dead but dying, with the result that the lament for Daphnis is at the same time, and perhaps more importantly, a protest of the victim *against* nature. We shall come back to this directly.

The most common formal element in the pastoral dirge is a feature we have discussed before—the refrain. We found earlier that the major function of the refrain is to stop movement in its tracks, to stabilize the flux, and exhaust the reservoir of the significant moment charged with feeling. To our jaded ears the refrain of the pastoral lament may cause embarrassment. E. K. Rand says about the refrain of Milton's "Epitaphium Damonis": "There is one tremendous infelicity, the refrain: 'Go to your folds unfed, my lambs, your master has not time for you.' This is well enough for three times or even four, but lambs that have to be liturgically shooed away seventeen times are either unusually hungry or unusually inquisitive; at any rate they become unusually monotonous."[39] Rand's jibe is a pity, for it indicates that he is not willing to enter into the compact between poet and listener, which is a prerequisite for the enjoyment of a poem modeled on the paradigm of oral communication, as the pastoral lament always is. Monotony can, under certain agreed circumstances, be a virtue, especially when the deadening drug helps us to overcome the sharpness of too great a grief. "Dead Mother Ida, hearken ere I die" is no doubt offensive to some ears, for the quality of its diction, perhaps, or because of its air of melodrama. But the charge of monotony should not be pleaded.

The pastoral lament tries to maneuver death into a position where it enters into a partnership with Epicurean pleasure. It is the complete fixing, the radical elimination of *ponos*, the absorption of motion and commotion by the noon shade. Pastoral laments that look at death in a different way, and that do not reach out for the joy of the ultimate *otium*, fail to exploit the advantages of the genre. Even "Lycidas," with its Christian message, is always on the point of abandoning the shaded cabinet for the heroic annihilation of drama. What is more, later pastoral often misunderstood Theocritus' "Where were you, Nymphs . . . ?" to mean that Nature has become flawed. Theocritus' question is, rather, designed to let us know that the herdsman is isolated from Nature; in some undetermined way the song is to rescue him from this isolation. Nature is whole and incorruptible, though it need not be sensitive; only man will now and then move away from it and set up his own music shop. The remarkable thing about Theocritus' handling of the dirge is that it is done with precisely that sense of distance and cool appraisal which some have criticized in Yeats' "Shepherd and Goatherd" from *The Wild Swans at Coole*.[40] Whereas Renaissance dirges spill their sadness over into the opening and closing conversation, in *Idyll* 1 the lament is scheduled as a performance, and framed by opening and closing sections which give no inkling of tragedy in the delicate courtesies and delights of a chance meeting between the performers. The frame insulates our responses against too immediate an identification with the suffering of the dying hero. Daphnis is put on display, not as a contemporary whose death should touch us, but as a fictional hero whose death in the past might interest us for the particular implications it holds.

As I have mentioned, Daphnis is dying, not dead. Instead of an accomplished fact confronting us, with a meaning whose pathos is easily accessible, Daphnis' dying is a puzzling affair. For once it raises so many questions that there is little time left over for mourning. We are tempted to sympathize with Daphnis, but first we wonder about his reasons for dying,[41] and we are shocked by the violence of his struggle against the flesh. There is nothing soothing or conciliatory about Daphnis. The call for nature to reverse itself is issued, not by the poet or by a mourner, but by the victim himself; and Daphnis thereby reveals a hubris that sets him apart even further. It is only because his boasts and complaints occur within the setting of the bower that his death strikes us as a possible and not unattractive extension of *otium*. The dirge of *Idyll* 1 exhibits a mixture of calm and strain, of *stasis* and *kinēsis*. Though availing himself of the equation of noon and death offered by the genre, Theocritus appears, momentarily, to squander the sorrow on a hero who is recalcitrant. But even here the pain and the wrangling are in the end outweighed by the sheer joy of living, and the accent on raw animal sex with which the poem, not untypically, closes. Mortification, even strenuous or surly mortification, is put in the proper perspective; the lasting mood is that of life, and liberty. Daphnis wills his own death, in the face of the gods and the companions who wish to save him. The rigor of his will and the absence of an intelligent reason why he should have to die constitute the triumph of freedom, and mark his death as, in its way, a conquest of death.

Virgil saw this, and in *Eclogue* 5 he decided to spell things out more clearly by joining a song of mortification with a hymn of apotheosis. The contributions of Mopsus and Menalcas are conceived as variations upon the same theme: the declaration of freedom on behalf of the herdsman-singer in his green abode.

Like Theocritus, Virgil does not give a reason for the death; like Theocritus, Virgil has the informant talk about the death-scene in the past tense. Apollo, like Theocritus' divinities, is completely naturalized; his presence at the bier is little different from that of the herdsmen and the animals. There are important differences; Daphnis is dead, not dying; his past exploits, narrated for our benefit, possess a Dionysiac grandeur. The call for obsequies (lines 40–44) proposes a memorial inscription (see also lines 13–15) and recommends a ritual procedure whose obscurity does not diminish its beauty and its larger appropriateness: *inducite fontibus umbras*, which must mean something like: "Draw a curtain of shade over the spring." Virgil pays more attention to the tranquillizing and enveloping powers of his silvan setting; but the effect of the epigraphic boast at the end, with its emphatic *ego* and its comparative *formosior ipse*, is not one whit less hubristic than the pugnaciousness shown by Theocritus' hero. Again, as in *Idyll* 1, the song is, at its termination, characterized as a performance. The joy that the listeners derive from it is more substantial than any mourning in which they may be encouraged to share. This is what simplifies the transition to the song of jubilation that follows. The pleasure that the herdsmen-listeners take in the musical offerings brought by their friends is a portion of the pleasure which the pastoral bower holds as its birthright. Against this background, the grief of a lament is dulled, as is the bravado of the dying hero and the veneration paid to his deified spirit. The simplicity of the pleasance endorses the freedom and the genuine aspirations of the herdsman; the relaxing beauty of the *otium* mutes the poignancy of the challenge. Note how quickly, in Menalcas' song of apotheosis, the celestial dimension is abandoned. After a very brief glimpse of the divine threshold we return to the woods and their joys. Pleasure and *otium*, the keywords of the grove, are shown to be in control of the millennial peace among animals and men that Daphnis' special standing has insured. Menalcas himself, addressed in the vocative, is drawn into the festive concert. In the end we sense that, though Daphnis dies and is translated, both events cause barely a stir in the solid balance of natural enjoyment. Lament and encomium, death and resurrection, experienced within the larger setting, are near-identical; freedom is all.[42]

Theocritus' Daphnis is a fictitious person. There is no point in trying to identify the dying herdsman of *Idyll* 1 with any one of Theocritus' friends or colleagues. Even if we knew more about Theocritus' private life than we do—it is symptomatic of the "anonymity" of the pastoral form that we don't—it would be futile to interpret the hymn of Thyrsis as a *poème à clef*. Theocritus shows by his practice in the *encomia* that have come down, notably *Idylls* 16 and 17, that he prefers not to mix pastoral with biography. Virgil surrenders this discretion when he puts the dying Gallus in a situation modelled on that of Daphnis. But then *Eclogue* 10 is a leave-taking from pastoral. To the degree that the dying Gallus is cast in the role of an expiring herdsman, the incident borders on the ludicrous, which is not, as we shall see in a later chapter (Chapter Eight), necessarily a disadvantage in a bucolic poem. I think we may safely say that Virgil recognized the incongruity of investing a moribund herdsman with the weaknesses and idiosyncrasies of a soldier-administrator well known to the poet's contemporaries. Later writers, beginning with Calpurnius, refuse to admit the awkwardness of the fixture; and so the pastoral lament for the death of a patron came into currency.

Such a lament must always, in the nature of things, also be an encomium. When Daphnis calls on nature to overturn her own laws, and when Virgil's Daphnis immortalizes his beauty in an inscription, the pastoral lament turns into a pastoral panegyric, an encomium *sui ipsius* on the part of the hero. In fact this is about as close as Theocritus ever comes to composing a pastoral encomium; other praises in the *Idylls* are either low-keyed demonstrations of mutual courtesy, or they are humorous. Virgil contrives, on the whole, to keep praise and lament fairly separate, in spite of the natural coincidence of the two. Nemesianus (*Eclogue* 1.49 ff.) has one of the rare ancient examples of an encomiastic dirge. In the European tradition, the encomiastic dirge comes to be a prominent subspecies of the pastoral. It is distinct from the pastoral encomium proper, from bucolic poetry written in praise of patrons and princely personages, such as Spenser's "Aprill" in honor of Queen Elizabeth,[43] or Ben Jonson's *Pan's Anniversarie*, or Drayton's *Shepheards Garland*, *Eglog* 3, a panegyric of Beta which lavishly combines classical and local pigments to honor the Queen. Much of this goes back to Ronsard and the Pléiade; earlier examples are provided by Boccaccio's "Daphnis and Florida," Petrarch's "Pamphilus and Mition," and Modoin's eulogy of Charlemagne.

The ancient source for many of these encomia is Calpurnius, who, in his *Eclogues* 1, 4, and 7, praises the emperor Nero as the guiding spirit of the new golden age. Calpurnius was aware of undertaking a comparatively new venture. This is revealed by his confession, in the last eclogue, that the praise of the emperor should be regarded as more valuable than the writing of pastoral:

> I wish I had not worn my rustic weeds;
> I would have seen my god close up.[44]

As it was, he combined the two, much as Virgil combined the praise of the unborn child (not an encomium so much as a prophecy) with pastoral motifs. It is clear, however, that the experiment was disastrous; for it helped, in the long run, to discredit the pastoral by showing that it lent itself, not only to escapism and artificiality, but to self-abasement and the flattery of unworthy patrons. Empson's obvious contempt for the whole genre (as distinguished from a few achievements on the frontier of it) is explained on the grounds that "the praise of simplicity usually went with extreme flattery of a patron . . .; it allowed the flattery to be more extreme because it helped both author and patron to keep their self-respect."[45] At the time of the Battle of the Books, the anti-classicists could enlist democratic sympathies to combat what they felt was a type of literature in the pay of the establishment.

A contemporary of Calpurnius, the writer of the two *Einsiedeln* pastorals, shows even more clearly to what extent the pastoral encomium is indebted to the hymns of flattery that originated in the Alexandrian age.[46] The *Einsiedeln* writer praises Nero as superior to Homer and Virgil, and puts him on one pedestal with Apollo. The spirit, though not the skill, is that of Callimachus in his *Hymns* to Zeus and Apollo, hymns which are only thinly veiled panegyrics of the ruling Ptolemy, extolling the artistic and cultural accomplishments of the patron prince. Callimachus is more tactful about the identification of ruler and god than the Roman writer; nor does he use pastoral colors to achieve his end. Theocritus' encomium of the same Ptolemy, *Idyll* 17, is more straightforward about its equation of ruler and Zeus; but he, too, refrains from applying the bucolic palette. The truth of the matter is that pastoral naiveté and the flattery of a patron are incompatible. At its best, as Theocritus' practice shows, the pastoral dramatizes a self-contained reality that has few points of contact with the world in which the poet lives. To argue or pretend, as the writer of the pastoral encomium must, that the eulogized patron is of a purity and refinement which makes him prefer the pastoral bower to the bustle of politics, is to present him with an offering which he might be expected to view with suspicion. In any case, the fiction of the man of action dallying in the bower breaks the spell of pastoral solidity, and raises all sorts of questions about the motives of the writer and the real meaning of the poem, questions that the pastoral is designed to discourage.

There are some successful pastoral encomia; Spenser's "Colin Clout's Come Home Again" is one. It is a mistake, I think, to suppose that the success has much to do with any tendency of pastoral imagery to point beyond itself.[47] The best that the pastoral language of an encomium can hope to accomplish is to embellish and glorify by means of beautiful speech; at their worst the pastoral tropes make for frigidity. Perhaps the most persuasive examples of pastoral eulogy in the English language are some of the sections in Book 4 of *Paradise Lost* (lines 411–439; 440–491; 610–688). The praises that Adam and Eve offer up to the Lord are couched in pastoral terms. The theme of pure love is developed against a background of the *locus amoenus*. This particular amalgamation of encomium and pastoral is successful, perhaps because it is part of a larger whole. The pastoral setting extends beyond the songs of praise, and is quite naturally made to provide an impetus for the spontaneous outburst of celebration. Again, Milton's praise of God is here fully and believably put forward as a character's praise of God; the poet keeps his own stake in the matter out of view. The crass self-interest, and the awkward isolation of the encomiastic strain, both of which are so apparent in Ronsard's political eclogues, are avoided. Finally, the pastoral praise of a god is less liable to cast a dubious light on the praiser than the praise of a temporal authority. God is the original non-mover; he is the only man of affairs whose enthronement in the peaceful cabinet can be accepted without a snicker.

꽃 꽃 꽃 꽃

We have said that the Epicurean allowance for the *Gottmensch* is one consequence of Epicurus' removal of the gods from effective control of the universe. It is now high time to discuss the standing of the gods in Theocritus. Once more, the parallel is very close. The gods, and religion, *have* no standing in the Theocritean bower.[48] Altars are mentioned in several of the epigrams, but in only one *Idyll*, 7, line 155, and there the altar stands only as a directional sign; it is associated with a drinking party rather than with sacrifices. In *Idyll* 5 (80–83) the non-singing contestants boast of sacrificing animals to the Muses and to Apollo; and in *Idyll* 7 a thanks offering to Demeter is contemplated (31–34, 155–157). But these are merely details in the concrete setting for a specific poetic development. The goddess herself matters less than the joyousness of the harvest festival; her cult creates the holiday atmosphere from which the poet generates the pastoral relaxation of the final scene. In any case, two altars briefly mentioned and three sacrifices remembered or forecast do not make a religion.

Virgil proceeds quite differently. In *Eclogue* 3 (60 ff.), the first two stanzas of the singing match are in honor of gods, Jupiter and Phoebus. Later in the contest, Damoetas voices his wish that the gods may hear Galatea's words to him (72–73). Finally Damoetas bethinks himself of a sacrifice (77): *cum faciam vitula pro frugibus*; "when I shall offer a heifer, on behalf of the harvest." Similarly, in *Eclogue* 7, lines 29–36, the contesting singers promise dedications to Diana and Priapus. Here the projected offerings to the gods are of the same order as the stakes in the contest; they are the sort of objects that have meaning in the competitive life of the herdsmen. Even a simple type of theology enters the picture; in *Eclogue* 8, line 35, Damon charges Nysa with thinking that the gods do not care. Thus the gods are drawn openly into the intimate ranks of the herdsmen. Their caring or not caring counts for as much as the passion or coldness of a human agent. The gods have a role to play and their feelings to contribute in the Virgilian bower.[49] The apotheosis of Daphnis in *Eclogue* 5 is invested with true religious emotion; altars and a simple ritual follow quite naturally (65 ff.). In his perceptive discussion of religion in the *Eclogues*, Hubaux finds that Virgil's gods have about them an air of *opéra-comique*.[50] They are invoked at moments when the singers are not necessarily at their devotional best. The way they are fitted into the pastoral scene puts them close to the woodland creatures whose comportment, in Hellenistic literature and its Roman succession, is rarely dignified. But it is also true, as Hubaux admits, that Virgil substitutes native Italic cults for the largely decorative institutions in the Hellenistic epigrams.[51] The combination of gaiety and rustic respectability communicates a genuine sense of faith.[52] Unlike the Theocritean pleasance, the Virgilian grove is full of gods, and the gods are such that, on occasion, they invite worship.

By the time of Horace, every poetic landscape has its altar:

> Color it green: a grove, and Diana's altar;
> An oxbow of water rushing through pretty fields.[53]

Horace's language recalls tapestries and painting. In Campanian wall painting, and the Hellenistic models on which it is based, pastoral panoramas, even beach scenes, usually contain a *sacellum*. Most painters attempt to make the idyllic landscape more interesting by the inclusion of architectural *vedute*. The artists are, it seems, averse to separating country from city entirely; likewise they tend to incorporate religious institutions into the natural grove. All this clearly connects landscape painting with the tradition of the epigram, especially the pastoral dedicatory epigram, and with Virgil, but not with Theocritus.

Medieval and Renaissance pastoral, under the impact of the Christian association of the herdsman with Christ, accelerates the religious tempo.[54] We need only mention Boccaccio's *Olimpia*, which deals with Christ's passion and triumph, his harrowing of Hell, and his second coming, and which furnishes a pastoral description of God enthroned, and the Virgin. A different sort of thing altogether, but equally in praise of God, is Mantuan's *Eclogue* 8, in which the two herdsmen award a prize to the absent Pollux for his good showing as a worshipper of Mary. At the end of the tradition, Pope could say, in his "Discourse": "An air of piety to the gods should shine through the poem, which so visibly appears in all the works of antiquity." *Not* in Theocritus. The divinity of the woodland creatures—Pan, Satyrs, and

Nymphs—was never anything more than a trope. Their presence is felt to contribute a special element of vitality or musical zest to the well-being of the pastoral group. Where the traditional divinities—Aphrodite, Hermes, Apollo—appear, they tend to have the same function. They are in no way central to the plan. Aristophanes made fun of the gods because they were members of the establishment he was expected to lampoon. Such lampooning made it possible for the good citizens to turn around and worship their gods with most of their grudges drained from their piety. Theocritus' gods are not members of the establishment; the religious revolution of the Hellenistic age had deprived them of their earlier privileged status. But even if they were, it would not matter. Theocritus is not a critic of the authorities. He either disregards them, or he proceeds as if the establishment had accepted passports to the grove. Hermes and Priapus, in *Idyll* 1, are both ignorant and ineffective, whatever else they may be. They are perplexed about Daphnis' stance and do not know how to help him. There is nothing to distinguish them from a Menalcas or a Lacon except their names. The tensions to which other poets respond, either by means of devotions or by means of persiflage, do not exist for Theocritus. He acts and his characters act as if gods and men fitted easily into one and the same society.

Theocritus' herdsmen, like Epicurus' disciples, refuse to acknowledge a control of their world outside themselves. Neither Fate, nor chance, nor gods, nor any external power exists to threaten the *otium* and the well-being that the bower makes possible. This, incidentally, is one of the reasons why unhappiness in love, where it occurs in the pastoral, is to be distinguished from amatory frustration in other genres, which permit the introduction of the motif of external compulsion. When Marvell, in "The Definition of Love,"[55] makes Fate responsible for the miscarriage of love, or when Euripides gropes for explanations in divine malice or ancestral conditioning, these alibis have the peculiar effect of putting the passion at issue into an even more desperate light. Theocritus' herdsmen have only themselves to blame, or the objects of their affections. As a result, the listener comes to accept the infatuation as both curable and excusable, the symptom of a healthy fallibility. The power-lessness of the gods in Theocritus is one of the important factors for the vitality of the pastoral scene. Whatever their temporary ailments may be, the author gives his herdsmen a clean bill of health, and they know this. They are not always sure of their own capacities and desires; but at every turn they are sustained by the assurance that they are free. Their actions and their songs document this conviction. Freedom, like simplicity and leisure, is an endowment that the pastoral surrenders at its peril.

6
The Animals

The wailings of a maiden I recite,
A maiden fair, that Sparabella hight.
Such strains ne'er warble in the linnet's throat,
Nor the gay goldfinch chaunts so sweet a note,
No mag-pye chatter'd, nor the painted jay
Nor ox was heard to low, nor ass to bray.[1]

Gay's famous lampoon stipulates a special kinship between animals and men. Under its aegis, men and women are given free passage into the animal kingdom and, conversely, animals are used primarily to create a distorted image of men. No doubt this burlesque has some justice on its side; it castigates the leveling tendencies that could be seen at work in Ambrose Philips and other "natural" pastoralists. But it would be wrong to go further and regard Gay's verses as a fair commentary on all pastoral. Theocritus, for one, does not advertise the sort of intimacy between herdsmen and beasts that provoked Gay's mirth. To be sure, we cannot, in Theocritus, look for a realistic appreciation of sheep and their needs. For that one has to go to Cato (*On Agriculture*) or Columella (*On Farming*, 7.2 ff., 7.6). Cartault's eminently useful lists of animals in Theocritus and Virgil are not meant to suggest that the pastoral permits itself to talk about animals as autonomous creatures, zoologically, or economically, or pictorially.[2]

"I think I could turn and live with the animals; they are so placid and self-contained." This saying of Walt Whitman's is used as a motto at the beginning of John Kipling's *Beast and Man in India*. In spite of the rather different sense which the pronouncement has for Whitman on the one hand, and Kipling on the other, the wording would commend itself to a pastoralist, with certain qualifications, which should emerge from what follows. Let us begin with the matter of the setting. The fact that animals are present on the scene stamps the scene as a pastoral one. The beasts capering about Adam and Eve in Eden (*Paradise Lost*, 4.340 ff.) have the function of decentralizing the composition, as it were, and reducing the human agents to a status that leaves them less exposed and less dominant. The ox and the ass attending Jesus at his birth bespeak an enlarged order of nature within which man is at every step conscious of his ties with the rest of creation. This, at least, is the feeling conveyed to the beholder or the listener, even if the herdsmen are sometimes shown to be curiously ignorant of the limitation. In Theocritus, as in most pastoral, man remains central; but the harshness of the centrality is softened by a sense of fullness. The spaces stretching out from the center are populated with other forms of life which, it is suggested, are potentially capable of filling the center position.

The animals are both tame and wild. Given the proposition that animals and men share common characteristics and that animals by their presence lend comfort and joy, the distinction between tame and wild is not so very crucial after all. It is less a question of behavior than a question of availability. The tame are always near at hand, they are companions, perhaps protégés, more rarely property; the wild need to be conjured up from the periphery when their cooperation becomes useful. By and large one may say that the domestic animals, and that includes insects, are prominent in conversation pieces and amoebean contests, while the wild beasts are held in reserve for lamentations and complaints. Bears, wolves, jackals, foxes, and other beasts that are usually hunted form choruses to express grief (less

commonly joy) at what befalls a Daphnis or a Comatas or a
Gallus, the heroized herdsman whose pride of freedom puts him
at odds with his native bower.

Mostly the animals are mammals. Other creatures referred
to, though more rarely in actual attendance, are birds, the cicada,
the frog, locusts, beetles, and the lizard. Some of them are partners
in the community because of their association with music.
The birds, particularly, are useful in proverbial priamels: "Jays
must not strive against nightingales; hoopoes must not strive
against swans" (5. 136–137; for priamels, see Chapter Twelve).
Even the frog may lend his voice to add to the chorus of musicians;
on another occasion, however, it is the simple needs of the frog
that count: "The frog is lucky, he has enough to drink" (10.52–53).
That is, the self-sufficiency of the frog, who is at the same time
not averse to sounding his basso profundo, makes him a suitable
paradigm for the personal qualities of the pastoral singer.[3]
The lizard is in a similar class. He is not only the main companion
and playmate of the lonely herdsman; he is also known for his
uncomplicated vitality. Cut a lizard in half, Aelian tells us in his
On the Nature of Animals (2.23), and each half will continue to
live and become a full lizard again. Sometimes the emphasis on
the life force of the animals is elaborated into an overt contrasting
of the cyclical eternity of the animal and vegetable kingdoms
with the mortality of men:

> As you, shrouded in silence, rest within the earth,
> The Nymphs decree that frogs should have eternal song.[4]

Theocritus avoids such general reflections.[5] He chooses to let
actions and desires speak for themselves. When the unhappy
Cyclops resolves to give up his fruitless courting and to look
after his sheep, the substitution of what is concrete and familiar
for what is evanescent and complicated is obvious. It is pro-
claimed also by the grossness of the proverbial formula that
follows (11.75): *tān pareoisan amelge*; "milk the one you have!"—

the vulgar equivalent of our "A bird in the hand. . . ." Sex takes the place of love, the physical relieves the spiritual, life conquers death, *kinēsis* swamps the precarious *stasis*, which needs to be refashioned again and again. The life swirl of sex is ever-present on the horizon, promising to spill over into the still heart of the setting. That is the meaning of the marginal references to lecherous bucks and skittish nannies, and equally excited men and women. Even the gentlest shepherds, we are given to understand, have the capacity for an honest day's work at sex, and they are prone to remind each other of past or future occasions when this would be true.[6] One recalls those inscriptions on the rocks and walls of the island Thera that record the names, with patronymics, of who fornicated with whom, as if the activity were a sacred game that won the agents favor in the eyes of the gods.[7] Epicurus, relying on the speculations of the Presocratics, implies that man developed from an animal state and has much of the nature of his ancestors within him.

As representatives of gross sexuality, animals are superior to men. But in another respect they stand a step below man; they do not think. Men supply the values and the perspectives.

> Know, man hath all which Nature hath, and more,
> And in that *more* lie all his hopes of good.[8]

Milton says in his "Epitaphium Damonis" (100 ff.) that when animals lose friends, they immediately find others.[9] Men are not so frivolous: *nos durum genus*. Animal simplicity, in other words, has its negative as well as its positive side. "The nightingale whose springtime song is so harmoniously charming has no knowledge of art. . . . Birds and animals act with numbers in making. Man is superior to them, not in acting with numbers but in knowing numbers."[10] Man has knowledge, animals do not; for in pastoral poetry, unlike the fable or the Gothic tale, animals are true animals. The herdsman is the composer, animals are the performers.[11] It is true that in many pastoral poems (here again

Theocritus set the fashion) the knowledge that herdsmen have is severely limited, as if the company of the animals were effective in reducing the distance between them and men. But the tension is always there, the tension which has each herdsman behave in his dual capacity as a friend and as a guide to his animal companions. The animals are not his equals; a contest between a herdsman and an animal is out of the question. Ambrose Philips' frantic enactment of a contest with a nightingale (*Eclogue* 5) is merely bizarre.

The animals are the instrumentalists; without their voices the *locus amoenus* might easily become still and barren.[12] Especially at moments of grief, the animal chorus furnishes both the corroboration and the consolation.[13] Even in situations where their active response is not required, as when two herdsmen engage in a singing match, they are welcome as listeners (Virgil, *Eclogue* 8.2–3), though Theocritus uses this element less than those after him. Sometimes the rudeness of the animals clashes with the refinement of the musician. In the third *Elegy* of Tibullus' second book (lines 19–20), the cattle interrupt the skilled song of Apollo, Admetus' herdsman, with their lowing; the ill-breeding of the countryside jars with the refinement of the artist. There are similar things in Calpurnius. Some animals, however, are more sympathetic with the singer's aspirations than others. The most musical animal, because it is pure music and little else, and has none of the qualities associated with sex and strength, is the cicada.[14] The literary tradition, from Homer to the *Anacreontea*, concerning cicadas and grasshoppers (they are not clearly distinguished) is full and virtually unanimous. They live on dew, or on nothing at all; their bodies are mere shells, but they have no wants. By way of compensation, they are marvellously gifted with speech[15] or song. Virgil's handling of the cicada motif is indebted to that of Meleager (*Anthol. Pal.* 7.195, 196), who is himself in the debt of Plato's *Phaedrus*.[16] In this branch of the tradition the cicada is above all an emblem of nature at her muscial best, a pinpointing of the quiet harmony into which man must allow himself to lapse. In Theocritus, I feel, though it is difficult to prove this, the cicada is unemblematic, concretely there; as in Hesiod and Aristophanes, the Theocritean cicada is a part of nature, enjoyable, but in the background, a member of the orchestra, not a heraldic sign.[17]

The green cabinet does not harbor hostile animals; when Calidore, chasing the blatant beast (*Fairie Queene*, 6.9.6) asks the shepherds whether they have seen it,

> They answer'd him, that no such beast they saw
> Nor any wicked feend, that mote offend
> Their happy flockes, no daunger to them draw:
> But if that such there were (as none they kend)
> They prayd high God him farre from them to send.

The naiveté is important; the herdsmen had, till then, not conceived of the possibility of the beast's presence. The boar of Adonis is an intrusion, just as much as the invaders in *Daphnis and Chloe*, and similar marauders later. The romance requires intrusions of violence because of its length; the pastoral lyric cannot withstand the shock of such an irruption of ferocity. It is true that the Theocritean herdsman sometimes thinks of himself in the role of hunting small animals, particularly rabbits (rabbits are never featured among the animal companions); and in pastoral epigrams Daphnis often appears as a hunter.[18] In Theocritus' *Epigram* 3, Daphnis the huntsman is hunted by Pan and Priapus, as if to make clear the contradiction that exists between Daphnis as herdsman and Daphnis as imitator of the huntsman Adonis. The same contradiction is at work also in the implied rebuke of *Idyll* 1, line 109, where Daphnis reminds Aphrodite of her association with the doomed Adonis.

Regardless of the realities in the life of a Greek shepherd, in literature hunting and herding were, to begin with, contrasted. Zethus comes in to go hunting, and upbraids the herdsman

Amphion for his lack of interest in the sport.[19] The reasons for
this disjunction are not far to seek. One need only glance at,
for instance, Nemesianus' *Cynegetica*, especially lines 10 ff. and
48 ff.; they exhibit a fine feeling for nature, but under the aegis
of *negotium* rather than *otium*. Nature is vividly experienced
precisely because the perception is enlivened by motion, attack,
purpose, action. Propertius' *Elegy* 19 of the second book illustrates
the point. The speaker addresses his love: "You are in the country, protected from the vices of the city, in a quiet environment
conducive to reflection and moral good. I shall come and hunt,
not fierce animals, but rabbits and such, with a ready eye for the
beauties of the country." It is *because* he hunts that the attractions
of the landscape, including the snow-white oxen taking a bath
in the Clitumnus, open up for the man, while his girl, in her
sedentary pose, has no eye for any of this. Ironically, then, the
torment of the lover, translated into the *ponos* of the huntsman,
readies him for a finer appreciation of what nature has to offer.
Somewhat like Marvell's Mower, the hunter promotes a more
complex relationship with nature. Pastorally, however, the increase in complexity is a loss.

There are intimations of this in Theocritus, but they are held
to a minimum in order to retain the mood that stamps animals
as companions and even friends of the herdsman rather than his
victims. A straw in the wind: Theocritus' herdsman does not, as
a rule, carry the stick or club which in Greek is called a "rabbit-
killer," *lagōbolon*. It is mentioned in *Idyll* 7 (128; see also lines
18 and 43); but its sole function there is to serve as the rustic
equivalent of the poet's laurel branch, the badge of office that the
older poet hands to the younger on the occasion of his investiture.
The herdsman's club is mentioned on two other occasions;
once it is a prize given for a song (9.23), in an *Idyll* generally
regarded as spurious; and the only other occurrence is in *Idyll*
4 (49) where the herdsman says he wishes he had a club to pummel
his cow with. By comparison with the later uses of the shepherd's

crook, then, Theocritus is found to practise a radical economy. In fact Reitzenstein, whose theory we have had occasion to mention more than once, was so impressed with the negligible role of the hunting motif in Theocritus, that he felt the bow and arrow in the hands of the herdsman could be explained only in terms of ritual necessity. He concluded that the *boukolos*, the servant of the god who looms so large in his speculations (see above, Chapter Two), was an armed hunter before he became a herder of cattle. This is a counsel of desperation, but excusable in the light of the very real paradox that is involved. Of the Renaissance critics, Scaliger and Colletet decried the use of hunters (along with fishermen and working men) in pastoral poetry.[20] In the romance pastorals of the fifteenth to the seventeenth centuries, it is worth noting, hunting is carried on chiefly by nymphs; as creatures of another order they are not bound by the decorum of the herdsmen.[21]

There are occasions in Theocritus when the relation between men and animals is less than perfect. The occasion can be humorous; the buffoon of *Idyll* 3 fears that the wolves will eat him (53): a palpable exaggeration designed to make us laugh.[22] Or the occasion is furnished by the closer approximation to sordid reality which is found in one or two of Theocritus' more pugnacious poems. At *Idyll* 5, lines 106 and following, for instance, certain kinds of animal aggressiveness are drawn into the acrimony of the contest: dogs hunt wolves, locusts hurt vines, cicadas provoke harvesters, foxes plunder vineyards, beetles chew up the figs—the long list of aggressive acts is terminated with a reminder of how one herdsman abused another. *Idyll* 5 is the most intransigent demonstration of the possibility of *ponos* and violence entering into the heart of the poem and subverting the pastoral vision. It is significant that the contestants do not sing, but speak;[23] and that they do not perform in one and the same *locus amoenus*, but hurl their paltry contributions at each other from separate bases. The poem is unusual, an extreme realization of certain tendencies that elsewhere are largely sublimated or held at arm's length.

More typically, then, the animal, tame or wild, is a companion. Animals share in the freedom, in the absence of mastery and servitude, that characterizes the relations between men. Unlike the romantic poet who emphasizes the fierceness of the "wild and wanton pard," the pastoralist desegregates, and makes brothers out of men and animals.[24] In the end, the herdsman may appeal to his friends the animals to sympathize with him in his complaints about the cruelty of his girl; example: Drayton, *Idea*, *Eglog* 9. This explains why the traditionalists found the piscatories so unpalatable. How can a man be on terms of fellowship with a fish? Quite apart from the fact that fish were not, until recently, known for the expressiveness of their voices.

In *Idyll* 4, Theocritus combines two animal motifs. Early in the poem (12 ff.) we are told that the cattle will not eat and are losing weight because their master is no longer with them. That is to say, they mourn for an absent friend. But toward the end of the poem (44 ff.), the cattle take to nibbling olive shoots from the trees; here the hubris motif, brute energy winning out over gentler feelings, comes into its own. The two themes, loyalty and vitality, are placed almost cheek by jowl; that they do not neutralize one another is one of the achievements of the pastoral form, with its delight in discreteness and its stress on variety. Polyphemus' dog, in *Idyll* 6, belongs to the same range of associations; a charming detail of genre painting, the dog zigzagging along the shore embodies a convincing combination of good fellowship and zest.

In the examples we have discussed, animals and men are comrades. Another way of putting this is to say that animals are used as extensions of man. The motif of companionship blurs the outline of human nature sufficiently so as to undercut the isolation of man and to adjust him to a larger natural world. But there is another use, one that de-natures man. This is the relationship between a master and his pet, a bond that is ego-centric, contrived, precious. The owner of a pet is an owner in the full sense of the word. The myriad tears wept by Lesbia over the grave of her sparrow do not blind us to the fact that she regards the animal as disposable, as a piece of property that belongs to her only, and to no one else. Ovid's "On the Death of Corinna's Parrot" (*Amores* 2.6) and countless Hellenistic specimens of the same genre, including the epitaphs for animals, testify to the popularity of this poetic rendering of the man-animal relationship. In Theocritus, pets are introduced only when the herdsman is made fun of as particularly short-sighted and not quite at home in the pastoral bower, as in *Idyll* 11 where the Cyclops boasts of the eleven fawns and the four bear cubs that he wants to bestow as gifts upon his Galatea. The over-breeding and the rarity of the creatures disqualifies them as inhabitants of the pleasance.

The giving or offering of animals that comes to be routine later is very rare in Theocritus.[25] In the Renaissance, built on centuries of Christian insensitivity to the charms and rights of animals, they are thought of as toys, instruments of pleasure to be handled at will. Their qualities are often described in detail to show off their prettiness, as one would praise a piece of mer-chandise. This treatment is in force even in so profoundly melan-choly a poem as Marvell's "Nymph Complaining," in spite of the fact that the fawn's poetic status is dignified by the many layers of symbolism invested in it.[26] In Theocritus, the disposa-bility of animals is handled with an extraordinary talent for promise and retraction. As a general rule we may say that the more contentious and abusive a poem is, the more straightforward is the acceptance of the principle of disposability. As we have seen before, the one pastoral idyll in which Theocritus talks about animal sacrifice is *Idyll* 5. Comatas brags that he has sacrificed two goats to the Muses (81); Lacon answers that he is fattening a ram for Apollo (82–83); Crocylus has slaughtered

a goat for the Nymphs (11–12); a lamb is to be sacrificed to the
Nymphs (139–140; 148–149). So much emphasis on sacrificial
killing is of a pattern with the threat Comatas addresses to the
buck at the very end of the poem:

> I'll be Melanthius if I don't castrate you!

Other references to sacrifice occur only in the epigrams and the
non-pastoral poems and in the post-Theocritean *pastourelle*.[27]
For the rest, the offering of animals as gifts and prizes in singing
contests is an abortive theme. In *Idyll* 1 (4–6, 9–11, 25, 143, 151)
the shepherd initially offers a goat, and the goatherd a sheep.
But these are only make-believe offerings, for eventually the
prizes are the cup, and a pipe, and the milk of a goat. Is the
chiastic arrangement of the promise—after all, one would
expect a shepherd to stake a sheep, and a goatherd a goat—designed to alert the listener to the implausibility of the offer? We
cannot be sure: in *Idyll* 5 (23 ff.) the competences of goatherd
and shepherd are kept distinct, but in *Idyll* 8 (49) Menalcas
addresses a goat, and it is true even today that a herd of sheep
is likely to contain a few goats also. Still, I am inclined to believe
that the neatness of the disposition in *Idyll* 1 is meant to draw
attention to the unreality of the scheme. Elsewhere, in *Idylls*
3 (34–36) and 8 (14–16), animal offerings are either not carried
out or immediately rejected. *Idyll* 5 (96, 132; 106) includes projected love offerings of a pigeon and a dog; but as we have
seen, this poem is unusual and the two herdsmen are improbable
lovers.[28]

It should be remarked in passing, though this comes under the
heading of economy rather than the use of animals, that the food
eaten in the pleasance does not, typically, include meat or fish;
milk, cheese, nuts, and fruits, the non-violent products of a
bountiful nature, are preferred. There is a cursory reference to the
eating of the flesh of the goat (1.5), but this is meant to mislead,
for the goat is *not* offered. More correctly, perhaps, the herdsmen

of the pastoral do not eat at all. They are shown living a life from which the grosser occupations—eating is, apparently, one of them —are excluded. This is one of the elements that distinguish the pastoral from the mime, which is often, unjustly, compared with it; contrast, for example, the meal detailed in *Idyll* 14 (14–17), which *is* a mime. Altogether then, there appears to be a clear understanding that the basic feeling of the pastoral, which brings men and animals together in a close nexus, does not permit an arrangement whereby the herd animals are treated as disposable, as chattel, or as canned goods.[29] The tendency is toward equal status; on the other hand one may doubt that Theocritus would go so far as to make a goat a go-between for lover and beloved, as the author of *Idyll* 8 (49–52) does.

The pastoral function of animals works by degrees; it may be thought of as fitting into a system of concentric rings. At the center, men and animals are completely equal and firmly united in an orchestra of congenial voices. At the periphery, the animals are endowed with objective features that set them aside from men: as mere embodiments of the sex instinct, or as the possessions of herd-owners. I would claim that in Theocritus and in the early pastoral lyric, the treatment is generally that of the central ring; the themes that derive from the outer circle are brought in only for momentary relief, or for strong conclusions.[30] This suggestion is confirmed by the striking scarcity of animal comparisons in Theocritus' *Idylls* and Virgil's *Eclogues*. There are a number of catalogues that list the characteristics or activities of animals side by side with those of men.[31] Though the terminal statement in each case makes certain that it is the man or woman whose qualities or needs provoke the comparison, the parallelism of the catalogue structure guarantees the animals a virtual independence. They do not have their rights subsumed under those of men. One of the fringe benefits of the catalogue is to stress the variety of natural life as much as its harmony. The egalitarian texture of the pastoral symphony, in which everybody is a soloist, is reflected in the patterning of priamel and catalogue and *praeteritio*. What is more, the pastoral catalogues often bear down on the senses; the tastes and looks and sounds that afford joy to the Epicurean herdsmen are listed side by side with impartial delight.

Other ways of comparing beasts and men are few, and, in the case of Theocritus, usually found in the non-pastoral poems. In the epyllia, animal similes are used in the traditional epic manner; men are like beasts that fight (22.72–74); Agave roars like a lioness (26.20–21). The mimes employ both straight comparisons and animal proverbs, often for the purpose of abuse.[32] All this is negative confirmation of what I am trying to say about the pastoral *Idylls*. The few comparisons and similes in the pastorals usually turn on the magnitude of a feeling;[33] or they mark the similarity of patterns of conduct that are linked to a feeling.[34] Once in the pastorals the special standing of a person vis-à-vis the animals is formulated by way of comparatives; the Cyclops calls Galatea

> Whiter than yogurt, softer than a lamb,
> Friskier than a heifer, glossier than a grape.[35]

The exaggeration is what we would expect of the Cyclops, whose pastoral credentials are adequate but not impressive. Compare also the comic treatment of *Idyll* 3, line 13: I wish I could become a bee and buzz around the entrance to your cave. That is to say, the animal comparison is used for a special effect, to pillory the adolescent with his boasts and his hyperboles. The exception proves the rule. In the same vein, the animal proverbs of *Idyll* 10 (11, 18, 52) are found only in the mouth of Milon, the Hesiodic partner in the exchange. The Hesiodic tradition deals with animals in terms of their practical uses and their zoological oddities. It also reflects the peasant's attitude toward the dumb beasts, which is usually less than gentle or humanitarian. Take, for an extreme example, what Aratus, a contemporary and perhaps a friend of Theocritus, says about sheep and cattle (*Phaenomena* 1104 ff.); they become interesting to him only when the imminence of rain affects their behavior. Thus animals become mere instruments in the life of the farmer, serving as warning signals so he may arrange his schedule properly. No thought is given to animals as living creatures with their own claims to dignity and grace.

We conclude, then, that the bucolic style on the whole frowns on animal comparisons. Neither in Theocritus nor in Virgil is there a single example of the type, lampooned by John Gay, "your . . . is like a sheep's" (or goat's, or pig's). Animals are not "used" to provide the raw material for similes that would redound to the greater glory, or at least to the greater illumination, of man. A comparison is felt to have the same effect as the making of animals into pets. The same danger may be observed when the animal is demoted to serve as a symbol; when, as in Calpurnius' *Eclogue* 3, the finding of the heifer turns into an omen for the recovery of the girl; or as in Drayton's ninth *Eglog* (185 ff.), where the animal symbolism makes for a playfulness that is pointed up with puns:

> A Milke-white Dove upon her hand shee brought,
> So tame, 'twould goe, returning at her call,
> About whose necke was in a Choller wrought,
> Only like Me, my Mistris hath no Gall.

It is interesting that Theocritus has comparatively little on birds, in spite of an acute awareness of the beauty of their song.[36] Where they occur, they are built into the scenery, rather than playing a part as other animals do. It is as if the poet wanted to avoid too close a proximity of men and birds in order to escape the symbolisms prefigured by the many myths that expose the cruelties that birds and men share in common. Marvell's soul that turns into a bird and sings in the boughs ("The Garden," stanza 7) draws on an ancient conceit, the *Seelenvogel* that is pictured in many paintings; but for all its mythic and pictorial respectability, the notion is unthinkable in the ancient pastoral.

Nor, for similarly obvious reasons, is the animal fable welcome. Like the animal comparison, it has its uses in a literary work that emphasizes the centrality and the uniqueness of man and proceeds to say something meaningful about him via non-human imagery. The pastoral, also, sets man aside from the rest of creation. But it eschews doing so by denying substance or autonomy to the rest of the community. The story of the fox and the kid told in the fifth eclogue of the *Shepherds Calender* deprives the animals of their franchise. They are hollow shells, thinly constructed markers for the dramatization of human ambitions and human failures. The type derives from another branch of Hellenistic letters, the Cynic diatribe with its simplified account of moral causes and its appeal to men to emulate the skills of animals. Both the moralizing and the exploitation of animal archetypes go against the grain of the pastoral idea Their presence in a pastoral poem is bound to generate an ethical density, an abrupt bulging of hortative muscle, that warps the delicate structure, the fragile parataxes of the old pastoral mode. In the pastoral pleasance, the animals are free; their vitality is such that it brooks no subjection to ulterior ends. Theocritus and Virgil knew this, and proceeded accordingly.

7
The Music

Fountains and yee, that warble, as ye flow,
Melodious murmurs, warbling tune his praise.
Joyn voices all, ye living Souls, ye Birds. . . .
Yee that in Waters glide, and yee that walk
The Earth, and stately tread, or lowly creep;
Witness if I be silent, Morn or Even,
To Hill, or Valley, Fountain, or fresh shade
Made vocal by my Song, and taught his praise.[1]

Thus Adam and Eve call upon all nature, including
plants and birds, to praise the Lord and witness the harmony of
his creation. Milton's conception of nature as a system of harmonies, and this summons to the world to let its harmonies
ring out, are too philosophical to fit easily into the pastoral scheme.
As we noted earlier, the world of the pastoral is very much
more restricted than the vast cosmos intuited by the ancestral
couple. The genius of the wood in *Arcades*, who raises his eyes
from the forest to the "nine enfolded spheres," bids us listen
to a music that can be produced only in cosmic concert and that
would puzzle a herdsman, if it did not shatter his ears. His
music is that produced by a small chamber orchestra, of which
the herdsman singer is the guiding spirit. It is modelled on the
conversation of cicadas at the dead of noon; "singing and con-
versing with one another," as Plato puts it in the *Phaedrus* (258E6

ff.), the cicadas invite us to converse also, without guile and without pretense, spontaneously and genuinely, and that means—musically.

Plato's rather jaundiced view of the music practiced in his own day is well-known. As is equally well-known, Plato's scorn was his response to the traditional assumption, to which he subscribed, that music has an ethical component and that it may be expected to exert a powerful influence on the listener's (and the singer's) soul. This assumption, which dominates the educational and social thought of classical Greece, was first challenged at the beginning of the Hellenistic age. The thinker with whom this challenge is most prominently associated is, not surprisingly, Epicurus. Though we do not know the precise details of his work *On Music* (Diogenes Laertius 10.28), we can tell something of its general import from the discussion it triggered among his successors, and especially from the polemics of Philodemus.[2] Epicurus appears to have held that music may serve as entertainment, but that, considered separately from the words to which it is set (this separation of words and music is itself an Epicurean innovation of sorts), it has no power to influence the soul for better or worse. Love songs, for instance, cannot be used to fire the object of one's love; nor, conversely, can they purge a person of the love he feels.[3] Music is pure sound; it appeals to the sensation, which has no power of understanding. In this way, completing the work of the Sophists and the Isocrateans, Epicurus demolishes the traditional status of music as an educator and shaper of character.

The Stoics were less radical and continued to teach that music works on the ethos of a man, and that it can reshape him, or purge him. In this disagreement between Stoics and Epicureans, the writers of poetry by and large chose to go along with Epicurus. Musical verse was spurned by the great authors of the third century; they relegated it to the realm of entertainment for the masses. High, serious literature came to be spoken literature exclusively. Only the unaccompanied and unsung word, it was felt, could register its full effect upon the soul of the listener. Music would only distract. Callimachus, Apollonius, and the epigrammatists score their poems for *Sprechstimme*, refined, cunningly modulated, but spoken nonetheless. Music and song was left to those who wrote for the stage and the music hall.

Now in this controversy Theocritus occupies a very special position. It is true that his *Idylls*, in conformity with the new Hellenistic practice, are written to be recited rather than sung; the dactylic hexameter guarantees this mode of performance. And yet, the music is there. Though the verse is spoken verse, Theocritus asks us to imagine that much of it is not really spoken at all, but sung. On one occasion, in the least musical of the pastorals (5.78), he refers to the activity of the contestants as "speaking." Ordinarily, however, we are given to understand that the passages uttered by the herdsmen in their contests and challenges and complaints are sung, and musical instruments are mentioned throughout as providing a simple musical background. Without this imagined, internalized music, the pastoral landscape would be poor and indeed meaningless. For in Theocritus song is nothing less than the documentation of the native nobility of man. Outwardly, then, Theocritus adopted the Epicurean line and stilled his lyre. But the reason for the lack of music is surely that Theocritus does not want to avail himself of the music of the *Odeum* or of the folk song for fear of burying under it a music more delicate and civilized. Theocritus suggests the music instead of putting it on the boards. He is thus in a position to turn tables on Epicurus and to revalidate a power which Epicurus, Socratic rather than Platonic, failed to give its due.

Music as an affective bond between man and man and between man and nature need not be thunderous. In the pastoral, it is the small and brittle sound that Theocritus characterizes as "dry," *kapyros*, and which is best produced on the reed pipe, Virgil's *fistula*.[4] One singer or piper is sufficient; two are better; a small band is, under certain circumstances, best. In Virgil, the music is echoed by a sympathetic nature; mount Maenalus becomes a sounding board for the song (8.22 ff.); animals, trees, and rocks are caught up in the rhythms of Silenus' performance (6.27).

> Nor to the deaf our mournful notes we sing,
> Each wood shall with responsive echoes ring.[5]

The prominence of responses from nature has prompted Marie Desport, in a perceptive book, to consider bucolic poetry, especially Virgil's, an art of incantation.[6] The poet-herdsman sings, and with his song he quickens the latent energies of nature. She agrees that there is little of this in Theocritus. I am inclined to think, however, that even in Virgil, "incantation" is too strong a word for what happens. It might easily suggest that the pastoral singer is invested with a sacred office, a *vates* in the succession of Orpheus, performing a ritual act upon a ceremonial stage. Pastoral, even in Virgil, is essentially a secular art; it is closer to the *psilos logos*, the sober speech, of Socrates than to the Hymns to Nature that we find in drama and in choral lyric. Echoing nature is not unknown in the epic; Apollonius, developing Homeric suggestions, shows us a nature reacting to tuneful impulses from abroad.[7] Perhaps "incantation" would be an appropriate term there. But pastoral does not favor the automatism of a conditioned reflex, nor the sacred mystery of a cosmic response. The sounds produced by sheep and bears, brooks and rocks in the Greek pastoral carry a stamp of spontaneity that distinguishes them from the field of ritual energy. Even the echoes that play so large a part in Virgil have an air of freedom about them, as if they were at once the reverberations of a human sound and the original utterance of a ubiquitous errant nymph, Echo writ large, as she appears in Lucretius' account of the way Pan first came to be imagined (see below, Chapter Eleven).

Horace has his own idea of the validity of echo, at least in a particular situation (*Satires* 1.4.76):

> suave locus voci resonat conclusus.

The vaulted chamber amplifies the voice; reading poetry in a sound chamber, like the baths, or the forum, pleases some but not me. Here resonance is literal and invidious; the public reciters get assistance from a law of physics. Is Horace making fun of a pastoral commonplace? Perhaps not; but it may be significant that the later pastoralists, apparently in a mood of dissatisfaction with the Virgilian motif, decided to silence nature and have the herdsman sing to a hushed audience. Astylus, in Calpurnius' *Eclogue* 6, refuses to sing near a brook whose babbling he considers inimical to music-making, and wanders off to a silent cave. In Nemesianus, likewise, music is strictly human; it may be interfered with, but is not supported by sounds elsewhere in the bower. Nature supplies an open stage, not a chorus. Even the cicada's song is felt to be obstreperous.[8] Virgil's resonant nature is gone, and the poets revert to an essentially theocentric conception. The motif of nature falling silent at the epiphany of a god is more at home in hymns to the gods and in religious drama.[9] Very much later Petrarch reintroduced the secular theme of nature musically responding; and in Sannazaro's Arcadia, the poet-singer is anything but alone. His songs are echoed and counterbalanced by the songs and *sampogne* of the shepherds, and by the trees and rocks that form the pleasance.

The musical relation between singer and companions can take the form instanced in Pope ("Autumn"):

> When tuneful Hylas, with melodious moan,
> Taught rocks to weep, and made the mountains groan.

The little word "taught" is crucial. According to this perception, which is also approximately that of Virgil, the singer is the teacher, and nature can do little more than take its cues from him. Now it is true that even in Theocritus the herdsman-musician is the exemplary producer of beautiful sounds. At bottom, music is the expression of feelings centered in a human soul; rocks and trees can utter their own music only to the extent that they are, however covertly, conceived on the human model. Be that as it may, what matters is that Theocritus does not work with echoes. The sounds he ascribes to the animate and inanimate comrades of the singer are usually the natural utterances that we would expect from them. A comparison of Theocritus with Virgil would suggest that in Theocritus the singer is the prompter rather than the teacher. Each member of the pastoral community has his own voice, and his own desire to sing. In Theocritus, music is a native ability accessible to all;[10] in Virgil it tends to be a special gift, drawn forth by exceptional circumstances and usually under duress (*Eclogue* 9). On this score, I would suggest, the European pastoral tradition conforms more closely to the Theocritean than to the Virgilian type.[11] In Castiglione's "Alcon," the loss of Alcon is felt by Iolas as a loss in musical energy. In Milton's "Lycidas," the Pilot of the Galilean Lake climaxes his castigation of the men whom he would gladly have sacrificed in the place of Lycidas by condemning their musicianship:

> And when they list, their lean and flashy songs
> Grate on their scrannel Pipes of wretched straw.

Lycidas' death, like Alcon's, is above all a "loss to Shepherds ear." This caps a priamel which audaciously hammers away at the theme of loss and pain. And when Arnold's Thyrsis ("Thyrsis," 41 ff.) is ill at ease in his landscape, the poet assigns to

> his piping too a troubled sound. . . .

Music is the natural language spoken, with varying skill, by all the inhabitants of the bower, depending on the degree of their attunement to the manners of pastoral society. One might argue that in Milton and Arnold the attunement is geared to poetic and religious reflections that subject it to certain limitations. In Theocritus music is less fleeting, less critical; it is a democratic dispensation confirming the goodness and the beauty of the natural order.

One experience that, even in Theocritus, is likely to stimulate the language of music is love. Bion formulates the connection in an argument, that is to say, in a non-Theocritean way: the Muses shun the non-lover and attend the lover; proof: only when I sing about love and my darling, does my music turn out perfectly.[12] When the occasion is love, music may play the ancillary role of a healing drug. *Idyll* 9 is our finest example of the combination of two motifs; the Cyclops sings because he is in love, and he sings to overcome his love. The latter purpose, however, is secondary; it is the superimposition of an ulterior motive upon what in origin is a natural act. Unhappy, unrequited love in particular is likely to express itself in music. It stands to reason that happy love (which in the grove and particularly on its borders is tantamount to successful love) has less cause to produce words or song. But all sorts of other feelings beside love, including the delight in beautiful things, press for music.

When all is said and done, the proposition that pastoral music in Theocritus is natural must be qualified in an important way. Drayton's *Muses Elizium* 1, "The Description of Elizium," concludes with the lines:

> Then on to the *Elizian* plaines
> *Apollo* doth invite you
> Where he provides with pastorall straines
> In *Nimphals* to delight you.

Here pastoral music is looked upon as entertainment, as a performance, whereby the musician hopes to delight others as well as please himself. Other kinds of poetry are addressed directly by the poet to the listener (epic), or by the singer to himself

(lyric). Pastoral has the extroverted dimension, the public character, that we associate with a staged performance. Earlier we
spoke of the peculiar detachment, the anonymity of the pastoral;
music is a guarantee of the disengagement. Even with the songs of
frustrated love, ostensibly addressed to the cruel beloved or
chanted to the suffering heart, the pretended musicality makes the
song take on the aspect of an aria. The element of play-acting
suggested by the singing breaks the spell of empathy and helps
us to disregard the suffering so as to enjoy the beauty more. The
lyrics of Sappho and Anacreon were sung, but their poetic
substance did not usually feed on the fuel of musical performance.
Hence it is possible to read a poem by Sappho and identify
oneself with the speaker's private despairs and hopes. In spite
of the original mode of delivery, the appeal of the poem is
direct; we are asked to look into the heart of one and only one
person; there is no obstacle to block the desired end of lyric
compassion. In the case of the pastoral, which is recited rather
than sung, the internal fiction of musical delivery makes the
music a part of the lyric substance. It sets up a buffer that makes a
direct identification much more difficult. Thus music in the
pastoral is not only designed to tell us something about the
characters and their standing in the pleasance; it also characterizes
the poetry as a non-private communication. Because we are all
musicians, we can appreciate the language spoken in the pastoral;
but because a musical offering is, after all, a performance, we can
keep our distance, much as the performing herdsmen keep their
distance. This saves us from losing ourselves and overindulging in
private wrongs. Pastoral suffering, like pastoral joy, calls for
applause rather than pity or fear. The appreciation is that of the
connoisseur, not of the bewitched sympathizer.

Because the music is not a mode of delivery, but an element of
the poetic substance, Theocritus and Virgil, and their successors,
are under an obligation to shape their verse so as to suggest the
sound of music. It has often been observed that the very first

line of the Theocritean corpus in its sounds imitates the dry rasp of a reed pipe. Sound painting, *poésie verbale*, was by no means the rule in Greek poetry prior to Theocritus. The few instances of it that we appear to have may be due to accident as much as to plan.[13] Theocritus is our first poet of whom it may be said with some assurance that he varies his verse and his speech patterns in accord with the poetic intentions. The parts that are supposed to be song have a greater sonority; their versification is slower,[14] they show deeper vowels and fewer fricatives than the lines representing conversation. Virgil goes even further; there is a softness to his pastoral speech that set the standard for the later pastoral tradition, "liquifying the line."[15] But Virgil's speech does not show the variety, the differentiation between talk and piping and song, between grave lamenting and zestful serenade, that is the norm in Theocritus.[16]

❧ ❧ ❧ ❧

Near the end of Book 18 of the *Odyssey* (365 ff.), Odysseus and Eurymachus have a conversation in which the latter proposes a rustic contest of scything and ploughing. In the place of the martial duels of the *Iliad*, the *Odyssey* suggests a sportive—though, in this case, by no means genial—substitute. The *Iliad* too makes some room for contests, on the occasion of the funeral games for Patroclus in Book 23. It has always been recognized that the love of formal competitions, with rules, umpires, and prizes, is one of the most enduring features of Greek communal life. Within this tradition of *agōnes*, the singing match occupies a very special place. The Great Panathenaic Games and their counterparts elsewhere, such as the Pythian Games, included both athletic and musical contests. The dramatic competitions in the theaters of Athens belong to the same vogue of communal entertainment organised along competitive lines.[17] These great occasions for the sublimation of communal rivalry must, I think, be distinguished from another, purely literary tradition of contests between great singers and musicians. The myth of Thamyris competing with the Muses, and other similar legends of gods vying with gods or gods with mortals, are not so much projections of the great musical *agōnes*, but more direct expressions of delight in the esthetically satisfying formulation of human combativeness. The contest between Daphnis and Menalcas, judged by Pan, which Sositheus put on the stage is a musical pendant to the reaping contest that the legendary ogre Lityerses demanded of his guests.[18]

Reitzenstein, as we have seen, was of the opinion that pastoral contests were the literary recreation of ritual contests. For example, he points to a Cnidian epigram in which a singer is invited to share in the worship of the divinities Antigonus and Phila by competing with a song, not improvised, but prepared ahead of time.[19] The glen contains an altar, and an image of Pan. Unfortunately there is nothing in the Cnidian epigram to suggest that the competition is amoebean. In point of fact all the ritual contests and communal competitions of which we have knowledge are arranged in such a way that each contestant presents the whole of his contribution before the next contestant or contestants enter into the fray.[20]

Rather than looking for the origins of literary contests in ritual practice, or in some eastern influence,[21] we ought to be able to appreciate pastoral confrontations in terms of the poem and its needs. It is useful, to begin with, to observe that pastorals staffed with only one character are in the minority. Although in real life, herdsmen tend to be alone with their animals and their chores, in the pastoral it is the norm to have a meeting of two. Of the twelve pastorals in the Theocritean corpus, only three are complaints uttered by solitary singers; the other nine present conversations and contests. Six of Virgil's *Eclogues*, and all but one of Calpurnius', are dialogues; and the Renaissance virtually abandons the solo complaint. Pastoral, it appears, relies on a modicum of dramatic conflict to work its charm. It has been suggested that without this grain of dramatic tension, pastoral drama would not have developed out of the eclogues of the cinquecento.[22] Pastoral herdsmen need to talk with friends; *negotium in otio* invites the pastoral play of bargaining and jockeying for position. Perhaps drama is too big a word for the minor collisions and gentle frictions that develop between the inhabitants of the bower. It is a drama of moods and of temperaments, not of issues and purposes. This is what distinguishes the dramatic scenes in Theocritus from seemingly similar situations in contemporary drama.[23] Pastoral dialogue shows two friends in the process of enjoying each other's company, and little more than that. This is true even in the slugging matches, where the friends appear to go at each other hammer and tongs. Though the degree of hubris and friction is greater, the self-sufficiency is the same; there are no plots, no plans, no intrigues, no objectives, beyond the expression of immediate wishes and perceptions.

The herdsman, in his role as lover, friend, and singer, must employ dialogue. Dialogue, as Socrates wished it to be, is the joint enterprise of like-minded men to find order and beauty in the world in which they live. Roughly the same is true of the *hetairoi* of the green cabinet. In the Socratic dialogue, the exchange may be heated and even insulting; so the pastoral conversation often permits a considerable latitude for aggressiveness. Theocritus wants his characters to show themselves as they are, without subterfuge, without the restrictions of a feigned politeness. They can indeed be courteous and gentle with each other; pastoral *otium* and the ease that comes with an inner freedom open the door to many delicate touches of conduct. Where the contestants do engage in scurrilous chaffing, the infighting is free of that special air of intrigue that is associated with the city or the court, where people are likely to say less than they mean, but hurt each other more severely.

The pastoral verse sees to it that the confrontations are developed with an eye to stylization and symmetry. As in the stichomythies of classical tragedy, the exchanges of the herdsmen tend to reduce themselves to equivalent patterns of weight and thrust. There is ample precedent for the regularity of the alternation; we have already mentioned the archaic *skolia* and their splendidly formalized art of repartee and vocal equilibrium (above, Chapter Two). The pastorals contain much that puts one in mind of the *skolia*, especially the amoebean contests, with their fireworks of improvisation, musical elaboration, and competitive zeal. The fiction within the poem distinguishes between speaking and singing. But in a sense pastoral singing contests are merely extensions of the potential that resides in the pastoral conversations. In fact it is occasionally difficult to decide whether a verse is conceived as a musical offering or not. Does the serenade of *Idyll* 3 start at line 40 or earlier? But usually there is a difference in the quality of the encounter, if not in that of the verse patterns. Conversation ranges all the way from courteous greetings and amiable acknowledgments to the contentiousness of *Idyll* 5. But in spite of this range, all conversations share in the quality of being personal. That is, conversation is the instrument whereby the impulses of the characters are given free rein to mesh or clash, with little attention being paid to the objective claims of the pleasance. In the songs and sung exchanges, on the other hand, the herdsmen prefer to rest their minds in the beauties and comforts of the world around them. The musical dialectic, therefore, is conditioned by the larger interactions and the broader issues as much as by the temperaments of the singers. It is, I think, fair to say that the truer pastoral colors are found in the singing contests, rather than in the introductory sections and the sparring that frame the singing. It is instructive to note that the conversations which feature the greatest amount of aggressiveness are also those in which the scheduled singing fails to come off: Theocritus' *Idyll* 5 and Calpurnius' *Eclogue* 6. The singing contest, it seems, can become operative only if the natural pugnaciousness of the two herdsmen is tempered by the demands of a gentler code. The singing match sublimates aggressive instincts under the aegis of the rules of music and refashions the spontaneous in the image of art. It cannot be undertaken, however, unless there is already an understanding on the part of the contestants that a form of contractual restraints is in order. The music, therefore, whether amoebean or in the form of successive arias, endorses the inherent Epicureanism of the genre. The pastoral singing contest, then, is not the literary imitation of a ritual datum, but the logical conclusion to the tendency at work throughout the genre: the matching of perceptive beings in a nexus of friendship and equality.

One further distinction is in order; it is between those contests that are conducted without the help of an umpire, and those more formal matches held in the presence of a referee who has the final decision. The former may be said to stand halfway between unstructured conversation and controlled debate. Where no umpire is present, the contestants face each other, as friends or quasi-foes; their lines are not entirely devoid of the element of personal reference that defines most of the conversations. Where an umpire *is* available, the contestants face away from each other, and the umpire forms an audience. In such a situation, the songs come closest to being performances;[24] the circle of friendship extends beyond the chance meeting of two men and involves a minimum of three, of whom one is a comparative outsider. Or, in other words, the pastoral group is less homogeneous; but its greater scope for differences helps, in turn, to temper the latent spirit of aggression even further.

Is it possible to distinguish a procedure for what the contestants are likely to take up in the course of their more or less discursive performances? The chances are that it is not; it may be easier in the case of Virgil than in the case of Theocritus. A comparison of *Eclogue* 3, lines 60 and following, with *Eclogue* 7, lines 29 and following, shows surprising similarities, which it is convenient to list in tabular form:

Eclogue	3.60	gods	*Eclogue*	7.29	gods
	64	beloved (Galatea +)		37	beloved (Galatea +) as frame
	92	*locus amoenus* endangered		45	*locus amoenus*
	104	gods and beloveds juxtaposed		57	gods and beloveds juxtaposed.

This shows, incidentally, how much the gods (or divine mythology) are part of the texture of Virgilian amoebean pastoral, irrespective of whether the poet is communicating religious feeling or not. The structural parallels are, however, more relevant. The similarities are in part an outgrowth of the use of the Polyphemus motif. Elsewhere in Virgil, and especially in Theocritus, it would be harder to pin down procedural paradigms of this type.

Virgil's *Eclogue* 7 gives a fine picture of a match, with its regular, symmetrically arranged quatrains. Typically, the singer who sings the first quatrain determines the shape and the ring of the quatrain that follows. The second singer, in each case, tries to do better than his opponent by deviating slightly, but only slightly, from the pattern set by his predecessor. Such symmetries with minor divergences are found also in some conversations, as in *Idyll* 5, where lines 55–59 echo lines 50–54. As we have suggested before, the symmetries help to corroborate formally the spirit of equality reigning in the pastoral bower.[25] They are often highly contrived; the type of stylization used reminds one of the antiphonal patterns of religious hymns. There are, however, secular parallels even in the Middle Ages and the Renaissance. One expert speaks of a *casuistique amoureuse* and a *mathématique du sentiment* in Montemayor and D'Urfé.[26] The roots of these may well lie deeply imbedded in the recesses of human psychology. But it is legitimate to look to the medieval *tensons* and *partiments* and *debats* for phenomena which are of the same order. There is a difference, however. The speakers and singers of the medieval poetic debates, especially in the Provençal *tensons*, deal with a specific question, which they develop by means of a progressive argument; the casualness of the ancient amoebean simply balances a series of lyrical impulses and responses, without harnessing the utterances to any one covering subject.

The symmetry of response creates one peculiar difficulty. Where there is a match, there should, it is hoped, be a winner.[27] If the palm is to go to the singer with the creative imagination, then it should go to the starter, since it is he who sets the pace initially. If, on the other hand, the victory should accrue to the more accomplished artist, then in many cases the second singer, who has his opponent's model to draw on, ought to get the prize. The dilemma is typical of the genre. Ideally, there is no victor, unless the poet by a deliberate distribution of accents wants to indicate that one of the singers is distinctly superior to the other. Some scholars have felt that they could demonstrate such a weighting of the balance. In Virgil's *Eclogue* 7, for instance, the question of why Corydon is declared the winner has been answered in various ways, but always on the supposition that there is something about Corydon's contributions, or at least about some of them, that signals their superiority over those of Thyrsis. That is to say, Virgil used his virtuosity to make Thyrsis' lines less effective than those of Corydon. One recent critic supplies what is probably the most plausible suggestion within the limits of this general point of view: what matters is not the whole of Thyrsis' performance—there are moments when Thyrsis is better than Corydon—but only the last stanza, in which he fails to measure up to the quality of the preceding stanza sung by Corydon.[28] The listeners move along from stanza to stanza, and when the victory of Corydon is announced, they remember the last two stanzas and little else.

What is attractive about this solution is the recognition that a pastoral poem need not and actually should not be appreciated as a total unit, but as a succession of discrete pronouncements. If so, the victory need not be for the entire series. What I find less persuasive about the proposal is the idea of a verdict that is necessarily tied to the poetic quality of the poem. We distinguish between the poem on the one hand, and the performance as a poetic fiction on the other. If the poet tells us that one of the singers has won, it is up to us to accept the information, and to leave it at that. It is useful to recall dramatic *agōnes*, like the quarrel between Creon and Tiresias in the *Antigone*. It would indeed be difficult to say whether Creon or Tiresias is the one who comes out on top in the exchange; that Tiresias in the end proves to have been the winner has nothing to do with the logic, or the attractiveness, of his argument. It is the poet's choice, not exactly arbitrary, to be sure, but inexplicable in terms of the speakers' utterances.

The awkwardness of the issue is most apparent in the contest that we have had occasion to mention several times already, the boasting match of *Idyll* 5, which has no singing, but is organized as a competition nonetheless. Comatas speaks the first lines; he also speaks the last. And he wins. Because he is a goatherd rather than a shepherd? If this were a reason one wonders why any self-respecting shepherd would want to enter into a contest with a goatherd. Because he is a more straightforward rascal than Lacon? If this were the reason, Morson might well have gotten some humor out of stating this openly. Because he loves a girl rather than a boy? But there is nothing in the pastoral tradition to suggest that one of the two loves is regarded in a better light. On the contrary, the two loves are needed for the refraction of symmetry that the pastoral prizes. No, the award of the palm is as irrational as the procedure of the match itself. Periodically each contestant turns to the judge and says: "Do you see how angry my opponent is getting?"; they go on with the match, but become more and more abrupt; the logical sequence turns increasingly jagged. Then, at line 134, the shepherd, instead of echoing the goatherd as he is supposed to do, turns his negative statement positive. This should be the end, since the goatherd started the contest; but now the goatherd has an additional turn in which he, limply, applies the technique of lines 92–95, originally a statement about the herdsman's love, to the relation between the two contestants. This strikes me as eminently feeble, but it is the signal for Morson to award the sheep to him. It is almost as if Theocritus decided, unfairly and indiscriminately, to have the victory decided at a point when he, the poet, got tired of the rally.

In the later pastoral, the honor of starting the singing contest often goes to the more distinguished of the two, or to the older, or to an injured party. He sets the theme, the number of verses, the meter. In the ancient pastoral tradition, no such favoring can be discovered, chiefly perhaps because as a rule the two contestants are scarcely differentiated. The choice of the beginner is haphazard; we assume that the declaration of the winner is equally so. We should remember that to lose under these circumstances is no disgrace. The temper of the contest promotes the impression that the loser gains as much from his defeat as the winner from his victory. He now has his chance to prove his respect for his friend-competitor by giving him the gift that is the token of his admiration or of his sense of solidarity.

The singing is always rewarded, no matter whether the award is formal, and at the discretion of a judge, or not. [29] In the balanced ecology of the pleasance, no effort is wasted. "Payment" is not the right way of putting it, for nothing could be further removed from the business transactions of the city than the freely given tokens of the green cabinet. Poggioli says that the herdsmen live by "home economics in the literal sense of the term." The phrase is witty, but it may mislead. For, strictly speaking, the herdsman has no home beyond the bower, the open-air arena where he meets his fellow herdsmen. Occasional references to watchful parents or filled larders are marginal and usually in the spirit of comedy. The herdsmen have no home, and they have no business. We have no way of finding out the details of their diet, or what daily routine they would observe if they had a home and practiced a home economics.[30]

In the bower, money has no meaning. When Calidore tries to offer some money to Meliboee for letting him stay in his cottage (*Fairie Queene*, 6.9.33),

> the good man, nought tempted with the offer
> Of his rich mould, did thrust it farre away
> And thus bespake: Sir knight, your bounteous proffer
> Be farre from me, to whom ye ill display
> That mucky masse, the cause of mens decay,
> That mote empaire my peace with daungers dread.

What in Spenser is an explicit and peremptory rejection of money, in Theocritus shows up as a tacit exclusion of it from the substance of the poetry. Talking of business and commerce as an evil is the task of the satirists and analysts: Ovid, in his "Silver Age;" Seneca, in the choruses of the *Medea*; Boethius, in the *Consolation of Philosophy* (3.3); Propertius, in his moralizing mood (3.7). Similarly, the virtue of poverty is preached by poets outside the pastoral tradition; the "Fishermen's Idyll" in the Theocritean corpus (21) is not a pastoral but a Cynic diatribe, written considerably after the time of Theocritus.[31] The Theocritean herdsmen do not concern themselves with wealth or poverty; their self-sufficiency permits them to turn their attention to more essential things.

It follows that the gifts and prizes offered in the bower are not to be evaluated by their monetary value, but by the special standards of the pastoral life. (I lump together prizes won in a contest, gifts offered freely by one singer to another, and gifts offered by lovers to their loves. I suggest that all these are presents of the same sort, tokens of affection and admiration, offered in a spirit that has nothing to do with economics.) In spite of the absence of labor from the pleasance, a gift in which the donor has invested some of his time and energy is especially welcome. Hence the cups lovingly chiselled, the pipes meticulously honed and waxed, and the garment newly oiled. The prize is usually an object of simple rustic manufacture, or, more rarely, a member of the flock, which, properly speaking, is not the herdsman's to give. The presents must not be costly, as Rapin saw,[32] but "yellow apples, young stock-doves, milk, flowers, and the like." The doves would, in an ancient pastoral, be exceptional; they are more appropriate to an epigram or a love elegy than to a pastoral contest. But their gentleness makes them a suitable member in the series proposed by Rapin.

Theocritus, as we have already seen (above, Chapter Six), is remarkably adept at getting around the difficulty of animal gifts. In *Idyll* 8, the first suggestion is that a calf be staked against a sheep (14). But subsequently, with the excuse that the parents count the animals, the singers settle for pipes. In this instance, the poet falls back on an almost explicit avowal that the herdsmen have no property of their own in order to dismiss the feasibility of animal prizes.[33] In *Idyll* 3 (34–36), the pathetic lover offers a she-goat with two kids as a love gift, but the offer is not taken up. The same happens with the fawns and bear-cubs offered by the Cyclops in *Idyll* 11 (40–41).[34] Only in *Idyll* 5 does the winner get a lamb for a prize (143–144); but after what we have said about the special status of this poem in the Theocritean corpus, it should not surprise us that the belligerent youngsters offend against one of the elementary conventions of the social contract within the bower.

In Virgil also, where the gifts offered are not really within the power of the donor to give, as for example the two dappled kids of *Eclogue* 2, lines 40–42, the emphasis is on their aesthetic qualities, on their contribution to the charms of a beautiful world, rather than on the transfer of ownership. It is as if the donor were saying: think of the wild goat, how beautiful it is, how shapely and energetic. It is a piece to fit into the mosaic of the pastoral grove. This, I think, is generally true of the gifts and prizes in the classical pastoral. They are rewards or signs of accreditation, as the pipe in *Eclogue* 2. But perhaps even more important, they must be regarded as integral pieces in the panorama of scattered elements that together form the world of the herdsman and give him pleasure. Whether a pipe is seen attached to the mouth of a player or is held out as a promise for the future, whether the sheep is pictured grazing in the clover by the elm or is offered as a (delusory) hope to the partner in the enterprise, does not matter; the distinction is merely technical. It is enough that the pieces are fitted in somewhere in this scene, which, because it is not constructed according to the laws of beginning, middle, and end, is tolerant of more than one way of organizing the material. It makes little difference whether the grove is the setting of the song, or the theme of the song, or a dream for the future; all that matters is that it puts in an appearance somewhere within the characteristically flexible structure of the poem. The pastoral has few surprises, not because it has a fixed pattern that must be followed, but precisely because there is no pattern. There are the predictable themes, but no table of organization.

Trouble does start, however, when the gifts and prizes begin to be inappropriate to the bower. In Calpurnius' *Eclogue* 6, Astylus wagers a tame stag, put before us in a sustained flight of description (32–47) which itself defies the Theocritean mode; [35] his opponent Lycidas stakes a horse. Now though we have ventured to show some affinities between epic and pastoral, it simply will not do to allow the epic hero's best friend an entry into the bower. Job's fighting charger, snorting his "Ha, ha," cuts a most peculiar figure amid the personnel of the greensward. Calpurnius is, as so often, straining at the limits of his genre. Later pastoralists labored hard and ingeniously to improve on their predecessors' conceits. A study of the gifts offered in

Mantuan, Sidney, Drayton, and others produces a veritable rogues' gallery of offensive commodities. Sidney knew what he was doing when he proposed a good cat and a bad dog;[36] at the end, the judge says:

> Enough, enough; so ill hath done the best,
> That since the having them to neither's due,
> Let cat and dog fight which shall have both you.

The good cat and the bad dog are rewards for bad singing; the pastoral freedom has become license, both moral and aesthetic; the commitment to simplicity is gone. Most of the Renaissance pastoralists do not have Sidney's sense of humor and list their outlandish prizes quite seriously.

Conversely, there are times when Theocritus' successors are more squeamish in the matter of gifts than he. One subtlety that goes against the grain of pastoral simplicity is the notion that the gifts are seasonally conditioned. We know this theme best from the humor Shakespeare strikes from it in Perdita's speech; earlier Mantuan has Candidus, in discussing what prize to award to Pollux, observe that rabbits may be offered in winter, geese in October and November, fruits in summer, lambs in the spring (*Eclogue* 8). Theocritus is familiar with this sophistication; but the only poem in which he employs it—Virgil never does— is *Idyll* 11: the Cyclops, the faintly Hesiodic bull in the pastoral chinashop, testifies to his lack of credentials by sneering at the absurdity of both the lily and the poppy being bound in the same nosegay. The Theocritean Cyclops would like to be a pastoral hero; there are analogies, strangely, with Virgil's Gallus. But the Cyclops is too violently caught up in the pains of adolescence to give himself fully to the bower, without questioning and without resentment. Hence the calculation, the Hesiodic timetable; his adolescence is backward and forward looking; it does not permit him to savor the moment. The pastoral *otium* eludes his grasp (see also above, Chapter Four).

It was to protest the excessive niceties and the gaucheries of the tradition that Philips in his sixth *Pastoral* abolished all concrete giving:

> Let others meanly stake upon their skill,
> Or Kid, or Lamb, or Goat, or what they will;
> For Praise we sing, nor Wager ought beside:
> And, whose the Praise, let Geron's Lips decide.

But Philips' revisionism, though laudable in principle, is evidence of a waning sensitivity to pastoral needs. The pastoral does not cherish abstractions, but things, objects to be sensed and enjoyed. When a pain is felt, it tends to be a physical pain, the piercing of the flesh by a thorn; when pleasure is experienced, the pleasure flows from a concrete occasion. Praise is too pale a thing to satisfy, not only the beneficiary but also the donor. For this reason the idea that a song may be given as a gift or prize is absent from Theocritus' pastoral poetry. It is significant that he does feature the *topos* in *Idyll* 16, a Pindaric encomium; in that tradition a song is the most precious gift that the poet has to give. In the pastoral, song is not a present but a natural event, a spontaneous way of voicing the feelings and longings that press for recognition. In singing, the herdsman is not doing anyone a favor; he is pleasing himself. The Pindaric singer has a profession, a business; to give his product free of charge is a benefaction. The herdsman has no profession; he exists to voice what is within him; in satisfying this need, he has done his job.

Calpurnius anticipates the stratagem of Philips; in *Eclogue* 3 Lycidas has his song conveyed to Phyllis as a love gift. In Tibullus' fourth *Elegy*, Book One, the "Song of Priapus," we learn that the best bribe for a worthy boy would be a song. Here, we feel, the sentiment is appropriate because of the emphasis on the intrigue and the hard work required in the courting. But such machinations have no place in the bower. It is amusing to see the Cyclops attempt to sing for a purpose (*Idyll* 11), and find out in the end that the singing has an entirely different and unexpected effect. In the pastoral, singing cannot be subjected to a plan; like the unselfconscious mimic energies of children it can only be channelled into games and brought under the control of certain minimal rules. Once it is subordinated to purposes that point it away from itself, it has lost its charm. That is how the music of the pastoral shares in the freedom that we have seen to be one of the most precious attributes of the pleasance.

8
The Humor

It is customary to distinguish between several ways of making fun of the written word, especially between parody and burlesque. Burlesque is said to mock a literary form by using it to say things not appropriate to that form; parody, on the other hand, makes fun of a genre by exaggerating its formal and thematic features. I am not sure that this distinction is always defensible; but broadly speaking it is correct, and useful. Let us, tentatively, say that Swift and Gay are masters of the burlesque; they use the patterns of the pastoral and add to its humorous possibilities by turning its attention upon city life. The town eclogue is, in effect, a literary joke based on a complete distortion of the original purpose of the tradition. Swift saw this quite clearly: "I believe farther, the pastoral ridicule is not exhausted, and that a porter, footman, or chairman's pastoral might do well. Or what think you of a Newgate pastoral among the thieves and whores there." [1] Thus Swift considered the pastoral conventions conducive to satirizing a subject; and Gay's work was the result.

Even Gay's *Shepherd's Week*, a persiflage of Philips instigated by Pope, would come under the heading of burlesque, since the world described is not that of the herdsmen, but the Hesiodic barnyard of uncouth peasants and half-witted sluts. The ending of "Monday, Or The Squabble" makes this clear:

> Forbear, contending louts, give o'er your strains,
> An oaken staff each merits for his pains.
> But see the sun-beams bright to labour warn
> And gild the thatch of goodman Hodges' barn.
> Your herds for want of water stand adry,
> They're weary of your songs—and so am I.

Such burlesque can be funny; it can also be disgusting, as Swift's pastoral dialogue between two weeders, Sheelah and Dermot, is.

Empson argues that the *Beggars Opera* exhibits a form of humor based on disenchantment with traditional values: "After what Dryden called the Deluge, the republic, one could not take the old symbolisms, even the Elizabethan poetic ones, for granted; one must go back to the simplest things and argue from them. . . . The assumption of humility in such flat plain-man writing, together with its analytic power of generalization, leads a stylist inevitably to irony." [2] This, I dare say, gives Gay too much credit for political philosophy, and underrates the amount of sheer playfulness immanent in his prose. More important, it introduces the critical notion of irony into a context where it is hardly warranted and can only muddy the waters. Burlesque employs the sledge-hammer humor; it opens wide with a broad grin, rather than letting us guess with the thin smile and the expert appeal that we associate with irony, especially with self-irony, the amused standing back from the commitments of the work. Such irony is rarely combined with burlesque, which has no commitments to begin with. It is more appropriate to parody, the mocking of traditional forms and themes by means of exaggeration and hints of self-consciousness. Self-mockery is common enough in English pastoral; Surrey's "Harpalus and Phyllida" is a case in point.[3] Like Jaques in the Forest of Arden, Surrey could not take pastoralism quite seriously:

> The Hart he fedeth by the Hynde
> The Bucke hard by the Doo,

The Turtle Dove is not unkinde
To him that loves her so. . . .

The material is not much different from that of Gay's lines cited at the beginning of our Chapter Six. But the mood is one of gentle irony, not rude burlesque. As the herdsman takes his position on the pastoral stage, he is made to realize the narrowness and the precariousness of that position; the awareness comes through in his speech, and lends it an undertone of surprise, amusement, and disbelief. Surrey's poem is said to be one of the earliest pastorals in the English language. It is of some interest that, as the genre makes its entry, irony and self-depreciation should already be in evidence.

They are by no means late arrivals. We have three lines of parody published soon after Virgil's *Eclogues*; they are reported in Donatus' *Life of Virgil*.[4] Such distortions of the tradition are more instructive than burlesques, for by their exaggerations they give us a clearer idea of what were felt to be the conventions. In Drayton's seventh *Eglog* of *Idea*, both songs, Borrill's against Love and Batte's for Love, are exaggerated statements of traditional attitudes. They are amusing, but from them we learn how Drayton defined those conventions. The same is true of Charles Churchill's *The Prophecy of Famine*, lines 273–402, a parody of Ramsay; again, the special qualities of Ramsay's pastoral art are thrown into clearer relief when we see what happens to them in Churchill's version.

The humor is harder to detect when, as in Surrey's poem, the parody is incidental rather than pervasive; when, in other words, the humor lightens the fabric of what is, otherwise, straightforward pastoral. Theocritus' *Idyll* 5 contains literal quotations of two lines from *Idyll* 1 (5.101 = 1.13, and 5.46 = 1.107). In the mouth of the blackguard who uses them, the courteous phrases sound barely convincing. But can we say for sure that in their original setting in *Idyll* 1 the lines are more "respectable"? The fact is, we cannot even be sure that *Idyll* 1 was written before

Idyll 5. The interdependence of questions of tone with questions of priority makes definitive judgments of the specific quality of a line very difficult. Precisely because the conventions of the genre are so easily imitated, they also lend themselves to various degrees of deflection, from light parody to travesty. And because the straight and the parodistic uses of the conventions are close neighbours, the listener is encouraged to practice the suspension of empathy which the pastoral demands.

There are two uses of parody. Either the author himself is having fun with the tradition; this happens in the portions of the poem given over to narration and description. Thus in Marot's "Loyse," following a pattern initiated by Virgil's fourth *Eclogue*, the description of nature's mourning makes for witty excesses: lilies turn black, and sheep grow black wool. *Or* it is the characters, in their speeches and songs, who exaggerate the old forms. Virgil's *Eclogue* 10, lines 46–49, cannot be read without recalling the words about Pan in Theocritus' *Idyll* 7, lines 111–112; a geographical survey, originally organized as a (half-humorous) threat to the god if he does not behave himself, turns into a vista of suffering endured by the girl whose elopement Gallus deplores. Both of these are elaborations of the geographical expansion which we had occasion to discuss above, and which is used more ingenuously—or so it would seem—in *Idyll* 7, lines 76–77; cf. also *Idyll* 1, lines 67–69. Again, can we be sure where self-parodying begins and primary usage leaves off?[5]

The second variety, parody put in the mouths of the characters, is more common, because direct speech forms the bulk of the material, but also because of the tendency of the pastoral to minimize the poet's chances to make his own personality felt. In Virgil's seventh *Eclogue*, for instance, the humor resides in the fact that, as champions of two views of the pastoral, the herdsmen represent their sides with more enthusiasm than tact.[6] Their exaggerations poke fun both at the conventions and at their own credentials vis-à-vis the conventions.

Corydon	Galatea, my Sea-goddess, sweeter than thyme,
	Whiter than swans, fairer than light-green ivy,
	Come to me when the bullocks return from pasture,
	If you have any feeling for your Corydon.
Thyrsis	You'll think me bitterer than Sardinian herbs,
	More grating than a rake, plainer than sea-weed,
	If this day hasn't been one long year already.
	Go home now, bullocks! where is your modesty?[7]

In the last analysis, of course, the credibility of the self-parodying must be charged to the writer and his control over the form. There are analogies with the medieval *pastourelle*. The manner in which the knight offers his love to the peasant girl leaves little doubt that the love is to be taken with a grain of scepticism and that he does not intend to marry her, though the terms he uses might, if taken in isolation, create that impression. The *pastourelle* being an aristocratic genre, the main character looks upon the pastoral scene from without and from above; the knight takes the long view, and exploits the simplicity of the herdsmen.[8] In the pastoral, the sources of the irony are more subtle; the herdsmen do not enjoy the advantages of education and status that the knight of the *pastourelle* has. It is the poet himself who has the perspective; but he must not exhibit the condescension which the knight has for the villains. On the contrary, he must be in sympathy with his rustics, and let them be both funny and dignified. This calls for a very delicate balance between humor and understanding, between innocence and substance, so as not to disrupt the unselfconsciousness of pastoral well-being.

Consider the parody of conventional rhetorical devices of praise in *Idyll* 10, lines 36–37:

> My darling Bombyca, your feet are knuckle bones,
> Your voice belladonna; your ways—I cannot say.[9]

The absurdity of the comparisons pales before the obvious innocence with which they are offered. The fundamental ambivalence of the role of the simile comes out beautifully in the fun that Theocritus has with it here and elsewhere. The awe, and the delight in beauty, in Bucaeus' utterance are touching; but the idea of comparing ankles to knuckle bones, and a voice to a velvety but poisonous plant, shows up the futility of reducing any item in the bower to serve as a means of glorification for another. The praise, it seems, mixes pleasure with self-deprecation. It is a very special trick of Theocritus; but it crops up again and again in the history of the pastoral.

Theocritus' *Idyll* 3, one of his slighter and thus more easily analyzed compositions, is a fine example of this kind of light-headedness. The form of the poem is that of a *paraklausithyron*, a complaint sung in front of the barred door of the beloved—except that it is sung in front of a cave rather than a city door and the lover is, not a man–about–town, but an untutored herdsman, who hands his goats over to a baby-sitter to obtain enough elbow room for his recital. The song proper is preceded by a series of summonses and recriminations. If we did not learn from the text that the singing does not start till line 40, we would naturally assume that the first portion of his addresses is also sung, for many of the feelings expressed are those found in amoebean sequences in other poems. Since we are not told specifically that the herdsman is *not* singing the first part, the subsequent announcement that he will begin to sing "leaning against this pine tree" comes as something of a surprise. The teasing continues as the poem develops. When the awkward clown wishes he were a buzzing bee so that he might find an entrance into the cave through the overhanging vines, we are asked to relish the incongruity between fumbling rustic and the insect that gets through. At the same time we pity his inexperience and his failure of nerve. The man's reliance on superstition—the poppy did not click; his eye throbs—rounds out the picture of helplessness. We cannot really take seriously the lamentations of an indolent clown; what are we to make of an unhappy

lover whose brooding on suicide is tempered with the practical
consideration:

> I'll take off my overalls and jump into the sea![10]

His song, when it comes, may well shock us; nothing would
seem to be more out of character than the spectacle of the country
bumpkin serenading his girl with an aria on mythological
subjects. He sings of the loves of Hippomenes, of Bias, of Adonis,
of Endymion, and of Iasion. As it turns out, the themes could
not have been better chosen, for the ladies named—Atalanta,
Peira, Aphrodite, Selene, Demeter—were a domineering lot,
and the wooers all went into a decline of one sort or another after
achieving union with them. Clearly, then, the poor herdsman
with his pathetic book learning has not the slightest idea what he
is singing about. If a love song is meant to furnish good auspices
for the action at hand, the present performance cannot help but
doom his fortunes for good. Even the ten apples promised to the
lady—the precise number is the right touch; are ten enough?—
are not likely to undo the damage.

The hero of this *Idyll*, like the Cyclops of *Idyll* 11, is not
entirely typical of the Theocritean swain. He lacks assurance; he
is more bumpkin than most, and the form of the poem, the
kōmos, thrusts him into a pose that aggravates his clownishness.
But his unsuspecting simplicity, his lack of insight into his own
defenselessness, is characteristic of many other Theocritean
herdsmen. We laugh at the self-dramatizing, the air of suffering;
nevertheless we are refreshed by the thought that the suffering
cannot be profound, and that the zest of living and the penchant
for pleasure will win out.[11]

It is this humorous dimension of the pastoral that makes it
such a useful instrument for relief when it serves as an enclave
within a larger structure of a different type. Pastoral interludes
in epic, notably in Tasso's *Gerusalemme Liberata*, help to relax the
tension and bring on a smile, no matter whether the herdsmen

are really courtiers engaged in a bit of play-acting, or whether they are genuine rustics who have strayed into an environment strange to them. In Homer, heroes and shepherds can live under the same roof; with the introduction of the pastoral as an independent literary form, this homogeneity is no longer possible. But the new compartmentalization produces its own benefits; the humorous pastoral enclave is one of them. In the love lyric, likewise, pastoral can be used to offset pain and bitterness with the fresh breeze of its pleasantry. But even within its own small frame, pastoral combines humor and seriousness; the mixture validates the insight, stressed in the Middle Ages, that a positive accent on life is as such "comic."[12]

There is another kind of humor in the pastoral that has nothing to do with parody or irony or the awareness of shortcomings. It comes, rather, from the effervescence of the vital spirit. We know this spirit well from the uninhibited sallies in the *Secunda Pastorum* of the Towneley Plays of the late fourteenth century. This animal vigor, which fires the bursts of energy we have had occasion to notice, declares itself especially in the brief but pungent sallies at the end of songs or of whole poems.[13] In the ancient rhetorical handbooks, these terminal explosions would come under the heading of *para prosdokian*, "that which is contrary to expectation." The classical treatment of this figure is furnished by Cicero's *De oratore*, 2, sections 255–290.[14] The examples given are largely puns, illustrating an earlier point in the discussion. But at 289, summing up the various kinds of humor, Cicero lists, among the jokes that derive their force from the matter itself, the defeating of expectations and laughing at people's natures.[15] Cicero does not analyze the workings of *para prosdokian* as such; ancient rhetoric is strangely reticent when it comes to the analysis of the rhetoric of humor. But the combination of the two points supplies part of the answer to the question of effect. What we would call the punch line is, in Cicero's discussion, understood to do its job by reinforcing surprise with aggressiveness. In pastoral, the terminal punch line and the surprise ending are especially at home; this is because the pastoral glories in its lack of structure. In a sense the discreteness of the parts mitigates the surprise; in a context made up of units whose interconnection is minimal, the surprise ending foregoes one of its usual advantages, its disconnectedness. Since the whole of the poem consists of paratactic elements, each of which begs to be appreciated individually, the punch line is not privileged over other lines. What matters about the pastoral punch line, then, is not so much that it stands by itself, but rather that it dispels the veil of courtesy which signals the contract of man with man, and introduces, in a relatively pure state, the combative excitement of the beasts. The pastoral frame is opened to admit the entry of vulgarity or abuse or some other equivalent shock to shatter, at least momentarily, the pastoral *otium*. This happens in a number of the *Idylls*. The ending of *Idyll* 1 may serve as an instance. The goatherd has just complimented Thyrsis on his song, and has given him the cup to endorse the compliment. He also hands over a goat for milking, and then turns to the other ewes:

> Stop your capering, girls, or the buck will come and get you![16]

This passage is, in one respect, untypical; usually it is the dominant character, or the winner in the contest, who achieves the humorous breakthrough designed to subvert the threat of overrefinement. The maneuver is analogous to another which Horace is said to have borrowed from Archilochus, the technique of deflating the listener's expectation by a radical reversal:

> So spoke the banker Alfius.
>   He wanted to buy a farm;
> And when he had called in his capital—
>   He loaned it out again.[17]

Archilochus and Horace use their reversals to shock the listener out of his complacency; in the end they leave him suspended, unable to lodge his sympathies anywhere in the poem. Theocritus, on the contrary, uses the surprise punch line to pump energy and lustiness back into a bower which, under the pressure of an Epicurean sensibility, is in danger of turning soft. The Theocritean punch line, like the echoes of *ponos*, toughens the fibre of the pastoral design.

In the hands of Theocritus' successors, the surprise ending has had varying degrees of success. Virgil is rather chary of it; in spite of the pugnacious tone of some of the contests and encounters, the Virgilian bower is too gentle a world to endure the buffeting provided by the punch line. The Renaissance poets come back to it, however. Mantuan's *Eclogue* 5 draws to a close with Candidus trying in vain to get the rich Silvanus to promise him a reward; after Silvanus has held him off with double talk, Candidus bursts out with

> To Hell with you! I hope you'll turn into another Midas.[18]

In Ronsard's "Adonis," Venus

> who but lately doted on
> Adonis, forgot him to love a certain Anchises.[19]

The poem concludes with a denunciation of women in love. It is as if the poet, in the process of availing himself of the pastoral punch line, found the energy released by it so strong that he had to follow through with it, and end up as a satirist. Once more, Frost is the better and purer heir. His

> At present I am living in Vermont[20]

coming as it does at the very end of a poem in praise of New Hampshire, provides the same shock of the unexpected and the same satyr's grin as Theocritus' terminal vulgarities. The wrench is considerable; after it, it would be difficult to find one's way back to the lyricism of the earlier experience, if this were desired. Perhaps this is the reason why Demetrius (*On Style*, 152–153;

cf. also 139) called the stratagem a *griphos* (literally, "fishing net;" hence: "maze," "conundrum"). The *griphos*, according to Demetrius, is a device whereby both psychological anticipation and logical connection are snarled. From the examples he gives, it is clear that he regards the arrangement as important; the shocker has to come last, so there will be no chance for a gloss that might unsnarl the tissue.[21] In actual fact, strong language and the figure *para prosdokian* are found also, though less frequently, within the body of the pastoral. The reason is obvious. Because the pastoral lyric does not rely on the unities but favors paratactic structuring, every line is potentially a terminal line. The listener is prepared to move, not along an extended arc, but back and forth with the miniature advances permitted by pastoral *stasis*. This means that in the pastoral poem, the *griphos* cannot destroy the mood as radically as elsewhere; or, to put it the right way round, the pastoral mood is a function of several unrelated elements. Humor is one of the elements. It is always close to the surface, either as irony—the detachment of the speaker who knows that the forms he uses are conventions; or as aggressive-ness—the grotesqueries of the herdsman who is also a satyr. Occasionally the humor takes control. The device of the final punch line is cognate with the pictorial device of the ivy tendrils framing the scenes on the cup; the poet summons the simple products of natural exuberance to insulate our feelings against other, more demanding excitements. Thus the humor is both part of the substance, and a protective shield. Most important of all, it is there, from the very beginning.

9
The Pleasance

Samuel Johnson (*Rambler* No. 36) believed that it was the business of the pastoral to capture men's passions by mirroring them in nature. The precise contribution of nature to the process of understanding the affections of men is not made clear in Johnson's discussion. Perhaps it is no more than the notion, often encountered in the writings of the eighteenth-century critics but by no means restricted to them, that there is an analogy between the state of our minds and the state of nature. "If the young and amorous are placed in a delightful grove, reclining on beds of flowers, in the midst of a happy country, and under a bright and serene sky, these beauties of nature will increase the pleasing sensations that arise from representations of love."[1] There may well be something more, however, than this informal expectation of analogies. Much of the pertinent discussion appears to assume a virtual identity, aesthetic and moral, between what charms us in the external setting and what interests us in human behavior, an identity which is confirmed by the double service of the word "nature."

Paul Elmer More, commenting on "Lycidas," called nature that "damnable word ... into which have been distilled all the fallacies of human wit through thousands of years."[2] Empson takes the opposite view, and finds much of value in the multi-plicity of the term: "There are three main ideas about Nature, putting her above, equal to, and below man. She is the work of God, or a god herself, and therefore a source of revelation; or she fits man, sympathizes with him, corresponds to his social order ... and so forth; or she is not morally responsible so that to contemplate her is a source of relief.... One reason for the force of Milton's descriptions of Eden is that these contradictory ideas can be made there to work together." [3] Frost has a facetious poem on the meaning of "nature," entitled "Lucretius versus the Lake Poets," [4] and addressed to a Dean, in which he gets witty mileage out of the fact that "nature" may mean either landscape or the world.

According to Empson, great poetry needs to operate with several conceptions of nature simultaneously. Faithful to his commitment to complexity and ambiguity, he is slow to predicate quality of any writing that moves on one level of understanding only. But the history of literature shows that great poetry has in fact been created with a very narrow working conception of nature. Hardy's apprehension of nature as an eminently hostile power shapes his vision of men in their world; nature is flawed, and the cruelties men practice upon each other is in tune with that flaw.[5] Comus' argument from nature, to convince the lady of the unnaturalness of chastity, is narrow and poetically effective. Much in Sophocles is upheld by the proposition of nature's inherent hostility or viciousness.[6]

Frost too has been said to view nature as essentially alien; "man's physical needs, the dangers facing him, the realities of birth and death, the limits of his ability to know and to act are shown in stark outline by the indifference and inaccessibility of the physical world in which he must live."[7] Perhaps this is too sharply focused; but it contains an element of truth, and it may serve as a reminder that the tragic poet and the pastoral poet can be at one philosophically. The corollary must be that it is not the philosophy of a poet, the way he looks at Nature and Man, or at least not exclusively this, which defines him as a

tragedian or a pastoralist. Still, a poet who wishes to be taken
seriously cannot do without that modicum of a stance, call it
philosophy or vision or what you will, that provides the listener
with his Archimedean point. It may turn out that the position
taken is that no one perception will do. In any case it is useful
to study the possibilities.

Under the aegis of the equation of nature with everything
that is, man is found to be part of that nature; an eternal harmony
binds them together. The view of nature as a carrier of world
harmony has its roots in ancient Platonism and Stoicism; it is
poetically exploited in the songs of the troubadours, with echoes
in Tasso[8] and many other poets, from Petrarch to Keats, who
propose a near-identification of nature with the beloved.[9] One
of the most impressive documents in this tradition is Tennyson's
"The Gardener's Daughter," which plunges the heroine, Rose,
into an organic setting of flowers and lights; the human, the
vegetative, and the atmospheric merge to form a homogeneous
canvas, in the manner of Titian and the Venetians.

> The fields between
> Are dewy-fresh, browsed by deep-udder'd kine,
> And all about the large lime feathers low,
> The lime a summer home of murmurous wings.
> In that still place she, hoarded in herself,
> Grew. . . .

With this British landscape, shimmering and continuous, we
should compare certain passages in Keats, especially "Endymion,"
I, line 436. Peona settles Endymion in her bower:

> So she was gently glad to see him laid
> Under her favorite bower's quiet shade,
> On her own couch, new made of flower leaves,
> Dried carefully on the cooler side of sheaves
> When last the sun his autumn tresses shook. . . .

The sequence is characterized as a dream; this does not detract
from its fullness, its avowed intention to achieve a fusion of

the human and the non-human in the verdant tapestry of Nature.

Others who seek to distill the wholeness of nature try to do so by emphasizing a more abstract quality which is thought to reside in nature and weld its constituents together. This is the appeal to *Stimmung*[10] or to the *Sympathiekosmos* featured in Stoic speculations and Senecan drama. Horace (*Epistles* 1.14) compares the *cultura animi* with the *cultura agri*,[11] if I may use Ciceronian terms. In Horace's lyrics, nature is the great paradigm. Organic nature—cyclical, growing and decaying—is introduced to alert man both to his greatness and to his mortality, and to provide a splendid setting for his music.[12] A comparison with Propertius is instructive. In Propertius, nature is usually little more than the locale, pleasant and innocuous, for his elegiac reflections. In Horace, with his profounder appreciation of the link between organic nature and man, we find more ambitious landscapes, more freshly experienced rural scenes. He has a better eye for what gives life to a setting.[13] Horace's landscapes enter into the action; the details are less contrived, the fields and woods breathe a spirit which locks into the spirit of the argument by means of powerful chiaroscuros. Sometimes, as in *Odes* 1.17, "On his Sabine Farm," Horace combines reminders of another tradition, the Hellenistic toreutic of fine distinctions and sharply pencilled contours, with touches of romantic organicism.[14] Propertius is committed to the Hellenistic motifs, to bees, fruits, rustling leaves, singing birds, aromatic breezes and, above all, caves and grottoes. Horace goes more directly to the nature he knows, to the woods and the water courses of his rural abode.

Still, lest we misunderstand the quality of Horace's genius, his *Stimmungslandschaft* usually has a villa at the center of it. His farm is a part of the world of business and culture because it is part of a larger harmony. Country and city are separated and contrasted because they are known to be one. This is, it seems to me, what disqualifies Horace as a pastoral poet; there is always a villa. The Campanian landscape paintings, themselves surely based on Hellenistic originals, include a villa or a temple or both in their rural scenes.[15] But this decorative world, in which country and city are combined in a pleasing pattern, is no more pastoral than the programmatic contrasting of country and city which we shall discuss below (Chapter Ten).

Stimmung, the quality of feeling "which extends over, and unites, a landscape and a man," is an important factor in the art of Horace, and also of Virgil; but not in Theocritus. The words are those of Leo Spitzer, who also cites related terms from antiquity, *temperamentum, consonantia, symphōnia.*[16] None of these have any meaning for Theocritus. In spite of the close collocation of shepherd and pleasance, the sights are trained on the first. Nature is the backdrop, and in some respects a shaper of attitudes, but on balance man is autonomous. Theocritus, as we observed in the chapter on freedom, stands not in the Pythagorean-Platonic-Stoic tradition of the *Phaedrus* and the *Timaeus* and Cleanthes and Posidonius and Seneca, but in the Socratic tradition of the *Symposium* and the *Protagoras*, in which nature supplies a scene, but not an umbrella. Only in the dirge of *Idyll* 1 are there approximations to having man and his passions absorbed into a larger order. But the approximations are subtle and discreet; Daphnis, one feels, remains great in death because he does not remit the rights of his differentness. The Theocritean herdsman is not a student of nature; he does not seem to care, except again in passing, whether the beings that surround him are friendly or hostile. He takes their songs, and their murmured responses, as his due, not as the verification of an axiom of natural philosophy. Invocations of the natural powers, of the night, the moon, the sun, and the like, are found in abundance in drama and in the lyric of passion, but only rarely in the pastoral. Typically, the most famous occurrence in Theocritus is in *Idyll* 2 (69), a city mime, or perhaps a little drama, but not a pastoral.[17] The *topos* of the lonely sufferer calling upon living nature to keep him company is premised on the assumption that there is a harmony. Further, the harmony stipulates that the creatures which comfort man with their presence, animals and plants and rivers and rocks, act and feel the way men do. This is what Ruskin castigated under the name of "pathetic fallacy."

It is easy enough to demonstrate the prominence of the pathetic fallacy in Renaissance and post-Renaissance pastoral; Miss Gerhardt cites passages from Garcilaso, Montemayor, Marot, Ronsard, D'Urfé.[18] In earlier pastoral this is rarer. When weeds displace flowers and crops in Virgil's *Eclogue* 5, lines 36–39, or harsh mountains form an appropriate backdrop to cruelty in *Eclogue* 8, lines 44–45, the trope is implicit rather than spelled out, and in the absence of the imputation of human feelings, perhaps not operative at all. Virgil's practice is more like that of Theocritus in *Idyll* 13, lines 64–65: Heracles, looking for the lost Hylas, is said to be moving among "untrodden brambles;"[19] the landscape in which he pursues his fruitless search has become faintly colored by the state of his soul.[20] But again, characteristically, this emphasis on the *locus vilis* occurs in a non-pastoral poem, an epyllion. The practice of the *Odyssey*, the fountain head of all epyllia, shows that this sort of interaction between soul and setting is more congenial to the epic than to the Theocritean pastoral.

Nature has very little to teach the herdsmen. Wordsworth's[21]

> One impulse from a vernal wood
> May teach you more of man,
> Of moral evil and of good
> Than all the sages can . . .

and Auden's[22]

> Old sounds re-educate an ear grown coarse,
> As Pan's green father suddenly raps out
> A burst of undecipherable Morse . . .

pay homage to nature as a source of refreshment and wisdom. The concept has its roots in Shaftesbury[23] and Thomson and the eighteenth-century Platonists, rather than in classical attitudes toward nature. In Petrarch and the Petrarcheggianti, nature's teaching is of a special kind: she activates the memory.[24] As the lover makes his way through the landscape which his sensibility links with his love, the recollection inflames his passion. In that sense, the poetry, the wisdom, is taught by the grove.[25] Significantly, however, the Petrarchan disciple of nature is alone. The lovers of Petrarch and Sannazaro, and the enthusiasts of Shaftesbury and the romantics, confront a nature that is untouched; they are the solitary disturbers of a virgin calm.

To this solitude which Petrarch, or perhaps his Provençal forerunners, introduced upon the European poetic scene, there is no equivalent in the ancient tradition. Potentially, one feels, it was there, ready to be tapped. Mythology, with its stories of Pan and nymphs and other godlike creatures surprising man in the woods and working their terror on him, shows that the magic of solitude was understood. From Plato's *Phaedrus* we know that the close-up of nature releases a sense of humility and awe; only the philosopher is capable of converting the *Angst* into a gentle mockery, an ironic contemplation of one's own god-likeness. But the poets were not, as far as we can tell, interested; and the pastoralists preferred to evade the issue of solitude by falling back on the protective mechanism of the group. Shepherds have friends as well as lovers; the impact of nature is cushioned as it is distributed over a wider front.[26]

If the Theocritean herdsman is not a disciple of nature, could the harmony of which Dr. Johnson speaks be realized the other way round? That is, could the swain be the teacher? In Virgil this is certainly so; the singer sings, and nature echoes his songs.[27] The woods and the mountain glens, like the rocks in a famous passage in Lucretius (4.570 ff.), supply the resonance which an ambitious musician desires. We have spoken of the herdsman as the singer and the animals as the instrumentalists. To this extent the herdsman is the leader, and the rest of creation takes its signals from him. But that is the limit of the knowledge imparted. After Virgil, when Calpurnius and Nemesianus remove the echo and insist on a seemly silence in their landscapes, even this small vestige of nature's discipleship is dropped from the pastoral plan.[28] In this respect, Theocritus shows greater affinities with the successors of Virgil than with Virgil. True, his pleasance is filled with sound; but the sounds are not the echoes of a human voice ricocheted from the resonant surfaces of a compliant landscape, but the freely offered comments of the creatures who join the herdsman singer in his noon concert. The Greek pastoral does not attempt to solemnize man's power over nature, or his response to nature's guidance, nor does it, overtly, assert any bond between man and nature. Instead, it directs attention to man's virtues, and especially to his promise as an enjoyer of the pleasures of life, by filling in the scene around him. There is no movement back and forth, no integration or bridging of gaps; only ways of setting the stage, of visualizing the conversation and the articulated feelings of the herdsmen against a background that allows them to move with some freedom, and with a maximum of congeniality, but with no awareness of obligation or authority.

The *locus amoenus*, then, is, at least in its origins, not a reduced picture of the world as a whole, not an emblem concealing all of nature,[29] a pinpointing of all that determines man, or all that he must face. On the contrary, the *locus amoenus* is a highly selective arrangement of stage properties. The character of the properties is décided, not by the ideals or the needs of man, but by the pastoral demand for freedom and pleasure. The stage is set in such a way that the herdsmen may pursue their objectives, their affections and their dreams, as easily as possible, against the smallest number of obstacles. The ease of the rural scene, with its tree, its greensward, and its brook, is a dramatic convenience, not a philosophical necessity. It is because the herdsman has no obligations whatever toward the trees or the brook, except for a laisser-faire attitude of respect and enjoyment, that he is placed among them. Neither the city, nor the fields and the pastures which call for work and hardship, would do. The importance of the background for converting momentary sadness into enduring pleasure is obvious; tragic isolation becomes difficult in a grove peopled with companionable spirits. But the function of the pastoral landscape is one of quiescence rather than positive influence. Herder assumed that any setting might do for an idyll, provided it was arranged in such a way that it did not prove burdensome or restrictive to the characters. In the Greek world there was less choice than in the leisured society of the modern West. The franchise of the *locus amoenus* could not be bettered. The setting remained roughly the same through the Middle ages and into the Renaissance. Unlike the rose garden of the Virgin Mary, the *locus conclusus* of chastity untrammeled and protected,[30] the *locus amoenus* of the pastoral carries with it no symbolic overtones, no weight of significance. Its weightlessness commended it to Theocritus' attention.

In the pastoral poem, the *locus amoenus* is rarely hoped for; it is there. It may, however, be present in two ways; either as the setting within which the singing competition or the aria is produced, or as a landscape touched upon in the song. In its second variety, the pleasance often is little more than an incidental reference, a brief cue to set a mood. In *Idyll* 7, lines 6–9, the mention of the host's ancestor generates a remark about a spring which foreshadows the later *locus amoenus* (135 ff.), itself a variation upon the type, for it houses not the singing competition (which, for once, is conducted in transit) but a pastoral picnic. The two *loci* are, topographically speaking, identical; framing the poem as they do, they gently lead the listener from the past to the present, from myth to reality, from legend to poetry. But all the time the setting is there, to furnish the beauty and the airiness that condition the pastoral delights and ready our perceptions for the music. In the songs themselves, also, the *locus* makes brief appearances; the oaks mourned for Daphnis, along with the hills (74); and, "I wish Comatas were here, reclining under oaks and pines" (88). The emphasis is on the pastoral concert, rather than on the tactile and visual beauties of the scene. But the boundary between the visual and the auditory facets of the pleasance is often tenuous.[31]

The use Theocritus makes of the *locus amoenus* in *Idyll* 5, the least musical of the poems, is particularly interesting. We count four *loci*, each of them proposed as the setting for a musical contest. Each mention forms a conciliatory gesture, to pave the way from the invective to the gentler communication which is the desired norm. But in this poem, for once, the spirit of battle is too strong; the potential singers remain talkers, and refuse to be enticed into the pleasances offered as bait. Each remains where he is, and the invocations of the bower remain abortive. In fact they serve to sharpen the sense of loss; the difference between what a pastoral is expected to accomplish, and what the present contest does, is bitingly defined by the quadrupling of the pastoral arbor.

The bucolic *locus amoenus* is obviously related to the sacred precinct, the god's habitat of Greek lyric poetry.[32] A typical example of the latter is furnished in a fragment of Pindar, transmitted by Plutarch and now augmented from a papyrus.[33] This is a description of the place where the good souls go; they enjoy perpetual sunshine dispelling the dark, red roses in the meadow, shade trees bearing frankincense, and orchards heavy with golden fruit. They entertain themselves with sports, with checkers, music, and conversation about the past and the present. Above all, the odor of sacrifices bathes the place in sanctity. Similar descriptions in a variety of writers, listing the attractions of the place favored by a divinity or of the place where the blessed dead assemble, testify to the widespread existence and the uniformity of the tradition. The emphasis is usually on the coolness and the protective shade of the refuge, on a pool or brook ringed with leafy trees, and aromatic with herbs and flowers. The residents of the sacred garden are often pictured in the process of celebrating and feasting. In comedy the enjoyment is of a distinctly material sort;[34] in other genres the pleasures are more spiritual. In all cases the holy grove invites the guest to share in the peace and the refreshment that the gods offer as their dearest gift.

The *topos* becomes especially popular in the *Greek Anthology*, where poem after poem is in the form of an invitation to a stranger to stop in the grove-precinct and take his ease.[35] Sometimes the grove is so thickly wooded that conflict is kept out by the massiveness of the greenery. In Callimachus *Hymn* 6, lines 25–29, the grove of Demeter at Dotium, where pines, elms, pears, and pomegranates encircle the spring, is said to be so dense that an arrow would pass through with difficulty. E. R. Curtius distinguishes between the grove and the pleasance, on the grounds, apparently, that the former has more the character of a forest, while the latter uses trees more sparingly. He further discusses the rise of the pleasance as an autonomous poetic form, and points to Petronius *Satyricon* 131, as the earliest example in Latin poetry,[36] an assertion which has not gone unopposed.[37] But these claim stakes are as hard to establish as to justify. Similar difficulties arise when we attempt to test Curtius' distinction between a pleasance and a grove on the grounds offered by him. Boccaccio's description of Elysium-Paradise, in *Olimpia*, lines 170–196, contains a wealth of the good things expected in such a place: clear light; various trees; flowers, streams, fruits; birds, goats, does, lambs, cattle, lions, griffins; sun, moon, stars; a good climate, without death or sickness; and, climactically, music. The scattering of blessing is so plentiful, and the role of trees so subordinate, that the question: grove or pleasance? becomes problematical. Much in Boccaccio's sacred place is modeled on Virgil's Elysium, in *Aeneid*, Book 6; though not nearly so densely populated, the abode of Anchises shares in the same roseate light, in the sun and the moon, the music, and the good cheer. Is Virgil's Elysium an early example of the pleasance, or the grove?

Fortunately neither the distinction between the two, nor the question of priority, is as crucial as another consideration which exercises a prior constraint: that the pastoral arbor cannot, properly speaking, be a precinct. As we have seen already, Theocritus' herdsmen lead entirely secular lives. They do not worship gods or perform sacrifices; the beauty of the landscape which surrounds them does not derive from divine grace, but is part of the natural world which guarantees their freedom. Ritual precincts appear in *Idylls* 25, lines 18–22; 26, lines 1–6; 18, lines 43–48; and in the epigrams, but not in the pastoral poems. If this were all, it would perhaps not be so very important, for a secular arbor and a divine arbor could, one might suppose, look very much alike. But the naturalness of Theocritus' bower carries with it a casualness that works against elaboration. Where ritual and the encomium of a god are at issue, the setting needs to be looked at carefully so as to make the properties worthy of the end; where the landscape is *merely* a setting, it does not need to draw attention to itself. Theocritus avoids the bravura stratagems that produced the opening prose of Sannazaro's *Arcadia*, or the description of the grove in Garcilaso's *Eclogue* 3, or Milton's Eden in *Paradise Lost*, Book 4.[38] These are cases of the *locus uberrimus*,[39] necessitated, I suspect, by the grandeur of the poetic designs into which they are fitted. The *uberrimus* appeals with its ripeness, its fullness, it luxuriant beauty; the *amoenus* tends to be composed of a few well-chosen details which suggest, rather than constitute, the liberating setting. Theocritus is the master of the *locus amoenus*; the *uberrimus* is too likely to engulf and absorb the swains, rather than set them free. Engulfment actually threatens in the one instance in which Theocritus chooses to avail himself of the *uberrimus*, at the end of *Idyll* 7:

> Cheerfully we stretched out on beddings of sweet
> Rushes and of the freshly cut vine leaves.
> Poplars and elms, tree upon tree, murmured
> Above our heads; the sacred water of the Nymphs

Was splashing downward from a cave nearby.
Tawny cicadas, on their shaded branches,
Were busy with their chirping; the tree frog
Was croaking on his distant perch in the thorns;
The larks and finches sang, the dove was sighing,
The yellow bees encircled the springs in flight.
There was a smell of harvest, of ripe fruits picking;
Pears in profusion rolled at our feet
And apples at our sides; branches hung down
Heavy, dark plums touching the ground.[40]

The picnic turns into a naturalist's orgy. With the tokens of fruitfulness and plenty liberally strewn around the feasters, nature is about to conquer man. But Theocritus extricates himself, in the nick of time. For as Simichidas and his friends drink the wine that might have put the finishing touch to their submersion, the speaker turns the wine over on his tongue, comments on its bouquet, and adds a mythological catalogue, ostensibly to ask whether any of the heroes named—Chiron, Heracles, Pholus, Polyphemus—ever tasted a wine as good as this, but more crucially to assert his standing as a man of taste, judgment, knowledge, a civilized man. The animal stupor is narrowly but decisively turned back; man's freedom is kept intact.

The experiment is singular; elsewhere in his pastorals, Theocritus avoids the temptation of allowing nature full play. Usually, as we have seen before, his scenery is lightly sketched in. This aspect of Theocritus' "dryness," his restraint in the matter of landscape, is not merely an economy in the distribution of furniture. One of the features of Theocritus' art is that he refuses to describe. Rapin is quite mistaken when he accuses Theocritus of descriptive prolixity: "In his First Idyllium [he] makes such a long immoderate description of his Cup, that Criticks find fault with him."[41] The cup is not a case of description at all, but, like the landscapes, a series of highly selective details put together for a purpose. Each of the panels—the old fisherman, the coy mistress, and the drowsy watchman—is given in its barest essentials;

together they remind us of the life of *ponos* which the herdsmen have left behind them, or so they think, though the poet knows better. By means of a few judiciously chosen figures and actions, the poet knows how to evoke a complex of ideas and a mood. Exactly the same is true of the natural scenes; save for the ending of *Idyll* 7, there is no fullness of description, no attempt to reproduce the streaks of the tulip. The genre sketch of *Idyll* 6, lines 10–12, of the dog barking at the edge of the surf, comes closest; the vivid portraiture of the *boukoliskos* in *Idyll* 20 is not by Theocritus. We discover more photography in Hylas' grove (*Idyll* 13.39 ff.) and in the positively Virgilian restoration-wish of the "Letter to Hieron" (*Idyll* 16.90 ff.) than in the pastoral proper. Generally speaking, extended description is more common in non-pastoral literature. The catalogue of trees which comes before the reunion of Odysseus with his father,[42] the lush pleasure garden of Calypso imitated by Apollonius in his *Argonautica*,[43] the fine topography in Dio Chrysostom's *Euboean Oration*,[44] the horticultural pyrotechnics of Achilles Tatius:[45] all show a willingness to linger over details at the expense of the drama and the human involvement.

As a rule, extended descriptions of landscapes in ancient literature occur in the form of enclaves, sealed capsules set aside from the larger action, to be enjoyed for their own sake. The effect usually comes close to that of *ecphrasis*, whereby an object described is made to look like a pictorial imitation of that object. The popularity of *ecphrasis*, from the scenes on Homer's "Shield of Achilles" on down, is indicative of the Greek reluctance to describe organic entities that fit into larger entities. An object whose contours are not easily definable is refashioned into a painting or a work of sculpture, and suspended, fixed and independent, within the larger whole.[46] This gets around the difficulty, especially acute in the case of landscapes, of doing justice to the subtle ties between the natural scene and the social action within and beyond it. The isolation of the natural from the social is especially noticeable when the whole poem is concerned with a landscape, as for instance Meleager's description of a country setting at springtime (*Anthol. Pal.* 9. 363). True, the poem places a herdsman or two in the field of vision, but they are merely the frills on a conception that has no business with human action or motivation.

Nevertheless, we must guard against the notion that the capsule treatment and *ecphrasis* stand for a desire to describe nature objectively, for its own attractions. The Greeks were not, so far as we can tell, interested in voicing a response to natural beauty. As a matter of fact, Meleager's poem has an ulterior purpose. The argument runs roughly as follows: seeing that plants and animals and men are having such a good time, should we not expect the poet also to honor spring by singing a beautiful song? In other words, the picture, despite the capsule format of its perceptions, leads beyond the segment of nature described; the response to nature becomes the premise for a moral inference. Quintilian (5.10.37; cf. also 3.7.27) has something to say about the rhetorical uses of *ecphrasis*. Even the "Shield of Achilles" is at its place in the *Iliad* less because the poet, and the readers with him, enjoy the spectacle of organic life and its cycles at work, though there is some of that. Rather, the sudden introduction of this life, by way of contrast with the stylized manners of heroic combat, encourages us to make inferences about Achilles' prospects and delusions, and about the claims of heroic society as a whole. The description of a larger nature, though kept meticulously distinct from the rest of the action, is not an end in itself.

Moreover, much of the *ecphrasis* of organic nature is as stylized as the environment into which it is put. The authors offer some lip-service but little actual commitment to the notion that it might be valuable to describe things precisely as they impinge upon the retina. The Hesiodic *Shield of Heracles*, taking up a hint from the "Shield of Achilles," repeatedly calls figures on the shield "life-like;" [47] but the author does not follow through to implement the promise contained in the announcement. Herodas, Theocritus' contemporary and the one writer of mimes whose work has come down to us, attempts a naturalistic picture of how the middle-class lives. But he does so, not by means of description, but rather by having the characters talk in a distinctive manner.[48] Neither Herodas nor anyone else in antiquity may properly be called a descriptive realist; and even if there was an approximation to realism, as in some pages of the Roman novel, it would not encompass the description of nature.

It was the romantics, from the Wartons and Rousseau and Saint-Lambert on, who created a misleading diversionary movement by demanding that pastoral present nature faithfully and clearly. They had their predecessors among the neoclassicists, such as Chetwood and Pope; and examples of descriptive realism may be found earlier in France and Spain.[49] The British made the description of the natural scene their own. James Thomson, Crabbe, and Allan Ramsay went to great pains to explore the continuities of the landscape. Ironically, Saint-Lambert objects to Thomson that the *Seasons* emphasizes nature at the expense of people. He himself, in his *Saisons*, attempts to weld men and nature into an integral whole of action and experience.[50] In the process, the description of nature is disrupted, and the patterning of pastoral, which is discontinuous, reemerges.

Ezra Pound, in *Make it New*, says: "Don't be descriptive; . . . when Shakespeare talks of the 'Dawn in russet mantle clad,' he presents something which the painter does not present. There is in this line of his nothing that one can call description; he presents." In his own way Johnson had meant the same thing with his warning against numbering the streaks of the tulip; and Aristotle's remarks about *mimesis* are generally understood to point in the same direction. These are remarks about poetry in general; Purney applies them to the pastoral: descriptions are wrong because they limit the reader's scope of imagination.[51]

This is good advice, though perhaps for the wrong reason. Certainly both Theocritus and Virgil avoid extended description. Among the several reasons for this restraint we should probably give the first place to the need for innocence. It will not do to have the poet display a power of sustained viewing for which the shepherd could not be expected to develop a taste. The lack of description is, therefore, connected with the very nature of the pastoral medium, its casualness, its lack of theme or thesis, its refusal to preach. This is an entirely different matter from the absence of description of scene in such "pastorals" as Tennyson's "Dora" and Wordsworth's "Michael." Both of these poems have a theme; they do not prize discontinuity. In their case, reticence is the function of a turning inward, a gaining of overtly spiritual dimensions which could only be disturbed by a stress on external nexus.[52]

It is commonly said that ancient landscapes tend to be gardens, that is, extensions of city culture, rather than the untouched wild. That the distinction between the two is difficult to maintain is shown by the beautiful confusion in Joseph Warton's "The Enthusiast," which sets out to contrast garden nature with wild nature:

> Can gilt alcoves, can marble-mimic gods,
> Parterres embroider'd, obelisks, and urns,
> Of high relief; can the long, spreading lake,
> Or vista lessening to the sight; can Stow,
> With all her Attic fanes, such raptures raise,
> As the thrush-haunted copse, where lightly leaps
> The fearful fawn . . . ?

He goes on to compare the natural scene to the forest where Numa and Egeria used to meet, watched over by Tiber:

> Old Tyber lean'd
> Attentive on his urn, and hush'd his waves.

Apparently without realizing it, Warton has crossed his own purposes by introducing the pretty conceits of a pastoral Versailles, complete with fountains and garden furniture, into the virgin

forest.[53] Marvell's *Mower* songs effect a more brilliant and a
more fruitful matching of garden with nature. Like Perdita
of *The Winter's Tale*, the poet of the *Mower* songs comes down
unambiguously on the side of Nature. This hatred for the garden,

> He first enclos'd within the Gardens square
> A dead and standing pool of Air. . . .

is not found in Theocritus. But this does not make Theocritus
into a garden poet. His landscape is neither a garden nor a forest,
neither a jungle nor a farm, but the only true pastoral habitat, a
pleasance. Because of this, the notorious conflict between Nature
and Art, without which the Renaissance pastoral is unthinkable,
has no standing in the Theocritean pastoral lyric.

Nor, on the other hand, could Theocritus avail himself of
Marvell's daring reversal whereby the hated garden comes to be
the setting for the mind's self-disciplining toward illumination
and goodness. The pastoral bower of Theocritus is not one of a
number of contrasting possibilities. It appears to be contiguous
with field and forest. This indeterminacy of locale is made
possible because the setting is not fraught with symbolic significance. The Greek landscape is setting, background, not trope;[54]
it shrugs off the moral interpretations that we find in the Christian
and Platonizing treatments of nature in the British pastoralists.
That is why Virgil can replace the Theocritean bower with
his silvan grove;[55] the result is a different poetic voice, but no
fatal jarring of the central idea. With some modifications, Virgil's
copse will do for the pastoral singer what Theocritus' more open
bower does for him. Neither author seeks to distinguish between
the natural and the contrived, except as utopia excludes the
hard work that the Hesiodic landscape carried with it. There is
no hardening of the setting into a prescribed canon of *topoi*,
the six "charms of landscape" which Curtius reports from
Tiberianus and Libanius.[56] At the same time we cannot, as
Empson does, dismiss the natural setting entirely.[57] Nature, in

the Alice books, is singularly unvital; soup tureens cannot replace bears and wolves, and Humpty-Dumpty's wall does not suggest a *locus amoenus*, not even a *locus conclusus*.

A rapid survey of plants in Theocritus shows that he mentions grasses and herbs, bushes and brambles, and a number of different kinds of trees.[58] Surprisingly, he has few flowers. What few flowers there are, are not cited for their colors; the plants exercise a magic which has nothing to do with their pigment. More important, he has none of the ornate catalogues of flowers which enliven, and sometimes stultify, later pastoral poetry. Suggestions of the catalogue of flowers do occur in Theocritus, Bion, and Virgil; and even before Theocritus enumerations of flowers and shrubs are not unknown.[59] Eupolis' comedy entitled *The Goats* (frag. 14) features a tidy list of the shrubs eaten by the goats. But all of these are brief, the merest hints of the possibilities that were to be realized later. The most celebrated ancient catalogue is that which gave the name to Meleager's "Garland" (*Anthol. Pal.* 4.1) in which, for the first time, flowers and herbs are used as emblems of the special qualities of individual writers.[60] During the Middle Ages, the flower catalogue is conspicuous by its absence. Nor does Petrarch come back to it. Sannazaro and Marot were the first moderns to revive what in antiquity had been a comparatively minor *topos*, and they gave it its character of pomp and circumstance.[61] Beginning with Spenser's Platonism and throughout their career in British letters, the flowers are used both for their sensuous charm and for their symbolic potential.[62] But the symbolism is in no way standardized. It is my impression that with few exceptions, any one flower or herb may have a variety of connotations and allegorical uses. Their display in the form of garlands and posies is at the discretion of the poets, for their sound, or for their *ad hoc* contribution selected from a large spectrum of meanings.[63]

But all this comes later. Theocritus has few flowers, fewer certainly than herbs and shrubs; his flora is *amoena* rather than *uberrima.* What is more, there is not the slightest hint of metaphor or allegory in the presence of the flowers that he offers. Roses and lilies and anemones are named because they are lovely, not because their moral or other associations help to establish a grid of values. The accumulation of several flowers into one paragraph, therefore, has the same effect as the accumulation of several proper names: the effect of the familiar and the pleasurable, and little else.[64] In the absence of a programmatic distinction between wild and tame, between forest and garden, the identity of the flower is less significant than its beauty. And the beauty is one of verbal texture, as much as of the recall of visual loveliness. The same is true of all the other elements of the pleasance: the trees, the herbage, the water courses. A pastoral pleasance is a setting which happens to be good and beautiful, and whose constituents are beautiful without prejudice to any other conceivable setting or combination of constituents. An emphasis on the special qualifications of certain flowers is likely to create pressures alien to the freedom of the grove.

The grove's main objective, as we have said, is liberation. It is a setting in which the singer, or the complainer, can move about without stubbing his toe or straining his voice against obstacles. The singer may be a poet or a philosopher. The pastoral pleasance is located on the same latitude as the grove of Orpheus and the valley of the Muses; seated in it the singer may, if he wishes, establish commerce with a divinity or with the animals. The isolation afforded by the *locus*—isolation, not solitude— permits the singer to devote himself to his task, and the thinker to concentrate on his deepest and most valuable thoughts.[65] Tacitus, an unexpected but welcome witness, confirms this: "The woods and groves and, altogether, the world of seclusion . . . bring me so much pleasure that I count it a principal benefit of poetry that it is not composed in the hubbub and ugliness of one's professional life. The mind withdraws into a place that is pure and innocent, and reaps the benefits of an unsullied abode."[66] Because the setting has little weight and complexity, the singer realizes his gifts without external resistance and, for that matter, without inhibitions or scruples.[67] The garden in which poetry is at home is of the same airiness as the cave where Hephaestus, unknown to others, creates his beautiful things for Thetis and Eurynome.[68] Petrarch (*De vita solitaria*, 1.5.2) praises the woods, fields, and streams as the best setting for contemplation, inspired composition, and peace of mind. In his essay he refers to Cicero, Virgil, Plato, and Cyprian as recommending the same. Boccaccio likewise (*Genealogy*, Book 14, chapter 11) pictures the poets as seeking lonely spots to do their composing; this gives him a chance to describe the *locus amoenus*, more fully than the ancient models—he includes trees, grass, flowers, fountains, songbirds, breezes, playful animals—but evidently intending to exclude what might prove distracting.[69] Philosophical biography is replete with notices that philosophers like to converse in the open country or in gardens.[70]

The Coans, we learn from Hermesianax, set up a bronze statue of Philitas, singing of his Bittis, under a plane tree.[71] Thus at least one poet came to be fixed in his grove, more particularly under the one tree which affords much shade and tends to be located close to a source of water. The motif of the philosopher-poet reclining, in imitation of the Socrates of the *Phaedrus*, under a plane tree is found in many quarters.[72] In these instances, as in the pastoral, the tree is a refresher, a liberator, but still little more than an appealing backdrop. By way of contrast, it is useful to consider Arnold's "Thyrsis," one of the few more recent successful pastoral poems, in which the elm tree is of an entirely different order, as indeed the whole landscape is. It has become unique, experienced, identifiable, conveying a specific, non-repeatable mood and atmosphere; a focus for memory, for sense of loss, and consolation. The main stimulus for this new way of handling a tree is perhaps provided by the elm of Thyrsis in Milton's "Epitaphium Damonis," line 20; but it takes Arnold's special combination of melancholy and pride of place to complete the change.

From here it is only a short step to the point where the poem and the setting in which it is composed are identified. This happens, for instance, at the beginning of Keats' "Endymion;" the concepts of bower, flowery band, beauty, and poetry itself are synthesized into a larger unit that absorbs them all. Antiquity is not unfamiliar with this venture. Statius' *Silvae* are poems; and some of the Hellenistic poets worked out a system of style symbols, using plants and shrubs to denote special qualities of poems. The oak, according to this system, stand for grandeur, while a stalk of grain stands for the *tenue poema*.[73] Meleager's *Garland*, in which each poet is designated by means of a flower or a plant symbol, has already been mentioned. It is worth repeating, however, that Meleager's practice does not seem to reflect a fixed pattern of associations, such as underlies the plant symbols in Callimachus. This is not surprising; Meleager's demand for specimens far exceeded the supply that any standard system, especially one of recent canonization, could have furnished.[74] At any rate, there is little of this in pastoral; Theocritus makes no distinction between the mighty oak and the tender stalk, between poplars and clover; any combination of plants, as long as it is economical and does not inhibit the exercise of pastoral concerns, will do. The reason is, again, the recalcitrance of the pastoral *topoi* to take on symbolic meanings. The association of plant types with types of writing is an enterprise which could have started only outside of the pastoral sphere. The flora of the pleasance is remarkably catholic. Weeds and brambles are avoided, unless they are introduced in connection with reminders of *ponos*. But such exclusions are minor, and unprogrammatic. Keats' identification of the grove with poetry does not come easily to the pastoral poet. The exclusiveness of the pastoral poem, in diction, versification, theme, and mood, is hardly commensurate with the catholicity of its flora. There are a few occasions in Virgil's *Eclogues* when *avena*, the oaten reed, and *calamus*, the reed, appear to turn into symbols of the pastoral craft, especially since *calamus* may also be understood to refer to the poet's pen. It is my feeling, however, that Virgil would not want to have these hints exaggerated. He is clearly aware of the Callimachean tradition of plant symbolism, and teases his listeners with its echoes. But on the whole he seems to shy away from the density of the artifice. In this he follows Theocritus, who led the way by keeping the pastoral free of suggestive syntheses. In the *Idylls*, the pleasance is a place *in which* songs are sung; that is all.

The philosopher-singer is not the only one who is at home in the grove; so is the lover. In the *Spiritual Canticle* of St. John of the Cross, the verdage is planted by the lover;[75] in *Iliad*, Book 14, we watch with amazement as the love of Zeus and Hera by virtue of its divine magic makes a grove spring up (346 ff.):

> The son of Cronus caught his wife in his arms,
> And from below the glorious earth broke into fresh grass,
> And the dewey lotus and crocus and hyacinth,
> Thick and soft, held them aloft, away from the ground.[76]

Homer, like most poets, likes to see love supported by a *locus amoenus*. The fashion can become too obvious; in Plutarch's *Amatorius* (749A) Flavianus asks Autobulus, who is about to talk about Eros, to strip his account of pastoral embellishments: "Leave out . . . the greenswards and the shades, and the runners of ivy and smilax and all the other things stolen from Plato: his Ilissus and the plane tree and the gently sloping bank of grass, *topoi* which indicate zeal rather than discretion."[77] Pastoral vegetation both accommodates and conceals love. Scaliger thought that the herdsmen made love one of their chief occupations because of their leisure, their scanty dress, their healthy and plentiful food, their youthfulness, and their proximity to animals.[78] Roman poetry is full of appeals to girls to join the lover in the country, in the sight of goats nibbling at the shrubs, and without fear of snakes and wolves.[79] Shakespeare's romantic comedies usually profit from a rustic setting, "under the greenwood tree;" the tragedies are located in castles or cities. The country, in Elizabethan drama, is the home of the insignificant, or of the refreshing and vital. In a non-pastoral context the *locus amoenus* may become a trap; this is shown by Theocritus himself, in two epyllia. Hylas is undone in a place which has all the marks of a pleasance (*Idyll* 13.39); and Pollux experiences great danger when Amycus confronts him, against the lovely backdrop of a fresh spring and a plot of grass (*Idyll* 22.37). In the pastoral, on the other hand, the charms of the grove normally ensure a full savoring of love, even if it is disappointed or abortive love.

There are, however, two ways in which frustrated love can affect the conception of the landscape; both of them are, in origin at least, humorous. For one thing, the *locus amoenus* may turn into a *locus inclusus*. In *Idyll* 3 the lover stands outside of it; to get to Amaryllis, the goatherd would have to be, he imagines, a bee. In *Idyll* 11, conversely, the Cyclops *owns* the cave, and cannot, figuratively speaking, get out of it to reach his girl. In spite of the fine vegetation festooned around the cave, the laurel, cypresses, ivy, and vines, Polyphemus' insistence on the enclosed space rather than an open bower tells against his success from the start. This nice distinction between the open pleasance and the enclosed cave was not to have much of a history. The Roman grotto and the Renaissance cavern came to be thought of as worthy seats of elegant living. Thereafter it was more difficult to distinguish between the grove and the cave for purposes of love.

The other modification of the natural environment was, however, of great historical consequence. This is the sorry literary convention of scratching erotic sentiments into the bark of a tree. It stands to reason that the pastoral had nothing to do with its inception. After all, as we have stressed repeatedly, the swain respects the rights of the world around him; just as he cannot, in the full sense of the word, use his animal friends, so he should not be able to tamper with the franchise of the flora. To mar the bark is to demote the tree to a subordinate standing, aesthetically and socially. The first occurrence of the motif is, as one might have expected, in Callimachus; Acontius complains to beeches and elms and vents his despair on them by cutting the name of Cydippe into their bark.[80] Theocritus does not adopt the conceit for his pastorals; Virgil does (*Eclogue* 5.13–14); Calpurnius follows Virgil's example (*Eclogue* 1.34–35); and with this the pretty vulgarism was off to a galloping start that was to influence all of subsequent pastoral poetry. Apparently the idea of bespeaking permanence by a rustic mimicry of archival recording was too enticing to be resisted by poets anxious to endure. In the end there were hardly enough trees to accommodate the dolorous or resigned messages gouged into them. The rapprochement of pastoral romance and epistolary novel encouraged the fad further. Nothing could be clearer evidence of the loss of purity, and plain confusion, which befell the pastoral soon after its foundation by Theocritus than this self-defeating attack upon the surface of trees. The pastoral pleasance exists to be enjoyed, to give protection, to furnish a solid background for the activities of the herdsmen. Virgil's easy adoption of Callimachus' mannerism is a straw in the wind; with the defacing of the arbor's texture, the tradition of the pastoral lyric was about to enter upon a new phase.

Appendix

Theocritus' use of adjectives provides additional information about his stand vis-à-vis the description of external reality. If we divide adjectival attribution in the *Idylls* into four major types, we find the following: (1) defining or value-giving adjectives, example: *empty* kisses (*Idyll* 3.20); (2) descriptive or specific adjectives, example: *black-browed* girl (*Idyll* 3.18); (3) analytic or generic adjectives, example: *heart-rending* pain (*Idyll* 3.12); (4) decorative adjectives, example: *sweet* voice (*Idyll* 1.65). We may further isolate two sub-groups: (2a) affective adjectives, example: *disagreeable* fellow (*Idyll* 5.40); and (3a) divine cognomina and geographical adjectives, example: *headland* Pan (*Idyll* 5.14). A rough compilation of all adjectival uses in the *Idylls* produces the following results. Words of group (2) are rarely used, except of persons and animals; groups (3) and (4) are more common. As against what is found in the epic, the adjectives of group (4) in the *Idylls* are always simple words. Group (1) is not really pertinent; this use of the adjective is closer to the predicative than to the attributive.

The conclusion is that Theocritus does not favor the type of adjective that would be most helpful to one who wished to describe the world around him. Three contexts prompt the use of significant adjectival modifiers: (a) the description of *objets d'art*; (b) addresses to specific persons; and (c) the definition of feelings and sensations. In the case of (a), the adjectives used are usually sophisticated; example: *deep, double-handled, freshly-made* bowl

(*Idyll* 1.27–28). In the cases of (b) and (c), they tend to be much simpler. For the rest, the employment of adjectives is remarkably sparing; where adjectives occur, they are mostly at a low level of semantic contribution, on the order of *sloping* hill (*Idyll* 1.13), *bitter* bile (*Idyll* 1.18), *sweet* fig (*Idyll* 1.147). The most common adjectives are: sweet, charming, beautiful, ugly, bitter, large, small, little. Water is either *hieron*, an epic term which is best reproduced by *pure*, or *kalon* which signals an unfocused hedonist response. All in all, both the comparative restraint in the use of adjectives, and their low level of sophistication, are reliable indices of Theocritus' lack of interest in elaborating the setting by means of descriptive variety. We may compare Josephine Miles' findings for Milton; she stresses Milton's role in introducing the eighteenth century to the efficacy of certain simple adjectives, such as "fresh, high, pure, sacred, new."[81] For Milton, this is only one side of the picture; we cannot overlook the kind of violence represented by his "blind mouths," a violence which is only slightly tempered by the knowledge that it has its roots in the Gospel according to St. John, and that it refers to poets as much as to bishops. But such "mystic oxymora," to use Kenneth Burke's famous phrase, have no place in Theocritus' pastoral. More important yet, the *Idylls* eschew color terms; Milton's "mantle blue" and Marvell's extravaganza of white, red, and green in stanza 3 of "The Garden" have no equal in Theocritus' unpainterly verse. The only color that appears with any frequency is white; green occurs twice in the *Idylls*, though it is not uncommon elsewhere in the Theocritean corpus. As a pastoralist, Theocritus prefers the non-specific "light," "shiny," and "dark."

10
Anatomy

In the course of our discussion we have noted already that Theocritus has remarkably little "praise of the country," a *topos* which is rare in Greek literature anyway.[1] Ruskin thought he could explain why the Greeks were insensitive to the beauties of nature, but his account is no longer acceptable.[2] Certainly beginning in the fifth century BC, if not earlier,[3] writers respond to the beauties of the world around them. But even so splendid an encomium of the country as the first choral ode of Sophocles' *Oedipus at Colonus* is less in praise of the countryside than of the political community of larger Athens, with many—largely rural—attractions. I think it is safe to say that there is more overt appreciation of the charms of flowers, fields and streams in choral songs and philosophical discourses dedicated to the praise of a city or a political idea, than there is in early pastoral poetry. Encomia traditionally tabulate the good points of the object of praise; pastoral is under no such obligation.

Praise is a type of argument, and presupposes a thesis, and perhaps an antithesis.

> Dear countryside, when shall I see you, to read
> The books of the ancients, and to doze and nod
> And tend the fruits of sweet forgetfulness. . . .[4]

Horace's *Satires* 2.6, from which this is taken (lines 60–62), terminates with the tale of the country mouse and the city mouse.

The few pastoral touches in the poem are merely starting points for the bulk of the performance, which is argumentative, philosophical. The characters are aware of the contrast between city and country, and their praise of the country[5] gets its credentials from an explicit condemnation of the city, or rather of that segment of the city which cannot be built into a larger country scene. Marvell's "Upon Appleton House," to take one of a number of seventeenth-century poems modeled on the *Epistles*, shares in the same perspective (though there is, of course, a great deal else, not the least the tentative identification of house and man[6]); and it is a mistake to regard the poem as in any important sense primarily a pastoral.[7] Fairfax's house is celebrated in a variety of ways; but it is always the unity of house and country, of privileged culture and rustic strength, of the artful and the living, that matters. The spirit is Pindaric rather than Theocritean; the encomium feeds on synthesis and comprehensiveness, on restoring a sense of the whole, of a total nature, that is in danger of being lost.

There is a greater temptation, however, to seek the pastoral in the more partisan enterprise of inveighing against urban narrowness. Outbursts against the city are as old as the city itself. From Juvenal to Mantuan[8] and Goldsmith,[9] the vices of the city have formed a ready subject for poets in the primitivist camp. It is commonly felt that pastoral, also, obtains some of its effects by playing the country against the city, and exploiting the tension between them.[10] To emphasize pastoral or rural happiness by placing the *locus amoenus* against a foil of court luxury or city misery is a technique that has appealed to many. Thomas Campion's *Pastorals* illustrate the point, and W. H. Auden continues the tradition:

And not even man can spoil you: his company
Coarsens roses and dogs but, should he herd you through a sluice
   To toil at a turbine, or keep you
  Leaping in gardens for his amusement,

Innocent still is your outcry, water, and there
Even, to his soiled heart raging at what it is,
   Tells of a sort of world, quite other,
  Altogether different from this one
With its envies and passports, a polis. . . .[11]

The tone is that of the stump-orator, halting and angular; the same is true of countless other praises of the country which are really harangues against the city. More often than not, the city vice castigated is greed; this is particularly common in the Roman examples and those based on them.[12]

If we look at the Roman pastoral that followed Virgil's, Calpurnius' *Eclogues* derive much of their charm from the poet's evident concern to balance town and country, the world of culture and the world of peace and goodness. The prophecy of Faunus in *Eclogue* 1 cut into the bark of a beech tree, constituting as it does a political prognostication, proposes to make the life of the city manageable within the *otium* of the bower. The accommodation is facilitated by Calpurnius' desire to introduce his own relationship to his patron, that is, the social and personal grounds of his writing, into the argument of the poem. We need not hesitate to regard this as a specifically Virgilian development; its beginnings are most obvious in Virgil's *Eclogues* 1 and 9. Virgil too plays the city against the country, but with a degree of sophistication which suggests that he is amusing himself at the expense of the shortcomings of a simpler approach, namely, the soap-box oratory according to which the city is all bad and the country all good. That simpler outlook is found in its purest state in Old Comedy. Aristophanes has a number of passages, especially in the *Acharnians*, that may be read as a pastoral protest against the unnaturalness and the coercions of the city.[13]

Still, one must be careful about this. In the *Birds* (lines 120 ff.), the villain heroes run from the city to find a *city* where they will get their chance to be idle, put on soft woolen cloaks, and stretch themselves on the ground. Momentarily, it appears, the polemic

against the city turns into a hope for a better city. Similarly, in a
fragment ascribed to Aristophanes,[14] the praise of the country
versus the city is formulated as follows: the country offers the
ownership of a yoke of cattle, it permits a man to listen to the
bleating of sheep and to the straining of lees; above all, the
country offers a simple but delicate cuisine, instead of the stale
but expensive fish which is the city diet. Here we have the wish-
dream of a man who is fed up with the sordid realities of the
marketplace, with three-day-old fish and cheating merchants;
he wants to have his own farm and his own team of oxen and
his own *fresh* food. But there is nothing pastoral about this;
note the emphasis on work, on ownership, and on gross physical
satisfactions. The ideal is Cynic rather than Epicurean. This is
characteristic; Aristophanic man, even in his dreams, is a small
entrepreneur; the domestic economy is important to his purposes,
if only to flout it for a little while. Deep down, therefore, Aristophanes does not treat city and country as natural enemies;
given the Attic realities of the time, the contrast would not have
made any sense. Throughout Old Comedy, city and country are
linked by mutual bonds of resentment and affection that defy
the broad separations of later polemics.[15] The same is true elsewhere in classical Greek poetry. Pindar's fourth *Paean*, for
instance, written for the Ceans, has them sing of their land: it is
simple, without the wealth of other places, but they love it and
have no desire for greater pastures elsewhere. In all these passages,
what appears at first glance to be a protest against the city turns
out to be a condemnation of certain types of city, but a continued
approval of the Greek political life which combines city and
country in a viable and attractive mixture.

Before we raise the question of the extent to which protest
against the city forms an element in Theocritus' poetry, we should
say a word or two about satire. According to Schiller, whose
reflections on this head are still worth considering, the "sentimentalische" poet is either satirical or elegiac, depending on

his attitude toward reality.[16] That is to say, Schiller, like most other critics of pastoral poetry, expects the poet to incorporate his feelings about the city within the poem, and supposes the feelings to be either resigned (elegiac) or aggressive (satire), with the aggressiveness again stipulated to be of two sorts, either lighthearted or punitive. The modern European tradition bears Schiller out; five of Spenser's twelve eclogues are "moral" eclogues, dealing with public issues in a manner so as to advertise the poet's feelings about the issues. The stance can be made to look like impartiality; Perdita's response to Polixenes' threats (*The Winter's Tale*, 4.4) is judicious and non-partisan:

> I was not much afeard; for once or twice
> I was about to speak, and tell him plainly
> The self-same sun that shines upon his court
> Hides not his visage from our cottage, but
> Looks on alike.

But actually from this studious posture of neutrality to satire is only a short step, and one that was taken with gusto in Renaissance pastoral.[17] Soon the city is epitomized into a constellation of sins, each of which may find its way into the catalogue of misdemeanors denounced in the pastoral. Samuel Daniel (*The Queen's Arcadia*, 3.1)[18] has a brilliant caricature of smoking, which is worth quoting for its own sake, and to show how far afield Renaissance pastoral could go in the tracking of what might conflict with the virtues of the bower:

> For whereas heretofore they wonted were,
> At all their meetings, and their festivals,
> To pass the time in telling witty tales,
> In questions, riddles, and in purposes,
> Now doe they nothing else but sit and sucke,
> And spit and slaver, all the time they sit;
> That I go by, and laugh unto my selfe. . . .
> That men of sense could ever be so mad,
> To sucke so grosse a vapour, that consumes

> Their spirits, and spends nature, dries up memorie,
> Corrupts the blood, and is a vanitie.

The onomatopoeia of heaped sibilants gives a special edge to this fine attack; but where, one may ask, are Virgil's gentle liquidities?

Petrarch, Mantuan, Spenser (*Eclogues* 5, 7, 9) and many others write satirical pastoral. Some, among them Ben Jonson, turned from satire to pastoral with little change of emphasis; his *Sad Shepherd* continues to berate the new urbanization and commercialization of the age; the Robin Hood legend is put to a moralizing use.[19] Even Michael Drayton, who wrote pretty good satires himself, and attempted to drown out the negative voice by concentrating on pastorals, cannot resist entirely the urge to express his dislike for "Felicia," as the world of urban man is ironically called by him; and the fourth "Nimphall" of his *Muses Elizium* is unadulterated Juvenalian satire.[20]

These Renaissance pastoralists paved the way for Milton's treatment of the church in "Lycidas."[21] In that poem, the condemnation of the church provides the center of gravity and the emotional heart of the dirge. By allying the listener with himself in a protest against forces which, it is suggested, were inimical to King, the anonymity of the poem, its airiness and detachment, are undercut, and the elegy takes on some of the qualities of a moral pamphlet. The question is: does such a procedure not impair elements which in a pastoral lyric deserve to remain intact? There is something self-defeating about an attempt to set up a pastoral world in which all vile and mundane passions are stilled, only to turn around and give vent to massive indignation, a sentiment perilously close to resentment and anger, two passions linked with the very city which is, *ex hypothesi*, excluded from the pleasance.

Horace, as well as Drayton and others, saw the absurdity of it. His *Epode* 2 is a successful demonstration of the nonsensical status of a moral posture in a primitivist idyll. The poem praises life and work in the country; the usual proofs are mentioned: simple food, useful labor, happy family relations, and so forth. The picture is almost too sweet, but the listener is sucked into the trap and goes along with the spun sugar, until at the very end he is rudely awakened: unexpectedly the poem turns out to have been in direct speech, and the speaker has been, not a merry farmer, but the usurer Alfius, about to choke off his debtors and invest his capital anew (cf. above, Chapter Eight). Horace's point is obvious; the closer a picture of the country comes to being a sermon, an act of advocacy, the less authentic it is as an appraisal of what the country has to offer. *In culpa est animus*, as he puts it in one of his comparisons of city and country (*Epistles* 1.14.13): the fault is with the disposition, not the place. A man always wants what he does not have; a desire for the country that is based on the rejection of the city promises to be as deceptive as the reverse.[22]

There is another point that needs to be made. When pastoral is used for the purposes of satire, or even when it pauses to indulge in a temporary contrasting of country and city, the natural life that is set against the vices of the city tends to be Hesiodic rather than strictly pastoral. Hesiod is the prototype of the writer who protests against an order which he thinks interferes with the rights and the norms of the village culture. The more strongly the writer condemns the sins of the enemy, the greater is his obligation to describe the society he favors in colors which suggest social responsibility, moral health, and economic vigor—all elements with which the pastoral has no truck. One Renaissance pastoralist who took up the satirist's rapier drew the only proper conclusion finally available to him.[23] A woodsman relates how he tried the Court, and then the City, and then the Country, and found them all to be full of falsehood and cabal. Finally he returns to the woods where he lives alone and contented. The moral fervor and the precedence of logic over gentleness anticipate Wordsworth and Emerson.

The result is, in the end, not pastoral but a form of mystic hymn, an anchorite's confession of sin and redemption.

Theocritus has his own criticism of the evils of commercialization and the dangers of the city; but characteristically the passage occurs, not in a pastoral idyll, but in his "Letter to Hieron" (*Idyll* 16.13). The reproach is Pindaric: no one wants to listen to poets, because no one wants to pay them; they are the victims of their own love of profit. There is nothing like this in the pastorals, not only because there Theocritus keeps reflections about his own station in life out of the picture, but also because the idea of the pastoral evidently excludes the discussion of public issues. The contrast between city and country is such an issue, better taken up in a Cynic diatribe or in a Menippean satire than in the genre given over to the direct communication of the feelings of simple men for whom the pleasance constitutes a world. Looking beyond the bower is beyond the abilities of the pastoral characters, though it may be the poet's privilege. Theocritus presents himself with a number of opportunities for animadverting on the disadvantages of life on the other side; but he drops the opportunities without further ado. He does not avoid reminders of suffering and injustice, as we saw earlier; but they are edged in pictorially, not analyzed or defined. Like the Epicurean saint who lives only for himself and his pleasure, and therefore spurns offices and functions in the larger world without making an issue of it,[24] the Theocritean herdsman refuses even to consider the possibilities of living elsewhere but in his bower. That is part of his simplicity; that is also why, as we noted above, so little attention is paid to the description of the bower. It is a *donnée*; its significance is not subject to discussion.

This gets us back to the point with which we started, the marked difference between Theocritus, on the one hand, and Roman pastoral, notably Virgil, on the other.

To think, Menalcas,
Of you, and all our solace, almost gone![25]

With the elimination of Menalcas, the herdsman would have lost also the flowers on the ground and the shade over the spring. Natural beauty is placed under the control of the poet, who is himself at the whim of the political world. In Theocritus, politics is at best marginal, conveyed via images and passing references that allow small glimpses of the realities ringing the bower. In Virgil, politics is the ever-present condition without which the pastoral fiction could not last. In *Eclogue* 1, the city and the country are compared and dovetailed in a series of subtle and, I fear, obscure manipulations. This is possible only because the bower has ceased to be the habitat of the herdsmen and has turned into the dream of the poet, a dream pressured by the constant query how the city, and the new covenant, measure up against a rustic simplicity that is largely lost. Virgil's pastoral is written in the comparative mode; the comparison affects even the amoebean machinery, so that the contest, which in Theocritus is one of smallish stimulus responses, turns into a matching of ideas, political and moral. The hedonist nonchalance, the paratactic buoyancy of the Theocritean idyll are left behind, and the pastoral starts on its journey toward an amalgamation with various kinds of anatomy, from Jonson's satire to Crabbe's manifesto, and finally to Rousseau's sustained onslaught on all social ills. In the end it became difficult to appreciate fully that it had once been possible to write pastoral that contained no measure of satire or argument, and which was, notwithstanding this lack, a poetic achievement of the first rank. In Theocritus, the absence of anatomy is not felt as a lack; on the contrary, the completeness of the artistry is sufficient proof of the irrelevance of what the poet chooses to leave out.

❧ ❧ ❧ ❧

The contrasting of country and city has a close parallel in what is conveniently termed Golden Age nostalgia. Virgil's fourth *Eclogue* is responsible for the critical commonplace that the theme of a distant golden age, placed either in the dim past or in an unascertained future, is appropriate to the bower, and may therefore be expected to play its part in a bucolic poem. The author of the *Aetna*, which has often been ascribed to Virgil but is now generally dated later, refers to the theme of the Golden Age as a standard *topos* in poetry, one of the many threadbare topics he is going to pass over as he tackles his unusual task. This is somewhat surprising; Ovid's "Five Generations," and certain other passages in the Augustans,[26] show the Golden Age to have been a readily accessible theme. But its use in the generation of Virgil and the generation immediately following is not so widespread as to suggest a literary bromide. In point of fact, on those occasions when the Augustans launch into Golden Age nostalgia, the procedure is often tortuous. In Tibullus, for instance, there is a surprising combination of nostalgia and revulsion: I long for the days, he says, of simplicity and free love, when people dressed their hairiness in stinking skins.[27] This aesthete's primitivism is an elaborate joke; it is what might be expected from a city dweller whose longing for an unalloyed simplicity is genuine but reluctant. Propertius constructs his Golden Age vision from elements which go back to the Neoterics, who shied away from the avowal of any passion that was obvious.[28] Finally, Virgil's own variation on the theme is an exercise in incompatibles; we shall return to that.

Golden Age nostalgia exists long before Theocritus. It is, in essence, an aristocratic scheme contrived when new political and social developments threatened to destroy the influence of the noble lords, and caused them to look back with longing to a remembered glory. In classical Greek literature, it is always directed to the past; the future dimension is not introduced until the cyclic theories of the historian-philosophers combined with the Messianic hopes of the East to produce an entirely different kind of yearning. Classical Golden Age nostalgia stresses an agricultural and ranching automatism; the Messianism of the later period stresses social utopia rather than economics, and paradox rather than automation. Hesiod set the tone with his "First Generation," the golden *genos* to which he gave the name. It is interesting to watch how the Boeotian peasant's son struggles to retain the aristocratic features of a myth which for him has considerably less meaning than the expectation of Zeus' victory in the distant future:

> All things were noble
> For them. The donor earth produced her fruit
> Unforced, rich and unstinting. They went after their tasks
> At leisure, freely, with many noble companions.
> Blessed with flocks, they walked with the mighty gods.[29]

Hesiod's Golden Age paradise is simple; he does not batter our senses with a picture of overripeness and Oriental felicity. There is, however, another version of the myth that underlines the theme of *plerōsis* and epiphany: the god appears, and the land flows with milk and honey. One example of many may serve; this is a fragment from a Pindaric *Maiden-Song*, in which Apollo is said to have appeared on earth and to have caused nature to give of herself freely to all:

> From all the flocks a gushing jet
> Like sturdy water from the well,
> The milk of ewes.
> The men rushed forth and filled their pails;
> Not a flask nor barrel took the day off,
> All buckets and pails were gorged to fill. . . .[30]

The epiphany of the god produces miraculous dislocations of natural law. Hesiod's Golden Age has no miracles, no *adynata* (impossibles), only realizations of hopes which can hardly be said to tax the imagination. It is the combination of Golden Age nostalgia with the theme of divine *plerōsis* which, along with touches of Oriental luxury, introduces the tradition of the impossibles: the oak that drips honey, the animal skins that

come in technicolor hues, the lion that beds with the lamb.[31]
Once we detach the paradisiac plenty from the distant age, and
generalize it on a foreign shore, we find ourselves in Cockaigne
or Schlaraffia, the comic land where fried geese fly of their own
volition into the perennially open jaws of gourmands with
unbreakable digestions. The Schlaraffia theme is pervasive in the
brute utopia of Old Comedy;[32] Eupolis' *Golden Age* probably
featured it in abundance.

In popular thought, then, Golden Age longing was a significant
factor. In the school philosophies of the Hellenistic age, however,
this type of thinking was not greatly in favor. Neither Stoicism
nor Epicureanism avails itself of its services, even though Stoicism, at least, was keen to utilize popular legends to broadcast its
message. Lucretius' description (5.1379 ff.) of man's early estate is
a construction working backwards from present achievements,
and has little to do with the traditional longing for the good
old days. His early man knows no surplus, much less automation.
To be sure, he is vigorous and even happy—to this extent the
wish-dream asserts itself—but his strength and well-being are a
function of his *autarkeia*, of his ability to manage with the little
that nature has always freely offered, and to wish for nothing
more. Nevertheless Lucretius in his turn furthered the notion
of a natural connection between pastoral and Golden Age, for
his picture of early man has affinities with the pastoral bower:

> That was the age of jests, of talk, of much sweet laughter,
> The age when the Muse of the countryside held sway.[33]

The jests, the happy discourse of the men who need little and
have all they need, are said to be inspired by the *agrestis musa*;
Lucretius adds that it was at this stage that men learned to make
music and to sing. Lucretius' analysis of the situation of early
man looks, in many ways, like a projection back into time of the
behavior witnessed in pastoral poetry, where innocence, *autarkeia*,
and musical spontaneity are similarly interdependent. It is a

plausible conjecture that Lucretius regarded the herdsmen of Theocritus and his successors as projections forward, into timelessness, of conditions which, according to his Epicurean models, prevailed at the beginning of civilized life.

Lucretius is not the only Epicurean, or the only philosopher, who placed aboriginal man in a setting of comparative hardship. Democritus, Epicurus' spiritual forerunner, was the first to construct a graduated succession of the stages of human development, from the plight of primitive savagery to the dishonesties of the corrupt present. One of his later imitators varies the picture somewhat in the direction of a gentler primitivism, and describes the life of early men as "simple and adequate and humane . . .; they had no kings or magistrates or tyrants, or armies, or acts of compulsion or forcible removal; the life they knew was distinguished by love of fellow men, freedom, and lack of luxury."[34] Later, the same author continues, with the invention of fire came softness and pleasure and indulgence. We have already mentioned Plato's fiction of the small groups left alive at the conclusion of each cosmic destruction. They have nothing left but a great deal of land and a few head of cattle and some goats (*Laws* 677E8–10). They have no tools, and no metallurgy; hence they know no war. They love one another, and do not have to fight for their food. There is no scarcity of pasture; they do not lack milk or meat. They practice hunting and the simple crafts of pottery and weaving for which no metal implements are needed. They are neither rich nor poor; their experience does not include hubris, or injustice, or resentment, or envy, or lying. Their social order is *dynasteia*, the absolute rule of the head of the household, as in the land of Homer's Cyclopes. Plato puts all this (678E2–680C1) into the past tense; though these beginners reemerge every time a great year begins anew, from the vantage point of the time in which we live, the age is best described as lying in the past, thousands of years ago. Some of the features outlined, especially the eating of meat and the patriarchal

organization, do not apply to the pastoral. But there is enough
that is similar to reinforce the assumption that the pastoral
bower is a revival of Golden Age hopes, and that yearning for the
Golden Age is itself a proper feature of pastoral writing.

The philosopher whose developmental scheme became the
most influential is Dicaearchus, the student of Aristotle.[35] As I
mentioned earlier (Chapter Four), Dicaearchus had men move
through three successive stages: the natural life, the pastoral
life, and the agrarian life. The first is the happiest; the second, the
vita pastoricia, represents a considerable decline: men undertook
to hunt down and domesticate wild animals, for the purpose of
having enough meat. Violence, the profit instinct, and the eating
and exploiting of beasts are the special features of this age,
which is morally inferior even to the age which succeeds it.
If now we look back at the characterization of early man in
Lucretius, we see that it is of the same sort. Logically speaking,
the naiveté and the self-sufficiency prized by the philosophers
and the pastoral poets cannot be realized on a level of development that also features the acquisition and distribution of herds
of animals. A Hellenistic pastoral poet, it seems, would have
considerable difficulty convincing his listeners that the pastoral
life and the Golden Age are one. Nor, on the other hand, could
one fairly expect him to present herdsmen yearning for a Golden
Age that is different from the pleasance in which they live.

Perhaps the pastoral ethos is closer to the less schematic arrangement of Dicaearchus' teacher, Aristotle, who in the *Politics*
unfolds a picture of lives.[36]

In the lives of men there is a great difference. The laziest are shepherds,
who lead an idle life, and get their subsistence without trouble from
tame animals; their flocks having to wander from place to place in
search of pasture, they are compelled to follow them, cultivating a
sort of living farm. Others support themselves by hunting, which is of
different kinds. Some, for example, are brigands, others, who dwell
near lakes or marshes or rivers or a sea in which there are fish, are

fishermen, and others live by the pursuit of birds or wild beasts. The
greater number obtain a living from the cultivated fruits of the soil.
Such are the modes of subsistence which prevail among those whose
industry springs up of itself, and whose food is not acquired by exchange and retail trade—there is the shepherd, the husbandman, the
brigand, the fisherman, the hunter.

All this is part of a chapter concerned with the art of acquiring
food. One surprising thing that jumps to the eye is that Aristotle's
order—the first arrangement, that is; not the scrambling in the
summary—is reflected in the pastoral scale of values. At the heart
of the bucolic poem, with the highest value attached to him,
there stands, or rather reclines, the idlest of the food-gatherers,
the herdsman. As we move out to the periphery, we pass fishermen, hunters, and farmers, akin to the herdsmen in the simplicity
of their lives, but not equally adjusted to the peace of the bower.

Aristotle's account differs from those of Democritus and
Lucretius and Dicaearchus in that it is concerned, not with
ages, but with lives or professions. Instead of historical reconstruction, he furnishes a typology of occupations and values. His
investigation is pragmatic rather than utopian; the Golden Age
has no place in his considerations. For this reason his ideas have
much greater relevance to the thinking that lies behind the
pastoral vision. The pastoral is not concerned with history, or the
sequence of evolutionary stages. Its time is here and now; its
attention is to what is best in man, not to what he can do at
one time or another. The mode of temporal discrimination sits ill
with the simplicity of the bower. Reminders or predictions of a
Golden Age, an age, that is, which contrasts with the present,
should be the concern of satire, or comedy, rather than of a
genre which filters out contrasts and lightly skips over the long
perspective. It is surely significant that when Golden Age nostalgia does make its triumphant entry into the Renaissance
pastoral, it is usually in the form of pastoral drama, as in Tasso's
Aminta, and Daniel's "A Pastoral," [37] not in pastoral lyric.

Virgil appears to have sensed the difficulty when at the start of the fourth *Eclogue* he apologizes for introducing the theme, and undoes the gentle quiet of the bower with a first line snap of prose:

> Let us, Sicilian Muses, turn up the volume.
> Not all are lovers of clover and small shrubs;
> For once we'll sing of woods of consular girth.[38]

The same hesitation is noticeable in Calpurnius' *Eclogue* 4. But in Calpurnius' *Eclogue* 1 and in the *Einsiedeln* eclogues, pastoral and Golden Age have entered into a new union, under the shelter of the imperial encomium. The emperor is praised, as in an earlier period the god was praised, for ushering in a time of bliss and plenty that has all the earmarks of the Golden Age.[39] It is clear that the marriage of the Golden Age theme with the pastoral is a Roman development. It began as an experiment, in full awareness of the paradox involved in turning the herdsmen's glances away from the bower, toward another bower more splendid and more humiliating; it proceeded with a decreasing sense of the experimental. There are other reasons, beside the greater prominence of encomium and epiphany in the Roman poetic experience, why this should have happened. The memory that Rome was settled by Arcadians, the antelunar paradise people (we shall discuss this in Chapter Eleven), helped to evoke thoughts of paradise. Again, because the pastoral in Rome was encumbered with socio-political messages, the protest against the city, which Theocritus omitted from the *Idylls*, came into its own. Satire was admitted into the body of the pastoral; the view was opened up for glancing backward and forward in time; and the Golden Age, the period before the invention of the city, became accessible to the artist. But lurking doubts about the legitimacy of the merger remained; and the contrived or cerebral quality of the Golden Age *topos* continues to be felt in, for instance, Drayton's *Pastorals, Eclogue* 4.

The naturalness of the connection between Golden Age longing and pastoral was challenged by the eighteenth-century rationalists. Dr. Johnson, in his essay in *Rambler* No. 37, presents specific arguments against the Golden Age—and, for that matter, Arcadia—as a necessary ingredient in pastoral poetry. Others went further. Allan Ramsay and Thomas Warton, forerunners of the romantic school, debated the question on two issues: whether the pastoral got its start during the Golden Age of mankind, which would make it the oldest genre, a view widely accepted in Renaissance criticism; and whether pastoral poetry must dramatize or summon up Golden Age conditions. On both issues the answer given was no. On the former, the reply was directed to those among the neoclassicists who tended to favor a very early origin of pastoral verse. The burden of the reply was that the genre was created by men who were tired of the city, and that consequently the invention could not antedate the full flowering of city culture.[40] On the other score, the supposed invocation or realization of Golden Age conditions in the pastoral, the opponents increasingly adopted Rousseauist notions of a primitive paradise on "some unsuspected isle in far-off seas,"[41] which effectively blocked the backward glance of the neoclassicists.

Schiller was sufficiently impatient with the Golden Age convention to write, against Gessner, that by returning man to a point prior to the commencement of culture, the pastoral performed the neat trick of placing the goal of his development at his back rather than in front of his eyes. Pastorals of this kind, he felt, could only serve to instil a mournful sense of loss, not the gaiety of hope.[42] Schiller goes on to say that in focusing on an age long past, the pastoral can stimulate us only when we are in quest of quiet, not when we long for movement and activity. They may bring healing to a sick mind, but they cannot give food to a healthy one. Schiller's objections are not only to Gessner, but to all pastoral, because of his acceptance of the neoclassical belief that the pastoral is a reevocation of the past, and of an irrecoverable past at that. His criticism is further shaped by his

conviction that serious literature stands or falls with its success
as a promoter of socially productive passions. Herder has a
broader understanding of the matter.[43] The Golden Age, he
finds, is a "schoene Grille," a handsome figment of the imagination. The Greek writers of pastoral know of a perfect Golden
Age only in the Elysium of the gods, and in the childhood of
the world, when there were heroes. The Corybantes drew
their ecstasy from streams of milk; but Theocritus' herdsmen
draw clear water. The meaning of Herder's remarks appears to
be that the ecstasy required to put oneself in the mood of the
Golden Age is foreign to the simplicity of the Theocritean herdsman. This is indeed true, for though Theocritus has some references to the Golden Age, they invariably occur in non-pastoral
poems, usually in encomiastic contexts such as were later, in
Rome, combined with the pastoral tradition.[44] It is generally
agreed that we have no evidence of a Greek pastoralist picking
up the Golden Age theme; Erycius, who is sometimes cited to the
contrary, is probably later than Virgil.[45]

Once more, therefore, we have had occasion to distinguish the
pastoral from the Hesiodic tradition, and from its philosophical
elaborations. As Poggioli put it: "Bucolic poetry is largely
indifferent to the lot of man in collective terms."[46] When
he goes on to cite exceptions to the rule, in Sidney, Shakespeare, Montaigne, Rousseau, and Saint-Simon, it should be
said that these writers are not pastoralists in the stricter sense of
the word. It is clear from Poggioli's remarks that they win
his admiration precisely insofar as they go beyond what he
calls the "pastoral of the self" and permit themselves to dream
dreams of a universal brotherhood. Such noble business, I
suggest, is not the business of pastoral. The documents in which
it is transacted do not exhibit the characteristic and analyzable
pastoral forms.

But I do not wish to be dogmatic about this. In spite of Theocritus' reluctance to admit the elements of anatomy into his

pastorals, it is indisputable that some degree of longing, some sense of a lack of fulfillment, is to be found in the *Idylls*. For the most part, the bower encourages gaiety and a kind of disciplined abandon. But there are intimations of an undercurrent of melancholy which now and then comes out into the open and for a short while dampens the good humor. Perhaps melancholy is too strong a term; but we have already seen that on occasion, especially when the pastoral turns lament, bucolic patterns can accommodate a mournful spirit. Pastoral melancholy is not unrelated to the nostalgia for a lost Eden; it is therefore not inappropriate that we should say a few words about it now, by way of addendum to our section on the Golden Age, and as the last topic to be taken up under the general heading of Anatomy.

ᔑ ᔑ ᔑ ᔑ

"The life of the fields is never without its undertone of sadness. . . . In the hush of the woods and pastures, the 'still sad music of humanity' is plainly audible. And if you go back to Theocritus . . . the echo of this music rarely ceases to sound."[47] The Christian tradition had its own reasons for coming down hard on the side of pastoral melancholy. Empson singles out the use of "weep" in

> Thus was this place
> A happy rural seat of various view:
> Groves whose rich Trees wept odorous Gumms and Balme. . . .[48]

I suspect the suggestion, as so much else in Empson, contains that pinch of exaggeration which he has perfected into a critical tool of great power. But the feeling that Eden must be lost so soon is endemic in the European versions of pastoral, no matter whether the Christian coloring is overt or not. Long before the introduction of the Fall, however, melancholy had been known among the inhabitants of the bower. Occasionally this sadness manifests itself as something very like *taedium beatae vitae*; the discovery that a contemplation of beauty and happiness may issue in tears has its value even for the criticism of ancient pastoral. One of the more striking instances of this possibility is furnished by one of the two puzzling pastorals from the time of Nero known as the *Einsiedeln Poems*, after the place where they were found. Lucretius'

> The flowers, too, distill a bitterness [49]

is perhaps alive in the secret hinted by Mystes in *Carmina Einsiedeln*. 2.7, when asked by his friend Glyceranus why he is silent and sad. Glyceranus, whose imagination is bounded by Theocritean precedent, guesses that perhaps Mystes' herd is in danger. No, answers Mystes,

> You're wrong; the cause lies deeper, out of sight. [50]

At first glance it looks as if the whole poem is given over to the realization of a romantic disenchantment with happiness. But there is a good chance that the poem is incomplete, and that the poet is more concerned with the moral dangers resulting from *otium* than with the inevitability of an existentialist *nausée*. [51] The melancholy of the voluptuary is, however, a fairly stable theme, from Aristippus and Epicurus to Keats and Pater. Keats' "Ode on Melancholy" canvasses suicide in terms of pastoral magic:

> Make not your rosary of yew-berries,
> > Nor let the beetle, nor the death-moth be
> > > Your mournful Psyche, nor the downy owl
> A partner in your sorrow's mysteries;
> > For shade to shade will come too drowsily,
> > > And drown the wakeful anguish of the soul.

In the end the speaker proposes to forego the suicide because he would thereby miss the delicious pleasure of suffering and sadness. [52]

Epicurus' pessimism stands at the head of the line; the cosmos is mortal, like any other living thing, with the exception of the gods, who are beyond involvement. The sum total of atomic matter is always the same; individuals and worlds alike die so that new bodies and groupings may be born. Philosophical optimism generated by the assurance that the universe as a whole can never die is undone by the private recognition that we are mortal, and that the garden is mortal also.[53] The *carpe diem* pastoralism of Bion (frag. 8) is one answer; we must use this short life of ours to sing sweet songs, or we might as well give up. "Hedonism disappointed"[54] is, however, not the usual pastoral response to the burden of mortality, nor is pastoral melancholy easily circumscribed by contrasting it, as is sometimes done, with a more profound Christian sadness. In actual fact, pastoral melancholy makes very little open reference to death. Poussin's "Et in Arcadia ego,"[55] with its insistence on the reality of death in a charming and seemingly vital landscape, is a motto more appropriate to a medieval *Moritat* than to ancient pastoral. Even the dirge, as we saw, started out not so much as an emphasis on mortality, but as a praise and near-deification of the dying herdsman-hero. The keynote in a pastoral lament is the sounding of life in death, not death in life. Consequently, we are not likely to find the springs of melancholy that we are seeking in the vicinity of the ancient pastoral dirge.

Sannazaro gave the pastoral lament its great impetus; it was Sannazaro, also, who developed the Petrarchan specialty of the sad song sung against a charming backdrop. In Sannazaro, as in Petrarch, sadness and even fretting are pervasive; they are beautified by the loveliness of the ambience. This coincidence of opposites makes for a species of harmony which, in Sannazaro at least, succeeds in dispelling the gloom. Sannazaro's herdsmen report their sufferings; the singers' passions are neutralized by the musical effect of the poetry, which is uniformly refreshing. Against the Italians, Sidney introduces those disturbing sounds that reverberate through his British woods, especially in the double sestina, "You Gote-heard Gods". A recent critic has a fine discussion of the enormity of these touches in Sidney, "the dreadfull cries of murdred men in forrests," "the mortall serene of an evening," and "The Nightingales doo learne of Owles their musique."[56] Sidney's dark glances set the mood for much British pastoral; melancholy received a cutting edge that takes us far beyond the occasional shadows darkening the sense of well-being in the ancient pastoral. Jonson's *The Sad Shepherd* is a comic animadversion on the theme; Aeglamour's monomania signals a state of comic disharmony with his pleasant surroundings. The lampooning, if that is not too strong a term, endorses the general tendency. Throughout the later Renaissance, melancholy reigns supreme in the pastoral; death, exile, unhappy love are the important themes. Miss Gerhardt has shown that the writers commonly regarded themselves as following in the footsteps of Virgil, especially of the "sad" *Eclogues* 2, 5, 10, and the complaint of Damon in *Eclogue* 8.[57] But, as so often during that period, the writers exaggerated their dependence on the Virgilian patterns.

In "Il Penseroso," Milton calls on Melancholy to appear with her train: Peace, Quiet, Spare Fast, Retired Leisure, Contemplation, and Silence. The catalogue constitutes a tabulation of the *mise-en-scène* associated with pastoral melancholy. It is worth remembering that Milton uses the bower both in "L'Allegro" and in "Il Penseroso." He wants it understood that the two moods, mirth and melancholy, are complementary in the design of the pastoral complex. "Forget thyself to Marble," the Miltonic equivalent to the "Ode on a Grecian Urn," is incomplete without its pendant on the side of cheer. But that is not the whole story.

> And when the Sun begins to fling
> His flaring beams, me Goddess bring
> To arched walks of twilight groves,
> And shadows brown that *Sylvan* loves
> Of Pine, or monumental Oake,
> Where the rude Ax with heaved stroke,
> Was never heard the Nymphs to daunt,

Or fright them from their hallow'd haunt.
There in close covert by some Brook,
Where no profaner eye may look,
Hide me from Day's garish eye,
While the bee with Honied thie,
That at her flowry work doth sing,
And the waters murmuring
With such consort as they keep
Entice the dewy-feather'd Sleep. . . .

Strangely this picture is more like that of the traditional pastoral pleasance than is the sun-drenched English village garden which forms the rustic setting of "L'Allegro." When a decision needs to be made, apparently, Milton links the pastoral tradition with melancholy rather than mirth. The diptych is not really a diptych, but an attempt to right the balance and add to the traditional picture of pastoral melancholy a dialectical opposite of happiness and cheer, which in the end turns out not to be pastoral after all. It remains for Marvell, by means of a Plotinian synthesis, to put the two complementary moods back into the same garden, on a level of philosophical virtuosity not dreamed of, and probably not wished for, by earlier pastoralists.[58]

Pastoral melancholy is usually associated with pastoral solitude, the precious, brittle modality introduced by Petrarch, and developed by the Pléiade.[59] For the later period this is undoubtedly correct. But in antiquity, solitude and melancholy do not go together. A brilliant account of solitude, of a man who isolates himself from society, occurs in a medical text, a letter spuriously ascribed to Hippocrates.[60] This description of an intellectual turning anchorite reads almost like a parody of the bucolic ideal. "He neglects his family, his property, and lives in caves and deserts and bowers and meadows or at streams. For this is the kind of thing that goes with people who suffer from melancholy. They turn silent and become lone wolves and lovers of solitude, and shun human intercourse, regarding the sight of a fellow man as completely irrelevant." The writer terms this not a madness but an excessive health of the soul, as if unsociability was a measure of a man's strength of character. Within the gregarious culture of Greece and Rome this view may have had a point; and even today, readers of Riesman's *The Lonely Crowd* may be tempted to agree. But there is not the slightest link between such revelling in solitude and the sensibility toward one's fellow man we have come to expect in the ancient pastoral.

Melancholy in the ancient pastoral has nothing to do with concentrating upon one's private needs, or with bemoaning the loss or absence of a beloved. It is a more subtle sensation, one that touches upon the very core of the pastoral experience. On the one hand, there are the delicate reminders of *ponos*, of the indignities of the empirical order. On the other, and equally unobtrusively, melancholy is triggered by the awareness, on the part of the herdsmen, that the bower in which they perform their songs and conduct their dialogues does not really exist, or if it did, it would most likely be a lair of Marathonian bulls. In other words, the precarious substance of the pastoral bower affects the hearts of the herdsmen roughly in the same way as the unreality of the heroic world affect the actions and motives of the heroes who must fight their stylized duels. George Thomson remarks on the "dynamic tension between them [sc. the poets] and their material, and . . . this tension appears as something internal in the heroes of the story."[61] This is the cause of what in mature pastoral emerges as a touch of melancholy; the more verdant the turf, and the more robust the swains, the more poignant the sadness or even malaise which a responsible poet will allow to communicate itself in the poem. It is, for instance, instructive to see how the maturing of Michael Drayton led to his revision of the pastorals by augmenting the vein of melancholy in them. The *Pastorals* of 1619 (but largely completed by 1606) are a reworking of the *Shepheard's Garland* of 1593. One of the most interesting changes is the removal, in *Eclogues*

8 and 9, of all suggestion that Rowland is languishing in hope-
less love. Similarly in *Eclogue* 1, the melancholy is not that of
the lover, but a distress that has to do with the poet's increased
detachment from his materials. The gain is substantial; for this
kind of melancholy, unlike the plain lover's grief, can be worked
in almost imperceptibly to add richness to the texture. The superior artistry of the *Muses Elizium* is the fruit of a deeper melancholy, to darken but not eliminate the joyousness of the
pleasance.[62]

Both Virgil and Theocritus were in full control of this kind
of darkening. In Virgil, remembrance and longing form vectors
that lead away from the present, and add their force to the
latent melancholy of the pastoral singers.[63] In Theocritus, the
part melancholy plays in rendering the pastoral music fuller and
more suggestive is hard to pin down. There are some obvious
moments of pensiveness; the goatherd's comment to Thyrsis:

> You know you cannot
> Salvage your song in unremembering Hades;[64]

Lycidas' regrets that Comatas is no longer alive to herd goats
with him and join in a concert under the trees;[65] Daphnis'
tabulation of what is harmful to trees, waters, birds, and men:
all of these are, in varying degrees of gravity, suggestions that the
pleasance is vulnerable, and that the pastoral existence is a mi-
rage.[66] At other times the melancholy is even less explicit, and
can be divined only from a change in pace or a sudden irresolute-
ness. But it is pervasive; without its resonance, Theocritus'
artistry would be merely frivolous or crude. Theocritus' herdsmen
have one advantage that is not enjoyed by others whose thinking
is tempered by melancholy: their naiveté. Though the ultimate
inaccessibility of pastoral happiness is reflected in moments of
wistfulness or dejection, the simplicity of the men and women in
the bower gives wings to the sadness, and prevents it from de-
generating into the self-conscious grieving which in the end

makes for pastoral opera. In Montemayor and in Monteverdi, sadness defines; in Theocritus sadness is a marginal mood which adds depth to the spirit of enjoyment. Above all, it is not programmatic; like satire, and like nostalgia, melancholy leads a subterranean existence in the Theocritean cabinet. The herdsmen are incapable of anatomy; the poet refrains from it; and this is true of such anatomy as melancholy, in her more aggressive moments, might undertake. Indeed, the underplaying of melancholy in the *Idylls* is the most persuasive proof of Theocritus' refusal to be an anatomist.

I I
Arcadia

"But you, Arcadians, will sing
Of this in the hills: masters of song, you alone,
Arcadians." [1]

One of the changes that Virgil wrought on the Greek
pastoral came to be of great significance for the later European
tradition. He replaced Theocritus' Sicily and Cos with Arcadia.[2]
Unlike Frost's Vermont or Wordsworth's Lake Country, Theocritus' Sicily is not a specific setting with a feel and a contour
of its own. It is little more than a cartographical pretense, a
cypher for the *locus amoenus* with its brooks, its pastures, its
groves of oaks and willows, and the occasional beach. If Theocritus were not a native of Sicily, and if he had not lived part of
his life in Cos, other regions might have lent their names to his
designs just as well.

Virgil's Arcadia is no more realistic than Theocritus' Sicily.
It is well known that Virgil's landscape is a composite one; the
fertile fields of the Po Valley and the barren hills of the heel of
Italy rub shoulders to produce a mixture that defies exact locali-
zation, least of all in the Peloponnesus. Why then did Virgil
bother to introduce Arcadia? The question is the more interesting because Virgil's innovation apparently failed to impress his
immediate successors; the post-Virgilian Latin pastoralists do not

avail themselves of Arcadia for their bucolic landscape. Perhaps this is due to a deeper understanding of what Virgil was about. Calpurnius and Nemesianus perceived that Virgil's choice of Arcadia was in fact a disclaimer of geographical realities. Consequently their own dispensing with the name of the country may be regarded as a continuation of what Virgil had begun.[3]

Theocritus himself, though averse to using Arcadia as a locale for his singers, has many references to the land of Pan.[4] Pan lives in the rugged hills; the names of Arcadian mountains abound in the *Idylls* and provide some of the most sonorous patterns: Mainalos, Erymanthos, Lykaios, Parthenios, Parrhasia. Wilamowitz suspected that Theocritus had studied an *Arkadika* from which he took not only the general associations of Pan, but also the more specialized lore, including the place names *Helikēs rhion* and *Aipytou tymbos* in *Idyll* 1; he speculated further that Theon's commentary on the *Idylls* is the source of Virgil's adoption of Arcadia as the prototypal pastoral landscape.[5] Arcadia, the central hill country, apparently excited the interest of Hellenistic authors, for its comparative remoteness from the developments of the day, and its preservation of a number of archaic institutions. Pausanias (8.5.7) reports an earlier tradition according to which there was an Arcadian prince Bukolion; and the geographer Mnaseas of Patrai or Patara, who lived a couple of generations after Theocritus, mentions a Bukolion, son of Pan, as the inventor of *boukolein*, the herding of cattle. Much of this is admittedly speculation *ex post facto*, involving learned combinations and popular etymologies. But Thucydides knows of an Arcadian place called Bukolion, on the upper Alpheius; and whatever the origin of the name, it is obvious that its availability was of some use to those who wanted to bring the Arcadian god Pan into some relation with bucolic poetry.

The story of the Arcadians in Greek literature before the Hellenistic period is easily sketched. The passages may be grouped according to certain well-defined cues:[6] Arcadia is called lovely

and well watered; she is said to be famous for her sheep; she is
the land of hunters; the Arcadian diet is notorious for its simplicity; the inhabitants are autochthonous, and in fact their race
is older than the moon. Two of these motifs are already combined in the Hesiodic *Marriage of Ceyx* (frag. 266, Merkelbach
and West), a riddle that reports the Pelasgians to have served
their mother's mother for food. The solution: mother = oak,
mother's mother = acorn. The passage is relevant because
Pelasgus was known as the ancestor of the Arcadians (frags.
160–168, Merkelbach and West); he grew out of the ground, like
a tree, in the hills. Plutarch (*Moralia* 286A) says that the Arcadians
were the first men to rise from the earth, as the oak was the
first plant.[7] This close connexion of the (Pelasgian) Arcadians
with the oak and the acorn testifies to their reputation as simple
folk who were satisfied with a rough diet, and therefore were
not prey to the sicknesses that befall more civilized people.[8]

The hard primitivism that appears to be at the bottom of
much of this[9] is reinforced by the legend that the Arcadians
are the original settlers of their land, and that their origins are
ante-lunar.[10] The themes are combined in another riddling
text, Lycophron's *Alexandra*, lines 479–483:[11]

> The second to come to the island is from the fields,
> A dry-land self-grown-food-man, child of the oak . . . ,
> Of those who, before the moon, heated their prop
> Of oak-wheat in red-hot ashes, at the height of winter.[12]

Antedating the moon, sons of oaks, the Arcadians roast acorn
bread in the chill of winter. They are the proverbially contented
people of long ago; theirs is a primitive Golden Age which has
lasted into our day, or at least until recently, before they discovered barley-bread and pork.[13] According to Theopompus,[14]
the Arcadians at their feasts admit both masters and slaves, and
set up one table, with the same buffet dinner and the same
mixing bowl for all. This sounds as if it came from an eighteenth-

century report about life with the happy savages in America; it accords well with the utopian touches found elsewhere in Theopompus' work. The choice of the Arcadians for the purpose of pointing up simplicity without guile and contentment without class barriers is of some interest.

I suspect that Virgil emphasized Arcadia because he is more interested in the Golden Age than his Greek predecessors (cf. above, Chapter Ten). True, the Golden Age and Arcadia are not used together in *Eclogue* 4. But the two concepts are the two sides of the same coin. In his *Georgics* Virgil drew on a tradition that Aristaeus left Ceos for Arcadia and practiced his bee-keeping there.[15] Usually Arcadia is less prominent in the Aristaeus legend than Thessaly or some other places. Once more it is a plausible conjecture that Virgil preferred this variant because the simple virtue that he wishes to associate with Aristaeus, and the simple diet for which he stands, fit best into the rugged paradise of legendary Arcadia.

We may go further and suggest that there was a popular tale in which Arcadia assumed the role of a fool's paradise. The simple countryman easily becomes the clown, as is shown abundantly in Elizabethan comedy. Theopompus reports that anyone who enters the sanctuary of Zeus in Arcadia loses his shadow; Polybius, in his comment on the passage (16.12), characterizes such tales as infantile foolishness. But they may help to explain a passage that has puzzled commentators. In Aristophanes' *Knights* (797 ff.), Cleon, reading from his oracles, promises to Demos that he will one day, if he waits long enough, be a juryman in Arcadia, at a fee of five obols a day. The usual explanation is to refer to the Spartan defeats in Arcadia, and to read the oracle as the prediction of an Athenian victory over Sparta.[16] But the outrageously high payment, and the comic associations of the juror's life, seem to me to point in a different direction. Cleon promises, not a military success, but a life of idleness and physical satisfaction, in a land which, to most Athenians at the time, in spite of the flourishing of alliances, was largely a mystery, remote from contemporary power struggles and a trap for unwary invaders: an ancient Shangri-la. In this capacity, Arcadia survives in the *Shepherd of Hermas.* In one of the visions, a figure dressed as a herdsman takes Hermas to Arcadia, to nine rugged and deserted mountains, until finally they arrive at the mountain which is the hoped for oasis.[17] Here Arcadia is the landscape of simple rustic virtue, but also a distant land of mystery, a combination that is appropriate for the planned pneumatic conversion. This use of Arcadia is fairly rare; Elysium and Paradise retained their privileged position. But even this single instance indicates the spiritual potential of the Arcadian theme.

That potential is evident also in the legend which made another Arcadia of the site of Rome, and particularly of the Palatine.[18] Book 8 of the *Aeneid* is Virgil's adaptation of the legend of the Arcadians who settled on the banks of the Tiber, under Evander and Pallas, and established a rustic utopia as the first nucleus of the *pax aurea.* Virgil's account is paralleled by versions in Varro, Dionysius of Halicarnassus, and Livy.[19] Dionysius' report is particularly interesting: the first inhabitants on the site of Rome were Sicels, who were displaced by Aborigines. Elsewhere these Aborigines are identified with the Arcadians. Thus Dionysius makes room for both Sicily and Arcadia in his narrative of the earliest simple life, when men lived without walls and without the machinery of civilization.

Servius, in his commentary on Virgil's *Aeneid*, Book 8, line 51, remarks on the name of the town Pallanteum, which the Arcadians established on the future site of Rome. Usually the name of the town is derived from the name of Pallas, one of its founders. But, Servius adds, others say that it got its name *a balatu ovium,* from the bleating of sheep. We recall that in *Aeneid,* Book 8, line 282, the officiating priests are clad in the skins of sheep and goats. Servius Danielis comments: that is because Pan, the god of Arcadia, is clad in skins. This connexion between Pan, Arcadia, sheep, and early Rome is stressed again and again, notably by Ovid in his *Fasti*.[20]

> An exile from Arcadia, Evander had come
>   To the fields of Latium, with his imported gods.
> Here, at the site of Rome, hub of the world, he found
>   A tree or two, much grass, few sheep and fewer houses.
>
> . . . .
>
> He taught the people many kinds of worship, but first
>   The rites of goat-horned Faun, and winged Hermes.

We conclude that there are many reasons why Virgil may have been prompted to adopt Arcadia as the country of his shepherd singers: because Arcadia is the land of Pan; because her people are said to have the simple diet that goes with simple strength and virtue; because they date back to time immemorial, which has given them a wisdom that comes from knowing the Golden Age at first hand. There was something else; Pan's identification with Faunus, the Italic woodland spirit,[21] played into Virgil's hand, for his own pastoral landscape is more silvan than that of Theocritus. The echo, the response of nature, is deeper and more resounding when caught and reverberated in a forest. Theocritus has groves; each of his trees has its own music, but there is no perception of echoes, no sense of whole blocks of nature reflecting the Orphean stimuli of the herdsman. Arcadia, a densely wooded highland region, fitted into Virgil's scheme, as Sicily and Cos or Southern Italy would not. The forest is, of course, an Italian forest; it is the same forest that shadows the progress of Aeneas' party as they make their way upstream to Pallanteum. Virgil's replacement of Theocritus' Sicily and Magna Graecia with Arcadia is, in an important sense, an Italicizing of the Greek material. That he chose Arcadia rather than a location in Italy is explained by the special character of his pastoral art. The more openly the political reality of his day is admitted into the *otium* of the pleasance, the greater the need for a "spiritual" landscape, to lift the experience above the mundane level of party strife.

Arcadia is Italy writ large, a spiritual Rome, a primitivist conception of the blessed land, remote and exotic, hence ideally suited to accommodate and reconcile the incongruities of Virgil's pastoral vision. In such a land, expropriations, deaths of patrons and the worship of princes can innocently consort with plaints of love, catalogues of myth, and the miracles of a Golden Age. Only a people older than the moon, with a digestion accustomed to acorns, are fit to sustain the added burdens imposed in the *Eclogues*.[22]

     ❧   ❧   ❧   ❧

  Sannazaro's tenth *Eclogue* presents a myth of the origins and the development of the pastoral. According to this version, the genre was introduced by the god Pan, and transmitted via Theocritus and Virgil to the herdsmen of Italian Arcadia.[23] There is an ancient tradition that Theocritus dedicated his poems to Pan.[24] These pious inventions reflect the truth that Pan is, by all accounts, the patron divinity of the *locus amoenus*. Hermes, the Nymphs, and the woodland creatures associated with the circle of Dionysus are welcome also; but usually they are thought of as accompanying Pan, or substituting for him in his absence. I have said before that there is no room in the bower for the cult of divinities. That is true also of Pan and his retinue. When they occur, they differ little from the rest of the pastoral population, except that Pan is on several occasions acknowledged as the master musician, and one whom it is best to count among one's friends. As the central occupant of the pleasance, he appears in countless bucolic epigrams by Anyte, Leonidas, and others.[25] Even in these poems, where the argument calls for a divinity that is worshiped with sacrifices and entreated for favors, it is hard to believe that Pan is anything more than a sculptured detail in a well-appointed cabinet, conjured up to facilitate pretty sentiments that have little to do with religion. A vast distance separates this occasional, rococo Pan from the charged symbolism of Shelley's "Hymn of Pan," in which the god has become a metaphor for all of lyric poetry.

Originally, as we have seen, Pan comes from Arcadia. Neither Homer nor Hesiod mentions him; in fact there are no references to him in literature prior to 490 BC, when he put himself squarely on the map by assisting the Athenians against their barbarian adversaries at the battle of Marathon. The oldest vase painting on which he appears is of roughly the same date.[26] After Marathon, because of the prestige acquired with the victory, Pan came to be widely known throughout the Greek world. In some quarters, including Athens and Attica, he was worshipped in cave sanctuaries, a practice into which the recent discovery and publication of Menander's *Dyskolos* has given us a better insight.[27] He was rarely worshiped alone; usually he was one of a consortium of spirits or divinities honored together. The vases show us that from the beginning he was a herdsman's god. Often he carries a *lagōbolon*, the Greek equivalent of the shepherd's crook, or he carries an animal on his shoulders, or he is pictured in pursuit of a herdsman who has ventured upon his territory without first making sure that it was permitted. We are reminded of the circumspection of the herdsman in *Idyll* 1; he knows that Pan is about and is reluctant to disturb him in his rest.

An Attic drinking song, unfortunately corrupt in the last line of the stanza that has come down, addresses the god:

> Pan, ruler of famed Arcadia,
> Dancer companion of dervish Nymphs,
> Smile, Pan, at my songs. . . .[28]

Pan is the protector of the little people. This gives special force to the flattery of Calpurnius, who imagines that the spirit of Nero creates a peace that makes even Pan feel more secure:

> The imperial grace shelters Arcadian Pan,
> To haunt his woods in peace; Faunus reclines,
> Calm in his shade; the splash of a gentle spring
> Cleanses the Nymph. . . .[29]

That the country people cherish him, and associate him with the
carefreeness of which, ordinarily, they can little more than
dream, is clear from comedy. Again and again Old Comedy
mentions Pan in contexts that celebrate the country as a source of
beauty, strength, and happiness. From Pindar through Aristophanes, and from Euripides to the "Hymn to Pan" composed
about 300 BC,[30] the concept of Pan hardly changes, though
toward the end of the fifth century the beard is given up, and
the shaggy hill creature turns smooth-shaven. Throughout
Pan remains what he was at the beginning, a brusque and uncomplicated protector of the rustic folk, not one of the august
divinities, and not overly refined, but effective and beneficent
nonetheless.

In Roman poetry, Pan was often associated and even identified with Faunus, as is the case in the poem of Calpurnius just
cited.[31] There are some slight differences between the two;
whereas Pan was *nomios*, that is, a god of the pasture, Faunus is
usually *agrestis*, connected with tillage. Horace's reference to
Faunus as a digger is typical:

> Gleefully the digger strikes the ground
> With a vengeful three-step.[32]

Unlike Pan, who is never linked with work in the fields, Faunus
fits smoothly into an agricultural calendar. He is part of a social
pattern, an emblem of productive economy, in a way that could
hardly be said to suit Pan. Faunus has prophetic gifts; prophecies
from the volatile and unceremonius Pan would scarcely be in
character. Faunus' oracular powers in Calpurnius' *Eclogue* I can
be explained as a function of his dual nature; besides being a member of the economic establishment, he is also a fellow of the
woodland *thiasos*. In fact the silvan role of Faunus is more pronounced than that of Pan. Faunus is the more complex personality; Virgil's use of him in the *Aeneid* testifies to this. Because of
this greater complexity, Faunus is a less useful symbol of pastoral

otium and simplicity. When the poem calls for an emphasis on playfulness or naiveté, the Roman poets usually enlist Pan in addition to Faunus, instead of merely using the Latin avatar.

That is not to say, however, that Pan is two-dimensional; that once he has been defined as a protector of herdsmen and herds, all has been said. His crook is an offensive weapon—*lagōbolon* means rabbit-killer—as much as it is used for defensive purposes.[33] Pan is a hunter. As we noted above in our discussion of the role of animals in the pastoral (Chapter Six), hunting occupies a precarious position in the structure of pastoral pursuits. It infringes on the privileged status of all animate life; the latent aggressive instincts that cannot be entirely silenced are roused afresh to vex the calm of the grove. The same is true of fishing; and there is some evidence that as early an author as Pindar explored Pan's interest in the rod.[34] Artemidorus tells us that the vision of Pan in a dream is a good omen for husbandmen and hunters, perhaps also for actors because like them he has no firm gait, but bad for all the rest.[35] In these manifestations Pan is an aggressor; the lusty instincts that elsewhere are acted out on the sexual plane[36] show up in reverse, as destructive impulses. What these facets have in common is an energy which is difficult to contain and threatens to erupt violently. Callimachus (*Epigram* 44, Pfeiffer) invokes Pan, along with Dionysus, by means of the image of a flame slumbering under the ashes; the concept is that of a force which, after a time of latency, breaks forth with renewed and sudden violence.

This is the assumption underlying the notion that Pan is behind the onrush of terror that we still call Panic. In the pastoral romance, beginning with Longus' *Daphnis and Chloe*, scenes of panic are common. In the original pastoral lyric, this aspect of Pan is rarely realized; but it is fair to assume a connection between panic, on the one hand, and the aggressive element, especially sexual exuberance, on the other. By an amusing coincidence, the only portion of Clearchus' essay "On Panic" of which we have knowledge concerns itself with sex habits in birds.[37] When we learn that Pan managed to seduce even the goddess of the Moon,[38] the affinity of terror and sex is not difficult to appreciate. But the story also shows that Pan's violence lends itself to the playful reduction in which mythology specializes. This is how Theocritus knows Pan, as a disturbing but ultimately absorbable element in the pastoral order. The herdsmen are aware of the fact that his presence portends tumult; the "acrid choler from his nostril" (*Idyll* 1.18) is a cause for wariness. But they do not permit this presence to throw them off their set course. Like the scenes on the cup, and like the reminders of brute sex elsewhere, Pan's availability helps to maintain the contact with animal energy and preserves the minimal tension without which the texture of the poem would be flabby.

The quality of Pan that is most relevant is his skill in music. A writer of Middle Comedy, Ararus, has a play entitled *The Birth of Pan*. According to this, when Pan was born he jumped up lightly and seized a pipe to play on it.[39] From the beginning, Pan is shown with a pipe, or a syrinx; because the herdsman tends his flock in lonely places, he amuses himself by playing tunes on a homemade pipe. The motif of Pan the piper appears to have been particularly prominent, if one may judge from the sorry remains we have, in Pindar's celebrated *Maiden-Songs*.[40] The combination of idyllic relaxation and sexual excitement embodied in Pan apparently suited the special purposes of the *Partheneion*; Pan's piping, moreover, was an appropriate emblem for the sort of music favored in the girls' "country-style" dances. But the pipe was not his only instrument. The Homeric "Hymn to Pan," whose date is late,[41] refers to Pan as *philokrotos* (*Hymn* 19.2), which probably means the same as *philokrotalos* (*Anthol. Pal.* 9.505d2), i.e., fond of clappers or castanets. That is to say, in addition to his pipes we should also picture

Pan as accompanying himself on a simple percussion instrument. Another interpretation is, however, equally likely; according to this, *philokrotos* is to be associated with *polykrotos*, an epithet of the sea. One may venture the guess that *krotos*, literally "clatter," is one of the fearsome sound effects associated with Pan in his capacity as a rouser of panic. The music of Pan, in other words, is more than just a pretty tune; in its essence it is an outcropping of a larger music; it is the natural sound of open nature, funnelled through the transformer of a simple instrument. The plausibility of this suggestion is confirmed by the frequent association of Pan with Echo. Lucretius speculates that Pan and his pipes are an invention of the country people stimulated by echoes reverberating in the mountains.[42] This is the rationalist's version of an older conception that links Pan, echo, and music in a pregnant image of acoustic consubstantiality.

From Pan as the communicator of the music of nature it is only a short step to the belief that Pan somehow incorporates the whole of creatural being in his hybrid body. This fiction is found in the Stoic sources that used the ancient legends to add color to their compendious and learned cosmologies. Plato's *Phaedrus* had introduced Pan as a figure to designate totality and many-sidedness. The woodland spirit, who is both man and beast, both smooth and rough, both gentle and cruel, had come to stand for a world whose wholeness is a function of its contradictions. The cosmic symbolism of Pan was further elaborated by the Neo-Platonists, by Proclus and Ficino, until in the end it reached Keats, Emerson, and Swinburne.[43]

> And God said "Throb!" and there was motion
> And the vast mass became vast ocean.
> Onward and on, the eternal Pan,
> Who layeth the world's incessant plan,
> Halteth never in one shape,
> But forever doth escape,
> Like wave or flame, into new forms. . . .

Emerson's homogenization of creator and creature, of material and plan, is a direct derivative of Stoic science. To adopt this conception is to swear off pastoral; the fiery mystery, the unity swarming with tension, have no point of contact with the bower and its variegated bloom. Interestingly enough, Marvell casts Pan in a role which is precisely opposite to that of the romantics; his Pan, in "Clorinda and Damon," is an invidious authority who spoils the enjoyment of nature. Damon cites Pan in his campaign *against* natural Love, in support of sublimation:

> Grass withers, and the Flow'rs too fade.

It is difficult to say with any certainty that this Pan is the moral law of Christendom, or, for short, Christ, interposing his spiritual command to choke off a pagan entertainment. The possibility is not to be rejected out of hand, because in fact Pan did become one of the pseudonyms of Christ as the pastoral ventured upon Christian ground. But the intricacy of Marvell's scheme is, as usual, such that it defies the simple identifications suggested by the history of ideas. What matters here is the plain fact that Marvell's Pan, like the entirely different Pan of Emerson and Keats, has acquired a universality that disqualifies him from his old fellowship in the pleasance.

One final development is usually chalked up to the Renaissance, namely the identification of Pan with the patron or the reigning prince. There are ancient precedents for Marot's and Ben Jonson's use of Pan in this fashion. We have some evidence that Hellenistic rulers liked to see themselves equated with Pan. From the *Life of Aratus*, the poet of the *Phaenomena*, we know that Aratus attended the wedding of Antigonus Gonatas, king of Macedonia, with Phila in 276 BC, and that the first poem recited for the pleasure of the king was a hymn to Arcadian Pan. We also know that Antigonus coined tetradrachms that show the image of Pan. It has been suggested[44] that the choice of the coin type was prompted by Antigonus' victory over Brennus and his

Kelts at Lysimachia in 277, and that the poet was flattering the king by insinuating that his triumph was as miraculous as the victory of the Athenians over the Persians at Marathon. But though the prince, an accomplished and cultured man, will have relished the compliment, that cannot be the whole story. The cities that honored Antigonus as a hero also dedicated an image of Pan in the precinct set aside for him. Thus the identification of the king as Pan was not merely temporary. Other Macedonian rulers were paid the same honors. Pliny reports that Archelaus asked Zeuxis to paint Pan; and Protogenes painted an image of Alexander and Pan.[45] We may assume that Aratus' "Hymn to Pan" was much like Callimachus' hymns to Zeus and Apollo in which the god assumes a virtual identity with Ptolemy. What it was in Pan that attracted Antigonus and his fellow princes is now impossible to guess. But for what it may be worth, we hear that in his youth Antigonus was a disciple of Zeno, the founder of the Stoa, and that throughout his life he attempted to put the Stoic theories into political practice.[46]

In any case, by the time of Spenser and Ben Jonson, everybody understood that Pan, in a pastoral poem, was likely to stand for the reigning prince, with some echoes of the other uses to which we have made reference. In *Pans Anniversarie, Or: The Shepheard's Holy-Day*, the Pan whom Jonson addresses in four hymns is King James. Sometimes the echoes overpower and smother the political significance of the name. In Spenser's "December," Pan is "half mere god of shepherds whom Spenser in his inspired days—like another Apollo—shamed in a music match, and half over-arching Providence which the repentant Spenser flatters with his *confessio amantis*."[47] In Spenser, Pan is both king and god, both figure of myth and ceremonial trope, both stock-in-trade of the pastoral vocabulary, and emblem of commitment. Pan's promotion is a striking index of the development of the pastoral lyric since its earliest days. Starting as a volatile but simple champion of the grove, without symbolic import or intimations of mystery, Pan ends up as a Protean configuration of multiple meanings, a favorite image of authors whose thoughts are fueled not just by the tradition of the pastoral but also by the contributions of Christianity, Stoicism, Greco-Roman art, and the court politics of their day.

12

Figures and Tropes

Earlier, in Chapter Three, I remarked on the affinity between pastoral naiveté and the refusal of the *nouveau roman* to interpret its subject in depth. According to Roland Barthes, the new novelist faces his world with no power other than the sharpness of his eyes, without recourse to psychology, confession, religious hypostasis, or any of the other instruments whereby the older novelists, including both romantics and naturalists, softened the hard outlines of the object.[1] Other writers, notably Natalie Sarraute and Jean-Paul Sartre, have similarly pleaded for a return to the pleasures of seeing without interpreting and internalizing. Metaphors, especially anthropomorphisms, are to be avoided, because they interfere with the direct appreciation of the surfaces of things.

Now, whether the poetics underlying the *Voyeur* is compelling or not—Alain Robbe-Grillet has written his own poetics in *For a New Novel* (1965)—there is much that rings familiar. It may be useful, to begin with, to consider how the writers of pastoral lyric proceed in the matter of anthropomorphisms, that is, the trick of reading human responses back into the external world, thus compelling the world to surrender something of its gleaming inviolability. As Robbe-Grillet puts it (p. 53): "To say that the weather is capricious or the mountain majestic, to speak of the heart of the forest, of a pitiless sun, of a village huddled in the valley . . . transports the reader (in the author's wake) into the imagined soul of the village . . . I am no longer entirely a spectator; I myself become the village, for the duration of the sentence, and the valley functions as a cavity into which I aspire to disappear."

When Ruskin wrote his derogatory comments on what through him came to be known as the pathetic fallacy, he proposed to rank pastoral poets among the second order of writers, those who feel strongly, think weakly, and see untruly.[2] His scathing words about Keats and Shelley are tame by comparison with what he would say about the pastoralists' imposition of human behavior upon external nature. Moschus' "Lament for Bion," for example, would have received his harshest condemnation; the sympathy of nature with the dead hero is expressed through an assortment of images all of which could be filed away under the rubric of anthropomorphism.[3] Nevertheless we must be careful here. Given the Greek tendency to hypostatize nature into woodland creatures and mythological fancies, does it make sense to apply the nineteenth-century yardstick, product of realism and scientism, of the pathetic fallacy? Again, is it legitimate to condemn, as pathetic fallacy, every case of the world's mourning in response to death and misfortune? Ruskin object to Keats' ascription of "wayward indolence" to a wave; is it possible to escape this kind of language entirely if one wishes to make a meaningful statement about external nature?

Fortunately these philosophical scruples need not worry us much. The fact is that good pastoral poetry features considerably less in the way of anthropomorphisms than is sometimes assumed. In "Lycidas" Milton can be observed avoiding the imputation of human feelings to nature, except in a very minor way. In this he appears to represent a position that was later voiced by Thomas Purney.[4] Purney disapproves of three kinds of thought in the pastoral lyric: the emblematical (he gives an example of Spenser), the allegorical (again he mentions Spenser as offending), and the refined. By the last he means an invocation of the type: "Nature, grieve with me!" Thus, Purney rejects the significant use of tropes. "'Twould be well if pastoral-writers would leave aiming at such thoughts as these and endeavour to introduce the Simple Ones in their stead." What Purney is in fact pleading for in pastoral poetry is the objective simplicity that Ruskin instances in Homer and Dante. But, as we have noticed before, Purney is nothing if not erratic. In a neighbouring passage (3.4) he says that pastoral, even more than epic, should be full of images (here, concrete expressions *and* tropes) but adds: "I need not make the Distinction between an Epick and a Pastoral Writer's manner of Imaging. They are widely different; nor can a Pastoralist Image so many Things as an Epick Writer. For he cannot consider Things as Persons, nor use the other Methods that Heroick Poetry takes to effect it." I take this to mean that the pathetic fallacy is admissible in epic, but not in pastoral, but I cannot be sure that Purney would want to be held to a rigid distinction.

Whatever the comparative claims of pastoral and epic in the matter of anthropomorphisms, Theocritus, for his part, has little room for the pathetic fallacy. In the *Idylls*, the externality of nature is taken at face value; nature is a population of creatures and beings each with a standing of its own. Further, the poet edges in the setting and the companions of the singer with so light a touch that a humanization of their role could only vulgarize the picture. True, the pine tree at the beginning of *Idyll* 1 is both a whisperer and a singer; it is only fair to assume that so prominent a piece of anthropomorphism at the head of the collection should have programmatic value. But the expectation is disappointed; there is nothing to equal this elsewhere in the *Idylls*. In the goatherd's answer, the water does not sing but tumbles down. Later, though the animals are said to grieve for Daphnis, the jackals and wolves show their grief by howling (*ōrysanto*). Theocritus seems to be making a conscious effort to avoid attributing to the animals and plants of the pleasance sentiments or utterances or conduct that is not specifically and generically appropriate to them.

The pathetic fallacy is a variety of metaphor. Perhaps it will be useful to broaden the inquiry and ask about the status of metaphor as a whole in pastoral. Offhand, one would guess that pastoral is more hospitable to metaphor than Homeric epic, which notoriously avoids this figure. The guess seems at first glance to be corroborated by a chapter in a celebrated book, Abraham Fraunce's *The Arcadian Rhetorike*.[5] To illustrate pastoral uses of metaphor, Fraunce cites, among other things, passages from Virgil's *Eclogues* 3 and 4; from Sidney's *Sonnet* 23, and prose portions of *Arcadia*; from Tasso's *Gerusalemme Liberata*; from Du Bartas' *Semaine*; and from Boscan's *Eclogue* 1. His list permits two conclusions; one, Fraunce does not, as a rule, go to the more famous pastoral poems to obtain his evidence; and, two, the metaphors harvested are remarkably discreet. The more adventurous usages are given in his next category, "hyperbolicall metaphores." Here, pastoral sources are rare. Since the name of his collection, *Arcadian Rhetorike*, suggests that he expected to find the figures in which he was interested especially well represented in Arcadian, i.e., pastoral writings, their relative absence from the list in this instance is interesting.

A recent critic has emphasized that Sidney's pastoral poems, both the more conventional poems in the body of *Arcadia* and the largely experimental eclogues attached to Books 1 and 2, are sparing with metaphor.[6] The meaning of the words is, to use Empson's terms, built up flatly and steadily. Evidently Sidney feels that the plain style of the pastoral tradition precludes a heavy investment of tropes. In our own day, with Frost, there is a similar dearth of metaphor. "Metaphor," says Lynen, "establishes an identity between diverse things, while the pastoralist's technique is to keep the image and the thing it resembles separate so that they may be compared."[7] This conforms to

Lynen's thesis, with which I hesitate to associate myself, that all pastoral invites the reader, by implication, to compare two worlds. Hence he continues: "The result is that pastoralism favors an anagogical form, a fact illustrated by its persistent tendency toward allegory—that is, extended analogy." We shall return to allegory. For the moment, let us simply take note of Lynen's point about the scarcity of metaphors in his author.

In Theocritus, overt metaphors are as rare as anthropomorphisms. Their only appreciable use occurs in the form of humorous addresses, as when the Cyclops calls his girl "my dear sweet-apple," *to philon glykymālon* (*Idyll* 11.39). The virtue of the apostrophe is that it does not lend itself to further development; its force is ephemeral. By way of contrast, when the Roman poet Florus (*Poems* 11-13) talks of a rose, he has in mind a girl to be loved; his statements about roses—they are to be plucked fresh; their stems may prick you—are designed to exploit the metaphor cumulatively. In later pastoral, the progressive exploitation of key metaphors becomes popular, and occasionally bizarre; in Thomas Lodge's "The Shepheards Sorrow, Being Disdained in Love," sheep and lambs are metaphors for the thoughts of the lover, and their behavior is constructed into an animated system of correspondences.[8] Theocritus, and indeed all ancient pastoralists, disdain such puzzles in their idylls. Even the scholiasts, constitutionally incapable of resisting the temptation to trace metaphor and allegory where a less preoccupied reader is unlikely to find them, are hard put to it to discover instances in Theocritus. Where they do find them, they are concerned more with *metaphora* in the ancient sense, word substitution under conditions when the primary word might be unsuitable or offensive.[9]

If metaphor is of little significance in the Theocritean pastoral, what about the simile?[10] Here again, pastoral and epic are felt to stand in a close relationship; more than any other genre of writing, it is thought, they favor similes and comparisons.

Rapin, in the third part of his *Dissertatio*, maintains that both Theocritus and Virgil have many comparisons; Fontenelle finds there are too many of them. In Virgil, he believes, they are acceptable, but in his imitators they are worn and threadbare.[11] Purney goes further and criticizes Virgil on this score (3.7): "SIMILIES in Pastoral must be managed with an exceeding deal of Care, or they will be faulty. . . . As I have hinted that *Theocritus* had a Genius capable of writing a perfect Set of Pastorals, his Similies are infinitely the best of any Swain's. . . . The chief Rule . . . is . . . that SIMILIES be contain'd in three or four Words," and that they not be cumulative. Unfortunately, in the sequel, Purney fails to distinguish cumulative similes from priamels, which work on a somewhat different principle. But this does not affect the validity of his basic assumptions, which agree with those of Fontenelle and others. By way of spoofing faulty cumulative similes, Robert Greene's "Doron's Description of Samela" parcels out comparison after comparison in a steady stream.[12]

> Thy lippes resemble two cowcumbers faire,
> Thy teeth like to the tuskes of fattest swine,
> Thy speach is like the thunder in the aire:
> Would God thy toes, thy lips, and all were mine.

The animal comparison is, as one might suspect, particularly common in the pastoral. The point of the comparison might be the looks, or the voice, or the movements or typical actions of the animal. In the epic, only behavior counts; when a hero is compared to an ox or a lion or a bird, the comparison focuses on energies that are not readily accessible to the senses. Man and animal are associated within a field of energies that is itself a segment of the larger system of forces defining the heroic world. In the pastoral, energy is not at a premium, sensory impressions are. Hence it is not surprising that so many of the animal similes should bear down, not on intangible tensions and springs of conduct, but on looks, and sounds, and on character to the degree that the character is an object of sensory cognition, especially when the comparison is not complimentary:

> Where, how many Creatures be,
> So many pufft in minde I see,
> Like to *Junoes* birdes of pride,
> Scarce each other can abide,
> Friends like to blacke Swannes appearing,
> Sooner these than those in hearing.[13]

Because of the emphasis on surface impression, pastoral similes tend to favor quantitative comparison.[14] First there is the likening of two beings for a property they share in common: your teeth are (like) boar's tusks. Then there is the explicitly quantitative comparison, via a comparative adjective: your teeth are longer than boar's tusks. Or the alternative: your teeth are as long (as white, as sharp) as boar's tusks. Mantuan's many animal similes furnish a more than adequate stock of illustrations. "I grieved like a nightingale," an example of the first variety, is actually a shorthand for: I grieved as loudly, or as tunefully, or as long, as a nightingale. "Her relatives opposed me as a cat opposes a mouse" is another case in point. The emphasis is less on what men and animals have in common, than on a quantum of opposition, more easily measured and perhaps more constant in the animal kingdom than among people. The quantitative dimension is most obvious in the more developed similes, as in Theocritus' *Idyll* 18, lines 41–42, where the girls sing: "We remember Helen as lambs remember the ewe."[15] For once, there is a certain awkwardness; is the relation between the girls and their queen really comparable to that between lambs and ewe? But then *Idyll* 18 is not a pastoral.

When we look at Theocritus' pastoral lyrics, the first thing that strikes us is the extreme paucity of animal comparisons. (I am not now concerned with other formal uses of the animal world, such as addresses to animals, or mere references to their presence or their conduct. That animals form an important

segment of the population of the bower is obvious.) Fully half
of the roughly ten animal similes in the pastoral *Idylls* occur
in *Idyll* 11, the "Cyclops." At the beginning of his complaint,
Polyphemus compares Galatea serially to a number of things—
yogurt, a lamb, a calf, a grape—by means of comparatives, and
tops the section off by likening her flight from him to the flight
of a sheep from the grey wolf.[16] The whole sequence is remarkable not only for its magnitude but also for the nature of the
comparisons. "Whiter than yogurt" and "sleeker than a grape"
are hyperbole, and do not easily square with the decorum of the
pleasance. The suggestion seems to be that the Cyclops is trying
his luck with a kind of flattery which, like his raising of deer and
bear cubs, smacks of the court at Alexandria rather than of the
simple bower. When at the end he compares the girl's response
to that of a sheep in the face of a wolf, the (unconscious) humor of
the complaint supports the impression of immaturity. The
four initial similes are appropriate to the genre in that they
cite the senses—color, texture, motion, luster; they go wrong
in that they "use" animals to say something about a human
being. As we noted above (Chapter Six), the pastoralist needs
to observe the fiction that the animals in the bower have the same
rights as men. Hence their function as raw material for pre-
dications concerning men is best played down.

If we scan the rest of the *Idylls* we find that, with the exception
of two or three contest comparisons in the manner of Alcman,[17]
there is practically nothing else. In *Idyll* 10, line 4, Milon accuses
Bucaeus of lagging behind his fellow reapers as a sheep lags
behind the herd when she has a thorn in her foot. It is significant
that the speaker who employs this elaborate figure is the reaper,
not the herdsman. The crusty, calculating man of the soil, the
amused critic of pastoral love, is just the sort of person to turn
a deaf ear to animal autonomy. In *Idyll* 7, lines 96–97, Simichidas
opens his song, which is not a pastoral, with the remark that he,
Simichidas, loves Myrto as much as the goats love spring. The

simile is quantitative; what is more, it does not posit an essential connection between man and beast, via an activity which
they share in common—see "lagging," above—but parallels two
distinct types of love. Its effect is close to that of a priamel, in
which several actions are put side by side for the purpose of a
better understanding of the action mentioned last. I shall come
back to this. In any case, the fact that this comparison appears in
the song of Simichidas rather than in that of Lycidas suggests
once again that for Theocritus, animal comparison and pastoral
are at odds. Only one more example of an animal simile remains,
in *Idyll* 8, which many consider spurious. Daphnis calls on the
pasture: if (you agree that) Daphnis makes music like the nightingales, then make his herd fat (37–39). And that is all.

Now it may be argued that by comparison with Homer, all
Hellenistic poets practiced restraint in their use of animal similes, as
if Homer's skill in this matter had preempted the field, and originality now had to be demonstrated along different lines.[18] But
though it is true that Apollonius of Rhodes, for instance, has
fewer animal similes than Homer, he does have a number that
are startlingly original.[19] Theocritus too has some skillfully
developed animal similes.

> (Like) a ravenous lion in his mountain lair who hears the call
> Of the fawn, and races toward the well-appointed table,
> So Heracles thrashed about . . .

or:

> (Like) the swallow who gives food to her young under the roof
> And swiftly flies off to gather another supply,
> More quickly she. . . .[20]

The comparisons of the racing lion with the utterly confused
Heracles, and of the purposefully volleying swallow with the
angry flute girl, are effective pieces of Hellenistic obliquity.
But note that the poems in which they occur, *Idylls* 13 and 14,
are not pastorals; one is an epyllion, and the other a city mime.

The prominence of these more ambitious animal comparisons in non-pastoral poems makes it likely that their relative paucity in the pastorals is deliberate. Theocritus, I submit, felt that animal similes have a way of compromising the status of the beasts in the grove, and ought to be held to a minimum.

The proposition may be checked against another traditional type of simile, the plant comparison. Here is a glimpse of how the figure was handled later, by Drayton (*Eglog* 2.53–60):

> Now I am like the knottie aged Oake,
> Whom wasting Time hath made a Tombe for dust,
> That of his branches reft by Tempest stroke,
> His Barke consumes with Canker-wormes and rust.
>
> And though thou seem'st like to the bragging Bryer,
> And spreadst thee like the Morn-lov'd *Marigold*,
> Yet shall thy sap be shortly dry and seere,
> Thy gawdy Blossomes blemished with cold.

Old Wynken falls back on plant lore to impress young Motto with the futility of his zest. The tree simile is known from Homer, where young men are likened to pliant olive trees, partly because of the synaesthetic quality of the image, but partly also because Homer wants us to visualize the planter of the tree, the parent who is about to be robbed of the son whom he has so carefully nurtured into young manhood. As usual, the epic simile teems with connotations and affective corollaries. The pastoral may not lose itself in such centrifugal maneuvers. The field of vision remains limited, and the eye comes to rest on little things, the outlines and the hues that mark the tree and make it comparable to the man.

On this score, Theocritus is no more liberal than in the matter of animal similes. Beside the Cyclops' comparison of Galatea with a grape, plant comparisons occur in only two genuine *Idylls*, and interestingly enough they are the least musical, *Idylls* 5 and 6. At *Idyll* 6, line 15, Galatea's hair is said to be dry "as from a thistle;" at *Idyll* 5, lines 92–95, the contestants claim that their beloveds are incomparable, and they express this by means of implied similes:

Comatas	Dogthorn and anemone cannot match the rose,
	Though they grow in plenty, lining the stone wall.
Lacon	And do not mix up acorns with wild apples;
	The acorn rind is thin and dry, apples are sweet.[21]

Ostensibly the talk is about flowers and fruits; the people are involved only by a tacit understanding that the comparisons and disjunctions apply to them. Elsewhere in this *Idyll*, lines 29 and 136–137, the same technique is used of birds. In all instances the focus is on the plant or animal, and the analogical element is suppressed, in order to keep the listener's mental eye riveted on the natural object, and retain for it its independence.

It is clear from this brief survey that Theocritus tends to use animal and plant comparisons primarily in agonistic contexts; in the place of the syntactic simile, which manipulates x to say something about y, the poet prefers a scheme of parallels. Flowers and animals, like men, are so constituted as to vie with one another. A contestant will refer to this natural competition to bolster his confidence, but also to acknowledge the democratic conditions which make the match possible and enjoyable. There is little of the decorative facade that prompted the snorts of Gay and Greene. What happens when Theocritus' restraint is dropped can be seen in the spurious *Idyll* 20, in which the speaker garnishes his complaint with a series of rococo comparisons: "I blushed from pain like a rose with dew" (line 16); "beauty blooms on me, like ivy on a tree" (22); "hair frames my temples like parsley" (23), and so forth. This is not the spirit of Theocritus.

Theocritus' own intentions are particularly manifest in his use of priamel and catalogue.[22] I would venture to say that the inventory, if I may use this term to cover all serial listing, is the single most effective and congenial literary device in the pastoral lyric. The loving enumeration of allied propositions or goods documents the discreteness of the herdsman's sensory experience, and his detachment-in-pleasure. At the same time, it furnishes proof that the grove is harmonious, a minuscule but well-ordered universe whose parts tend to group themselves together for purposes of inspection and enjoyment. The tenor of the inventory is both distributive and associative. The democracy of the bower encourages this formal combination of a delight in separateness with an insistence on kinship.

The longest priamel in Theocritus occurs in a poem of doubtful authenticity, *Idyll* 8. In addition to a series on *hādy*, sweet, and a series on *kosmos*, ornament (76 ff.), it contains a series on ills (57 ff.), specifying what is bad for trees, for water, for birds, for beasts, and for man. Logically, it should be possible to convert such a priamel into a series of similes: my trouble is for me what x is for a beast and y for a bird, and so on. But the paratactic arrangement allows the listener to relish each item of the series for its own sake. The capping proposition comes at the end, and it is not prepared for by a conjunction "as" or "like" preceding the earlier units. Elsewhere also, especially in the Homeric epic, the *comparatum* or *comparata* precede the *comparandum*; but the conjunction makes the hierarchy explicit, and conditions us to regard the *comparatum* as auxiliary to the *comparandum*. This is avoided in the priamel.

The inventory is found in Theocritus' non-pastoral poems as well. In *Idyll* 12, lines 3–8, an amatory epistle without bucolic coloration, the theme of the comparative itself is glossed in the following manner: as spring is sweeter than winter; as apple is sweeter than sloe; as the ewe is deeper of fleece than her lamb; as a maiden surpasses a woman thrice wed; as a fawn is fleeter-footed than a calf; as the clear-voiced nightingale sings more sweetly than all winged creatures: so you have gladdened me with your coming. . . . Strictly speaking this is an extended quantitative simile, but the length of it makes us forget the built-in connectives, and lets us savor the variety of the items in the listing. There is nothing quite so extensive in the pastoral *Idylls*; there is nothing quite so vague either. The range of qualities within which the comparative is illustrated—sweetness (two exempla, one abstract, the other concrete), shagginess, beauty (presumably), speed, and musical artistry—is so broad as to negate the intention of the analogic series, which is to validate the final proposition by a review of affinities. The context indicates that humor is not intended. The author emphasizes a purely cerebral concept, degree of difference, without direct dependence on the realm of experience, by choosing his instances from a broad spectrum of heterogeneous reality; note especially the reference to a woman who has gone through several husbands. In the pastoral, such abstraction is not desired.

Similarly, in the "Encomium of Helen" (*Idyll* 18.29–31) Theocritus has an extended simile on *kosmos*: As some tall cypress adorns the fertile field or garden in which it has grown, or as a Thessalian steed adorns its chariot, so rose-complexioned Helen adorns Lacedaemon. The multiplicity of relations here approaches the complexity, though not the subtlety, of one of Homer's extended similes. But by that token it functions in a way that would be deleterious to a pastoral. It removes itself from the appreciation of surface and contour, and draws us to an inquiry into hidden values, into the sources of beauty rather than the sheen of it. On the level of direct sensation, the inventory is preposterous; the shapes and the motions of the units clash, without providing the mutual reinforcement that we might reasonably hope for. The simile does not clarify, nor does it further the cause of simplicity. But then the universe of discourse is not the pleasance, but the Spartan commonwealth.

Now it must be stressed that there are a number of similes and inventories in the pastoral *Idylls* that resemble the *kosmos*-simile of *Idyll* 18 in their angularity and apparent incongruousness.

One of the most famous of these is almost literally imitated by Virgil.[23] I cite both texts in the original and in translation.

Theocritus ἀ αἴξ τὰν κύτισον, ὁ λύκος τὰν αἶγα διώκει,
ἀ γέρανος τὥροτρον· ἐγὼ δ' ἐπὶ τὶν μεμάνημαι.

The goat pursues the clover, the wolf pursues the goat,
The crane pursues the harrow; and I burn for you.

Virgil Torva leaena lupum sequitur, lupus ipse capellam,
florentem cytisum sequitur lasciva capella,
te Corydon, o Alexi: trahit sua quemque voluptas.

The lioness pursues the wolf, the wolf pursues the goat,
The frisky goat pursues the verdant clover;
Corydon pursues Alexis: each has his own desire.

Each of these priamels consists of four propositions. In the case of Virgil's version, the first three propositions are arranged transitively. As in an animated cartoon in which the small fish is swallowed by a bigger fish, and that in turn by one yet bigger, the beasts here are stationed in an order of violence, descending rather than ascending, but the principle is the same. Pursuit forms the connecting link between the three; it is pursuit of the same sort: gluttony. The fourth proposition is separate from the other three, because now the pursuit is amorous rather than alimentary. But the language remains the same; the relationships between wolf and goat, and between Corydon and Alexis, are stated in the same elliptic fashion. The effect is comical, especially because of the massive and uniform build-up leading into the last member of the series. At the very end, the explicit moral, reminiscent of the animal fable, confirms the humor and ties the units together into one package.

Theocritus' pursuit priamel is disconnected throughout. He starts with the small item which in Virgil's version comes third, the goat pursuing the clover. Next he ascends on the scale by citing the wolf who pursues the goat. But just as we are getting ready for a transitive series of animal cannibalism, the chain is

interrupted by the notice of the crane following in the tracks of
the harrow, an entirely different meaning of pursuit; and the
erotic item which caps the series adds further to the incongruity
of the sequence. In Virgil's formula, the curve of violence
descends while the curve of pleasure or aesthetic appreciation
rises. This crossover is itself indicative of the wit with which
Virgil has molded the pattern. In Theocritus, there is no sustained curve at all, either ascending or descending; it is as if he
had decided to construct a priamel that would frustrate the very
idea of the priamel, which is to lead up to an effective and
affecting terminus by means of a crescendo of expectation and
understanding. Significantly, Theocritus' lines do not issue in a
moral; anything that might shift the weight to the end of the
series is avoided. In other words, Theocritus' priamel, at least
in this instance, is a mock-figure; it is true to the spirit of pastoral
discontinuity, and in the process turns upon itself qua priamel,
with some further gain on the side of humor.[24]

The same type of humor is observable elsewhere in the pastoral
Idylls.[25] We have already had occasion to refer to that daring
series of asyntactic similes in *Idyll* 10, lines 36–37:

> My darling Bombyca, your feet are knuckle bones.
> Your voice belladonna; your ways—I cannot say.

The absurdity of the equations is planned; the combination of
wit, naiveté, and sheer craziness is a fitting formula for the pastoral vision.[26] Theocritus refuses to use his similes and inventories
for the purpose of constructing a larger unity. On the contrary,
comparisons and catalogues are employed to the end of high-
lighting the discontinuities. Once more we are made aware
of the consistency with which Theocritus shapes his material.
Combinatory rhetoric and synthetic figures clearly are not
wanted, except incidentally, in a world that is *only* a *locus
amoenus*, and not a unified cosmos with a tightly organized set of
relationships.

Before we turn to some larger implications of this, we should comment briefly, by way of a digression, on two or three tropes that are related to the types we have discussed. One trope that may be discounted right away is personification, a stratagem that in Greek literature is intimately linked with the Hesiodic tradition. Renaissance pastoral, in the wake of Prudentius and medieval allegorical drama, employs a considerable apparatus of personae of a more or less abstract character. An example is Daniel's *The Queen's Arcadia*, with its Techne, its Colax, its Pistophanax, and so forth. In addition, Stoicism and its mediate heirs had fashioned a concept of Nature and her handmaidens who could be depended upon to deliver sermons and issue warnings to the herdsmen. This feature became one of the chief inspirations for the early Wordsworth, of the Lucy poems and "The Fountain." In the Greek pastoral, personifications do not appear either as actors in the bower or as objects of addresses. Since the accent is on simple characters with strong and uncomplicated but human feelings, abstractions and hypostatizations are avoided. This is one of the great differences between pastoral and comedy. The latter favors personification; comedy requires an issue, or at least a fulcrum of reflection, that permits a more or less conceptual definition; and this in turn presses for the sort of personnel whom we still encounter in political cartoons: War with his blood-drenched hands, Justice balancing her scales, and the Russian bear fishing in troubled waters. The language is public, the signals are pre-arranged, and the personae are shorthand for complex issues and experiences. In pastoral we watch a slice of life, the advent of genuine sentiments, and the chance meeting of spontaneous souls, not the resolution of conflicts or the arbitration of moot issues. Thus pastoral has no use for personifications; and personifications in Renaissance pastoral are melancholy proof of how far the genre of the time has moved into the camp of theological controversy, or social satire, or ideological debate, away from the lyricism of the bower.

Another device that came to distinguish some of the later examples of pastoral poetry is periphrasis, especially mythological periphrasis. The nightingale is likely to go under the name of Philomel; being indebted to Theocritus turns into having drunk the waters of Arethusa; and to provoke Aphrodite means to write a poem about a subject recalcitrant to love. The periphrastic mode is found as early as Bion and Moschus,[27] and it is not absent from Theocritus' poems, notably *Idyll* 2, lines 147–148, where it is used to indicate the time of day:

> when the chariot was racing up the sky
> Carrying rose-colored Dawn from her ocean shelter. . . .[28]

This particular type of periphrasis, which in Theocritus imparts an air of lightheartedness and solace, became one of the most predictable staples of later pastoral. Even Pope, who is capable of making delightful fun of the convention, cannot, in his own bucolic poetry, resist the temptation of temporal periphrases.[29] In the battle of the books, the emulators of the ancients could be distinguished from the anti-classicists by their greater reliance on periphrasis. Philips uses it less than Pope. Periphrastic expression of place is less common than periphrasis of the time of day.[30]

As might be expected, Theocritus does not employ periphrasis in his pastoral *Idylls*. The figure is too precious, too redolent of Hellenistic learning and courtly self-consciousness, to flourish in the bower. On a few occasions, Theocritus seasons his dish with a pinch or two of mythology, just enough to introduce a slightly discordant note, usually for the sake of undercutting what might otherwise have turned into high seriousness. But the minor dislocation that is thus engineered never turns into pendantry or merely formal convention. The Hellenistic learning, or almost-learning, is offered by the characters rather than by the poet, and the characters do not employ periphrasis. The beginning of *Idyll* 7 shows the narrative simplicity of Theocritus' pastoral time indications at its best. The transition from morning to noon is brought about naturally, without explicit references to the hours, and certainly without celestial or astronomical superstructure. Nor is there any trace of periphrasis of place. The plain style does not encourage such frills.[31]

One overtly rhetorical figure which occurs with some frequency in the *Idylls* is the pastoral *adynaton*, the assertion or appeal via impossibles. One critic who has analyzed the material finds that the *adynata* in the Theocritean pastorals are close to popular speech, and least modified by the elaborations of Alexandrian wit.[32] His conclusion, that the pastoral *adynata* remain close to a rustic simplicity, is predicated on the assumption that Theocritus is deliberately portraying the rustic life. Peasants do not, however, discourse in the form of *adynata*. I think we must admit that the figure is a literate invention, modeled on a species of curse or prayer which is itself part of the literary, particularly the epic, tradition. What is more, the suggestion that pastoral *adynata* are simpler than those of other genres is hardly borne out by the evidence, particularly by the remarkable sequence at *Idyll* 1, lines 132-136, where Daphnis calls upon nature to reverse itself in response to his downfall. The structure of the appeal is unusual, with organic absurdity encircling his doom as if it were a soothing balm.

> May all the brambles, may all thorns sprout violets,
> And fair narcissus blossom on the junipers;
> May order turn disordered, and the pine grow pears—
> For Daphnis is to die—and deer tear at the hounds;
> And may the hillside owls hoot to the nightingales![33]

Once again, as in the priamels discussed above, the natural tendency toward terminal weight is blocked; the death of Daphnis has come to be, not the overwhelming disaster for which the other monstrous events serve as foil, but merely one of the several *monstra* envisioned in tabular form. But there is nothing simple about this; the imprecation generates a pressure which makes for a momentary surrender of pastoral moderation. Decorum is stripped away; for a few seconds, injured pride shatters the balanced noon peace. Inventory is put at the service of disorder; the turbulence of the passion and the enormity of the prospects mock the composure of serial sequence.

A less extravagant and more typical series of *adynata* occurs at *Idyll* 5, lines 124–127. Each of the two contestants rather routinely mentions certain conditions associated with paradise, hence unrealizable in their own lives: rivers that flow with milk, honey, and wine; reeds that bear fruit; and wells that produce honeycombs. One wonders what the "singers" may have in mind when they voice these wishes. The rest of their utterances show that the contestants are solidly rooted in their world which, for once, is harsher and more depressing than usual. They are not temperamentally equipped to imagine themselves transplanted into a life of beauty and inexhaustible cheer. The answer must be that the men offer their *adynata* because they know they are appropriate to a pastoral encounter. Such wish-dreams are simple, concrete, and benighted. They are, of course, entirely different from the fiery remonstrances of the dying Daphnis. But their kind is more common; their artless utopianism is more easily built into the pastoral *otium*.

The fact remains that Daphnis' imprecations are also part of the tradition, and they captured the imagination of Theocritus' successors. Virgil imitates the passage three times, once in *Eclogue* 1, lines 59–62, again in *Eclogue* 5, lines 34–37, and finally in *Eclogue* 8, lines 52–57, the only straightforward imitation of Daphnis's outburst. In the first instance, the effect is the opposite of the one intended in Theocritus. His memory of Caesar, Tityrus says, will not fade until nature has been overturned. Like similar assertions in the epic, this is not a challenge to nature, but an appeal to her granite stability. In the second passage, Virgil retains some of the despair of the Greek lines; with the death of Daphnis, Mopsus complains, the gods have left the fields, and weeds have won out over the grain and the flowers that used to embellish the countryside. Again, however, the changes are more significant that what the passages have in common. The shift from the future to the past tense robs the despair of its sharp edge; fury is replaced by pathos. In fact the *adynata* are gone, superseded by a picture of nature stripped of its bloom. The world implored by Theocritus' Daphnis is the large arena of all organic life, whose laws are put in jeopardy. The death of Virgil's Daphnis is shown to have affected a narrower sphere, causing the impoverishment and death of beauty in the fields. Milton's "Bid Amaranthus all his beauty shed," a call on nature to divest herself of her loveliness, stands halfway between Theocritus' challenge and Virgil's elegy. In one respect, however, it is Theocritean rather than Virgilian; the living nature invited to share in the death of the hero is not the fertile soil of the Italian farmer but the hedonist's pleasance, the "green terf" whose "quaint enameld eyes" have but one function, to support the herdsman in his *otium*.

How is it possible that Theocritus, who puts so much stock by naturalness of speech and naiveté of imagination, should allow his herdsmen to engage in *adynata*? In the epic, *adynata* are the privilege of weighty personages, to lend additional authority to their promises or warnings. The figure is augmentative; it adds to the impression of mass and magnitude. Is there not something peculiar about the herdsman, in his miniscule world, throwing off these grand effusions and conjuring up absurdities? Again, I think, we must hazard the guess that the intention is not, or only secondarily, to produce pathos, but has something to do with the pastoral desire for distance and self-deprecation. For once, however, the consciousness of the artifice does not extend to the character; he is merely the instrument of the poet's strategy. By settling on the herdsman the thunder of his *adynata*, the poet endows him with mock-epic dimensions, and makes us more than ever aware of his limitations. The point is, I suggest, that the *adynaton* in the pastoral lyric is designed to grate on the senses; it is meant to be noticed as a foreign element, an epic enclave, in an environment which resists it. This is so in spite of the fact that the terms of the *adynata* are usually fully assimilated to the flora and fauna of the grove. It is the tone of the device, its air of hubris and dissatisfaction, that stands out. It is part of a mechanism of alienation which interposes itself between character and listener, and kills off those stirrings of empathy which the pastoral disavows. The *adynaton*, that is, endorses disengagement.

ใช้ ใช้ ใช้ ใช้

In the previous section, I have discussed the role of metaphor and comparison and allied figures and tropes. In the course of the argument it became evident that a trope need not be restricted to a single term or phrase, that it need not be incidental to the larger meaning. Florus' image of the rose, Thomas Lodge's exercise in sheep, suggest that a trope can, either on its own or in combination with others, work toward a broader objective. Conversely a poem, which on the face of it uses few or no tropes, may in its entirety convey a message that is unmistakably figurative, difficult though it is to define the metaphor involved. It is possible for the herdsman as poet, the herdsman as lover, or the herdsman as moralist or satirist to present himself simply as a guardian of his flocks and as the amiable associate of other herdsmen. The pastoral vehicle remains intact; but by the imponderable force of the poet's shaping, the symbolic extensions become incontestable.

> Together both, ere the high Lawns appear'd
> Under the opening eye-lids of the morn,
> We drove a field, and both together heard
> What time the Gray-fly winds her sultry horn,
> Batt'ning our flocks. . . .

The lines that prompted Dr. Johnson's ridicule perpetuate a "sunken" trope which, by Milton's time, had become a conventional implement in the pastoral armory. Pasturing as a trope for the studying and writing of verse is only one of the possibilities. Pastoral can become a vehicle for poetic speculation on religious mysteries, on the hierarchy of the church, and sundry other subjects; and the temptation to articulate these issues by leaning on the language of the herdsman's life was always strong.[34] Modoin of Autun, in the early ninth century, devotes the first part of his *Ecloga* to a discussion of poetry;[35] Spenser's *Shepheards Calender* contains two eclogues, "June" and "October," which in different ways are about the writing of poetry. The theme of "October," whether one ought to write pastoral or more substantial verse, is Virgilian; similar weighings of the merits of one kind of poetry against another are common in Renaissance and post-Renaissance pastoral. The mode can be exploited for humorous purposes; at the end of Sir William Jones' *Arcadia* (1772), after a discussion of the various species of pastoral and their advantages and disadvantages, the piscatory idylls are thrown into the sea.

But we must distinguish between open considerations of poetry within a pastoral setting, and pastorals whose ostensible dramatization of life in the bower conceals comments on the writing of poetry. We are concerned with the latter. The degree to which Virgil's *Eclogues* offer a poetics is a question to which various answers have been given. My own feeling is that the matter can be exaggerated. It is true that in the second half of the collection, and especially in *Eclogue* 9, the subject of poetry is more prominent than in the first half.[36] It is also true, as we have seen, that Virgil seems to be aware of the figurative potential of such a term as *calamus*, which designates both reed pipe and reed pen. But there is no fixed grid of analogies, no agreed design for a pastoral poetics. The medieval love of systematic allegory was needed to make this development possible.

Servius is mistaken when, commenting on *Eclogue* 10, lines 16–17:

> Here are his sheep; they think no ill of us,
> So think no ill of them, my poet-hero,[37]

he proposes that the lines are allegorical, meaning: do not blush at the thought of writing pastorals.[38] The poet is not recommending that Gallus write pastoral poetry. Rather, Virgil is suggesting that Gallus should not blush at being placed, in the poem, in a bucolic setting despite the fact that Gallus himself, an elegiac poet, did not work in the pastoral medium.

Virgil's restraint is the more striking since poetics in the form of a poetry that is ostensibly about something else is of ancient vintage. It has recently been argued, with considerable success, that Pindar's statements about his poetic principles are not always overt. *Isthmian* 5, for instance, seems to be concerned with the writing of poetry as much as with the celebration of the victor.[39] In other poets this sort of thing is more obvious. The writer's workshop is likely to appear in the guise of the grove of the Heliconian Muses, and poets picking flowers in that grove are understood to be composing poetry.[40] Aristophanes, Hellenistic epigrammatists, as well as Plato, avail themselves of this apparatus, which in the end gives us Milton's variant

> Shatter your leaves before the mellowing year.

Milton is addressing laurel, myrtle, and ivy; he will scatter their leaves on the tomb; that is to say, he will sing a dirge. Here the strewing of flowers or leaves is a trope for the composing of funerary pastoral, just as the winding of garlands and the giving of posies may be a trope for the composing of encomia (cf. above, Chapter Nine).[41] Particular plants are elected to be images of style; likewise the voices of particular animals are sounded to suggest a commitment in the art of poetry.[42] The voices of the animals are programmatic in the very earliest examples of

Greek lyric poetry. Alcman's first *Maiden-Song*, for example, has the contending singers compare themselves and their opponents to swans and owls. Similar analogies crop up again and again in agonistic poetry.

Pastoral lyric, with its interest in the singing match, and with its natural scenery of plants and beasts, would seem to be a logical exploiter of the figurative uses of flora and fauna to define choices of style and mood. The voice of the cicada is central; it is a testimonial to the plain style, the utterance of the dry mouth, as Theocritus puts it in *Idyll* 7, line 37.[43] Theocritus' pride in the *style sec* is in line with Callimachus' repudiation of the grand style, which is itself expressed as a preference for cicadas over asses (*Aitia*, 1.29–30). But there is a difference. The Callimacheans, especially the Roman neoterics, provide the listener with frequent reminders of how much sweat and pain has gone into making the poem, thin and airy as it is. In pastoral, on the other hand, this will not do. *Ponos* is not alien to the bower; but it must not be associated with the glimpses into his workshop that the poet chooses to incorporate in the poem.

For Theocritus, however, we can go further. The question is whether Theocritus makes *any* figurative use of shepherding to talk about the making of the pastoral poem. The answer is, largely, no. In fact Theocritus' verse has rarely suggested anything of the sort.[44] His herdsmen are poets of a sort, to be sure; but their sheep are real sheep, and their pipes are tangible pipes, not more or less transparent keys to something else. Theocritus, and his herdsmen with him, are too firmly settled in the grove to cast their eyes beyond it to paler latitudes. He is not a theorizing poet like Callimachus, although on one or two occasions he has a singer come out with an explicit statement of literary allegiance. When this happens, the language is direct; the pastoral frame is momentarily forgotten. A Theocritean pastoral scene is never an apologia or a *recusatio* of the poet as poet. For one thing, such a procedure would introduce the element of autobiography, which offends against the Theocritean principle of authorial detachment. Or again, it would set off a preoccupation with development. This is what happens in Marot's "Eglogue au Roy;" the seasonal cycle absorbs much of the initial energy of the poem and is counteracted only by the unvarying homage to the king. Theocritus would frown on this refurbishing of bucolic *topoi* for the appraisal of real lives and temporal instability. The herdsmen's bower is the only reality; to employ it as a transparency through which to catch glimpses of other, more important, lives would be unthinkable. This is true even of the complex seventh *Idyll* in which two different types of poets match their skills. Their difference is documented by what they produce, by the poetic achievements they put before us, not by anything the author says about them or by what the singers say about themselves *as* herdsmen.

Theocritus' reluctance to mean more than he says does not confine itself to the subject of poetics. For the sake of contrast, let us look at one of his later successors. In the second eclogue of the *Einsiedeln* poet, it will be recalled, Glyceranus asks Mystes why he is sad, and wonders whether his sadness is caused by trouble in his herd. Mystes answers (7):

> altius est, Glycerane, aliquid, non quod patet: erras.

"You are wrong; the cause lies deeper, out of sight." Here the pastoral poet relinquishes the empirical mode usually observed by his peers, and has his character admit frankly that there are dimensions not open to view. This first step led to a development which E. W. Tayler recently described as follows (cf. also the passage from E. K. Chambers quoted above in Chapter One):

Broadly speaking there are two sorts of pastoral verse, two main traditions within the same genre: one is the allegorical or symbolic pastoral, which is no longer generally recognized for what it is; and the other is the "decorative" or "sugared" pastoral, which is no longer fashionable. Dr. Johnson appears to have had little or no

imaginative understanding of the former—the successful religious
use of the form died with the seventeenth century—but he was familiar
enough with the decorative tradition to want to judge all pastoral
in terms of it. . . . hence those vigorously commonsensical criticisms
of "Lycidas" that have reappeared in our own day in the naive notion
that the pastoral is a cotton-candy genre.[45]

I submit that Dr. Johnson was right to analyze "Lycidas" in
terms of the criteria that apply to the simple pastoral; and that
both Johnson and Tayler are wrong in shrugging off the simple
pastoral as cotton candy.

The difficulties of the word "symbol" are notorious. In a
discussion of the pastoral, the term may refer to the mechanisms
of the *Schluesselgedicht*, with its tantalizing substitution of certain
codable names for other more familiar ones. Or it refers to the
Christian allegory of the shepherd who looks after his flock.
Or again it signalizes the richly imaginative procedures of the
sixteenth- and seventeenth-century British pastoralists who
transcend the conventional analogies and construct their own
systems of meaning. Tayler notes that "Before reaching Spenser
and Shakespeare it was necessary that the entire form become
'allegorical', an emblem or trope of the world at a particular
moment in spiritual history: genre had to become metaphor."[46]

This is the notion of the pastoral form as trope. Before I
turn to it, let me say that I am not going to concern myself with
the specifically Christian pastoral. There is room for some attention to the function of Christian overtones in non-theological
pastoral. But the tradition of Christ the shepherd, derived
substantially from the Gospel of John (10.11–16),[47] forms a vast
subject, with its own objectives and formal characteristics. I am
not competent to deal with it; in any case, to include it would
mean to enlarge our task beyond seemly limits. A distinction
should be made between the old bucolic allegory of Christ and
his flock, on the one hand, and the management of traditional
bucolic patterns for the expression of religious ideas, on the other.[48]

From what I have said earlier, it is clear that the absorption of religious elements into the pastoral generates difficulties and dislocations. Even so simple a fiction as Orpheus taming the beasts, if taken as a religious allegory (*logos* taming the passions), introduces a strain and an opacity that are foreign to the original pastoral impulse.

All pastoral symbolism, whether religious or not, tends to build up toward crises and revulsions. This has been recognized again and again. After Boccaccio, Petrarch, and Mantuan, who perpetuated medieval patterns of symbolic extension, the High Renaissance went back to the pre-Virgilian writers and discovered Theocritus' combination of detachment and immediacy. Sannazaro, Montemayor, Sidney, even Spenser, yearn for the pure air of pastoral innocence, doctrinal or ideological innocence, that is. In spite of the satire of the church in "May," "July," and "September," the pastoral art of the *Calender* is relatively free of the pervasive symbolisms that we associate with the Middle Ages, and that are so prominent in the *Fairie Queene*. The critics, on the other hand, were slower to break with the earlier demands. Of the Renaissance critics who pronounced on the pastoral, only Scaliger comes out clearly against the insistence on symbols, and anticipates eighteenth-century critics in arguing for a pleasing representation of rural life and little else.[49] After pastoral allegorism had received a powerful boost from the metaphysicals, Fontenelle and his British disciples took up Scaliger's cudgels. Pope's judgment of Spenser's *Calender*, of all things, is characteristic: "He is sometimes too allegorical, and treats of matters of religion in a pastoral style, as *Mantuan* had done before him."[50] This does not prevent Pope from labelling his own "Messiah" a "Sacred Eclogue, in imitation of Virgil's Pollio."

Let us look more closely at one or two stages in this tale of trial and error. When Dante was beginning to write the *Paradiso*, he wrote a Latin eclogue in which he answered a friend who had reproached him for not writing the *Commedia* in Latin. In this he imitated Virgil, who had chosen the introduction to an eclogue for answering the similar question of why he was not writing epic or political verse. But unlike Virgil, Dante made his introduction part of the pastoral. He promises to send ten pails of milk, i.e., the ten books of the *Paradiso*, when they are ready. He calls himself Tityrus, and his friend Mopsus, and pretends to be talking about rustic commodities. He proceeds elaborately, even mischievously, taking an obvious delight in the infinite possibilities of the *poème à clef*. There is no attempt to be either mysterious or profound. The poet expects the reader, that is, his friend, to perceive the truth with a minimum of difficulty; the whole enterprise, consisting of two letters each by Dante and his correspondent, is one of almost conspiratorial enjoyment and spirited invention.[51] As in Virgil's fourth *Eclogue*, the pastoral color is used to impart an air of jollity; the message is determined by the medium, but the wit does not embarrass the decipherment.

It is quite different with the Latin eclogues written by Petrarch and Boccaccio. Both authors prized their achievements for their cryptic quality; they assumed the message to be undecipherable, and supplied keys to help their friends untangle the allegory of names and arguments.[52] These keys are to be found in the poets' letters; they are designed only for intimates. Thereby pastoral became a kind of closet poetry, esoteric and inbred, a development which Dante would not have wished, and which makes a sham of the original mandate of the genre. Though later pastoral hardly ever again achieved the degree of mystification realized in this poetry of Boccaccio's, the fashion was not quickly abandoned. Mantuan's ninth *Eclogue*, for instance, ostensibly discourses on the diseased and unnatural behavior of the animals and the dreariness of the landscape. That the talk is really about the corruption in the Roman curia becomes apparent only from the eventual compliment paid, by way of contrast, a papal official. On the surface the poem is rambling, unfocused, impenetrable; the clue to a more consonant vision is supplied late in the game, and even then it is accessible only to those who have a nose for this sort of allegory. In Mantuan's second *Eclogue*, likewise, the motif of the flood appears to be introduced not for its own sake, but for what it says, through symbolic extension, about the perils of unlimited passion.

After Mantuan the manner was continued by the vernacular pastoralists, by Marot and the Pléiade,[53] and by Spenser. Here the accent is more on the substitution of names than on broader symbolic techniques. In "Colin Clouts Come Home Again," every character stands for a poet or for a member of Elizabeth's court; Elizabeth herself is Cynthia. From two lines in the *Calender* that derive from Virgil, it appears that Spenser associated the technique of the *poème à clef* and personal allegory with Virgil's pastoral procedure.[54] There have always been critics who have tried to recognize historical persons in the herdsmen of Virgil's *Eclogues*. The seventeenth-century Spanish critic La Cerda argued that in the seventh *Eclogue*, Corydon is Virgil himself, while Thyrsis stands for Theocritus.[55] Other writers have read even more complicated correspondences into the sets of personae of the *Eclogues*,[56] including the recently offered suggestion that the Cyclopes stand for the enemies of Augustus. Curiously enough it was Virgil's originality that prompted much of this extravagant prosopographical speculation. It was felt that where he did not obviously imitate Theocritus, the reason was that his hand was forced by the circumstances of his life, and by his wish to include biographical information under the cover of bucolic masks.[57] The majority of modern critics, although conceding that in some of his pastoral characters Virgil has dramatized experiences which have their origin in his own social existence, prefer to think that it is impossible to set up equations of the sort that were the pride of Boccaccio and Mantuan. The *Eclogues* are not a confessional exercise in fancy dress, but dramatic realizations of issues and moods that transcend the lives of specific individuals.

The same is true, to a much greater extent, of Theocritus. Reitzenstein's well-known and at one time extremely popular theory that the *Idylls* featured a Coan circle of poets, recognizable by the application of certain keys, has few adherents left. Throughout his discussion the keyword is *griphos*, "conundrum."[58] Reitzenstein felt that Theocritus was, like Lycophron in his *Alexandra*, appealing to the problem-solving abilities of his listeners and readers. A typical example: in *Idyll* 10, Bucaeus is really Callimachus, while Milon is Sositheus (cf. *Anthol. Pal.* 7.707). Sanity returned when Wendel showed, against Reitzenstein and his followers, that only a few names in Theocritus refer to real persons, and that of them only two seem to be pseudonyms.[59] Wendel claimed that even Lycidas is the name of a real person. This I find hard to believe; but the conservatism of Wendel's treatment is an admirable corrective to the wild speculations that preceded it. In the end, Wendel finds that even Simichidas and Sicelidas are not made-up names, but *gentilicia*, on the order of Callimachus' *Battiadēs* (*Anthol. Pal.* 7.415).[60] He recognizes the difference between *Idyll* 7 and the rest of the *Idylls*; in the latter the herdsmen sometimes talk about real people, while in the "Thalysia" real people dress up as herdsmen. But there is no attempt to conceal identities, no preoccupation with obscurity or transference. With the exception of *Idyll* 7, which we may or may not want to call autobiographical, Theocritus' herdsmen, even more than those of Virgil, *are* herdsmen and not cyphers for politicians or poets or anybody else in the writer's life. There is no *Schluesseldichtung*, because Theocritus' conception of the pastoral takes its commitment to *otium* and a life away from civilization seriously. The aesthetics and the epistemology that underlie the genre demand that life in the grove not be unhinged by extrapolations. If the herdsmen and the animals were only a front behind which a cast of an entirely different persuasion were hiding, the basic purpose of the poetry, to show man at his simplest and at his unencumbered best, would be defeated. *Idyll* 4 indicates how important this is to Theocritus. The poem is set in the country near Croton. If Theocritus' pastoral were designed to mirror, or to enable us to infer, the realities of the poet's life, there should be a reference, overt or hidden, to the terrible fate which Pyrrhus visited on Croton in 279 BC. A Renaissance pastoral would have it; Theocritus does not.

We are now prepared to return to the larger question of the pastoral as trope. What about symbolisms that are implied rather than pushed at us; that are not conditioned by a code of substitution, but follow spontaneously from the poet's handling of mise-en-scène and action? Take Marvell's "The Nymph Complaining." D. C. Allen has argued[61] that "the poem is not, as critics have said, about kindness to animals, or the death of animals, or the death of Christ, or the British Church: on the contrary, it is a sensitive treatment of the loss of first love, a loss augmented by a virginal sense of deprivation and unfulfillment."[62] Allen holds that the understanding of the poem must be neither literal nor metaphorical in the conventional way, but allusive. We are to sense, implied in the argument of the poem, a realm of experience that is hinted at rather than formulated. It is the special virtue of this poetry of allusion that there are no systematic correspondences which would allow us to construct a deeper understanding from a number of small clues. But if this is so, how can we, as critics, be sure of our readings? The temptation is to be more definitive than the evidence permits. One critic says, with reference to Milton: "In *Lycidas* and the *Epitaphium* he employs, as the tradition of the pastoral monody fully sanctions, a species of allegory which is midway between direct statement and dramatic projection."[63] The preciseness of the formulation gives us pause; are we, after all, to plot the meaning on an orderly grid of limiting terms? In some sections of the poems this may be possible; but I doubt that they are the really important sections, and that the allegory contained in them will help us far.

Much better, with Rosemond Tuve, to regard the pastoral as a "continued figure;"[64] the poem as a whole is a trope, rather than any one portion of it. The figurative element of early pastoral is not figurative in the sense that we are asked to isolate a *relatum* or a set of *relata* behind the surface, but rather in the sense in which all non-descriptive writing is figurative. That is, the pastoral, with its accepted machinery and its predictable moves, generates an appreciation of beauty that carries the listener beyond the grove, and permits him, for himself, to compare small with great. I doubt, however, that this process is the result of a conscious design. On the contrary, it seems to me important to remember that the pastoral achieves its special effect by forcing the imagination to dwell on little things—note the riddles at the end of *Eclogue* 3—rather than to leave its moorings and divine larger matters. Once more it appears that Dr. Johnson's instincts were truer than the instincts of many modern critics nurtured on a fare of Ronsard, Donne, and Marvell. He insists that the pastoral be unpretentious. What, apparently, he declines to see is that the pastoral, to be fully effective, must also be something more than a literal statement.

What is the nature of the trope, and how do we distinguish it from the anagogic structure that Empson reads into everything *he* considers pastoral? If the traditional pastoral is granted an extension beyond its obvious semantic limits, is there not a risk of involuntary humor, as Johnson and Empson castigate it in Milton? Marvell's Mower, it has been suggested, is hardly a real mower but "a literary clown, a hard-laborer suddenly overwhelmed with the refined sensibility that courtly love brings with it. In 'The Mower's Song' . . . this incongruity reaches its highest pitch in the comic, symbolic extensions of the Mower figure. . . ."[65] This is an important insight, and one that is not always sufficiently taken into account. Did Virgil obtain symbolic depth without converting incongruity into ludicrousness? For, as Boccaccio has it, Virgil hides some meanings beneath his bark, whereas Theocritus intends no other meaning besides what the bark of his words shows.[66] This distinction between the founding fathers of the species is of ancient ancestry.[67] I believe that it is false, and that Theocritus and Virgil are at one in disallowing precise metaphorical extension, but offering another kind of openness.

Theocritus resists decoding. It is snatching at straws to aver, as one recent writer does, that when Polyphemus looks into the water and discovers himself to be beautiful, we should understand him to be looking at Galatea (a water nymph), and gaining an insight into his own looks by a contemplation of the beloved. Polyphemus' looking into the water—what else would he have used for a mirror?—and his delusion about himself accord well with the character Theocritus has given him. His thoughts are childish, not profound; self-contained, not allusive or figurative. Still, even the most naive poem of Theocritus allows for a tension between the reality described and the promise of a larger response.[68] Let us take so simple an action as that in *Idyll* 4. While Battus moans over his dead girl, the cattle stray into the olive grove, and as he runs after a heifer, he cuts his ankle on a thorn. There is an immediate moral (56–57): when you go into the hills, watch out for brambles. But the quality of the poem is such that we cannot be completely satisfied with so mundane a lesson. Unlike Calpurnius (*Eclogue* 3), Theocritus does not suggest, in so many words, that we are to make a connection between the lost girl and the strayed heifer. There is, in fact, no pressure upon us to enlarge the horizon of our understanding. It is the charm of the poem that its scene is small, insulated, and clearly focused, as if it were seen through the wrong end of a telescope. If, nevertheless, we feel that the poem has more to tell us than it actually states, it will not do to examine individual words or phrases for figurative secrets, or to look at the action, or the subactions, as condensations of a larger meaning. If the poem strikes us as more meaningful than its parts, we must go back to our original contention about the affinity between the pastoral and the Epicurean creed.

In Chapter Nine, I argued that the pastoral does not describe a life in the country, but arranges elements taken from the country in such a manner as to permit the full flowering of another order: the life of the soul, the *otium* of the free. This is the point at which the figurative presence of the poem comes into its own. The picture of the herdsman grieving over the death of his beloved and pursuing his herd into the thicket is sufficient unto itself as a credible and affecting scene. But it also serves to remind us of the simplicities available to all good men if only they can free themselves of the constraints of the commonwealth. "Remind" is, probably, too strong a term. The temper is not nostalgic, nor is it hortatory. Neither the poet nor the poem is in the business of therapy, of social adjustment or ideological conversion. The Epicurean strain is there, but only as an undertone, an aesthetic concomitant. This is a crucial point. In the Theocritean pastoral lyric, the symbolism is, as it were, accidental, an additional dimension, rather than the shaping vision that it is in other kinds of poetry. The psychological impact of the symbolism may be powerful. But that does not permit us to assign to it an importance that it does not have. The experience of pastoral teaches us that there are various degrees of symbolic commitment. In its own case, the commitment is unexacting. We cannot miss it; but all it does is to enrich our enjoyment of the grove, not to compel our devotion to a hidden creed. The freedom of the Garden turns out to be a part of the "message." Because of it, the symbolism is persuasive, but has no binding force. It makes itself available to the listener, ready to be caught, but tolerant if it is not.

The swain's innocence is, somehow, understood as an exemplum of what is possible under the aegis of friendship and liberty. The principal tropical burden of the Theocritean pastoral lyric is Epicurean. Put as baldly as this, and without the modifications of the scheme that each poem demands, the conclusion seems trite, and hardly intriguing enough to engage a good poet's interest. But it must be remembered that we are talking about the meaning of a whole genre, and not of an individual poem which will, naturally enough, produce its own special variation upon the theme. It is also true, however, that the pastoral genre is different from other genres in the nature of its figurative impact. A pastoral poem, qua pastoral, exercises a symbolic effect that is logically and aesthetically prior to the particularities of the individual work. Marvell and Donne push the special insights of each poem into what is at times an almost self-defeating tension with the generic trope. Others, among them Theocritus, choose to hold such tensions to a minimum by permitting the generic trope to operate in relative purity. This is not to say that the Theocritean pastoral is more unadornedly philosophical than that of the metaphysicals, or of Virgil; but only that its conceptual implications are more consistently traceable from poem to poem, and that they are less subject to the twists of vision imposed by the poet's intrusive ego.

Beyond this it would be rash to venture; the artlessness of the *Idylls* warns us not to probe too deeply. Epicurus' own recommendation to avoid all *paideia* probably includes a warning against literary criticism. Now that we have reached the end of our study, I suspect that Theocritus and Epicurus, reclining jointly in the garden reserved for the free, are laughing in their sleeves, like the Lycidas of *Idyll* 7, at the pretensions of those who argue before they fall in with the singing. Between Lycidas' smile and Pan's choler, the pastoral lyric invites but a limited response. It is up to us to observe a critical decorum commensurate to the scope of the object. There are certain kinds of literature that demand to be approached with the utmost restraint. The pastoral lyric is one of them. It is impossible for any one who tries to say something useful about Theocritus or Virgil to come away without feeling that he has used the steam shovel where he should have wielded a toothpick and a brush. For his sins, the critic begs forgiveness of those who know the secrets of the green cabinet and protect it from academic herbalists. Perhaps, who knows, a prayer to Epicurus is in order, if only to mark an end, before returning to the city!

REFERENCE MATTER

Abbreviations Used in the Notes

A J Phil.	*American Journal of Philology*
Anthol. Pal.	*Anthologia Palatina*
C & M	*Classica et Mediaevalia*
CQ	*Classical Quarterly*
GGA	*Goettingische Gelehrte Anzeigen*
GRBS	*Greek, Roman, and Byzantine Studies*
HSCPh.	*Harvard Studies in Classical Philology*
JAW	*Jahresbericht ueber die Fortschritte der Altertumswissenschaft*
JHI	*Journal of the History of Ideas*
JHS	*Journal of Hellenic Studies*
MH	*Museum Helveticum*
PMLA	Publications of the Modern Language Association
RE	*Real-Encyclopaedie der klassischen Altertumswissenschaft*, edited by A. Pauly, G. Wissowa, and W. Kroll.
REA	*Revue des études anciennes*
REG	*Revue des études grecques*
RhM	*Rheinisches Museum fuer Philologie*
SP	*Studies in Philology*
TAPA	*Transactions of the American Philological Association*
WS	*Wiener Studien*

Notes

Chapter 1

1. For a recent example, see D. J. Gillis, "Pastoral Poetry in Lucretius," *Latomus*, 26 (1967), 339–362. The author collects all or most of the rustic passages in Lucretius, on the supposition that rustic and pastoral are the same.

2. H. Tennyson, *Tennyson: A Memoir* (London 1897), Vol. I, 265.

3. Dr. Johnson's comments on the pastoral are to be found in his Rambler essays, Nos. 36 and 37; his *Lives* of Milton, Pope, and Philips; *Rasselas*, chapter 19; and the *Adventurer* No. 92. *Rambler* No. 37, rather more sympathetic than No. 36, is still about the best short discussion of the pastoral. Cf. E. W. Tayler, *Nature and Art in Renaissance Literature* (New York 1964), p. 180; F. Kermode (ed.), *English Pastoral Poetry from the Beginnings to Marvell* (London 1952), p. 11; J. E. Congleton, *Theories of Pastoral Poetry in England, 1684–1798* (Gainesville 1952), pp. 101 ff. For an anticipation of Johnson's jibe, see the "Remarques" added by Charles Sorel to the second edition of his *Le Berger Extravagant* (1633).

4. Servius on Virgil's *Eclogue* 3.1: "Qui enim bucolica scribit, curare debet ante omnia, ne similes sibi sint eclogae." Thomas Purney, more than a generation before Samuel Johnson, condemns pastoralists who imitate their predecessors: *A Full Inquiry into the True Nature of Pastoral* (London 1717; Los Angeles 1948, ed. by Earl Wasserman), 3.8; he finds borrowings from the Canticles less offensive than borrowings from Virgil and Theocritus.

5. lines 38–39:

> quid tum, si fuscus Amyntas?
> Et nigrae violae sunt, et vaccinia nigra.

6. For some of the dominant features that appear again and again in European pastoral lyrics, see the list furnished by M. I. Gerhardt in her very good *Essai d'Analyse Littéraire de la Pastorale* (Assen 1950), pp. 293–295.

7. Cited by René Rapin in his *Dissertatio de Carmine Pastorali*, translated by Thos. Creech and prefixed to his translation of the *Idylliums of Theocritus* (Oxford 1684), pp. 18–19. A similar view was held by G. J. Vossius; see Irene Behrens, *Die Lehre von der Einteilung der Dichtkunst, Beihefte zur Zeitschrift fuer romanische Philologie*, Heft 92 (Halle 1940), 129–130.

8. Some modern critics, also, refuse to grant pastoral an independent standing. E. Schwartz, *Charakterkoepfe aus der Antike* (Stuttgart 1943; first edition, 1903–1910), p. 154: "Hirtenpoesie und Alexandrinertum sind aus modernen Verhaeltnissen hervorgegangene, ungeschichtliche Begriffe, die das schwierige Verstaendnis Theokrits nur noch schwieriger machen." See also G. Rohde, *Studien und Interpretationen zur antiken Literatur, Religion und Geschichte* (Berlin 1963), in an essay originally published in 1932.

9. For Proclus and J. Tzetzes, see Behrens, *Die Lehre*, p. 31, note 93. Hugo of St. Victor's *Eruditio Didascalica* (before 1141) has no slot for the pastoral; but Matthew of Vendôme, in his *Ars Versificatoria* (before 1175) has Pastoral Poetry appear to him along with other genre figures; cf. Behrens, p. 44.

10. Behrens, *Die Lehre*, pp. 85 ff.

11. In line 39, Bentley's reading (adopted by Housman) *ritus pastorum* for the MS *pecorum ritus* can hardly be right. The emphasis is throughout on the behavior of the natural order, including animals; astronomic lions, bucolic sheep, and pharmacological snakes are treated as members of the same poetic universe.

12. J. C. Scaliger, *Poetices libri septem* (1561). Pastoral is discussed in Book 1, chapter 4, and Book 5, chapter 5; the latter is a comparison of Theocritus and Virgil, to the advantage of the Greek. A summary of Scaliger's views, drawn from F. M. Padelford (ed.), *Select Translations from Scaliger's Poetics* (New York 1905), will be found in Congleton, *Theories of Pastoral Poetry*, pp. 17–18.

13. For the details of the quarrel, see Thomas Purney, *A Full Inquiry*.

14. W. Empson, *Some Versions of Pastoral* (Norfolk 1950).

15. R. Poggioli was working on a book on the pastoral when, in 1963, he was killed in a car accident. For his views we must, therefore, depend on the following articles, always with the understanding that he would probably have wished to refine them further in the publication to which they stand in the relation of sketches: "Zampogna e cornamusa," *Inventario*, 8 (1956), 216–247; "The Oaten Flute," *Harvard Library Bulletin*, 11.2 (1957), 147–184; "The Pastoral of the Self," *Daedalus*, 88 (1959), 686–699; "Naboth's Vineyard or the Pastoral View of the Social Order," *JHI*, 24 (1963), 3–24.

16. Graham Hough, *Legends and Pastorals* (London 1961).

17. Cf. W. Leonard Grant, "New Forms of Neo-Latin Pastoral," *Studies in the Renaissance*, 4 (1957), 75–76.

18. Cited by I. A. Richards, in T. A. Sebeok, *Style in Language* (Bloomington 1960), p. 9. Richards further quotes from Wordsworth's "The Prelude," ii. 221–224, where Wordsworth reminds Coleridge that they are no friends of

> that false secondary power, by which
> In weakness, we create distinctions, then
> Deem that our puny boundaries are things
> Which we perceive, and not which we have made.

Ben Jonson applies the same healthy skepticism to definitions of the pastoral in the "Prologue" to the *Sad Shepherd*. He makes fun of those who feel that pastoral does not permit humor:

> As if all poesie had one character
> In which what were not written, were not right.

19. See A. Hulubei, *L'Eglogue en France au xvie siècle* (Paris 1938), p. 18; also W. Leonard Grant, "Early Neo-Latin Pastoral," *Phoenix*, 9 (1955), 19.

20. An elegiac amoebean commentary on the marriage of Ronsard's protectress, Marguerite of Savoy (1559). For this and other pastoral productions of the Pléiade, see Hulubei, *L'Eglogue en France*, pp. 417 ff.

21. Congleton, *Theories of Pastoral Poetry*, p. 198: G. Colletet's *Discours du poème bucolique* (1657) was the first separately printed study of the pastoral.

22. R. F. Jones, "Eclogue Types in English Poetry of the Eighteenth Century," *Journal of English and Germanic Philology*, 24 (1925), 33–60.

23. Hulubei, *L'Eglogue en France*, pp. 705–706.

24. I have not been able to verify references to Donatus found in some of the modern literature. For the form *egloga* or *egloge* in antiquity, see H. Schuchardt, *Der Vokalismus des Vulgaerlateins* (Leipzig 1866), Vol. 1, 124.

25. Present scholarship favors the view of popular origins, represented by W. P. Jones, "The Pastourelle and French Folk Drama," *Harvard Studies and Notes in Philology and Literature*, 13 (1931), 129–163, as against the notion that the form is a learned development of the latin eclogue: E. Faral, "La Pastourelle," *Romania*, 49 (1923), 204–259. But cf. W. Theiler, "Liebesgespraech und Pastourelle," in H. Dahlmann and R. Merkelbach, *Studien zur Textgeschichte und Textkritik* (Cologne 1959), pp. 279–283.

26. For the difficulties of εἶδος and εἰδύλλιον, see the account of A. S. F. Gow (ed.), *Theocritus* (Cambridge 1952), Vol. 1, lxxi f.

27. J. G. von Herder, *Saemmtliche Werke*, ed. B. Suphan, Vol. 23 (Berlin 1885), 298–306: a section entitled "Idyll," forming part of the second volume of *Adrasteia* (1801). Cf. also Herder's comparison of Theocritus and Gessner in his *Fragmente ueber die neuere deutsche Literatur* (1767), conveniently reprinted in P. Merker, *Deutsche Idyllendichtung, 1700–1840* (Berlin 1934), pp. 98–101.

28. "... der sinnlichste Ausdruck der hoechst verschoenerten Leiden-
schaften und Empfindungen solcher Menschen, die in kleineren Gesellschaften
zusammen leben." Herder's whole discussion is still eminently readable,
especially for his refusal, against F. Schlegel and M. Mendelssohn, to make
nice distinctions between various types of pastoral poetry.

29. The title is Moses Hadas', in his translation of Dio's seventh oration in
his *Three Greek Romances* (New York 1953).

30. Thomas Purney, *A Full Inquiry*, pp. 6 ff.

31. E. K. Chambers (ed.), *English Pastorals* (London 1895), pp. xvii–xviii.

32. See, e.g., E. W. Tayler, *Nature and Art*.

33. C. W. Truesdale, "English Pastoral Verse from Spenser to Marvell"
(unpublished Ph.D. dissertation, University of Washington, 1956), pp. 317ff.;
see also W. W. Greg, *Pastoral Poetry and Pastoral Drama* (London 1906), pp.
416 f. On p. 1 of his great work, Greg says:

It is characteristic of the artificiality of pastoral as a literary form that the
impulse which gave the first creative touch at seeding loses itself later and
finds no place among the forces at work at blossom time; the methods adopted
by the greatest masters of the form are inconsistent with the motives that
impelled them to its use, and where these motives were followed to their
logical conclusion, the result, both in literature and in life, became a byword
for absurd unreality.

34. E. Staiger, *Die Grundbegriffe der Poetik* (Zuerich 1946), pp. 157 ff.

35. That Theocritus himself regarded the pastoral epigram in a different
light from the pastoral lyric is shown, to take one instance, in his handling of the
gods. The epigrams are usually associated with a cult act or a cult implement,
both of which are conspicuously missing from the pastoral lyric, which is
secular. For a more extended discussion of this point, see below, Chapter Five.
Where the occasion for the epigram is a tomb, the emphasis on mortality is
greatly in excess of what is found in the lyric, which, even in the dirge, invokes
the vitality and beauty of life. Virgil's seventh *Eclogue* contains two ritual
epigrams, one to Diana, the other to Priapus. On this score, as on others,
Virgil synthesizes older forms. J. Hubaux, *Les thèmes bucoliques dans la poésie
latine* (Brussels 1930), Chapter 2 is entitled: "Epigramme et Bucolique."
In it he deals with the Roman neoterics, especially Porcius Licinius and
Mucius Scaevola, without touching on the genre problems involved.

36. Some scholars have, therefore, resigned themselves to the conclusion
that the pastoral genre is formally and procedurally indeterminate from its
beginnings. G. Rohde, *Studien und Interpretationen*, pp. 73–81: "Bukolik ist
kein formbestimmtes literarisches *genos*." It is obvious that I cannot go along
with this counsel of despair.

37. Compare Scaliger's derivation of this variety from early forms of intercourse: Padelford, *Scaliger's Poetics*, p. 21.

38. P. Steinmetz, "Gattungen und Epochen der griechischen Literatur in der Sicht Quintilians," *Hermes*, 92 (1964), 454–466. Steinmetz refers to the collection of material by J. Kayser, *De veterum arte poetica quaestiones selectae* (Leipzig 1906).

39. W. Leonard Grant, *Neo-Latin Literature and the Pastoral* (Chapel Hill 1965).

40. See, e.g., Hallett Smith, *Elizabethan Poetry* (Harvard 1952), pp. 31 ff.

41. For a recent appraisal of the contest in *Eclogue* 7, see V. Poeschl, *Die Hirtendichtung Virgils* (Heidelberg 1964), p. 108.

42. J. F. Lynen, *The Pastoral Art of Robert Frost* (New Haven 1960), p. 77: Frost's "casual speaking manner, which digresses at every turning into anecdote and whimsical speculation, creates the illusion that the poem is just a specimen of back-parlor conversation."

43. J. C. Ransom, "A Poem Nearly Anonymous," *American Review*, 4 (1933); reprinted in C. A. Patrides (ed.), *Milton's Lycidas* (New York 1961), pp. 64–81. The words quoted appear on p. 66.

44. This is argued by M. I. Gerhardt, *Essai*, pp. 300–301.

45. R. Poggioli, "The Pastoral of the Self."

46. *Don Quixote*, Part 1, chapter 12.

47. The view that pastoral offers moral instruction is already found in the section, less than a page, on the pastoral in Sidney's *Apologie for Poetrie*. See G. Gregory Smith (ed.), *Elizabethan Critical Essays* (London 1904), Vol. I, 175.

48. For the details, see below, Chapter Two.

49. According to W. C. Helmbold and E. N. O'Neill, *Plutarch's Quotations* (1959), Plutarch cites Theocritus only twice. He has nothing from Bion, Moschus, or Philitas.

50. Cf. the essay in *The Mirrour*, Vol. III (1779), No. 79, mentioned by M. K. Bragg, *The Formal Eclogue in Eighteenth Century England* (Orono 1926), pp. 115–116. The anonymous author suggests that rural poetry take the place of the formal eclogue. It may be of interest that on p. 116 of his book, Bragg prints a wonderful drawing by Thackeray; it shows a gentleman in fashionable garb sitting on a stile and playing a horn for a group of nonchalant pigs.

51. In Herder's "Idyll" from *Adrasteia*:

Aus der Hirten- ward eine Schaeferwelt, aus dem wirklichen ein geistiges Arkadien, ein Paradies unsrer Hoffnungen und Wuensche, ein Paradies also der Unschuld und Liebe.... Die Stunden unsrer Seele, da wir uns dem zartesten Glueck und Unglueck am naechsten fuehlen, wurden dazu Eklogen, erlesene Situationen und Momente.... Es ist ein Land, das nie war, schwerlich auch je seyn wird, in welchem aber in den schoensten Augenblicken des Lebens unsre dichterische Einbildung oder Empfindung lebte.

52. *Schiller: Ueber naive und sentimentalische Dichtung*, ed. W. F. Mainland (Oxford 1951), p. 54. Schiller's praise of Voss's *Luise* shows that he was not making a tidy distinction between pastoral and other forms of country poetry. Consequently he finds himself in a quandary whether to apply his term "naiv" to the idyll or not.

53. From the *Rambler* No. 36.

54. Lynen, *The Pastoral Art of Robert Frost*, p. 58.

55. Contrast Reuben A. Brower, *Alexander Pope* (Oxford 1959), p. 19: "The ideal shepherd, like Daphnis, is a man living in a mysteriously close relation to physical nature." Brower's picture of the herdsman appears to be based on Tasso and Spenser, rather than on Theocritus or Virgil or, for that matter, the Augustans.

56. Calpurnius 4.147–151:

> rustica credebam nemorales carmina vobis
> concessisse deos et obesis auribus apta;
> verum, quae paribus modo concinuistis avenis,
> tam liquidum, tam dulce cadunt, ut non ego malim,
> quod Paeligna solent examina lambere nectar.

57. M. Marchio, "Un componimento georgico sulle orme di Virgilio: L'egloga v di Calpurnio Siculo," *Giornale Italiano di Filologia*, 10 (1957), 301–314.

58. W. Richter (ed., comm.), *Vergil: Georgica* (Munich 1957), pp. 347–348.

59. For an ancient forerunner of James Thomson, J-F. de Saint-Lambert, and E. C. von Kleist, see the long fragment usually ascribed to Pamprepius of Panopolis (ca. AD 500), detailing various activities in the countryside in the course of rapidly changing seasons of the day. The poem and a translation are conveniently available in D. L. Page (ed., trans.), *Greek Literary Papyri* (London 1941), pp. 564–583.

60. M. Puelma, *Lucilius und Kallimachos* (Frankfurt 1949), p. 116 ff.

61. R. Vischer, *Das einfache Leben* (Goettingen 1965), p. 170; and R. Hoeistad, *Cynic Hero and Cynic King* (Lund 1948), *passim*.

62. For *ponos* in Epicurus, see Chr. Jensen, "Ein neuer Brief Epikurs," *Abhandlungen der Universitaet Goettingen, philosophisch-historisch Klasse*, 3.5 (1933) 35, note 4.

63. E. R. Curtius, *European Literature and the Latin Middle Ages*, trans. W. Trask (New York 1963), p. 185, with references to Homer as a forerunner of the pastoral.

64. *Fairie Queene*, 6.9, stanza 19, Calidore speaking.

65. Pauca tamen suberunt priscae vestigia fraudis.

66. Hugh Blair, *Lectures on Rhetoric and Belles Lettres* (Philadelphia 1858), p. 435.

67. E. W. Tayler, *Nature and Art*, pp. 151–153, tries to find an explanation for this sudden violence, which he considers inimical to the pastoral tradition, in some symbolic purpose, but despairs, and concludes: "Like the Nymph's Faun the Mower reveals a capacity for harmony with Nature, but as always in Marvell the relationship of man and Nature is precarious, liable to be lost in a moment." I would suggest that this insight is not foreign to the ancient pastoral at its best.

68. For this friend of Paulinus of Nola (fourth century AD), and his *De mortibus boum* in thirty-three Asclepiad stanzas, see W. Schmid, "Tityrus Christianus," *Rh M*, 96 (1953), 124 ff. The models are Virgil's *Georgics* 3.478 ff. and Ovid's *Metamorphoses* 7.585 ff., both of which go back to Lucretius 6.1138 ff.

69. *Idyll* 4.55: ὁσσίχον ἐστὶ τὸ τύμμα, καὶ ἀλίκον ἄνδρα δαμάσδει.

70. L. A. Post, "Subtleties in Menander's *Dyscolus*," *A J Phil.*, 84 (1963), 51.

71. See E. K. Chambers, *English Pastorals*, p. 269.

72. J-F. de Saint-Lambert, *Les Saisons* (Amsterdam 1769), pp. xix–xx.

73. See Aulus Gellius 9.3.4; J. Hubaux, *Le réalisme dans les bucoliques de Virgile* (Paris 1927), chapter 5. For Hesiodic influence in the *Eclogues*, see R. Hanslik, "Nachlese zu Vergils Eclogen 1 und 9," *WS*, 68 (1955), 5–19.

74. W. Hebel (ed.), *The Works of Michael Drayton* (Oxford 1932), Vol. III, 245 ff.

75. Truesdale, "English Pastoral Verse," pp. 300 ff.

76. For a witty muddying of Hesiodic and pastoral waters, see the anonymous poem printed by Kermode, *English Pastoral Poetry*, p. 182. The beggar says:

> A hundred head of blacke and white,
> Upon our downes securely feede,
> If any dare his master bite. . . .

Under the impact of proletarian realities, the sheep have turned into lice and bedbugs.

77. From "The Village," in *The Poetical Works of the Rev. George Crabbe*, by his son, Vol. II (London 1838), 73.

78. See especially P. G. Heimgartner, *Die Eigenart Theokrits in seinem Sprichwort* (Freiburg, Switzerland 1940). A few remarks on this dissertation may be in order. The writer classifies proverbs in five groups: (1) simple complete sentences (example: *Idyll* 10.17); this is the largest group by far; (2) paratactic compound sentences (example: 6.17); (3) sentences without copula (example: 16.18); (4) imperatives (example: 15.90); (5) proverbial comparisons (example: 3.54). The classification is not entirely natural; and in fact Heimgartner offers yet another classification, by metrical structure. This is based on his (now antiquated) belief that the hexameter developed from a *Kurzvers*, and

that early versions of the proverbs were often more or less metrical, hence analyzable in terms of *Kurzverse*. In the course of his discussion, Heimgartner offers many fine remarks. He observes that the didactic force of proverbs in Theocritus is virtually nil; and that many proverbial passages in Theocritus make for relief and even humor. But he does not choose to see that the function and frequency of proverbs varies with the kinds of characters whom Theocritus puts on the stage. Further, he is too prone to assume that the mere presence of a proverb enhances the dramatic quality of a piece. Finally he is wrong to assume that, since in many cases Theocritus is our first author to record a particular proverbial phrase, he must have gotten it directly from the people. But the dissertation is a model of tidiness, and a useful and conscientious piece of work.

79. *Proverbiorum Chilias prima, Prolegomena,* in *Desiderii Erasmi Opera Omnia,* Vol. II (Leyden 1703), 10F: "accedunt ad proverbii speciem et illa, bucolico carmini familiaria: ἀδύνατα, ἀναγκαῖα, ἄτοπα, ὅμοια, ἐναντία, i.e., impossibilia, necessaria, absurda, similia, contraria."

80. For further remarks on *impossibilia,* see below, Chapter Twelve.

81. On this subject, see the acute remarks of R. Preyer, "Victorian Wisdom Literature: Fragments and Maxims," *Victorian Studies* (March 1963), pp. 245–262. See also Archer Taylor, *The Proverb* (Harvard 1931), pp. 200 ff.; and Aristotle *Rhetoric* 2.21.1359a2 ff., trans. Buckley:

The employment of maxims becomes him who is rather advanced in life; and particularly as respects subjects about which each happens to be well informed. Since for one not so advanced in age to sport maxims is bad taste ... and argues a want of education. There is a sufficient sign of the truth of this; for the boors of the country are of all other people most fond of hammering out maxims, and set them forth with great volubility.

82. Demetrius *On Style* 156.

83. U. von Wilamowitz-Moellendorff, *Das Schiedsgericht* (Berlin 1925), p. 151.

84. Cf. Bion frags. 4 and 15: the drops that hollow out a stone; and "women are embellished by beauty, men by strength."

Chapter 2

1. Aristotle *Metaphysics* 3.3, 5.2, 9.8, 13.2; *Categories* 12–13. Cf. also the sources cited by S. H. Rosen, "Thales: The Beginning of Philosophy," *Arion,* 1.3 (1962), 48–64.

2. René Rapin, *Dissertatio de Carmine Pastorali,* trans. Thos. Creech (Oxford 1684), p. 2.

3. J. E. Congleton, *Theories of Pastoral Poetry in England, 1684–1798* (Gainesville 1952), p. 126.

4. Cf. M. H. Shackford, "A Definition of the Pastoral Idyll," *PMLA*, 19 (1904), 583–592. For a more judicious management of the same idea, see Stanley Stewart, *The Enclosed Garden* (Madison 1966).

5. For Scaliger and his sources, see F. M. Padelford (ed.), *Select Translations from Scaliger's Poetics* (New York 1905), p. 21. For the Golden Age, cf. below, Chapter Ten.

6. For the contribution of Fontenelle, see below, Chapter Four.

7. A. Lang (trans.), *Theocritus, Bion and Moschus* (London 1880), pp. xix ff. Cf. also R. Mandra, "Theocritean Resemblances," *Revue Belge*, 28 (1950), 5–28.

8. F. Kermode (ed.), *English Pastoral Poetry from the Beginnings to Marvell* (London 1952), p. 18. D. Petropoulos, "Θεοκρίτου Εἰδύλλια ὑπὸ λαογραφικὴν ἔποψιν ἑρμηνευόμενα," Λαογραφία, 18 (1959), 5–93.

9. Diodorus Siculus 4.84; Aelian *Varia Historia* 10.18; Parthenius 29. All go back to Timaeus.

10. See G. Pasquali in *Atene e Roma*, 19 (1916), 93, questioning the reconstruction of the legend by A. Rostagni in the second chapter of his *Poeti Alessandrini* (Turin 1916).

11. Athenaeus 14.619A–C. See G. Knaack, "Bukolik," *RE*, 3 (1899), 1001 ff., and Supplement 1 (1903), 260.

12. For the view of E. Kapp and E. Panofsky, see B. Snell, *Die Entdeckung des Geistes* (third edition, Hamburg 1955), p. 371. *Contra*, H. Dahlmann, "Vates," *Philologus*, 97 (1948), 348 ff.

13. A. Reisch, *De musicis Graecorum certaminibus* (Vienna 1885), has nothing about rustic contests prior to Diodorus, in the first century BC.

14. For literary *gephyrismos* in Theocritus' own time, see Apollonius Rhodius 4.1719 ff.

15. E. Schwartz, *Charakterkoepfe aus der Antike* (Stuttgart 1943; first edition, 1902), p. 163: Theocritus "ist schwerlich auf die einsamen Bergweiden seiner Heimatinsel gestiegen, um von den eintoenigen Rufen und Pfiffen der Hirten sich inspirieren zu lassen; bei den verwilderten, raeuberischen Gesellen, welche die ihre weiten Fluren billig bewirtschaftenden Grundherren in der Oede verkommen liessen, war keine Poesie zu holen."

16. See now the detailed analysis by E. Cremonesi, "Rapporti tra le origini della poesia bucolica e della poesia comica nella tradizione peripatetica," *Dioniso*, 21 (1958), 109–122.

17. C. Wendel, *Scholia in Theocritum Vetera* (Leipzig 1914), pp. 2–3, 8–9.

18. A. Meineke, *Analecta Alexandrina* (Berlin 1843), pp. 360 ff.; cf. Pausanias 3.10; Lucian *De saltatione* chapter 10; Athenaeus 14.629B. For a good survey of the ritual theory, see R. Y. Hathorn, "The Ritual Origin of Pastoral,"

TAPA, 92 (1961), 228-238. On pp. 233 ff., he tabulates his reasons for believing that we should credit the theory. But the counter-arguments of Welcker still hold: F. G. Welcker, "Ueber den Ursprung des Hirtenlieds," *Kleine Schriften*, I (1844), 402-411.

19. I. Trenscenyi-Waldapfel, "Werden und Wesen der bukolischen Poesie," *Acta Antiqua*, 14 (1966), 1-31.

20. Richard Reitzenstein, *Epigramm und Skolion* (Giessen 1893), chapter 4.

21. For the evidence, see A. Dieterich, "De 'bubulcis' Orphicis," in *Kleine Schriften* (1911), pp. 70-78. Now also Erika Simon, "Ein Anthesterien-skyphos des Polygnotos," *Alte Kunst*, 6 (1963), 11, note 36; and T. B. L. Webster, *Hellenistic Poetry and Art* (New York 1964), p. 196, note 4.

22. Cf., however, A. P. Smotrytsch, "Ὁ καλὸς νεανίας καὶ αἴπολοι," *Helikon*, 1 (1961), 118-126, on Herodas *Mime* 8. He argues that the youth is Dionysus, and that the αἴπολοι (*not* the Coan circle) are the περὶ τὸν Διόνυσον τεχνῖται, who included at that time not only actors but also writers, hence the circle of the Museum. Herodas is against the αἴπολοι; he honors the king (equated with Dionysus) but is at odds with the court writers.

23. Wendel, *Scholia in Theocritum Vetera*, p. 4: κρατιστεύοντος τοῦ ζῴου.

24. B. A. van Groningen, "Quelques problèmes de la poésie bucolique grècque," *Mnemosyne*, 11 (1958), 293-317, and especially 12 (1959), 24-53.

25. J. Lavinska, "Certamina bucolica et comica comparantur," *Eos*, 53 (1963), 286-297.

26. Examples: Οἱ Μαλθακοί, frag. 98 Kock; Χείρωνες, frag. 239 Kock.

27. B. Snell, *Scenes from Greek Drama* (Berkeley 1964), p. 73.

28. T. C. W. Stinton, *Euripides and the Judgment of Paris* (London 1965), chapter 2, and the remarks of E. R. Schwinge in *Gnomon*, 39 (1967), 649-650.

29. Theognis 993-996:

εἰ θείης, ᾿Ακάδημε, ἐφίμερον ὕμνον ἀείδειν,
ἄθλον δ᾽ ἐν μέσσῳ παῖς καλὸν ἄνθος ἔχων,
σοί τ᾽ εἴη καὶ ἐμοὶ σοφίης πέρι δηρισάντοιν,
γνοίης χ᾽ ὅσσον ὄνων κρέσσονες ἡμίονοι.

30. Cf. W. Aly, "Praxilla," *RE*, 22.2 (1954), 1762-1768. For Praxilla, see also below, Chapter Three.

31. T. G. Rosenmeyer, "Alcman's *Partheneion I* Reconsidered," *GRBS* 7 (1966), 331-332. Whether the Boeotian school of poetesses (Myrtis, Corinna) are of interest in this connection is difficult to tell because of the sorry state of their literary remains.

32. The story is told by Athenaeus, 14.619C-D. For the date of Clearchus, see F. Wehrli (ed., comm.), *Die Schule des Aristoteles*, Vol. III: *Klearchos* (Basel, 1948), 45.

33. Athenaeus 15.670C.

34. U. von Wilamowitz-Moellendorff, "Parerga," *Hermes*, 14 (1879), 173.

35. On this score I agree with Wilamowitz, against G. Rohde, *Studien und Interpretationen* (Berlin 1963), pp. 89–90, who speaks of "religioeses Erregtsein durch die Natur," the very last thing we expect to find in Theocritus. Anyte's epigrams are now available in A. S. F. Gow & D. L. Page (edd., comm.), *The Greek Anthology: Hellenistic Epigrams* (Cambridge 1965), Vol. I, 35–41; Vol. II, 89–104. Cf. also R. Vischer, *Das einfache Leben* (Goettingen 1965), p. 126 ff.

36. O. Jahn, "Satura," *Hermes*, 3 (1869), 180 ff. See also T. B. L. Webster, "Alexandrian Epigrams and the Theatre," in *Miscellanea Rostagni* (1963), pp. 531–543, especially p. 536.

37. Frag. 1 Powell. Cf. also the earlier treatment of the Polyphemus tale in the dithyramb of Philoxenus.

38. For the details, see A. S. F. Gow, *Theocritus* (Cambridge 1952), Vol. II, 118.

39. For the spelling, rather than Philetas, see W. Croenert, "Philitas von Kòs," *Hermes*, 37 (1902), 212 ff., on the basis of Coan inscriptions.

40. Frag. 16 Powell:

γηρύσαιτο δὲ νεβρὸς ἀπὸ ψυχὴν ὀλέσασα
ὀξείης κάκτου τύμμα φυλαξαμένη.

Cf. A. Nowacki (ed.), *Philitae Coi fragmenta poetica* (Muenster 1927), p. 67.

41. See M. Pohlenz, "Die hellenistische Poesie und die Philosophie," *Charites Friedrich Leo* (Berlin 1911), p. 111.

42. Nowacki, *Philitae Coi fragmenta poetica*, p. 21.

43. G. Lohse, "Die Kunstauffassung im vii Idyll Theokrits," *Hermes*, 94 (1966), 413–424.

44. With Bekker's apostrophes: ὡς λύκοι ἄρν᾽ ἀγαπῶσ᾽, ὡς παῖδα φιλοῦσιν ἐρασταί.

45. It might be asked whether some of the epigrams ascribed to Plato, notably 26 and 27 Diels, are not by Plato after all, in spite of the doubts expressed by most recent scholars. Cf. U. von Wilamowitz-Moellendorff, *Platon* (Berlin 1929), Vol. I, 451, note 1. But even if the poems in question cannot be vindicated, the fact that a later generation could ascribe them to Plato is not without interest. It was felt, apparently, that Plato was the one philosopher capable of pastoral conceits.

46. Note especially Plato's *Laws* 3.677B, and the remarks on the passage in the Budé edition by E. des Places (Paris 1951).

47. *The Moralists*, ed. John M. Robertson (London 1900), Vol. 11, 27–31. Cf. Erwin Wolff, *Shaftesbury und seine Bedeutung fuer die Englische Literatur des 18. Jahrh.*, (Tuebingen 1960), pp. 96–98.

48. See, e.g., Chrysippus' tenet lampooned in Cicero *Academica* 2.93 (frag. 277, Vol. II, von Arnim).

49. See the warnings of Pohlenz, "Die hellenistische Poesie und die Philosophie," pp. 90, 101.

50. See Diogenes Laertius 10.25; he mentions, among the students of Epicurus, "the two Ptolemies from Alexandria, the dark-haired and the blond." See also Plutarch *Adversus Coloten* 1107D–E; *De cohibenda ira* 9.458A. The monograph of A. Pridik, "Koenig Ptolemaios I und die Philosophen," *Acta Universitatis Tartuensis*, B. Vol. XXX, fasc. 1 (1933) is inadequate.

51. E. Bignone, *Teocrito* (Bari 1934), p. 50. See also R. Poggioli, "The Oaten Flute," *Harvard Library Bulletin*, 11.2 (1957), 154: "As a conscious or unconscious philosopher, the shepherd is neither a stoic nor a cynic, but rather an epicurean; and observes with natural spontaneity the ethics of that school. His eudaemonism is not only spiritual but physical as well: and includes the practice of hedonism." Poggioli has in mind the herdsmen of the later European pastoral as well as the ancient; and his picture of what it is to be Epicurean is not entirely favorable.

52. For the problem of the cosmogony in *Eclogue* 6, see the discussion prompted by the paper of A. La Penna, "Esiodo nella cultura e nella poesia di Virgilio," in *Entretiens Fondation Hardt*, 7 (1962), 213–270. See now also A. Traina, "Si numquam fallit imago: Reflessioni sulle Bucoliche e l'epicureismo," *Atene e Roma*, 10 (1965), 72–78; Traina explains *Eclogue* 2, lines 25 ff., as an echo of the Epicurean theory of mirrors. His conclusion: the *Eclogues* are built on a substratum of Epicureanism.

53. Tenney Frank, *Vergil: A Biography* (New York 1922), pp. 102 ff., especially p. 109.

Chapter 3

1. A. O. Lovejoy, *Essays in the History of Ideas* (Baltimore 1948), p. 72.

2. J-P. Sartre, *Literary and Philosophical Essays* (New York 1955), pp. 37 ff.

3. R. Barthes, *Essais Critiques* (Paris 1964), pp. 29–40; also pp. 175–187, concerning Michel Butor's *Mobile*.

4.   Δάκρυά μοι σπένδουσαν ἐπήρατον οἰκτρὰ Θεανώ
     εἶχον ὑπὲρ λέκτρων πάννυχον ἡμετέρων·
     ἐξότε γὰρ πρὸς Ὄλυμπον ἀνέδραμεν ἕσπερος ἀστήρ,
     μέμφετο μελλούσης ἄγγελον ἠριπόλης.
     οὐδὲν ἐφημερίοις καταθύμιον· εἴ τις Ἐρώτων
     λάτρις, νύκτας ἔχειν ὤφελε Κιμμερίων.

5. On symmetry, cf. below, Chapter Four.

6. V. Poeschl, *Die Hirtendichtung Virgils* (Heidelberg 1964); Brooks Otis, *Vergil: A Study in Civilized Poetry* (Oxford 1963), chapter 4. See also below, Chapter Seven.

7. From "The Village." Crabbe later changed the lines to: "For no deep thought the trifling subjects ask; / To sing of shepherds is an easy task. . . ." Cf. *The Poetical Works of the Rev. George Crabbe*, by his son, Vol. II (London 1838), 75.

8. Thos. Purney, *A Full Inquiry into the True Nature of Pastoral* (London 1717).

9. René Rapin, *Dissertatio de Carmine Pastorali*, trans. Thos. Creech (Oxford 1684).

10. J. E. Congleton, *Theories of Pastoral Poetry in England, 1684–1798* (Gainesville 1952), pp. 35–36.

11. *Ibid.*, p. 106. The reference is probably to Rémy Belleau and his imitators, but would apply equally to many non-dramatic eclogues.

12. *Ibid.*, pp. 265, 275. Boileau's critique appears in *L'art poetique* (1674), Chant ii, lines 1 ff.

13. J. Hubaux, *Le réalisme dans les Bucoliques de Virgile* (Paris 1927), pp. 98 ff. Example: *Eclogue* 3, line 1: *cuium pecus*.

14. T. G. Rosenmeyer, "Alcman's *Partheneion I* Reconsidered, " *GRBS*, 7 (1966), 325 ff.

15. A. S. F. Gow, *Theocritus*, Vol. I (Cambridge 1952), lxxii ff.

16. S. T. Coleridge, *Biographia Literaria*, chapter 17.

17. See Josephine Miles in C. A. Patrides (ed.), *Milton's Lycidas* (New York 1961), p. 100:

One reason that his individual emphases do not sound idiosyncratic to us today is that the language of *Lycidas* has had a powerful effect on English, especially American, poetry. . . . Thus the special vocabulary of *fresh, high, pure, sacred, new, fountain, hill, leaf, morning, shade, stream, shore, star, wind*, while extremely rare as dominant vocabulary before *Lycidas*, becomes dominant in the mid-eighteenth century, with poets like James Thomson, Collins, Dyer, Blake, and Wordsworth.

18. Servius *Proem. in Vergilii Bucolicon*, ed. G. Thilo (Leipzig 1887), 3.1–2; Hermogenes περὶ ἰδεῶν 2.3. L. Spengel, *Rhetores Graeci*, Vol. II (Leipzig 1854), p. 351, compares the simplicity of Theocritus with that of Anacreon.

19. The procedures he recommends are very similar to those recommended under the headings of the majestic and the rounded styles. I suppose Demetrius would suggest that there is a difference in the details to be presented.

20. It may be relevant, in the light of our interest in Epicurus, to mention that the ancients held a similar view of the writing style of that philosopher.

According to Diogenes Laertius 10.13, 31, Epicurus avoided the semblance of learning in his language; he used only expressions that were in general currency, and demanded clarity as the chief desideratum of spoken language. From what we have of his written work, we know that Epicurus employed a variety of styles, depending on the task at hand; cf. W. Schmid, "Epikur," *Reallexikon fuer Antike und Christentum*, 5 (1961), 708–714. Apparently his views of what the fitting speech of a wise man should be impressed itself sufficiently on the minds of his contemporaries to color the tradition about his own stylistic habits.

21. Leigh Hunt, *A Jar of Honey from Mount Hybla* (London 1897), p. 94.

22. Coleridge, *Biographia Literaria*, chapter 17.

23. Cf. above, Chapter One.

24. J. F. Lynen, *The Pastoral Art of Robert Frost* (New Haven 1960), pp. 86 ff., 94.

25. René Rapin, *Dissertatio*, p. 40.

26. J. C. Scaliger, *Poetices Libri Septem* (Heidelberg 1607), 5.5: ubique laxus et prolixus. Noster parcus, pressus, politus, rotundus, solidus.

27. This may be the place for a comment or two on the question of a larger syntax. Whether Virgil meant his collection to be read and appreciated as a whole rather than as independent pieces cannot be answered definitively, in spite of the readiness of most critics to accept the idea of a unified collection. But there can be little doubt about the architectonic design of such diptychs as *Eclogues* 5 and 8; they show a tightness of structure which is foreign to Theocritus. Sannazaro's decision to connect the eclogues of his *Arcadia* by means of prose is a development of tendencies first latent in Virgil. But even in Sannazaro the Theocritean discontinuities are still apparent. The first really continuous pastoral collection does not come till fifty years later, with Montemayor's romance *Diana*.

28. Cicero *De finibus* 1.18.57: O ... apertam et simplicem et directam viam! Cf. A. M. J. Festugière, *Epicurus and his Gods* (Oxford 1955), p. 50, note 80.

29. Diogenes Laertius 10.6; Epicurus *Sententiae Vaticanae* 58. A. Ronconi, "Appunti di estética epicurea," *Miscellanea Rostagni* (1963), pp. 7–25, rightly condemns efforts to minimize Epicurus' condemnation of παιδεία. At best, Epicurus' theory, like Plato's, does not match his practice; his life does not furnish a radical execution of the primitivism advanced by the theory.

30. Cf. E. Bignone, *Teocrito* (Bari 1934), p. 75, who compares the primitivist notions of Dicaearchus, frag. 59 Wehrli. See also A. O. Lovejoy and G. Boas, *Primitivism and Related Ideas in Antiquity* (Baltimore 1935), *passim*, a book in which Epicureanism gets short shrift, and pastoral poetry is omitted entirely.

31. *Sententiae Vaticanae* 63; in spite of considerable textual difficulties, the meaning must be that excessive self-sufficiency is just as bad as excessive lack of control. Cf. also below, Chapter Five.

32. See Congleton, *Theories of Pastoral Poetry*, pp. 138–139. Also Hunt, *A Jar of Honey from Mount Hybla*, p. 129.

33. See G. Castor, *Pléiade Poetics: A Study in Sixteenth-Century Thought and Terminology* (Cambridge 1964), pp. 77–85.

34. H. Herter, "Das Kind im Zeitalter des Hellenismus," *Bonner Jahrbb.* 132 (1927), 250 ff. Cf. also the same author's essays in *Bonner Jahrbb.* 161 (1961), 73–84, and *Jahrbuch fuer Antike und Christentum*, 4 (1961), 146 ff.

35. *Idyll* 10.33–35:

> χρύσεοι ἀμφότεροί κ' ἀνεκείμεθα τᾷ 'Αφροδίτᾳ,
> τὼς αὐλὼς μὲν ἔχοισα καὶ ἢ ῥόδον ἢ τύγε μᾶλον,
> σχῆμα δ' ἐγὼ καὶ καινὰς ἐπ' ἀμφοτέροισιν ἀμύκλας.

Cf. also Callimachus *Epigrammata* 30.6 Pfeiffer.

36.

> He would not defeat me with his songs, neither Thracian Orpheus,
> nor Linus; even if his mother assisted the one, his father the other,
> Calliopea Orpheus, handsomé Apollo Linus.

37. We should compare also the prattling anaphora in the children's song cited by Athenaeus 14.629E:

Tell me, where are the roses, where the violets, where the lovely parsley? Here are the roses, here the violets, here the lovely parsley.

38. No. 747 in *Poetae Melici Graeci*, ed. Page (1962):

> κάλλιστον μὲν ἐγὼ λείπω φάος ἠελίοιο,
> δεύτερον ἄστρα φαεινὰ σεληναίης τε πρόσωπον,
> ἠδὲ καὶ ὡραίους σικύους καὶ μῆλα καὶ ὄγχνας.

39. W. Empson, *Some Versions of Pastoral* (Norfolk 1950), pp. 253–254.

40. See below, Chapter Nine, Appendix.

41. See below, Chapter Eight.

42. Varro *On Agriculture* 2.10.1.

43. Aristotle *Rhetoric* 2.13.1390a19 ff.

44. Cf. D. C. Allen, *Image and Meaning: Metaphoric Traditions in Renaissance Poetry* (Baltimore 1960), pp. 2–3. He compares Philitas in *Daphnis and Chloe*.

45. R. Poggioli, "The Oaten Flute," *Harvard Library Bulletin*, 11.2 (1957), 157.

46. Purney, *A Full Inquiry*, 3.3.3.

47. Poeschl, *Die Hirtendichtung Virgils*, p. 34, refers to the "Ueberzeugung und Erfahrung des Dichters, dass kindhafte Einfalt und hoechste Weisheit konvergieren."

48. The poem is, of course, much more than a pastiche of echoes from Theocritus 11 and, to a lesser extent, 6. But Hubaux, *Le réalisme*, goes too far

when he claims that Virgil is more dependent on Meleager, especially *Anthol. Pal.* 12.127, than on Theocritus. For Virgil's originality, see now also E. W. Leach, "Nature and Art in Vergil's Second Eclogue," *A J Phil.*, 87 (1966), 427–445; and G. K. Galinsky, "Vergil's Second *Eclogue*," *C & M*, 26 (1965), 161–191.

49. Virgil, *Eclogue* 2, lines 4–5: incondita . . . jactabat.

50. E. Staiger, *Grundbegriffe der Poetik* (Zuerich 1946).

51. In *American Review*, Vol. 4; now reprinted in Patrides, *Milton's Lycidas*, pp. 64–81.

52. F. Kermode, *Romantic Image* (London 1957), p. 36.

Chapter 4

1. H. Usener, *Epicurea* (Leipzig 1887), p. 163.4–5: κρεῖττον δέ σοι θαρρεῖν ἐπὶ στιβάδος κατακειμένῳ ἢ ταράττεσθαι χρυσῆν ἔχοντι κλίνην καὶ πολυτελῆ τράπεζαν.

2. Diogenes Laertius 10.85.

3. *Idyll* 7.21–23:

Σιμιχίδα, πᾷ δὴ τὺ μεσαμέριον πόδας ἕλκεις,
ἀνίκα δὴ καὶ σαῦρος ἐν αἱμασιαῖσι καθεύδει,
οὐδ' ἐπιτυμβίδιοι κορυδαλλίδες ἠλαίνοντι.

4. J. M. André, *L'Otium dans la vie morale et intellectuelle romaine des origines à l'époque augustéenne* (Paris 1966), is the most recent treatment of the subject of *otium*. See also H. Lenzen, "Senecas Dialog de brevitate vitae," *Klassisch-Philologische Studien*, 10 (1937), pp. 31 and 72 ff. J. M. André, "Recherches sur l'otium romain," *Annales Littéraires de l'Université de Besançon*, 52 (1962), 5, refers to Bede, *De orthographia*, ed. H. Keil, in *Grammatici Latini* (Leipzig 1880), Vol. VII, 282: *Otium et silentium ex uno graeco venit, id est* ἡσυχία.

5. André, "Recherches sur l'otium romain," p. 8.

6. Kenneth Clark, *Landscape into Art* (Harmondsworth 1949; the 1950 edition is entitled: *Landscape Painting*), pp. 29–30.

7. R. Poggioli, "The Oaten Flute," *Harvard Library Bulletin*, 11.2 (1957), 149.

8. Diogenes Laertius 9.112, citing Antigonus of Carystus.

9. *Anthol. Pal.* 9.359 is representative. Posidippus is in the tradition of Hesiod, and of Theognis 603 ff. Note especially Posidippus' remark, line 3, that "in the fields, toil aplenty." A thorough-going pessimist, he finds both city life and country life equally disastrous. Cf. also A. Grilli, *Il problema della vita contemplativa nel mondo greco-romano* (Milan 1953), pp. 167 ff. Grilli

attempts to discuss bucolic poetry along the same lines, with less satisfactory results: pp. 182 ff.

10. See A. Kiessling and R. Heinze, Q. *Horatius Flaccus, Oden und Epoden* (sixth edition, Berlin 1917), p. 345, on *Odes* 3.18.

11. Tennyson's Lucretius testifies to the inadequacy of the rustic picnic. After describing the picnic in conservative Epicurean terms, he continues: "But now it seems some unseen monster lays / His vast and filthy hands upon my will. . . ."

12. The poem is conveniently available in F. Kermode (ed.), *English Pastoral Poetry* (London 1952), pp. 150–153.

13. M. P. Parker, *The Allegory of the Fairie Queene* (Oxford 1960), pp. 259 ff. For a close analogue to Lodge's poem, see Florimel's song in the third "Nymphall" of Drayton's *Muses Elizium*.

14. Lucretius 1.459 ff.

15. Diogenes Laertius 10.117, 119. The textual difficulties of 117 do not affect the point at issue. Cf. also *Sententiae Vaticanae* 21. Note, however, that on the subject of love, Epicurus' views are substantially different from those of the pastoral. Cf. below, this chapter.

16. Euripides *Antiope* frag. 194; cf. B. Snell, *Scenes from Greek Drama* (Berkeley 1964), p. 88.

17. Xenophanes frag. 2 Diels.

18. E. Fraenkel, *Horace* (Oxford 1957), pp. 211–214 sees in the poem a subtle polemic against the ending of Catullus 51. K. Latte, "Eine Ode des Horaz (II 16)," *Philologus*, 90 (1935), 294, stresses the topical relevance of this *otium*.

19. W. F. Mainland (ed.), *Schiller: Ueber naive und sentimentalische Dichtung* (Oxford 1951), pp. 54–55:

Ihr Charakter besteht also darin, dass aller Gegensatz der Wirklichkeit mit dem Ideale, der den Stoff zu der satirischen und elegischen Dichtung hergegeben hatte, vollkommen aufgehoben sei und mit demselben auch aller Streit der Empfindungen aufhoere. Ruhe waere also der vorherrschende Eindruck dieser Dichtungsart, aber Ruhe der Vollendung, nicht der Traegheit; eine Ruhe, die aus dem Gleichgewicht, nicht aus dem Stillstand der Kraefte, die aus der Fuelle, nicht aus der Leerheit fliesst. . . . Aber eben darum, weil aller Widerstand hinwegfaellt, wird es hier ungleich schwieriger. . . . die Bewegung hervorzubringen, ohne welche doch ueberall keine poetische Wirkung sich denken laesst.

20. The type is of some interest to ancient medical writers; cf. "Hippocrates," *Epistle* 12.1, p. 293 Hercher. Also A. Grilli, *Il problema della vita contemplativa*, p. 186. See also below, Chapter Ten.

21. Fontenelle, "Of Pastorals," trans. Motteux (London 1695), p. 282; cf. J. E. Congleton, *Theories of Pastoral Poetry* (Gainesville 1952), pp. 66–67.

22. Hesiod *Works and Days* 119. See also Plato *Republic* 565A, for the same combination of healthy work and absence of toil.

23. Seneca *De tranquillitate animi* 2.6–12. For *otium* in Catullus 51, see now A. J. Woodman, "Some Implications of *otium* in Catullus 51.13–16," *Latomus*, 25 (1966), 217–226.

24. Columella *De re rustica* 7.3.26:

He who follows the flock should be observant and vigilant . . . and when driving them out or bringing them home he should threaten them by shouting or with his staff . . . nor should he withdraw too far from them nor should he lie or sit down; for unless he is advancing he should stand upright, because the duty of a guardian calls for a lofty and commanding elevation from which the eyes can see as from a watch-tower . . . lest a thief or a wild beast cheat the shepherd while he is day-dreaming.

25. Plato *Laws* 677A ff; cf. *Timaeus* 22D and *Critias* 109D.

26. Frags. 48–51 Wehrli; they come from Dicaearchus' *Life of Greece*. Cf. Varro *De re rustica* 2.1.3; also 1.2.15. Book two of Varro's work contains a full discussion of the conditions of various types of ranching.

27. Hallett Smith, *Elizabethan Poetry* (Harvard 1952), pp. 8–10: "The central meaning of pastoral is the rejection of the aspiring mind."

28. *Eclogue* 5.46–47:

> quale sopor fessis in gramine, quale per aestum
> dulcis aquae saliente sitim restinguere rivo.

29. Theocritus *Idyll* 1.15–18:

> οὐ θέμις, ὦ ποιμήν, τὸ μεσαμβρινὸν οὐ θέμις ἄμμιν
> συρίσδεν. τὸν Πᾶνα δεδοίκαμες· ἦ γὰρ ἀπ' ἄγρας
> τανίκα κεκμακὼς ἀμπαύεται· ἔστι δὲ πικρός,
> καί οἱ ἀεὶ δριμεῖα χολὰ ποτὶ ῥινὶ κάθηται.

Literally the last word is "sits" rather than "rises" as I put it in the translation; "sits," though awkward in English, is the more appropriate word, given the suspension of movement in the scene. G. Kirk, "Objective Dating Criteria in Homer," *MH*, 17 (1960), 204, calls the whole phrase "strained, bizarre, and indeed almost meaningless." Cf. however *Odyssey* 24.318.

30. From Joseph Hall's "Defiance to Envy," cited by Congleton, *Theories of Pastoral Poetry*, p. 45. For the amorous pastoral in France, see Alice Hulubei, *L'Eglogue en France au xvie siècle* (Paris 1938), chapter 15, pp. 568 ff. Ronsard was the chief promoter of the amatory eclogue. In Sannazaro's *Arcadia* and

Guarini's *Pastor Fido*, the choral songs are mostly about Love. In Sidney, the antinomy between love and heroism is endemic. For love as an overt or covert theme of all pastoral poetry, see R. Poggioli, "Zampogna e cornamusa," *Inventario*, 8 (1956), 227 ff., 244. Poggioli's article is a brilliant discussion of a number of different issues associated with love in the pastoral. Much of his speculation is psychological; he analyzes pastoral love as an illusory rejection of sexual realities, later reversed by the eighteenth-century protests against social restraints on love. Poggioli is an erudite and sympathetic critic; but the psychological approach permits an element of condescension and even impatience. This is not surprising; in the eyes of a critic who looks to pastoral to play its role in a healthy body politic, pastoral must be found wanting. Both Poggioli and Empson show their Platonism most openly when they explore the handling of the topic of love.

31. For the time of Mnasalcas, see now A. S. F. Gow and D. L. Page, *The Greek Anthology: Hellenistic Epigrams* (Cambridge 1965), Vol. II, 400; the poet (Gow prefers the form Mnasalces) appears to have been roughly contemporary with Theocritus. His attack on love in the pastoral may be connected with his evident anti-Epicureanism in No. 17 Gow-Page; but cf. my remarks on Epicurus and love, later on in this chapter. It is difficult to say whether Mnasalcas is talking about a general tendency, or about a particular poet or collection. For the presumption that the pastoral is naturally about love, see also Propertius' estimate of Virgil's *Eclogues* in his *Elegies* 2.34.67 ff.

32. R. Poggioli, "The Oaten Flute," p. 159.

33. R. Poggioli, "The Pastoral of the Self," *Daedalus*, 88 (1959), 699.

34. *Idyll* 3.25–27:

> τὰν βαίταν ἀποδὺς ἐς κύματα τηνῶ ἀλεῦμαι,
> ὧπερ τὼς θύννως σκοπιάζεται Ὄλπις ὁ γριπεύς·
> καὶ κα δὴ 'ποθάνω, τό γε μὲν τεὸν ἀδὺ τέτυκται.

35. Contrast C. Fantazzi, "Virgilian Pastoral and Roman Love Poetry," *A J Phil.*, 87 (1966), 171–191; and G. Lawall, *Theocritus' Coan Pastorals* (Boston 1967), *passim*.

36. H. Usener, *Epicurea* (Leipzig 1887), frag. 483 (Hermias, *in Platonis Phaedrum*, p. 76): σύντονον ὄρεξιν ἀφροδισίων μετὰ οἴστρου καὶ ἀδημονίας. Cf. also Lucretius 4.1037 ff.

37. Lucretius 4.1160–1161:

> nigra melichrus est, inmunda et fetida acosmos,
> caesia Palladium, nervosa et lignea dorcas.

Cf. Theocritus *Idyll* 10.26–27. C. Bailey (ed.), *Titi Lucreti Cari de rerum natura* (Oxford 1947), Vol. III, 1310, comments: "The large number of Greek words suggests that this passage may be modelled on some Greek original, possibly contained in Epicurus' Περὶ ἔρωτος, though the model was more likely poetry; . . . Plato, *Republic*, 474d ff. deals with the same topic, and there are parallels to individual words and phrases in Theocritus and in the *Anthology*." It is probable that Plato, too, had a particular poet in mind; cf. M. Pohlenz in *GGA*, 197 (1935), 395, note 1.

38. See now also the speech of Chaereas in Menander's *Dyskolos* 58 ff. This and other parallels suggest that the idea was in the air, and that the writers of the early Hellenistic period found it fashionable to make use of it.

39. *Satires* 1.2.119. See also Lucilius, Book 29, satire 3. On the subject of Epicurus' views about love, I side with R. Flacelière, "Les Epicuriens et l'amour," *REG*, 67 (1954), 69–81, against A. M. J. Festugière in *REG*, 65 (1952), 259.

40. Note particularly lines 60–68: Gallus seems to be saying that pastoral activity and song will not help him to overcome his passion. Actually, he is describing pastoral activity in terms of its opposite: strenuous climbing, hunting, exposing himself to heat and cold; that is, a soldier's life. Gallus is toying with pastoral memories, but the memories are colored by what he knows best. He wishes he could be, or have been, a herdsman-poet-lover, but his pastoral life would have been . . . just like the active life he *has* led. Thus elegy, the soldier-poetry of Tyrtaeus, Theognis, Solon, and Gallus, is brought into humorous confrontation with the pastoral; in the process, elegy swallows the pastoral, and the gain in insight is nil.

41. See E. K. Chambers (ed.), *English Pastorals* (London 1895), p. 84. Chambers ascribes the poem doubtfully to Sir Walter Raleigh.

42. From Sir Philip Sidney, "Disprayse of a Courtly Life," cited by Kermode in *English Pastoral Poetry*, p. 141.

43. For further remarks on this subject, see below, Chapter Six.

44. For a radical *otium* of this sort, see Calpurnius *Eclogue* 2. The realization of *otium* at the beginning of the contest is exhaustive; the effect is tantamount to lowering the house lights.

45. Note the constant shifting of tenses in *peribat* (10), *fleverunt* (15), *stant* (16), *vēnit* (19), *inquit* (22, 28, 31), *detinet* (45), and so forth.

46. There are slight references to other seasons in the spurious *Idyll* 9, lines 12–13 and 20–21; and a reference to past beauty in the spurious *Idyll* 20, lines 21 ff. For the similarity of *Idyll* 27 to a medieval pastourelle, see W. Theiler, "Liebesgespraech und Pastourelle," in H. Dahlmann & R. Merkelbach, *Studien zur Textgeschichte und Textkritik* (Cologne 1959), pp. 279–283. Theiler suspects a direct line of dependence between it and Walter of Chatillon's poem No. 32 Strecker.

47. Compare the sad experience of Tiresias in Callimachus' *Hymn* 5; he too came to grief because his mother had failed to introduce him to her lady-friend.

48. The unusual standing of *Idyll* 11 in the pastoral corpus is indicated also by its metrical irregularities, commented on by U. von Wilamowitz-Moellendorff, *Die Textgeschichte der griechischen Bukoliker* (Berlin 1906), p. 159 note, and R. Stark, "Theocritea," *Maia*, 15 (1963), 373.

49. H. M. Richmond, "Polyphemus in England," *Comparative Literature*, 12 (1960), 229–242.

50. For the evidence, see A. Kambylis, *Die Dichterweihe und ihre Symbolik* (Heidelberg 1965), pp. 60–61.

51. A Cameron, "The Form of the Thalysia," *Miscellanea Rostagni* (1963), 301. See also the article "Meridianus Daemon" in *RE*, 15 (1931), 1030.

52. *Pace* K. J. McKay, *The Poet at Play: Kallimachos, The Bath of Pallas* (Leiden 1962), p. 38, I doubt that the noon-time peace in Callimachus *Hymn* 5.72, 74 contains an element of foreboding.

53. Cf. also below, Chapter Five.

54. For the latest discussion of the shape of the cup and its decorative scheme, see C. Gallavotti, "Le coppe istoriate di Teocrito e di Virgilio," *La Parola del Passato*, fasc. 111 (1966), 421–436.

It is interesting to see how 'each imitator of Theocritus adapts the *topos* of the decorated cup to his own uses. Virgil (*Eclogue* 3) has a pair of cups, of beechwood, each with its own panel, the portrait of a scientist. Nothing is said about the poses of the scientists; the panels are lifeless, the pictorial realization of an idea. But the identity of the subjects reminds us of Virgil's tendency to link the life in the country with the life of science. This is the source from which Virgil draws the energy which is to enliven the silvan *otium*.

Alamanni reverts to the Theocritean version of several panels on one cup (*Eclogue* 1). But now the panels are four in number, representing the four seasons: a peasant pruning, another cutting grain, a third sacrificing to Bacchus, and a fourth sitting near the stove preparing his tools for the coming year. Alamanni chooses to register the totality of rustic effort to enhance the value of the gift. See T. P. Harrison and H. S. Leon (edd.), *The Pastoral Elegy* (Austin 1939), pp. 121–122.

Ronsard has a number of descriptions of cups. Cf. the comment of M. Y. Hughes, "Virgil and Spenser," *University of California Publications in English*, 2 (1928–1929), 281: "Dramatic action is the essence of all Ronsard's descriptions of carved cups. They are always plays within plays, tiny idyllia within idyls. Ronsard must have regarded them as one of the final technical refinements of the pastoral, and as a delicate application of the (falsely interpreted) Horatian principle, *Ut pictura poesis.*"

Spenser's "mazer ywrought of the Maple warre" ("August," 25–42), has two panels, or one panel comprising two scenes; they show bears and tigers fighting with each other, and a shepherd running to save a lamb from the jaws of a wolf. Thus Spenser goes considerably beyond Theocritus in incorporating aggression and ugliness into the bucolic scene.

In Milton's "Epitaphium Damonis" (180–197), finally, we have the most ambitious treatment of the motif. Milton had received two books from Giovanni Battista Manso, the friend of Tasso. In the poem, the books turn up as two cups, decorated with subjects that may well coincide with the contents of the books. Between them—the distribution is not entirely clear—the pictures show the Red Sea and its wooded shores, the phoenix, the sky, Olympus, and Amor firing the souls of the gods. This bare listing does not do justice to the atmospheric qualities of Milton's panorama; among other details, for instance, the cups show *odoriferum ver*, "fragrant springtime." Perhaps the grandeur of the composition, its amalgamation of many diverse elements, was stimulated by the plans of the epic poem announced just previously. Pagan and biblical, epic and lyrical components merge, near the end of the pastoral poem, to prepare the ground for a new, non-pastoral construction.

55. John Keats, "On Indolence," stanza 2, lines 15 ff.

56. B. A. van Groningen, *La poésie verbale grecque* (Amsterdam 1953), has a full discussion of the subject. Cf., however, the reservations expressed by H. Herter in *Gnomon* 27, (1955), 254–259. On the subject, see also W. B. Stanford, *The Sound of Greek* (Berkeley 1967), especially chapter 5.

57. An exception: *Idyll* 5.66, in the least relaxed of the *Idylls*. Virgil, Calpurnius, and Nemesianus offer no exceptions to the rule; cf. J. Hubaux, *Le réalisme dans les Bucoliques de Virgile* (Paris 1927), p. 102.

58. See the essays of J. C. Ransom and F. T. Prince in C. A. Patrides (ed.), *Milton's Lycidas* (New York 1961), pp. 72 and 153 ff.

59. *The Poems of Alexander Pope*, vol. I (New Haven 1961), 31.

60. D. Kalstone, *Sidney's Poetry* (Harvard 1965), p. 84.

61. U. von Wilamowitz-Moellendorff, *Reden und Vortraege*, Vol. 1 (fourth edition, Berlin 1925), 265, in a paper entitled "Daphnis."

62. H. Schwabl, "Aufbau und Struktur des Prooimions der hesiodischen Theogonie," *Hermes*, 91 (1963), 385–415; A. Heubeck, "Zum Aufbau von Hesiod, *Theogonie* 161–206," *Hermes*, 94 (1966), 233–236.

63. On bucolic symmetry, cf. below, Chapter Seven.

64. ἁδύ τι τὸ ψιθύρισμα καὶ ἁ πίτυς, αἰπόλε, τήνα,
ἁ ποτὶ ταῖς παγαῖσι, μελίσδεται, ἁδὺ δὲ καὶ τύ
συρίσδες· μετὰ Πᾶνα τὸ δεύτερον ἆθλον ἀποισῇ.
αἴ κα τῆνος ἕλῃ κεραὸν τράγον, αἶγα τὺ λαψῇ·
αἴ κα δ' αἶγα λάβῃ τῆνος γέρας, ἐς τὲ καταρρεῖ
ἁ χίμαρος· χιμάρω δὲ καλὸν κρέας, ἔστε κ' ἀμέλξῃς.

ἅδιον, ὦ ποιμήν, τὸ τεὸν μέλος ἢ τὸ καταχές
τῆν' ἀπὸ τᾶς πέτρας καταλείβεται ὑψόθεν ὕδωρ.

αἴ κα ταὶ Μοῖσαι τὰν οἴιδα δῶρον ἄγωνται,
ἄρνα τὺ σακίταν λαψῇ γέρας· αἱ δὲ κ' ἀρέσκη
τήναις ἄρνα λαβεῖν, τὺ δὲ τὰν ὄιν ὕστερον ἀξῇ.

65. See, e.g., F. J. Hemelt, "Points of Resemblance in the Verse of Tennyson and Theocritus," *Modern Language Notes*, 18 (1903), 115–117. Hemelt regards cases of word repetition in Tennyson as proof of the poet's dependence on Theocritus. That is the wrong way of looking at what is a pervasive feature in pastoral. For anaphora after bucolic diaeresis, see Callimachus frag. 27 and Pfeiffer's comments; also *Epigrammata 22, et al.*

66. Seneca *Medea* 426–428:

> Sola est quies,
> mecum ruina cuncta si video obruta;
> mecum omnia abeant.

67. W. Empson, *Seven Types of Ambiguity* (London 1930), p. 41.

68. In Leslie Fiedler's perceptive essay on a sestina by Dante: "Green Thoughts in a Green Shade," *The Kenyon Review*, 18 (1956), 241.

Chapter 5

1. *Eclogue* 2.33: Pan curat ovis oviumque magistros.

2. For the subject, see A. Cartault, *Etude sur les Bucoliques de Virgile* (Paris 1897), pp. 425 ff. Note, however, that in *Eclogue* 2, Virgil stresses the servile status, and indeed the depressing circumstances, of the characters.

3. Ovid *Metamorphoses* 8.635–636:

> nec refert dominos illic famulosque requiras;
> tota domus duo sunt, idem parentque iubentque.

4. Chrysippus said of the Homeric heroes that they looked after their own needs and prided themselves on their facility in household matters; cf. M. Pohlenz, "Die hellenistische Poesie und die Philosophie," *Charites Friedrich Leo* (Berlin 1911), p. 84. In the non-pastoral poems, Theocritus has the Greek words for "house" (οἶκος and its derivatives, and δόμος) more than thirty times. In the pastorals, on the other hand, there are only three occurrences. I except *Idyll* 27.37–38; in a *pastourelle*, the tempter must offer the bait of a solid home and a good family background. In *Idyll* 11.64, the Cyclops implores Galatea not to go home; at *Idyll* 6.24, Damoetas engages in an apotropaic gesture by suggesting that the prophet Telemus take his sordid prophesies home with him for his children; and at *Idyll* 7.46, Lycidas states his preference for a short poem by deprecating the craftsman who wants to build a house as high as a mountain. The only passage in which a herdsman refers to his *own*

home occurs in a doubtfully ascribed poem, *Idyll* 9.33: "may my home be filled with music," a wish expressed by the unidentified but pastoral reporter of the poem. The conclusion is evident: Theocritean herdsmen have no homes. Their existence is circumscribed by the *locus amoenus*. It is instructive to see how even as late a writer as Longus appears to be uncomfortable with the domestic trappings necessitated by his fusion of the pastoral tradition with the bourgeois romance. As for Virgil, he supplies his herdsmen with lowly cottages and with the whispered promise of business security. For living conditions and housing in Virgil and Theocritus, see Cartault, *Etude*, pp. 457 ff.

5. Spenser, *Fairie Queene*, 6.3.1.

6. See J. W. Beach, *The Concept of Nature in Nineteenth-Century English Poetry* (New York 1936), pp. 385 ff.

7. *Idyll* 7.35–36:

ἀλλ' ἄγε δή, ξυνὰ γὰρ ὁδὸς ξυνὰ δὲ καὶ ἀώς,
βουκολιασδώμεσθα· τάχ' ὥτερος ἄλλον ὀνασεῖ.

Cf. also the humble *humanitas* voiced at *Idyll* 25.50, a gentle rejoinder to the epic flattery of lines 38–41.

8. See, e.g., Lucilius Book 29, satire 1: "On Friendship;" and M. Puelma, *Lucilius und Kallimachos* (Frankfurt 1949), chapter 1, par. 4: "Die Welt der *amici* als Lebensboden des lucilischen Sermostils." Epicurean statements about friendship are collected most conveniently by A. M. J. Festugière, *Epicurus and His Gods* (Oxford 1955), p. 37.

9. J. Ferguson, *Moral Values in the Ancient World* (London 1958), p. 72.

10. For a recent collection of the relevant passages, see R. Schottlaender, "Menanders *Dyskolos* und der Zusammenbruch der 'Autarkie'," *Schriften Akademie Berlin*, 50 (1965), 33–42.

11. Cf. Seneca *Epistles* 7.11: egregie hoc ... Epicurus, cum uni ex consortibus studiorum suorum scriberet: haec ego non multis, sed tibi: satis enim magnum alter alteri theatrum sumus. Note the anti-Stoic polemics implied in the last phrase. For the position of Epicurus in ancient epistolography, see the article of J. Sykutris in *RE, Suppl.* 5 (1931), 185 ff.

12. Horace *Epistles* 1.4.16, refers to the Epicurean circle as a *grex*. It is tempting to read pastoral associations into the term. Unfortunately he adds "of pigs"—or does *Epicuri de grege porcum* mean: the one piglet who strayed into the Epicurean flock of sheep? In any case, *grex* appears to be a regular Roman way of referring to any kind of circle, including even the Stoics; cf. the note *ad locum* in A. S. Wilkins (ed.), *The Epistles of Horace* (London 1919). I cannot find a Greek term to correspond to *grex*.

13. Occasionally the pastoral technique is found even in Aristophanes; see, e.g., *Peace* 1154–1155. Is it a coincidence that the setting here is a rustic picnic?

14. Epicurus' anti-Platonism reduces justice to an uncertain status (Diogenes Laertius 10.150): justice is nothing absolute, but a kind of contract for mutual protection of people, taking its specific nature from the occasion and the locale.

15. In Book 6 of the *Fairie Queene*, courtesy is a flower of virtue in the heavenly garden:

> Amongst them all growes not a fayrer flowre,
> Than is the bloosme of comely courtesie.

If Theocritus had been willing, like Spenser, to talk about the pastoral virtues in the abstract, one wonders what the Greek equivalent of courtesy might have been; εὐτραπελία? κομψότης? More important, Theocritus' courtesy, unlike Spenser's, involves a dash of irony.

16. R. Poggioli, "Naboth's Vineyard or the Pastoral View of the Social Order," *JHI*, 24 (1963), 3–24.

17. R. Poggioli, "The Oaten Flute," *Harvard Library Bulletin*, 11.2 (1957), 175.

18. For the *Gottmensch*, in this case Demetrius Poliorcetes, as superior to the traditional gods, see the verses cited by Athenaeus 6.253D–F, and the comments of A. M. J. Festugière, *Epicurus and His Gods*, pp. 51–52 and L. Alfonsi in *RhM*, 106 (1963), 161–164. Cf. also the *Hymns* of Callimachus, and Theocritus *Idyll* 15.106 ff., and *Idyll* 17 *passim*. For the whole phenomenon, see L. Bieler, *Theios Anēr* (Vienna 1935/6).

19. The evidence, including an important papyrus, is cited by E. Bignone, *L'Aristotele Perduto*, Vol. II (Florence 1936), 170, 210–211, 240. The papyrus is printed in A. Vogliano, *Epicuri et Epicureorum scripta* (Berlin 1928), p. 70, frag. 8, col. 1; its content is given by Festugière, *Epicurus and His Gods*, p. 22 as follows: "Those who live a dissolute life (?, defect in pap.) must not be admitted, nor those who groan in anxiety of soul; on the other hand, those who keep in mind the appearance of the perfect and altogether blessed beings (i.e., the gods) must be invited to feast themselves and laugh like the others, not forgetting any of the members of the Epicurean family nor indeed any of the outsiders. . . . we shall call to mind all those who show us good will, that they may help us to celebrate the ritual banquets which are right and proper for those who philosophize together so as to attain blessedness."

20. See W. Schmid, "Goetter und Menschen in der Theologie Epikurs," *RhM*, 94 (1951), 97–156; also Ph. Merlan, *Studies in Epicurus and Aristotle* (Wiesbaden 1960), pp. 38 ff.

21. W. F. Otto, *Das Wort der Antike* (Stuttgart 1962), pp. 293–333, in an essay originally published in 1958.

22. Festugière, *Epicurus and His Gods*, chapter 4.

23. Plutarch *Adversus Coloten* 17.1117B.

24. C. Bailey (ed.), *Epicurus: The Extant Remains* (Oxford 1926), frag. B 31, is inclined to take this and similar evidence (cf. *Sententiae Vaticanae* 33) as pieces of irony. But cf. Ph. Merlan, "Epicureanism and Horace," *JHI*, 10 (1949), 445–451.

25. For the lament in Greek poetry, see E. Reiner, *Die rituelle Totenklage der Griechen* (Stuttgart 1938). For the pastoral lament in Europe beginning with the Renaissance, see G. Norlin, "The Conventions of the Pastoral Elegy," *A J Phil.*, 32 (1911), 294–312. I prefer the term "lament" to the term "elegy" because of the historical uncertainties of the latter.

26. D. Kalstone, *Sidney's Poetry* (Harvard 1965), p. 13: "laments for the dead, laments for the passing of the Golden Age, but primarily lovers' laments."

27. *Anthol. Pal.* 7.189 ff.; cf. G. Herrlinger, *Totenklage um Tiere in der antiken Dichtung* (Stuttgart 1930), pp. 15 ff.

28. D. C. Allen, *Image and Meaning* (Baltimore 1960), p. 113.

29. Cited by M. K. Bragg, *The Formal Eclogue in Eighteenth-Century England* (Orono, Maine 1926), p. 41. William Congreve has two pastoral elegies: "The Mourning Muse of Alexis," a dialogue lament for the Queen's death; and "The Tears of Amaryllis for Amyntas," a monologue.

30. See the excellent bilingual edition of the principal examples of the genre by T. P. Harrison and H. J. Leon, *The Pastoral Elegy: An Anthology* (Austin 1939).

31. M. Jacobs, *The Content and Style of an Oral Literature: Clackamas Chinook Myths and Tales* (Chicago 1959), p. 204.

32. "Moschus," "Lament for Bion," 14 ff., 86 ff.

33. *Idyll* 7.74–77:

χὢς ὄρος ἀμφεπονεῖτο καὶ ὡς δρύες αὐτὸν ἐθρήνευν
Ἱμέρα αἵτε φύοντι παρ' ὄχθαισιν ποταμοῖο,
εὖτε χιὼν ὥς τις κατετάκετο μακρὸν ὑφ' Αἷμον
ἢ Ἄθω ἢ Ῥοδόπαν ἢ Καύκασον ἐσχατόωντα.

I suspect that the geographical identities are less important that the contribution of the open vowels to the sound pattern.

34. Cf. Horace *Odes* 3.25. Aeschylean geography is another obvious parallel.

35. Servius, in Thilo and Hagen, 3.21–22. Cf. also *Eclogue* 1.65, where according to Servius, *ad loc.*, Meliboeus appears to think that the Oaxes is in Crete.

36. B. Snell, *The Discovery of the Mind* (Oxford 1953), p. 282 calls them "borrowed words, cultured and strange, with a literary, an exotic flavour."

37. Poggioli, "The Oaten Flute," p. 165. Cf. also A. S. P. Woodhouse, "Milton's Pastoral Monodies," *Studies Norwood* (Toronto 1952), p. 264; and C. W. Truesdale, "English Pastoral Verse from Spenser to Marvell," unpublished Ph.D. dissertation, University of Washington, 1956), pp. 244 ff.

38. As detailed by G. Norlin, "The Conventions of the Pastoral Elegy," *A J Phil.*, 32 (1911), 294–312, the conventions include the following: (1) a pastoral setting; (2) a dramatic introduction and a postlude which acquaint us with the circumstances occasioning the poem; (3) a refrain; (4) a description of the mourning of nature, often involving the pathetic fallacy; (5) a call upon nature to reverse its course, that is, to die along with the victim; (6) a complaint to the denizens of nature (nymphs, satyrs, and the like) for being absent, and letting the victim die without a chance of appeal; (7) a parade of friends and interested parties who come and ask questions; (8) the strewing of flowers upon the corpse or the grave; (9) an expression of despair or disbelief: why did he have to die? (10) reflections on mortality and immortality: he is not dead.

Some of the features are more common than others; the scattering of flowers (8), for instance, comes in only gradually; and the contemplation of the contrast between life and death (10) gets a special impetus from Christian modifications of the pagan tradition.

39. E. K. Rand, "Milton in Rustication," *S P*, 19 (1922), 126.

40. See F. Kermode, *Romantic Image* (London 1957), 36. The poem, about a friend lost at war, is not one of Yeats' most successful achievements, but it does not, in my opinion, merit Kermode's charge of "stoic coldness." Precisely what passions, or what mixture of passions, a particular poem is supposed to elicit is a debatable question. But it can be argued that the business of the pastoral lament is to allay grief as much as to provoke it. In the process of the exchanges between the old goatherd and the young shepherd, the grief is diminished or, shall we say, distributed over a wider area, until the original griever is relieved of his solitary burden. Cf. also above, Chapter Three, note 52.

41. The puzzlement has produced one or two piquant suggestions. G. Lanowski, "La passion de Daphnis," *Eos*, 42 (1947), 175–194, speculates that Daphnis is dying because he has been castrated; R. M. Ogilvie, "The Song of Thyrsis," *JHS*, 82 (1962), 106–110, argues that the death of Daphnis is by drowning in the Anapus, after falling off a rock. One supposes that he says what he has to say while Hermes and Priapus administer artificial respiration.

42. I suspect that the strange vagaries of "Et in Arcadia ego" may have something to do with this natural reluctance of the pastoral to grant death a neatly isolable scope within its scheme. See E. Panofsky, "Et in Arcadia Ego: Poussin and the Elegiac Tradition," *Meaning in the Visual Arts* (New York 1955), pp. 295–320.

43. Cf. also the shortened version, entitled "Hobbinoll's Dittie in prayse of Eliza Queen of the Sheepheards" which appears as No. 6 in *England's Helicon*, ed. Rollins.

44. *Eclogue* 7.79–80:

> O utinam nobis non rustica vestis inesset:
> vidissem propius mea numina.

45. W. Empson, *Some Versions of Pastoral* (Norfolk 1950), p. 13.

46. For a discussion of the *Einsiedliana*, see W. Schmid, "Panegyrik und Bukolik in der neronischen Epoche," *Bonner Jahrbb.*, 153 (1953), 63–96.

47. For this view, see, e.g., Truesdale, "English Pastoral Verse," chapter 2. Cf. below, my Chapter Twelve.

48. C. Wendel, *De nominibus bucolicis* (Leipzig 1900), p. 22, emphasizes, against Reitzenstein, that *in ipsis Theocriti carminibus nulla religionis vestigia inveniuntur*. Wendel's little monograph is one of the unsung classics of pastoral criticism.

49. Cf. also *Eclogue* 8.103: Daphnis is said to care neither for the gods nor for *carmina* (incantations?). Once again the gods have become both objects of worship and denizens of the grove; the tricky *curat* conceals the equivocation.

50. J. Hubaux, *Le réalisme dans les Bucoliques de Virgile* (Paris 1927), p. 104.

51. See also Cartault, *Etude sur les Bucoliques de Virgile*, pp. 493–502.

52. For the lack of commitment on the part of Hellenistic authors toward the pastoral divinities, see Callimachus frag. 217 Pfeiffer: Apollo sets up the horns of a buck that has been—milked by him. This is an extreme example of the human frailty that Hellenistic poets liked to read into their gods. To them we may apply what Longinus 9.7 says about Homer, that he made men into gods, and gods into suffering men. Cf. also my remarks on the *Gottmensch*, above.

53. Horace *Art of Poetry* 16–17:

adsuitur pannus, cum lucus et ara Dianae
et properantis aquae per amoenos ambitus agros (sc. describitur).

54. For the Christian pastoral tradition see W. Schmid, "Tityrus Christianus," *RhM*, 96 (1953), 101–165; and the same author's article "Bukolik" in *Reallexikon fuer Antike und Christentum*, 2 (1954), 786–800. For nativity pastorals, especially in sixteenth-century France, see Alice Hulubei, *L'Eglogue en France au xvie siècle* (Paris 1938), p. 715.

55. ed. H. M. Margoliouth (Oxford 1927), Vol. I, 36–37.

Chapter 6

1. John Gay, *Shepherds Week*: "Wednesday, Or The Dumps."

2. A. Cartault, *Etude sur les Bucoliques de Virgile* (Paris 1897), pp. 461 ff.

3. It should be noted that the passage occurs in a Hesiodic rather than a strictly pastoral song. Hence the greater emphasis on self-sufficiency.

4. "Epitaphium Bionis" 105–106:

καὶ σὺ μὲν ὦν σιγᾷ πεπυκασμένος ἔσσεαι ἐν γᾷ,
ταῖς Νύμφαισι δ' ἔδοξεν ἀεὶ τὸν βάτραχον ᾄδειν.

Cf. also the immediately preceding lines, 99–104, about mallows and parsley and fennel dying off but growing back the year after, while men, "big, strong, and clever," once dead, sleep through the rest of time.

5. Note, however, that *Idyll* 8, which some consider spurious, contains a tacit *synkrisis* of human and animal; the flirtatious maid is spurned in favor of a sweet-voiced heifer.

6. Servius has several comments such as that Virgil *verecunde rem inhonestam supprimit, quam Theocritus aperte commemorat* (on *Eclogue* 2.51); or again, *quod suppressit verecunde, licet Theocritus aperte ipsam turpitudinem ponat et exprimat* (on *Eclogue* 3.8). Virgil has decorum; Theocritus does not. Cf. also below, Chapter Eight.

7. E. Hiller von Gaertringen, *Die archaische Kultur der Insel Thera* (Berlin 1897), pp. 25 ff.; see also J. Beazley, *Proceedings of the British Academy* (1947), pp. 6–7, plate 2B.

8. From Matthew Arnold's "In Harmony with Nature."

9. Cf. the "Lydia" in the *Appendix Virgiliana*: the dying herdsman contrasts the companionship among animals with the loneliness among men.

10. E. Chapman, *St. Augustine's Philosophy of Beauty* (New York 1939), pp. 69, cited by L. Spitzer, *Classical and Christian Ideas of World Harmony* (Baltimore 1963), pp. 56–57.

11. Cf. "Epitaphium Bionis" 46–47: Bion taught the birds to sing. Note once more that the conceit is overt, rather than implied as it would be in Theocritus.

12. Cf. M. Puelma, *Lucilius und Kallimachos* (Frankfurt 1949), pp. 223 ff.: "Tierstimmen, stilsymbolisch."

13. For the sympathetic grief of the creatures, see the note in the *Variorum Spenser: The Minor Poems*, edd. C. G. Osgood and H. G. Lotspeich (Baltimore 1943), p. 249, on "Januarie," lines 31–42.

14. For a survey of the use of the grasshopper and the cicada in ancient literature, see D. C. Allen, *Image and Meaning* (Baltimore 1960), pp. 83–86. For additional references, see E. K. Borthwick, "A Grasshopper's Diet," *CQ*, 16 (1966), 103–112.

15. Note Homer's comparison of elderly orators with cicadas, *Iliad* 3.151. The later tradition, exemplified and further stimulated by *Anacreontea* 34, saw in the cicada the self-sufficient and articulate philosopher. On this, see now A. Dihle, "The Poem on the Cicada," *HSCPh*, 71 (1966), 107–113.

16. J. Hubaux, *Le réalisme dans les Bucoliques de Virgile* (Paris 1927), p. 50.

17. Hesiod *Works and Days* 582 ff.; *Scutum* 393 ff.; Aristophanes *Peace* 1159 ff. The last passage is worth quoting because of its remarkably pastoral quality:

ἡνίκ᾽ ἂν δ᾽ ἀχέτας
ᾄδῃ τὸν ἡδὺν νόμον,

διασκοπῶν ἥδομαι
τὰς Λημνίας ἀμπέλους. . . .

The only non-pastoral touch is the periphrastic designation of the cicada; but note the Doricism.

18. For Pan as the divinity of hunters, see below, Chapter Eleven.

19. B. Snell, *Scenes from Greek Drama* (Berkeley 1964), p. 73.

20. See J. E. Congleton, *Theories of Pastoral Poetry in England, 1684–1798* (Gainesville 1952), p. 32.

21. M. I. Gerhardt, *Essai d'analyse littéraire de la Pastorale* (Assen 1950), p. 295. Miss Gerhardt adds that there is no line-fishing at all; that occurs only in the pastorals written in the country of the *Compleat Angler*.

22. Contrast the status of the wolf in medieval pastoral, based probably on John 10.12 (the false shepherd forsakes his sheep and flees; and the wolf seizes them, and tears them), and summed up in "Lycidas," lines 128–129:

> Besides what the grim Woolf with privy paw
> Daily devours apace. . . .

Note that in Theocritus *Idyll* 1.71 wolves join in the dirge for the dying Daphnis.

23. λέγειν in line 78 as a term denoting the delivery of the contest is unparalleled in the corpus, and must mean "to speak," without the help of music.

24. See the excellent commentary of W. Richter (ed.), *Vergil: Georgica* (Munich 1957), pp. 290–291, on *Georgics* 3.242–285. Richter contrasts the humanization of the feelings and values of animals, found elsewhere in Virgil, with the integration of man into the community of animals.

25. For example, see Drayton's *The Muses Elizium* 2; Lalus and Cleon offer to Lirope a lamb, a kid, sparrows, doves, etc. etc.

26. Calpurnius *Eclogue* 6.32–45 shows this convention in full flower.

27. *Idylls* 16.26, 36–39; 17. 126–127; 18. 43–48; 25. 18–22; 26. 1–6; 27. 64.

28. For prizes, see further below, Chapter Seven.

29. The Theocritean imitator of *Idyll* 9 does not understand this principle. He has his swain engage in some heartless talk about how his animals lost their hides.

30. For the strong conclusion, cf. below, Chapter Eight.

31. See *Idylls* 8.57–59, 76–77; 9.7–8, 31–35; 10.30–31; 12.3–8. *Eclogues* 2.63–65; 3.80–83; 10.29–30.

32. *Idylls* 14.22, 39–40, 43, 51; 15.28, 40, 45, 73, 89, 121; 21.36. 19.7 and the inconography underlying the whole of *Idyll* 19 confirm the generally accepted view that the poem is not by Theocritus.

33. *Idyll* 4.39: you were as dear to me as my goats; *Idyll* 7.97: Simichidas loves Myrto as much as the goats love spring. Cf. also Virgil's *Eclogue* 8.85 ff.

34. *Idyll* 8.89: the lad jumped for pleasure, as a fawn might leap around its mother. Cf. also below, Chapter Twelve, for a further discussion of comparisons.

35. *Idyll* 11.20–21 (cf. *Eclogue* 7.38 ff.; also 7.65 ff.):

λευκοτέρα πακτᾶς ποτιδεῖν, ἁπαλωτέρα ἀρνός,
μόσχω γαυροτέρα, φιαρωτέρα ὄμφακος ὠμᾶς.

36. Cf. A. Pischinger, *Der Vogelgesang bei den griechischen Dichtern* (Eichstaedt 1901).

Chapter 7

1. *Paradise Lost*, 5.195 ff.

2. See L. P. Wilkinson, "Philodemus on *Ethos* in Music," *CQ*, 32 (1938), 174–181. Wilkinson's view that Epicurus' rejection of music was not complete cannot be maintained. For the whole topic see now the excellent discussion of A. J. Neubecker, "Die Bewertung der Musik bei Stoikern und Epikureern," *Akademie Wissenschaften, Berlin: Arbeitsgruppe fuer hellenistisch-roemische Philosophie*, 5 (Berlin 1956).

3. Philodemus *De musica* iv, col. 13.

4. For music in Theocritean and Virgilian pastoral, see the still estimable discussion by A. Cartault, *Etude sur les Bucoliques de Virgile* (Paris 1897), pp. 480 ff.

5. *Eclogue* 10.8, trans. Joseph Warton: non canimus surdis, respondent omnia silvae.

6. M. Desport, *L'incantation virgilienne: Virgile et Orphée* (Bordeaux 1952). See also Ph. Damon, "Modes of Analogy in Ancient and Medieval Verse," *University of California Publications in Classical Philology*, 15.6 (Berkeley 1961), chapter 3.

7. Apollonius Rhodius 4.1296–1304; cf. also 1338–1340, *et al.*

8. Nemesianus 1.1–2: dum . . . raucis immunia rura cicadis. Cf. also 1.30–31 where the shelter of elms and beeches is preferred to that of the pine tree, which is said to chatter in the wind.

9. Examples: Aristophanes *Thesmophoriazusae* 39 ff; Callimachus *Hymns* 2.17 ff; Euripides *Bacchae* 1084 f.

10. Note that the *adynaton* at *Idyll* 1.132 ff. terminates in a reference to music; nature's upheaval climaxes in the confusion of what is normally most fixed: birds' voices.

11. Cf. the pertinent remarks in A. Kappelmacher, "Vergil und Theokrit," *WS*, 47 (1929), 87–101.

12. Bion frag. 9.8–11:

ἦν μὲν γὰρ βροτὸν ἄλλον ἢ ἀθανάτων τινὰ μέλπω,
βαμβαίνει μοι γλῶσσα καὶ ὡς πάρος οὐκέτ᾿ ἀείδει·
ἦν δ᾿ αὖτ᾿ ἐς τὸν Ἔρωτα καὶ ἐς Λυκίδαν τι μελίσδω,
καὶ τόκα μοι χαίροισα διὰ στόματος ῥέει αὐδά.

Cf. also frag. 10, where Eros acts the singing teacher.

13. See B. A. van Groningen, *La poésie verbale grecque* (Amsterdam 1953).

14. See R. Stark, "Theocritea," *Maia*, 15 (1963), 372, note 28.

15. H. Fuchs, "Zum Wettgesang der Hirten in Vergils siebenter Ekloge," *MH*, 23 (1966), 218–223 has a discussion of *molle* in Horace's *molle atque facetum*. *Satires* 1.10.43 ff.

16. I am speaking on the basis of rough impressions. In this area the collecting of statistics concerning the use of vowels and consonants and word endings is of doubtful validity, since we cannot be sure about the sensibilities of the poet's contemporaries. Note that Demetrius *On Style* 185 seems to imply that the sound of the syrinx is heavy and legato rather than light and reedy. Cf. also Plato *Republic* 3.399D. I also wonder whether it is easy to accept the findings of Ph. Legrand, "L'Arcadie et l'Idylle," *REA*, 2 (1900), 108, note 5, that Theocritus, as against Virgil, keeps ἀείδειν and συρίζειν clearly distinct, except once, *Idyll* 7.28, where a poet is called a συρίκτας. For the distinction, Legrand cites *Idylls* 1.15 ff., 19 ff.; 4.31; 11.38–39; 5.22; as against Virgil *Eclogue* 3.25 ff. But the fact that birds and even stones (*Idyll* 7.26) are said to ἀείδειν shows that it need not be articulate song. And in fact in *Epigram* 5.1 we find the expression διδύμοις αὐλοῖσιν ἀεῖσαι. The epigram is perhaps not by Theocritus (A. S. F. Gow wavers; in his edition [1950] he calls it a pastiche from Theocritus; but in *The Greek Anthology: Hellenistic Epigrams*, Vol. II [Cambridge 1965], 536, he tones this down: "It is difficult to believe that the lines are Th's."). But whether genuine or not, it is Theocritean in a larger sense. The same is true of *Idyll* 8, in which both Menalcas and Daphnis are called singers and pipers. We conclude that though the ideas of ἀείδειν and συρίζειν are distinct in Theocritus, he is not averse to picturing pipers who sing and singers who pipe, and exploiting the metaphoric possibilities of ἀείδειν. All this makes it likely that a musical mimicry of vocal and instrumental sounds would not insist on keeping the two entirely and recognizably apart. On the other hand it is possible, now and then, to catch effects that are clearly designed to remind us of either singing or piping.

17. See J. Duchemin, *L'AGON dans la tragédie grecque* (Paris 1945).

18. Cf. scholiast on Theocritus *Idyll* 8, argumentum, in A. Nauck, *Tragicorum Graecorum Fragmenta* (second edition, Leipzig 1889), p. 821.

19. G. Kaibel, *Epigrammata Graeca ex lapidibus conlecta* (Berlin 1878), p. 781; cf. R. Reitzenstein, *Epigramm und Skolion* (Giessen 1893), pp. 226–227.

20. H. Usener's explanation of the connection between Antigonus and Pan, in *RhM*, 29 (1874), 25 ff., is more convincing. There is nothing surprising about a wayfarer being invited to compete. It might also be mentioned that Hellenistic poetry is full of characters posing as contestants. A good example is Callimachus *Epigram* 8 Pfeiffer: the speaker poses as a writer of drama, that is, as a contestant. τὰ μὴ ἔνδικα: the tragic stance? Or does ἔνδικος here mean: good verse? In any case, the idea of the contest is employed to supply the poem with an obliqueness that is one of the desiderata in Hellenistic poetry.

21. Th. Zielinski, *Die Gliederung der altattischen Komoedie* (Leipzig 1885), pp. 236 ff. has a theory that the amoebean (which for him includes the epirrheme) derives from the East, and from the habit of *aulodoi* to alternate piping with singing; while one contestant sings, the other plays the pipe to accompany him. Zielinski himself, p. 235, suspects that his theory is not going to find ready acceptance.

22. J. E. Congleton, *Theories of Pastoral Poetry in England, 1684–1798* (Gainesville 1952), p. 249. Cf. also J. F. Lynen, *The Pastoral Art of Robert Frost* (New Haven 1960), p. 132: "It is a striking fact that when [Frost] writes in the pastoral vein, he tends to write dramatically." Cf. also above, Chapter One.

23. Wilamowitz compares the second act of Menander's *Arbitration*, the scene of the two slaves, with Theocritus: U. von Wilamowitz-Moellendorff, *Menander: Das Schiedsgericht* (Berlin 1925), p. 123. Characteristically, however, the two characters in Menander are more vigorously differentiated than similar duos in Theocritus; one is half-educated, the other totally uneducated. Furthermore, the conversation in the *Arbitration* turns on a plot; pastoral has no plot.

24. But note that *Idyll* 6 and *Eclogue* 8, which takes its cue from it, though without a judge and not terminating in a final decision, exhibit songs that are performances in the maximal sense of the word; the singers adopt roles which have no relation to their own presumed characters. This sort of play-acting has its dangers; it goes against the pastoral simplicity, and shades off into Stoic moods.

25. See also the material collected by J. Duchemin, *L'AGON dans la tragédie grecque*, p. 229. Under the heading "Le cliquetis de mots," she gives examples of words or word patterns being repeated by the antagonist.

26. J. Marsan, *La pastorale dramatique en France* (Paris 1905), pp. 107–127, cited by M. I. Gerhardt, *Essai d'analyse littéraire de la Pastorale* (Assen 1950), pp. 180 and 203, note 67. For the medieval *debat*, see H. Walther, *Das Streitgedicht in der lateinischen Literatur des Mittelalters* (Munich 1920).

27. For the topic of victory, see A. S. F. Gow, *Theocritus* (Cambridge 1952), Vol. II, 92 ff.

28. O. Skutsch, in *Gnomon*, 37 (1965), 165–168. For another view, see H. Dahlmann, "Zu Vergils siebenten Hirtengedicht," *Hermes*, 94 (1966), 218–232; and C. P. Segal, "Vergil's 'Caelatum Opus'," *A J Phil.*, 88 (1967), 306–307.

29. For prizes, cf. also above, Chapter Six.

30. Compare my remarks above, Chapter Five.

31. L. Gil, "Comentario a pseudo-Teocrito, *Idil*. 21," *Emerita*, 30 (1962), 241–261, dates the poem at the end of the second century AD. The article is learned and sane; nevertheless I wonder whether, in this area of the literary formulation of popular ethics, our dating methods are sufficiently scientific to permit so precise a result.

32. René Rapin, *Dissertatio de Carmine Pastorali*, trans. Thos. Creech (Oxford 1684), p. 25.

33. Cf. also *Idyll* 8.86: "I will give you a goat;" an empty promise, which is not meant to be fulfilled.

34. Cf. also *Idyll* 5.96 for a similar situation.

35. For Theocritus' avoidance of extended description, cf. below, Chapter Nine.

36. In "Nico and Pas," in the 1590 edition of *Arcadia*: W. A. Ringler, ed., *The Poems of Sir Philip Sidney* (Oxford 1962), 56. For a humorous parade of gifts, see Drayton, *Muses Elizium, Nimphall* 2.

Chapter 8

1. Swift's letter to Pope, dated August 30th, 1716, quoted by R. F. Jones, "Eclogue Types in English Poetry of the Eighteenth Century," *Journal of English and Germanic Philology*, 24 (1925), 42.

2. W. Empson, *Some Versions of Pastoral* (Norfolk 1950), p. 203.

3. H. E. Rollins (ed.), *Tottel's Miscellany* (Harvard 1928), Vol. I, 132–135.

4. C. Hardie (ed.), *Vitae Vergilianae Antiquae* (Oxford 1954), lines 178–180. For other parodies, see G. Thilo and H. Hagen (edd.), *Servii Grammatici Commentarii*, Vol. III (Leipzig 1887), 22.

5. For humor in *Eclogue* 10, see M. Pohlenz, "Das Schlussgedicht der Bucolica," *Studi Virgiliani* (Mantua 1930), pp. 205–226, reprinted in *Kleine Schriften*, Vol. II (1965), 97–115.

6. Cf. V. Poeschl, *Die Hirtendichtung Virgils* (Heidelberg 1964), p. 119. He speaks of "Selbstpersiflage."

7. *Eclogue* 7, lines 37–44:

> Nerine Galatea, thymo mihi dulcior Hyblae,
> candidior cycnis, hedera formosior alba,

cum primum pasti repetent praesepia tauri,
si qua tui Corydonis habet te cura, venito.

Immo ego Sardoniis videar tibi amarior herbis,
horridior rusco, proiecta vilior alga,
si mihi non haec lux toto iam longior anno est.
ite domum pasti, si quis pudor, ite iuvenci.

8. See A. Hruby, "Die Kuerenbergerstrophe MF 9, 21–28," *Orbis Litera-rum*, 18 (1963), 139–154.

9.

Βομβύκα χαρίεσσ', οἱ μὲν πόδες ἀστράγαλοί τευς,
ἁ φωνὰ δὲ τρύχνος· τὸν μὰν τρόπον οὐκ ἔχω εἰπεῖν.

10. Line 25: τὰν βαίταν ἀποδὺς ἐς κύματα τηνῶ ἀλεῦμαι.

11. With *Idyll* 3, compare Ambrose Philips' *Eclogue* 1. The worst that can be said about the poem is that Lobbin is apparently meant to be taken seriously.

12. "Like the swain of the pastoral, [the logger] can be lighthearted yet earnest at the same time, because he lives in a sphere where experience is so coherent that fundamental realities emerge from commonplace events": J. F. Lynen, *The Pastoral Art of Robert Frost* (New Haven 1960), p. 73, discussing the logging scene in Frost's "New Hampshire," lines 343–354. Cf. also his statement, p. 105, *à propos* of Frost's "The Code": "Such bits of humor result from the fundamental irony of pastoral. Crude, simple things take on a comic seriousness just as the humble and commonplace take on an unexpected dignity."

13. See also above, Chapter Six.

14. Cf. also Aristotle *Rhetoric* 3.11.1412a19 ff., and Lane Cooper, *An Aristotelian Theory of Comedy* (New York 1922), pp. 146–149.

15. Expectationibus enim decipiendis et naturis aliorum irridendis. . . .

16. οὐ μὴ σκιρτασῆτε, μὴ ὁ τράγος ὕμμιν ἀναστῇ. Cf. also *Idylls* 4.58–63; 5.147–150; 7.126–127; 9.35–36; 10.57–58.

17. Horace *Epodes* 2.67–70:

Haec ubi locutus fenerator Alfius,
iam iam futurus rusticus,
omnem redegit idibus pecuniam,
quaerit calendis ponere.

For the debt to Archilochus, see. A. Kiessling and R. Heinze, *Q. Horatius Flaccus, Oden und Epoden* (Berlin 1917), p. 504, and E. Fraenkel, *Horace* (Oxford 1957), pp. 60–61, who cites Lachmann. I find none of this persuasive. As satirists of human weaknesses, Horace and Archilochus are bound to use similar stratagems.

18. Vade malis avibus numquam rediturus . . . more Midae, quando virtus tibi vilior auro.

19. Lines 361–362:

> Qui estoit n'agueres tant eprise
> D'Adonis, l'oublia pour aimer un Anchise. . . .

Here the poem ceases being a pastoral and becomes satire. This is confirmed by the moralizing *epimythion*: "telles sont et seront les amitiez des femmes, / qui. . . ." This is almost an anticipation of Gay's "And Susan Blouzelinda's loss repairs."

20. From "New Hampshire."

21. Aristophanes *Clouds* 179; Xenophon *Anabasis* 1.2.27.

Chapter 9

1. J-F. de Saint-Lambert, "Discours Préliminaire" to his *Saisons*, translated in *The Monthly Review*, 41 (1769), 496; cf. J. E. Congleton, *Theories of Pastoral Poetry in England, 1684–1798* (Gainesville 1952), p. 191.

2. P. E. More, "How to Read *Lycidas*," from *On Being Human* (Princeton 1936); reprinted in C. A. Patrides (ed.), *Lycidas: The Tradition and the Poem* (New York 1961), p. 85.

3. W. Empson, *Some Versions of Pastoral* (Norfolk 1950), p. 187.

4. *The Complete Poems of Robert Frost* (New York 1949), p. 558.

5. Thomas Hardy, *Tess of the D'Urbervilles*, chapter 13. Cf. J. W. Beach, *The Concept of Nature in Nineteenth-Century English Poetry* (New York 1936), p. 506. See also the pessimism of the later Ruskin, discussed by Kenneth Clark, *Ruskin Today* (London 1964), p. 88.

6. C. P. Segal, "Nature and the World of Man in Greek Literature," *Arion*, 2 (1963), 42.

7. J. F. Lynen, *The Pastoral Art of Robert Frost* (New Haven 1960), p. 146.

8. See L. Spitzer, *Classical and Christian Ideas of World Harmony* (Baltimore 1963), p. 97; the reference is to *Gerusalemme Liberata*, 16, stanzas 12 and 16.

9. H. M. Richmond, "'Rural Lyricism': A Renaissance Mutation of the Pastoral," *Comparative Literature*, 16 (1964), 199 ff.

10. L. Spitzer, *Classical and Christian Ideas*, p. 5, quotes Amiel's "Le paysage est un état d'âme;" he connects this with the Germanic strands in Amiel's Swiss background.

11. Cf. Cicero *Tusculans* 2.13: ut ager quamvis fertilis sine cultura fructuosus esse non potest, sic sine doctrina animus. W. Wili, *Horaz* (1948), pp. 289–290, claims that Cicero was the first to use the comparison, or to use the image of

cultura animi. But the parable of the sower is anticipated in Plato's *Phaedrus* 276E, and elsewhere. For the implied harmony of nature and soul, see also Theocritus *Idyll* 8.41–48. Those who do not accept the poem as Theocritean may take comfort from the fact that this conception, with its Stoic overtones, is not found elsewhere in Theocritus; cf. G. Perrotta, "Teocrito e il poeta dell' idillio VIII," *Atene e Roma*, 27 (1925), 72.

12. S. Commager, *The Odes of Horace* (New Haven 1962), chapter 5.

13. I. Troxler-Keller, *Die Dichterlandschaft des Horaz* (Heidelberg 1964), p. 70: "Die Lebendigkeit und Weite seines Bildes machen den Dichter*hain* zur Dichter*landschaft*."

14. See *ibid.*, p. 108 ff.

15. See W. Helbig, *Untersuchungen ueber die campanische Wandmalerei* (Leipzig 1873), chapter 12; A. Adriani, *Divagazioni intorno ad una coppa paesistica del Museo di Alessandria* (Rome 1959), a study which traces the bucolic landscape in painting back to the third century BC, and notes cross-references to Theocritus, many of them, it seems to me, of a doubtful character; P. H. von Blanckenhagen and Charles Alexander, "The Paintings from Boscotrecase," *Mitteilungen des deutschen archaeologischen Instituts, Roemische Abteilung, sechstes Ergaenzungsheft,* (1962), pp. 60–61, again, I think, misjudging Theocritus in terms of Longus and his successors; and W. J. T. Peters, *Landscape in Romano-Campanian Mural Painting* (Assen 1963).

16. Spitzer, *Classical and Christian Ideas*, pp. 5 ff.

17. For other examples of the invocation of nature, see B. Lavagnini, *Studi sul romanzo greco* (Messina 1950).

18. M. I. Gerhardt, *Essai d'analyse littéraire de la Pastorale* (Assen 1950), p. 294.

19. ἐν ἀτρίπτοισιν ἀκάνθαις. Other suggestions of the *Sympathiekosmos* may be found in *Idylls* 2.38, and 8.43–44 and 47–48 (I do not accept Gow's dislocations).

20. For a further discussion of the pathetic fallacy, cf. below, Chapter Twelve.

21. From "The Tables Turned;" cf. Beach, *The Concept of Nature*, p. 29. Compare also the beginning of "Michael."

22. From W. H. Auden's "Woods," in *The Shield of Achilles* (1955), p. 15. Note how Auden refers to the "austere philologist."

23. "O glorious Nature! supremely fair and sovereignly good! ... wise substitute of Providence....": Shaftesbury, *Characteristics*, Vol. II, 1732 edition, p. 345. Cf. J. R. Foster, *History of the Pre-Romantic Novel in England* (London 1949), p. 10. Foster explores the relation between philosophical deism and the growth of sensibility. I suspect that a study of the connection between deism and the pastoral, centered around Fontenelle and his influence, would produce interesting results.

24. Note the power of the grove over man in Garcilaso's *Eclogue* 3.

25. Cf. David Kalstone, *Sidney's Poetry* (Harvard 1965), p. 15.

26. In this connection, see the interesting remarks of H. M. Richmond, "'Rural Lyricism,'" on Ronsard's *Odes*, such as the one to the Forest of Gastine, in *Oeuvres Complètes*, ed. Cohen, Vol. 1 (Paris 1950), 452. This and similar poems by Ronsard, but not the conventional églogues, deal with nature in a way that combines the complexities of the Petrarchan view with the immediacy of British nature poetry.

27. Cf. above, Chapter Seven, and Philip Damon, "Modes of Analogy in Ancient and Medieval Verse," *University of California Publications in Classical Philology*, 15.6 (1961), chapter 3.

28. Damon: "The basic function of forests in post-Virgilian pastoral is not to produce echoes, but to provide a ready supply of writing material."

29. Theocritus never has φύσις: κόσμος appears twice, in the sense of "decorum."

30. For the *locus conclusus*, see now S. Stewart, *The Enclosed Garden* (Madison 1966). Also Kenneth Clark, *Landscape into Art* (Harmondsworth 1949), p. 9.

31. The oaks are members of the pastoral chorus. Hence the oaks in *Idyll* 1.106 cannot be used to countermand the pastoral vision. This must mean that beginning with line 105, with his references to Anchises, Adonis, and Diomedes, Daphnis is severing his ties with the pastoral scene, in anticipation of his adieus at lines 115 ff.

32. Moses Hadas, *Hellenistic Culture* (New York 1959), chapter 16, has a discussion of "Blessed Landscapes and Havens" from Homer via Hesiod, Pindar, and other archaic and classical poets down to Luxorius and Tiberianus.

33. Frags. 129–131 Snell.

34. Aristophanes *Peace* 1140–1158.

35. See *Anthol. Pal.*, 9.313–315, 668; 16.227, 228, 230; and many others. *Anthol Pal.*, 9.668, on the grove of Eros at Amasia near the Black Sea, is by Marianus, a poet of ca. AD 500, who is known, among other things, to have translated the Theocritean corpus into 3150 iambic trimeters to make the ancient author more palatable to his contemporaries. The poem in the *Anthology*, consisting of seven elegiac couplets, describes the flora and fauna of the grove, and extends an invitation to share in the simple hospitality of the precinct.

36. E. R. Curtius, *European Literature and the Latin Middle Ages*, trans. W. R. Trask (New York 1953), p. 195.

37. H. M. Currie, "Locus Amoenus," *Comparative Literature*, 12 (1960), 94–95.

38. Cf. also *Paradise Regained*, 2.298 ff.; contrast *Paradise Lost*, 4.131 ff., the description of Eden as it appears to Satan. It is not a pleasance, for two

reasons: (1) it is visualized by a traveler, hence the perspective is wrong; (2) it is visualized from outer space, and appears as a convex surface. A pleasance is level and small, for ease of living and accessibility.

39. My distinction between *amoenus* and *uberrimus* is related to Poggioli's distinction between the pastoral of innocence and the pastoral of happiness, but the line of demarcation is not exactly the same. See R. Poggioli, "Naboth's Vineyard or the Pastoral View of the Social Order," *JHI*, 24 (1963), 18.

40. Lines 133–146:

> ἀδείας σχοίνοιο χαμευνίσιν ἐκλίνθημες
> ἔν τε νεοτμάτοισι γεγαθότες οἰναρέοισι.
> πολλαὶ δ' ἄμμιν ὕπερθε κατὰ κρατὸς δονέοντο
> αἴγειροι πτελέαι τε· τὸ δ' ἐγγύθεν ἱερὸν ὕδωρ
> Νυμφᾶν ἐξ ἄντροιο κατειβόμενον κελάρυζε.
> τοὶ δὲ ποτὶ σκιαραῖς ὀροδαμνίσιν αἰθαλίωνες
> τέττιγες λαλαγεῦντες ἔχον πόνον· ἁ δ' ὀλολυγὼν
> τηλόθεν ἐν πυκιναῖσι βάτων τρύζεσκεν ἀκάνθαις·
> ἄειδον κόρυδοι καὶ ἀκανθίδες, ἔστενε τρυγών,
> πωτῶντο ξουθαὶ περὶ πίδακας ἀμφὶ μέλισσαι.
> πάντ' ὦσδεν θέρεος μάλα πίονος, ὦσδε δ' ὀπώρας.
> ὄχναι μὲν πὰρ ποσσί, παρὰ πλευραῖσι δὲ μᾶλα
> δαψιλέως ἀμῖν ἐκυλίνδετο, τοὶ δ' ἐκέχυντο
> ὄρπακες βραβίλοισι καταβρίθοντες ἔραζε.

41. René Rapin, *Dissertatio de Carmine Pastorali*, trans. Thos. Creech (Oxford 1684), p. 65.

42. *Odyssey*, 24.245 ff., 336 ff. For landscapes in the *Odyssey*, see M. Treu, *Von Homer zur Lyrik* (Munich 1955), p. 101, note 2.

43. *Odyssey*, 4.63–73; *Argonautica*, 2.731–747. For Apollonius' description of localities, see H. Herter, "Bericht ueber die Literatur zur hellenistischen Dichtung seit dem Jahre 1921: ii: Apollonios von Rhodos," *JAW*, 285 (1944–1955), 298–299.

44. Dio *Orationes* 7.14–15.

45. Achilles Tatius *Clitopho and Leucippe* 1.15.

46. For particulars concerning *ecphrasis*, see E. Rohde, *Der griechische Roman* (third edition, Leipzig 1914), p. 360; and E. Norden, *Die Antike Kunstprosa*, Vol. 1 (second edition, Berlin 1909), 285; also P. Friedlaender, *Johannes von Gaza und Paulus Silentarius* (Leipzig 1912).

47. The key terms are ἐοικώς and ἴκελος.

48. S. Luria, "Herondas' Kampf fuer die veristische Kunst," *Miscellanea Rostagni* (1963), p. 407 suggests that Herodas' championing of realism is a deliberate declaration of war on the artificial court poets whom in *Mime* 8 he calls *aipoloi* (goatherds), and whom in *Mime* 4 he castigates under the pretext

of criticizing the opponents of the realist Apelles. From this he argues further that *Mime* I is a polemic against the rococo artificialities of Theocritus' *Idylls* 2 and 4. I find all this difficult to accept, mainly because the "realism" of Herodas is so limited. Luria also seems to me to overemphasize what he calls the artificialities of the Callimachean school.

49. Cf. M. I. Gerhardt, *Essai*, pp. 241-245. Note that contrary to the practice of Sannazaro, Ronsard, and their successors, Remy Belleau keeps his fresh and delightful descriptive pieces separate from his pastorals.

50. See Congleton, *Theories of Pastoral Poetry*, p. 131.

51. T. Purney, *A Full Inquiry into the True Nature of Pastoral* (London 1717), pp. 2-3. Purney has a knack for arriving at the right results on unconvincing grounds. Note his statement, 3.3.1: "If long Descriptions are faulty in Epick poetry, as they prevent the Curiosity of the Reader and leave him nothing to invent . . . they are in Pastoral much more disagreeable."

52. Even the description of items of dress, which is a prominent feature of later pastoral (Mantuan, Ronsard, Robert Greene) is not favored in the ancient pastoral. The only extended description of dress in Theocritus is that of Lycidas, again in *Idyll* 7. But even here the detailing is economical, and the effect is to single out what strikes the eye of his friends from the city, rather than to weave a full tapestry of sartorial elements.

53. The poem terminates with a wish for emigrating to America. Cf. Horace's *Epode* 16. Warton's contrasting of nature, on the one hand, with art, refinement, luxury, war, and life in the city, on the other, indicates a primitivist scheme, in the tradition of satire. Warton's poem is printed in Chalmers' *The Works of the English Poets*, Vol. 18 (1810), 159-161.

54. Cf. also below, Chapter Twelve.

55. *Eclogue* 6.2: neque erubuit silvas habitare. Cf. also *Eclogue* 1.2: silvestrem tenui musam meditaris avena.

56. Curtius, *European Literature and the Latin Middle Ages*, p. 197: "Causes of delight are springs and plantations and gardens and soft breezes and flowers and bird-voices."

57. Empson, *Some Versions*, pp. 261 ff.

58. For the plants of Theocritus and Virgil see the tabulation in A. Cartault, *Etude sur les Bucoliques de Virgile* (Paris 1897), pp. 467 ff. Cartault stresses Virgil's independence, pp. 448 ff. But in spite of the differences, and the greater love of Virgil for the plants and trees of his homeland, the general conception of the role and prominence of plants within the pastoral is the same. For the flora of the *Georgics* see R. Billiard, *L'agriculture dans l'antiquité d'après les Géorgiques de Virgile* (Paris 1928), and E. Abbe, *The Plants of Vergil's Georgics* (Ithaca 1965); both works are illustrated.

59. Theocritus *Idyll* 11.54-59; Bion, "Epitaphium Adonis," 75; Virgil *Eclogues* 2.45-55; 4.19 ff.; 5.36-40.

60. See the commentary by Denys Page in A. S. F. Gow and D. L. Page, *The Greek Anthology: Hellenistic Epigrams* (Cambridge 1965), Vol. II, 593–596; also index, s.v. "Trees," p. 716. Meleager's identifications were, it seems, influenced by Theophrastus' *Historia Plantarum*.

61. See C. Ruutz-Rees, "Flower Garlands of the Poets Milton, Shakespeare, Spenser, Marot, Sannazaro," *Mélanges Abel Lefranc* (Paris 1936), pp. 75–90. She shows that the "Culex" was an important source for Sannazaro and Marot. For other general discussions of the subject see T. P. Harrison and H. J. Leon (edd.), *The Pastoral Elegy: An Anthology* (Austin 1939), pp. 292–293, and the literature mentioned there.

62. Among the more prominent occurrences of the flower catalogue, the following are especially noteworthy: Spenser's "April" *Eclogue*, 136 ff.; Drayton's *Muses Elizium*, "Fifth Nimphall" (compare also the "Third Nimphall": a catalogue of disagreeable flowers and plants); Shakespeare's *The Winter's Tale*, 4.4.73 ff.; Milton's "Lycidas," 133 ff. (cf. Wayne Shumaker, "Flowerets and Sounding Seas," in Patrides (ed.), *Lycidas*, pp. 125 ff.); Keats' "Ode to a Nightingale," stanzas 4 and 5; Arnold's "Thyrsis," 62 ff.; Oscar Wilde's "The Garden of Eros."

63. For the details of the spectrum, see T. F. Thiselton Dyer, *Folk-Lore of Shakespeare* (London 1883); H. N. Ellacombe, *The Plant-Lore and Garden Craft of Shakespeare* (second edition, Exeter 1884); E. and J. Lehner, *Folklore and Symbolism of Flowers, Plants, and Trees* (New York 1960).

64. In an interesting but, it seems to me, basically mistaken essay entitled "Originality of Milton's Harmonious Use of Proper Names," Leigh Hunt (L. H. and C. W. Houtchens (edd.), *Leigh Hunt's Literary Criticism* [New York 1956], pp. 230–238) criticizes John Black, who in his *Life of Torquato Tasso* (1810) had argued that Milton uses proper names for beautification, and that he owes this technique to Tasso. Hunt disagrees: "Till the time of Milton, names appear to have had a privilege of exemption from harmony." But cf. the remarks of Bruno Snell on Virgil's use of series of Greek proper names: *The Discovery of the Mind* (Oxford 1953), p. 286.

65. For untrodden paths, see Lucretius 1.922 ff.; Callimachus *Epigram* 28 Pfeiffer. For other uses of the motif, see V. Poeschl, "Dichtung und dionysische Verzauberung," *Miscellanea Rostagni* (Turin 1963), pp. 621 ff.

66. Tacitus *Dialogus de oratoribus* 1.12:

nemora vero et luci et secretum ipsum . . . tantam mihi adferunt voluptatem ut inter praecipuos carminum fructus numerem quod non in strepitu . . . nec inter sordes ac lacrimas reorum componuntur, sed secedit animus in loca pura atque innocentia fruiturque sedibus sacris.

67. Contrast the willful heresy of Mantuan, *Eclogue* 8: Pollux addresses a long prayer to the Virgin Mary, asking protection from pastoral dangers.

In more than one poem in Mantuan's collection, nature is experienced as a scene of threats, discomforts, and disasters.

68. The poet's garden: Plato *Phaedrus* 276D; *Ion* 534A; Pindar *Olympian* 9.27. The cave of Hephaestus: *Iliad* 18.400–403.

69. Contrast with this the deep forest of *Olimpia* in which he presents himself under the name of Silvius, because, as he explains in a letter, *in silva quadam huius egloges primam cogitationem habuerim*. The experience here is not philosophical or pastoral, but religious.

70. See Diogenes Laertius 3.8, about Plato and Isocrates; 9.112, about Timon of Phlius. I like to think that the notice in Athenaeus 12.542A about Hiero II of Syracuse is not to be filed along with notices about philosophers' gardens, in spite of the fact that Hiero called the garden *Mythos*. Apparently Hiero used it to combine business with pleasure; Book 12 of Athenaeus' *Deipnosophists* is chiefly about lechery.

71. Frag. 7.75–78 Powell (Athenaeus 13.597B). Compare also Philitas frag. 14 Powell (Athenaeus 5.192E).

72. See Cicero *De oratore* 1.28–29, and A. Nowacki (ed.), *Philitae Coi fragmenta poetica* (Muenster 1927), p. 81. W. Richter (ed.), *Vergil: Georgica* (Munich 1957), p. 301, has some fine remarks about the richer symbolic status of the shade-giving tree in Virgil's *Georgics*.

73. See M. Puelma, *Lucilius und Kallimachos* (Frankfurt 1949), p. 240. Cf. also below, Chapter Twelve.

74. Compare also Ruskin's remarks on the pine, in *Modern Painters*, Vol. V, Chapter 9, par. 4–5, cited by Kenneth Clark, (ed.), *Ruskin Today* (London 1964), pp. 91–92:

The pine, placed nearly always among scenes disordered and desolate, brings into them all possible elements of order and precision. . . . Also it may be well for lowland branches to reach hither and thither for what they need . . . but the pine is trained to need nothing, and to endure everything. It is resolvedly whole, self-contained, desiring nothing but rightness, content with restricted completion. Tall or short, it will be straight.

75.

> O bosques y espesuras:
> Plantadas por la mano del amado. . . .

76.

> καὶ ἀγκὰς ἔμαρπτε Κρόνου παῖς ἦν παράκοιτιν·
> τοῖσι δ' ὑπὸ χθὼν δῖα φύεν νεοθηλέα ποίην,
> λωτόν θ' ἐρσήεντα ἰδὲ κρόκον ἠδ' ὑάκινθον
> πυκνὸν καὶ μαλακόν, ὃς ἀπὸ χθονὸς ὑψόσ' ἔεργε.

77.

ἄφελε τοῦ λόγου τὸ νῦν ἔχον ἐποποιῶν τε λειμῶνας καὶ σκιὰς καὶ
ἅμα κιττοῦ τε καὶ σμιλάκων διαδρομὰς καὶ ὅσ᾽ ἄλλα τοιούτων τόπων
ἐπιλαβόμενοι γλίχονται τὸν Πλάτωνος ᾽Ιλισσον καὶ τὸν ἄγνον
ἐκεῖνον καὶ τὴν ἠρέμα προσάντη ποὰν πεφυκυῖαν προθυμότερον ἢ
κάλλιον ἐπιγράφεσθαι.

78. See A. Hulubei, *L'Eglogue en France au xvie siècle* (Paris 1938), p. 718.
79. Two random examples: Horace *Odes* 1.17; Tibullus 2.3.
80. Callimachus frag. 73 Pfeiffer; cf. Aristaenetus *Epistles* 1.1. Also Theocritus *Idyll* 18.47: the name of Helen is inscribed on the bark of a plane tree,
to commemorate her wedding. The poem is not a pastoral; the sentiment has
nothing to do with love.
81. J. Miles, "The Primary Language of *Lycidas*," in C. A. Patrides (ed.),
Milton's Lycidas (New York 1961), pp. 95–100.

Chapter 10

1. Menander Rhetor περὶ ἐπιδεικτικῶν 2.1 has a chapter entitled "How
one must praise the country" (L. Spengel, *Rhetores Graeci*, Vol. III [1856]
344–346), which turns out to recommend the procedures followed, for example, in the Hippocratic *Airs Waters Places*: the author is invited to consider
the geographical location, the climate, the soil, and generally the geophysics
of the place with which he is concerned, with no thought given to the country
as a source of aesthetic pleasure.

2. John Ruskin, *Modern Painters*, Vol III (New York 1885), Part 4, chapter
13, pp. 176 ff. He argues that the Greeks had no interest in or feeling for nature
because (1) they tended to focus on the gods animating nature; (2) surrounded
as they were by great beauty, they were familiar with it, hence not excited by
it; (3) they preferred to find beauty in the human form; (4) they lived healthy
lives, and thus were not prey to the moods that find relief in taking refuge in
nature; and (5) their love of order made them afraid of everything disordered.
Almost all of Ruskin's evidence is from Homer. He admits that other writers,
especially Aeschylus and Aristophanes, have "more of modern feeling . . . but
then these appear to me just the parts of them which were not Greek." If
Ruskin had said "epic" instead of "Greek" his argument might be more
persuasive. At any rate, his assertion is contradicted, not only by Sappho and
Euripides and some of the epigrammatists, but by Homer himself whose eye
for natural beauty, especially in the *Odyssey*, cannot be gainsaid.

3. C. P. Segal, "Nature and the World of Man in Greek Literature,"
Arion, 2 (1963), 45 puts this development only in the fourth century.

4.

O rus, quando ego te aspiciam quandoque licebit
nunc veterum libris, nunc somno et inertibus horis
ducere sollicitae iucunda oblivia vitae. . . .

5. Compare also Horace's *Epistles* Book 1, nos. 7, 10, 14, 16.

6. For this, see D. C. Allen, *Image and Meaning* (Baltimore 1960), chapter 7, who cites some of the ancient precedents for the identification. Note especially his reference to Seneca's *Thyestes*, a notable example of the Stoic *Sympathiekosmos*.

7. This is done by H. M. Richmond, "'Rural Lyricism': A Renaissance Mutation of the Pastoral," *Comparative Literature*, 16 (1964), 209.

8. Note the speech of Cornix in *Eclogue* 6.

9. O. Goldsmith, *The Deserted Village* (London 1772). The poem ends with an impressive vista of emigrants leaving for a land which has not yet been infected with urban culture and industrialization.

10. See, e.g., J. F. Lynen, *The Pastoral Art of Robert Frost* (New Haven 1960), p. 10. He follows Epmson in believing that the pastoral makes for a renewed sense of solidarity between rich and poor, non-simple and simple.

11. W. H. Auden, *The Shield of Achilles* (New York 1955), pp. 28 f., stanzas 9–11 of "Streams."

12. The chief Roman models are: Horace *Epistles* 1.14; *Epode* 16; Tibullus *Elegies* 2.3; Propertius *Elegies* 2.19, 3.13. Also, Virgil *Georgics* 2.493 ff.

13. Aristophanes *Acharnians* 163 ff., 836 ff., 929 ff.; *Peace*, 556 ff., *et al.*

14. From Aristophanes' *Islands* frag. 387 Kock.

15. Passages in Old Comedy that deal with the beauty or the pleasures of life in the country are collected by R. Vischer, *Das einfache Leben* (Goettingen 1965), pp. 58 f., 131 f.

16. W. F. Mainland (ed.), *Schiller: Ueber naive und sentimentalische Dichtung* (Oxford 1951), p. 27.

17. Hallet Smith, *Elizabethan Poetry* (Harvard 1952), pp. 57 ff., has some remarks on the susceptibility of pastoral to satire, and comments on the variety of the objects attacked.

18. I owe my knowledge of the passage to the Ph.D. dissertation of C. W. Truesdale, "English Pastoral Verse from Spenser to Marvell" (University of Washington, 1956).

19. According to Gilbert Highet, "The Philosophy of Juvenal," *TAPA*, 80 (1949), 254–270, the proximity of pastoral and satire may be exemplified in Juvenal himself, whose philosophical position, if he may be said to have had one, is that of an Epicurean. For possible Hellenistic sources, see M. Puelma, *Lucilius und Kallimachos* (Frankfurt 1949).

20. Outside of Nimphall 4, satire proper appears only in 7 and, fleetingly, in 10. It seems that Drayton became aware of the precariousness of satiric pastoral, of the possibility that the real gains of pastoral were likely to be canceled out by anatomy and ridicule.

21. For attention to the church in pastoral, T. P. Harrison and H. J. Leon (edd.), *The Pastoral Elegy* (Austin 1939), p. 292 compare Radbert's *Ecloga*, Petrarch's *Eclogue* 6 (St. Peter rebukes Pope Clement), Mantuan, *Eclogue* 9, and Spenser's "September." Cf. also Spenser's "May." If I may venture a layman's opinion on a matter which calls for tact and erudition, I cannot help feeling that there is a certain ingenuousness about the superscription "And by occasion foretels the ruine of our corrupted Clergy then in their height." It is missing in the MS, and does not appear in the first printing in 1638. If we did not have it (from the second edition, of 1645), much of what is now interpreted as an attack on churchmen might well be read as an attack on bad poets, especially pastoralists. "Blind mouths" is more appropriately said of poetasters than of crooked churchmen. It is true, on the other hand, that the clock mechanism of the two-handed engine (cf. C. A. Thomson, "That Two-Handed Engine Will Smite," *SP*, 59 [1962], 184–200) is rather too imposing a piece of artillery to move up against literary rivals; and the superscription is, after all, a fact. In any case, there is no doubt that we are dealing with satire, no matter whether the butt is clerical, or just scribbling.

22. Compare also *Epistles* 1.16 which starts out with a loving description of the natural setting of the farm, but then continues with an encomium on virtue in public life.

23. "The Woodsman's Walke," by Sheepheard Tonie (probably Anthony Munday), No. 140 of *England's Helicon*, ed. Rollins.

24. Cf. H. Usener (ed.), *Epicurea* (Leipzig 1887), frag. 8: "Since Epicurus says that everything must be done for the sake of pleasure, he excludes the wise man from offices and public life, and asserts that he must live only for himself." Life itself is important, not filling a position or performing a function. By practicing *otium*, man becomes a god among men.

25. Virgil *Eclogue* 9.17–18:

> heu tua nobis
> paene simul tecum solacia rapta, Menalca.

26. Horace *Epode* 16; Tibullus *Elegies* 2.3 (cf. also *Elegies* 1.10.9; 2.5.27); Propertius *Elegies* 3.13.

27. Tibullus 2.3.76: horrida villosa corpora veste tegant.

28. See especially Propertius *Elegies* 3.13.25–46; the ending is translated from Leonidas, *Anthol. Pal.* 9.337.

29. *Works and Days* 116–120:

> ἐσθλὰ δὲ πάντα
> τοῖσιν ἔην· καρπὸν δ' ἔφερεν ζείδωρος ἄρουρα
> αὐτομάτη πολλόν τε καὶ ἄφθονον· οἱ δ' ἐθελημοί
> ἥσυχοι ἔργ' ἐνέμοντο σὺν ἐσθλοῖσιν πολέεσσιν,
> ἀφνειοὶ μήλοισι, φίλοι μακάρεσσι θεοῖσιν.

For the reasons why line 120 is likely to be genuine, in spite of the doubts generally expressed about it, see T. G. Rosenmeyer, "Hesiod and Historiography," *Hermes*, 85 (1957), 282–283. The reference to sheep helped to confirm the popular notion that Golden Age nostalgia and pastoral were made for each other. The subsequent lines about a Golden Age, in connection with the freeing of Cronus (169–169e), are post-Hesiodic.

30. Pindar frag. 104b Snell (cf. also *Olympian* 2), transmitted by Plutarch *De Pythiae oraculis* 29.409A:

> προβάτων γὰρ ἐκ πάντων κελάρυξεν,
> ὡς ἀπὸ κρανᾶν φέρτατον ὕδωρ,
> θηλᾶν γάλα· τοὶ δ' ἐπίμπλαν ἐσσύμενοι πίθους·
> ἀσκὸς δ' οὔτε τις ἀμφορεὺς ἐλίνυεν δόμοις,
> πέλλαι γὰρ ξύλιναι πίθοι ⟨τε⟩ πλῆσθεν ἅπαντες . . . .

31. Note the *adynaton* in Horace *Epode* 16.25.

32. See H. Langerbeck, "Die Vorstellung vom Schlaraffenland in der alten attischen Komoedie," *Zeitschrift fuer Volkskunde*, 59 (1963), 192–204. Cf. also Crates frag. 14–15 Kock, Teleclides frag. 1 Kock; Pherecrates frags. 108, 130.

33. Lucretius 5.1397–1398:

> tum ioca, tum sermo, tum dulces esse cachinni
> consuerant; agrestis enim tum musa vigebat.

34. Tzetzes, scholiast on Hesiod, in Th. Gaisford (ed.), *Poetae Minores Graeci*, Vol III (Oxford 1820), p. 58: βίον ἁπλοῦν καὶ ἀπέριττον καὶ φιλάλληλον εἶχον . . . οὐ βασιλεῖς, οὐκ ἄρχοντας, οὐ δεσπότας κεκτημένοι, οὐ στρατείας, οὐ βίας, οὐχ ἁρπαγὰς ἀλλὰ φιλαλληλίαν μόνον καὶ τὸν ἐλεύθερον καὶ ἀπέριττον βίον ζῆν εἰδότες.

35. For Dicaearchus, and the adoption of his scheme by Varro, whence it entered into the mainstream of European anthropology, see F. Wehrli, *Die Schule des Aristoteles*, Vol. 1: *Dikaiarchos* (Basel 1944), frags. 47 ff.; also above, Chapter Four.

36. Aristotle *Politics* 1256a29 ff. I forgo the privilege of citing the Greek, and present the passage in Jowett's translation.

37. For the latter, see E. K. Chambers (ed.), *English Pastorals* (London 1895), p. 77. For the Golden Age in Renaissance pastoral, see P. Meissner, "Das goldene Zeitalter in der englischen Renaissance," *Anglia*, 59 (1935), 351–367.

38. *Eclogue* 4.1–3:

> Sicelides Musae, paulo maiora canamus.
> non omnis arbusta iuvant humilesque myricae.
> si canimus silvas, silvae sint consule dignae.

For the prose quality of the first line, see H. G. Gotoff, "On the Fourth Eclogue of Virgil," *Philologus*, 111 (1967), 67.

39. Cf. W. Schmid, "Panegyrik und Bukolik in der neronischen Epoche," *Bonner Jahrbb.*, 153 (1953), 70 ff; also O. Skutsch, in *RE*, 5 (1905), 2115 ff., "*Einsiedlensia Carmina.*"

40. See Hugh Blair, "Pastoral Poetry," *Lectures on Rhetoric and Belles Lettres* (third edition, London 1787), Vol. III, 114–115.

41. R. F. Jones, "Eclogue Types in English Poetry of the Eighteenth Century," *Journal of English and Germanic Philology*, 24 (1925), 33–60.

42. W. F. Mainland, *Schiller*, p. 51. See also Ad. Frey (ed.), *Gessners Werke: Auswahl* (Berlin and Stuttgart, n.d.), p. xxxi.

43. J. G. von Herder, *Fragmente ueber die neuere deutsche Literatur, Zwote Sammlung*, Section IV: *Von der griechischen Literatur in Deutschland: Theocritus und Gessner* (1767), 198; reprinted in P. Merker, *Deutsche Idyllendichtung, 1700–1840* (Berlin 1934), pp. 98 ff.

44. The chief passages are *Idylls* 12.16; 16.90 ff.; 25.120 ff.

45. See W. Schmid, "Eine fruehchristliche Arkadienvorstellung," *Festschrift Konrat Ziegler* (Stuttgart 1954), p. 127 note. Also B. Snell, *Die Entdeckung des Geistes* (third edition, Hamburg 1955), p. 372, notes 1 and 2; and A. S. F. Gow and D. L. Page, *The Greek Anthology*, Vol. II: *The Garland of Philip* (Cambridge 1968), 279.

46. R. Poggioli, "The Oaten Flute," *Harvard Library Bulletin*, 11.2 (1957), 170.

47. E. K. Chambers, *English Pastorals*, p. xliii.

48. W. Empson, *Some Versions of Pastoral* (Norfolk 1950), p. 186.

49. Lucretius 4.1134: surgit amari aliquid, quod in ipsis floribus angat.

50. Altius est, Glycerane, aliquid, non quod patet; erras.

51. For the two possibilities, see W. Schmid, "Panegyrik und Bukolik," pp. 65 ff., and H. Fuchs, "Der Friede als Gefahr," *HSCPh*, 63 (1958), 363–385. For Lucretius' melancholy, see J. B. Logre, *L'anxieté de Lucrèce* (Paris 1946).

52. See also Douglas Bush, *Mythology and the Romantic Tradition in English Poetry* (Harvard 1937), p. 461, on Walter De la Mare's "Tears" (in: *Poems* [1906]): "Mr. De la Mare, in his own exquisite way, denied the death of Pan,

not, like most poets, in the name of facile pagan joys, but finding amid the violets 'Tears of an antique bitterness.'"

53. Cf. F. Solmsen, "Epicurus On the Growth and Decline of the Cosmos," *A J Phil.*, 74 (1953), 34–51; and more generally G. E. Mueller, "Wie lebt man sinnvoll in einer sinnlosen Welt? Der Begriff der Verzweiflung in der hellen-istisch-roemischen Ethik," *Studia Philosophica*, 21 (Basel 1961), 111–156.

54. The phrase is Poggioli's, "The Oaten Flute," p. 161.

55. Cf. E. Panofsky, "Et in Arcadia Ego: Poussin and the Elegiac Tradi-tion," in *Meaning in the Visual Arts* (Garden City 1955), pp. 295–320.

56. D. Kalstone, "The Transformation of Arcadia: Sannazaro and Sir Philip Sidney," *Comparative Literature*, 15 (1963), 249; cf. the same author's *Sidney's Poetry* (Harvard 1965), p. 83. Kalstone argues that for some of his dissent from Sannazaro, Sidney returns to the models in Petrarch.

57. M. I. Gerhardt, *Essai d'analyse littéraire de la Pastorale* (Assen 1950), p. 296.

58. R. Poggioli, "The Pastoral of the Self," *Daedalus*, 88 (1959), 698: "Marvell neglects the very dialectics Milton has exemplified in his famous diptych, *L'Allegro* and *Il Penseroso*. Melancholy and solitude are one and the same thing; and the soul is at once pensive and mirthful when it keeps its own rendezvous with itself."

59. Cf. H. M. Richmond, "'Rural Lyricism,'" pp. 202–203. Richmond emphasizes the role of Ronsard in helping to perfect the poetry of solitude.

60. "Hippocrates" *Epistle* 12.1, p. 293 Hercher; cf. A. Grilli, *Il problema della vita contemplativa nel mondo greco-romano* (Milan 1953), pp. 186–187. The pertinent passage runs as follows:

ἐν ἄντροισι καὶ ἐρημίῃσι ἢ ὑπὸ σκέπῃσι δενδρέων καὶ ἐν μαλθακῇσι ποίῃσι ἢ παρ' ἡσύχοισι ὑδάτων ῥεέθροισι· ξυμβαίνει μὲν οὖν τὰ πολλὰ τοῖς μελαγχολῶσι τοιαῦτα· σιγηλοί τε γὰρ ἐνίοτε καὶ μονήρεες καὶ φιλέρημοι τυγχάνουσι, ἀπανθρωπεύονταί τε ξύμφυλον ὄψιν ἀλλοτριωτάτην νομίζοντες.

61. G. Thomson, *Aeschylus and Athens* (London 1941), p. 66, cited by F. Kermode, *English Pastoral Poetry from the Beginnings to Marvell* (London 1952), p. 16.

62. For a good account of the changes in Drayton's pastorals, see W. Hebel (ed.), *The Works of Michael Drayton*, Vol. V (Oxford 1941), 183 ff.

63. Cf. V. Poeschl, *Die Hirtendichtung Virgils* (Heidelberg 1964), p. 57: "Nicht Gegenwart wie bei Theokrit, sondern Erinnerung und Sehnsucht bestimmen die Schilderung....Das Glueck ist aus der Perspektive des Schmerzes gesehen."

64. *Idyll* 1.62–63:

τὰν γὰρ ἀοιδάν
οὔ τί πᾳ εἰς 'Αίδαν γε τὸν ἐκλελάθοντα φυλαξεῖς.

65. *Idyll* 7.86–89.
66. *Idyll* 8.57–59.

Chapter 11

1. *Eclogue* 10.31–33:

> 'tamen cantabitis, Arcades' inquit
> 'montibus haec vestris, soli cantare periti
> Arcades.'

2. For this, see Ph. Legrand, "L'Arcadie et l'Idylle," *REA*, 2 (1900), 101–116, especially pp. 113 ff.; Herta Wendel, *Arkadien im Umkreis bukolischer Dichtung* (Giessen 1933), pp. 8 ff. In Legrand's view, Virgil's bucolic landscape continues to be Sicily. *Eclogue* 8.22–24, he feels, has a didactic flavor; it is a footnote to explain the justification for the refrain, thus suggesting that Virgil was not basing the notion of an Arcadian pleasance on a literary tradition. None of this is very persuasive.

3. Wendel, *Arkadien*, p. 45.

4. *Idylls* 1.123 ff., 7.106 ff., and elsewhere. For Pan's association with Arcadia, see F. Brommer, "Pan," *RE*, Suppl. 8 (1956), 949 ff. We should discount Anyte's association with Arcadia, pleaded as a contributory cause by Wendel, *Arkadien*, pp. 24 ff. Tegea is hardly part of the rugged Arcadian landscape. Other poetic uses of Arcadia cited by Wendel (Leonidas, *Anthol. Pal.* 6.188; Mnasalcas, *Anthol. Pal.* 9.324; cf. also the passages cited by Legrand, "L'Arcadie et l'Idylle," p. 102) do not bear out the inferences she draws from them. Her final statement, p. 30, shows that she is aware of the uncertainty of much of her *Quellenforschung*. As for Virgil's originality on this score, it is sometimes claimed that Erycius, *Anthol. Pal.* 6.96 preceded Virgil. One of those who argue for this position is G. Jachmann, "L'Arcadia come paesaggio bucolico," *Maia*, 5 (1952), 161–174: it cannot be Virgil who introduced the pastoral Arcadia, he argues; if it were, his Arcadia would be more concrete and convincing in its details; hence he must be drawing on an earlier tradition; Erycius, therefore, preceded Virgil; there were other Hellenistic examples of the tradition, but they are now lost. But the date of Erycius is quite uncertain, and it is much simpler to assume that it was Erycius who learned from Virgil, not the other way round. Cf. above, Chapter Ten, note 45.

5. U. von Wilamowitz-Moellendorff, *Die Textgeschichte der griechischen Bukoliker* (Berlin 1906), p. 111, note 1. For doubts concerning the role of Theon, see A. S. F. Gow (ed.), *Theocritus*, Vol I (Cambridge 1952), lxi. For authors of an *Arkadika*, see Legrand, "L'Arcadie et l'Idylle," p. 110, note 3.

6. The references, from the *Iliad* to Menander, are given by Legrand, *op. cit.*, p. 104.

7. For all this, see M. L. West, "Hesiodea," *CQ*, 11 (1961), 142-145.

8. Cf. F. Wehrli, *Die Schule des Aristoteles*, Vol. 1: *Dikaiarchos* (Basel 1944), 57; and W. Spoerri, *Spaethellenistische Berichte ueber Welt, Kultur und Goetter* (Basel 1959), pp. 152 ff. Menander frag. 397 Kock has a cook say about the Arcadians that, being landlocked, they are snared by λοπάδια. The word usually means some kind of shellfish; could it here be a humorous term for acorns?

9. M. Pohlenz, "Die hellenistische Poesie und die Philosophie," *Charites Friedrich Leo* (Berlin 1911), p. 86.

10. Servius on Virgil's *Georgics* 2.342, with references to Cicero and Statius.

11. Cf. also Apollonius Rhodius 4.263 ff.; Callimachus *Iambi* frag. 191.32 and 56 Pfeiffer; "Pindar" frag. 985.7-8, in *Poetae Melici Graeci*, ed. D. L. Page (Oxford 1962).

12.   ὁ δεύτερος δὲ νῆσον ἀγρότης μολών,
             χερσαῖος αὐτόδαιτος ἐγγόνων δρυός

             . . . .

             τῶν πρόσθε μήνης φηγίνων πύρνων ὀχήν
             σπληδῷ κατ' ἄκρον χεῖμα θαλψάντων πυρός.

13. Hecataeus of Miletus, as reported by Athenaeus 4.148E.

14. *Philippika* 46, as reported by Athenaeus 4.149D.

15. Servius on *Georgics* 1.14. The motif goes back to Pindar frag. 251 Snell.

16. See, e.g., J. van Leeuwen (ed.), *Aristophanes: Equites* (Leiden 1900), p. 145, who cites Herodotus 1.66, an earlier oracle, to support his position.

17. W. Schmid, "Eine fruehchristliche Arkadienvorstellung," *Festschrift Konrat Ziegler* (Stuttgart 1954), pp. 121-130. The passage occurs in *Pastor Hermae, visio* 5.1.

18. M. Dolc, "Sobre la Arcadia de Virgilio," *Estudios Clasicos*, 4 (1957-1958), 242-266.

19. Varro's *On the Life of the Roman People*; cf. H. Dahlmann, "T. Terentius Varro," *RE*, Suppl. 6 (1935) 1243-1246; Dionysius of Halicarnassus *History of Rome* 1.8.1; also 2.1.2; Livy 1.7. Cf. further Varro *De lingua latina* 5.101; Pliny *Natural History* 3.5.9.56: Latium was at various times held by, in this order, Aborigines, Pelasgians, Arcadians, Sicels.

20. *Fasti* 5.91 ff.; 2.289 ff.; 2.423 f. The first passage, translated in the text, runs:

    exul ab Arcadia Latios Evander in agros
       venerat, impositos attuleratque deos.
    hic, ubi nunc Roma est, orbis caput, arbor et herbae
       et paucae pecudes et casa rara fuit.
    . . . sacraque multa quidem sed Fauni prima bicornis
       has docuit gentes alipedisque dei.

21. For the connection between Faunus and the *Saturnia aetas*, see H. Dahlmann, "Vates," *Philologus*, 97 (1948), 349. But Dahlmann's thesis that *vates* is especially connected with the spirit of the forest is not convincing on the evidence presented.

22. It is clear from the text that I agree with Jachmann, "L'Arcadia," pp. 164 ff., against E. Kapp, B. Snell, E. Panofsky, and now F. W. Walbank, *A Historical Commentary on Polybius*, Vol. I (Cambridge 1957), 465 ff., in questioning the importance of Polybius' account (4.20-21) of musical contests in Arcadia for Virgil's Arcadia.

23. The fiction probably derives from *Idyll* 1.123 ff., where Pan's relation to Daphnis appears as a curious mixture of master, successor, and friend.

24. See the drawing in Codex Paris. graec. 2832, fol. v. 58, of the fourteenth century. The illustration goes back to ancient models; cf. V. Buchheit, *Studien zum Corpus Priapeorum*, *Zetemata*, 28 (Munich 1962), 9, note 2.

25. Anyte, *Anthol. Pal.* 9.745, 16.231, 16.291, perhaps 16.229; Leonidas, *Anthol. Pal.* 6.188, 6.154.

26. Amsterdam 2117/8; cf. R. Herbig, *Pan* (Frankfurt 1949), plate vii.2. Also F. Brommer, "Pan," *RE*, Suppl. 8 (1956), 956-958.

27. See especially N. Cistjakova, "Pan und Phyle in Menanders *Dyskolos*," *Schriften Akademie Berlin*, 50 (1965), 139-145.

28. Athenaeus 15.694D (*Poetae Melici Graeci*, p. 887):

> ὦ Πὰν 'Αρκαδίας μεδέων κλεεννᾶς
> ὀρχηστὰ βρομίαις ὀπαδὲ Νύμφαις,
> γελάσειας ὦ Πὰν ἐπ' ἐμαῖς
> . . . ἀοιδαῖς.

29. Calpurnius 4.132 ff.:

> Numine Caesareo securior ipse Lycaeus
> Pan recolit silvas et amoena Faunus in umbra
> securus recubat placidoque in fonte lavatur
> Nais . . . .

30. *Inscriptiones Graecae*, iv.1.[2] 130; or *Poetae Melici Graeci*, p. 936, from Epidaurus.

31. See C. L. Babcock, "The Role of Faunus in Horace, *Carmina* 1.4," *TAPA*, 92 (1961), 13-19. For Faunus as a spirit of the tillage, see W. F. Otto, in *RE*, 6 (1909), 2070. Cf., however, above for the connection of Faunus with the forest.

32. *Odes* 3.18.15-16:

> gaudet invisam pepulisse fossor
> ter pede terram.

33. But *not* in Theocritus, where only Lycidas carries the crook. Cf. above, Chapter Six.

34. Pindar frag. 98 Snell; cf. A. Boeckh, *Pindar: Epinicia, Interpretatio Latina* (Leipzig 1821), p. 594. For Pan as hunter, see, e.g., Rhianus frag. 66 Powell; also Leonidas, *Anthol. Pal.* 9.337: Pan declares himself a patron of hunting and piping.

35. R. A. Pack (ed.), *Artemidori Daldiani Libri V* (Leipzig 1963), p. 167.

36. Cf. the name vase of the Pan-painter, in J. D. Beazley, *Der Pan-Maler* (Berlin 1931), plate 2: Pan desires a shepherd boy.

37. Athenaeus 9.389 f.; C. and T. Mueller (edd.), *Fragmenta Historicorum Graecorum*, 2.324 frag. 71b.

38. Virgil *Georgics* 3.391. Cf. also Robert Browning's "Pan and Luna" (1880), and Douglas Bush, *Mythology and the Romantic Tradition in English Poetry* (Harvard 1937), p. 377. For a useful compilation of the material concerning Pan as an instigator of panic, see G. Gerhard, "Der Tod des grossen Pan," *Sitzungsberichte der Akademie, Heidelberg, philosophisch-historische Klasse*, 5.52 (1915). We may discount Gerhard's adherence to the anthropological obsessions of his day, which induces him to look for vegetation spirits and house demons to explain the roots of the tradition.

39. Araros frag. 13 Kock. The motif is obviously modeled on the lyre playing of the infant Hermes in the Homeric "Hymn to Hermes."

40. For ancient passages documenting Pan the musician, see Ph. Legrand, "L'Arcadie et l'Idylle," p. 111, note 1.

41. The Stoic interpretation of the name Pan to signify *pan* (all), for which see further below, points to the Roman period, not the Hellenistic, as has been suggested.

42. Lucretius 4.580-589; cf. also Plutarch *Quaestiones conviviales* 8.711E.

43. For Keats, see the "Hymn to Pan," in "Endymion." For Swinburne, see "The Palace of Pan," a near-pantheistic apprehension of the mystery of Nature. For Emerson, see "Woodnotes" (*Poems*, p. 58), cited by Douglas Bush, *Mythology and the Romantic Tradition*, p. 487. The lines cited in the text are Emerson's; cf. J. W. Beach, *The Concept of Nature in Nineteenth-Century English Poetry* (New York 1936), p. 364.

44. H. Usener, "Ein Epigramm von Knidos," *RhM*, 29 (1874), 43 ff. Curiously Brommer, "Pan," has nothing on the Hellenistic rulers' use of Pan.

45. *Natural History* 35.36.63 and 106.

46. For Antigonus as a philosopher king, see W. W. Tarn, *Antigonos Gonatas* (Oxford 1913).

47. M. Y. Hughes, "Virgil and Spenser," *University of California Publications in English*, 2 (1928/9), 301.

Chapter 12

1. R. Barthes, *Essais Critiques* (Paris 1964), p. 39.

2. John Ruskin, *Modern Painters*, Vol. III (New York 1885), 152 ff.

3. For the pathetic fallacy in ancient poetry, see F. O. Copley, "The Pathetic Fallacy in Early Greek Poetry," *A J Phil.*, 58 (1937), 194–209; for the pathetic fallacy in ancient pastoral, see B. F. Dick, "Ancient Pastoral and the Pathetic Fallacy," *Comparative Literature*, 20 (1968), 27–44.

4. Thos. Purney, *A Full Inquiry into the True Nature of Pastoral* (London 1717), 3.6.

5. *The Arcadian Rhetorike* was published in 1588. Cf. the edition by Ethel Seaton (Oxford 1950). The chapter at issue is No. 7.

6. D. Kalstone, *Sidney's Poetry* (Harvard 1965).

7. J. F. Lynen, *The Pastoral Art of Robert Frost* (New Haven 1960), 23.

8. Printed in F. Kermode (ed.), *English Pastoral Poetry from the Beginnings to Marvell* (London 1952), p. 150. Cf. Nicholas Breton's "A Solemn Long Enduring Passion," (Kermode, p. 169); also Sir Philip Sidney's lines beginning "My Sheepe are thoughts," from *Arcadia* (Kermode, p. 132, and W. A. Ringler [ed.], *The Poems of Sir Philip Sidney* [Oxford 1962], p. 39).

9. See C. Wendel (ed.), *Scholia in Theocritum Vetera* (Leipzig 1914), pp. 166 ff., on *Idyll* 5, lines 43c, 112–113bd, 86–87 f. A comparison with Servius on Virgil shows how much more often Virgil is allegorically explained.

10. It is difficult, in principle, to distinguish between a metaphor, on the one hand, and an asyntactic simile—"your voice is belladonna"—on the other. I am inclined to believe that where the case is doubtful, we should read the instance as an asyntactic simile, designed not to merge two separate entities under the cover of one name, but to list them side by side, correlating and separating them in one stroke.

11. J. E. Congleton, *Theories of Pastoral Poetry in England, 1684–1798* (Gainesville 1952), pp. 61, 286.

12. From *Menaphon*; cf. E. K. Chambers, *English Pastorals* (London 1895), p. 56.

13. From Sidney's "Disprayse of a Courtly Life;" cf. Kermode, *English Pastoral Poetry*, p. 142.

14. For the general subject of animal comparisons in classical literature, see E. Majer, *Mensch- und Tiervergleich in der griechischen Literatur bis zum Hellenismus* (Tuebingen 1949).

15.

πολλά τεοῦς, Ἑλένα, μεμναμέναι ὡς γαλαθηναί
ἄρνες γειναμένας ὄιος.

16. The point of the comparison is the whiteness of her skin, hence yogurt, still a favorite dish in Greece, rather than cheese. Cf. Shakespeare's "good sooth, she is / The queen of curds and cream," *The Winter's Tale*, Act 4, Scene 4. Leigh Hunt has a somewhat precious but occasionally perceptive essay entitled "An Effusion upon Cream, and a Desideratum in English Poetry," in which he suggests that Fletcher's "that meat, / Which the great god Pan doth eat" must be Pancake, that is cream. The essay includes a hymn to cream, composed by "Horace" for a Manchester newspaper in 1853: L. H. and C. W. Houtchens (edd.), *Leight Hunt's Literary Criticism* (New York 1956), pp. 528 ff.

17. *Idylls* 5.29 and 7.41. The former comparison is asyntactic, approximating to a metaphor; the latter is syntactic.

18. See H. Herter, "Bericht ueber die Literatur zur hellenistischen Dichtung seit dem Jahr 1921: ii: Apollonios von Rhodos," *JAW*, 285 (1944–1955, publ. 1956), 264, and the modern discussions cited there.

19. See *Argonautica* 3.1259 ff.; 2.88; 2.1023; 2.25; etc. etc. In most of these cases, the animal imagery is less ambitious than the manner of application. Apollonius takes traditional epic material—the prancing horse, the glowering bull—and uses it to cast a lurid light upon the novel situations of his Antihomer.

20. *Idyll* 13.62–64:

> νεβρῷ φθεγξαμένας τις ἐν οὔρεσιν ὠμοφάγος λίς
> ἐξ εὐνᾶς ἔσπευσεν ἑτοιμοτάταν ἐπὶ δαῖτα·
> Ἡρακλέης τοιοῦτος . . . .

Idyll 14.39–41:

> μάστακα δοῖσα τέκνοισιν ὑπωροφίοισι χελιδών
> ἄψορρον ταχινὰ πέτεται βίον ἄλλον ἀγείρειν·
> ὠκυτέρα . . . .

21.

> ἀλλ᾽ οὐ συμβλήτ᾽ ἐστὶ κυνόσβατος οὐδ᾽ ἀνεμώνα
> πρὸς ῥόδα, τῶν ἄνδηρα παρ᾽ αἱμασιαῖσι πεφύκει.
> οὐδὲ γὰρ οὐδ᾽ ἀκύλοις ὁρομαλίδες· αἳ μὲν ἔχοντι
> λεπτὸν ἀπὸ πρίνοιο λεπύριον, αἳ δὲ μελιχραί.

22. I use priamel to designate a series of brief statements or propositions which are felt to be based on an underlying pattern, and which usually lead up to a terminal proposition of somewhat greater weight. A catalogue, on the other hand, tends to be a series of terms rather than propositions, and usually does not exhibit terminal weighting. A third figure which is often mentioned in association with the other two, *praeteritio*, need not concern us here; pastoral shuns the suggestion that the material is too full, or too unpleasant, for the telling.

23. *Idyll* 10.30-31; *Eclogue* 2.63-65. J. Hubaux, *Le réalisme dans les Bucoliques de Virgile* (Paris 1927), p. 131, denies that Virgil here imitates Theocritus. I find this hard to accept, though I agree with Hubaux that what matters is the difference between the two passages.

24. It is worth recalling that Theocritus' crazy priamel—"crazy" in the sense of "crooked", "askew"—is anticipated by Socrates at *Phaedrus* 241D1, in the speech of the lover who pretends to be debunking love (I cite the line in Bekker's version; both it and the vulgate reading produce a hexameter): ὡς λύκοι ἄρν' ἀγαπῶσ' ὡς παῖδα φιλοῦσιν ἐρασταί. Cf. also above, Chapter Two. Here the incongruity of the comparison is obvious, and the humor unmistakable. For a later inventory on the theme of pursuit see Plutarch, *A Young Man's Guide to Poetry*, 11.30D. The bee, Plutarch writes, pursues the flower, the goat pursues the twig, the hog pursues the root, other animals pursue seeds and fruits; similarly in the reading of literature, one man harvests the fruits of history, another roots out the beauty and the arrangement of words. Plutarch's essay is moralistic and downright anti-lyrical; I suspect that the humor of the passage is entirely involuntary.

25. Note especially *Idylls* 9.7-8; a priamel on "sweet;" 9.31-32: a priamel on "dear;" 10.28-29: a sequence on "black."

26. Cf. also *Idyll* 7.76: Daphnis melted χιὼν ὥς τις. The formulation seems awkward. Is χιὼν τις a bit of snow? A snowflake? A snow drift? Whatever the correct explanation, the indefinite article helps to maintain the pastoral perspective: separative, diminutive, naive to the point of gaucherie.

27. See H. J. Rose, *The Eclogues of Vergil* (Berkeley 1942), pp. 12 and 222, note 14.

28.

> ἀνίκα πέρ τε ποτ' ὡρανὸν ἔτραχον ἵπποι
> 'Αῶ τὰν ῥοδόεσσαν ἀπ' ὠκεανοῖο φέροισαι . . . .

29. The details are given in Dorothy S. McCoy, *Tradition and Convention: A Study of Periphrasis in English Pastoral Poetry From 1557-1715* (The Hague 1965), pp. 35-36.

30. *Ibid.*, p. 96.

31. There is room for a new discussion of periphrasis in ancient poetry. The material should be tested for the contextual presence, absence, and frequency of the figure, and for its various uses: pedantry, pride of learning, delicacy, mollification, and so forth.

32. E. Dutoit, *Le thème de l'adynaton dans la poésie antique* (Paris 1936), pp. 31 ff. Cf. now also G. O. Rowe, "The *adynaton* as a Stylistic Device," *A J Phil*, 86 (1965), 387-396; he argues that the *adynaton* is, according to the ancient handbooks, not a figure but a trope, and that it belongs into the same category as the proverb.

33.

νῦν ἴα μὲν φορέοιτε βάτοι, φορέοιτε δ᾽ ἄκανθαι,
ἁ δὲ καλὰ νάρκισσος ἐπ᾽ ἀρκεύθοισι κομάσαι,
πάντα δ᾽ ἄναλλα γένοιτο, καὶ ἁ πίτυς ὄχνας ἐνείκαι,
Δάφνις ἐπεὶ θνάσκει, καὶ τὰς κύνας ὤλαφος ἕλκοι,
κῆξ ὀρέων τοὶ σκῶπες ἀηδόσι γαρύσαιντο.

34. Cf. Kermode, *English Pastoral Poetry*, p. 19; also R. Poggioli, "The Oaten Flute," *Harvard Library Bulletin*, 11.2 (1957), section ix, on the pastoral as self-appraisal of the artist and his art.

35. See M. Manitius, *Geschichte der lateinischen Literatur des Mittelalters*, Vol. I (Munich 1911), 550.

36. *Eclogue* 9 strikes capital from the absence of Menalcas, just as *Idyll* 4 takes its cue from the absence of Aegon. But while Aegon is a man of action, Menalcas is the poet. Battus and Corydon are conscious of being deprived of animal comforts; Lycidas and Moeris are conscious of being underprivileged poetically. They are memorizers rather than creators, and the brief snatches and halting delivery emanating from them makes us fellow-yearners for sustained poetic achievement. In Theocritus, singing is natural and spontaneous; in the ninth *Eclogue* it is, by implication, characterized as a special gift and a trained skill; cf. the references to Cinna and Varius (line 35). Cf. also C. Becker, "Virgils Eklogenbuch," *Hermes*, 83 (1955), 317.

37.

Stant et oves circum (nostri nec paenitet illas,
Nec te paeniteat pecoris, divine poeta).

38. allegoricos hos dicit: nec tu erubescas bucolica scribere.

39. M. R. Lefkowitz, in *HSCPh*, 67 (1963), 205–209.

40. See the passages cited by I. Troxler-Keller, *Die Dichterlandschaft des Horaz* (Heidelberg 1964), pp. 31–32.

41. V. Poeschl, *Die Hirtendichtung Virgils* (Heidelberg 1964), p. 12, note 5, cites a number of passages in which the weaving of a basket is used as an image of poetic creation. I think we must distinguish the two images, basket and garland, both for their immediate associations—after all, a basket is to contain something (cheese, or a cricket) which is likely to color the significance of the trope—ánd also for what the two images seem to imply about the craft of poetry. With the garland, the accent falls on freshness and the flush of spring; with the basket, the emphasis is on labor and off-season leisure time.

42. For this, see M. Puelma, *Lucilius und Kallimachos* (Frankfurt 1949), pp. 223 ff. and 240.

43. For the plain style, the *genus tenue*, see the references collected by Poeschl, *Die Hirtendichtung Virgils*, pp. 11–12.

44. Cf., however, Reitzenstein: the poems are *griphoi*, veiled representations of polemics between known and recognized poets.

45. E. W. Tayler, *Nature and Art in Renaissance Literature* (New York 1964), pp. 6–7. Cf also above, Chapter One.

46. Tayler, *Nature and Art*, p. 170.

47. See W. Schmid, "Tityrus christianus," *RhM*, 96 (1953), 101–165.

48. For a discussion of religious eclogues during the religious wars before and after 1570 in France, see A. Hulubei, *L'églogue en France au xvie siècle* (Paris 1938), pp. 544 ff.

49. See Congleton, *Theories of Pastoral Poetry*, pp. 172–173.

50. In his "Discourse on Pastoral Poetry," written in 1704. For other neo-classical protests against philosophy in pastoral, see N. J. Perella, "Amarilli's Dilemma: The *Pastor Fido* and Some English Authors," *Comparative Literature*, 12 (1960), 348–359.

51. The four poems may be studied in the edition of P. Fraticelli (ed.), *Dante: Opere minori*, Vol. I (Florence 1887), 405 ff.

52. W. Leonard Grant, "Early Neo-Latin Pastoral," *Phoenix*, 9 (1955), 21 ff. is frankly puzzled, not only by the obscurity of the poems, and the poets' delight in mystification, but also, in the case of Petrarch, by the faultiness of the verse. It is of some interest that Petrarch applies his artistic principle, that allegory is the heart of poetry, only to his Latin verse, and not to his poems in the vernacular (but contrast Boccaccio, whose *Ameto* is an elaborate *Schluesselgedicht*).

53. If one wishes to find the genuine pastoral spirit, unencumbered by symbolisms, in Ronsard, one has to go to his "Voyage de Tours" and other poems which are not, officially and formally, pastorals. On the other hand it should be noted that allegory may have the effect of enhancing the detachment which a good pastoral favors; see, e.g., the remarkable impersonality of Scève's *Arion*, a marine dirge with pastoral connections.

54. For the details, see M. Y. Hughes, "Virgil and Spenser," *University of California Publications in English*, 2 (1928/29), 294.

55. Cf. Poeschl, *Die Hirtendichtung Virgils*, p. 101. The equation gains in plausibility from the practice of Calpurnius, who in his *Eclogues* identifies Tityrus with Virgil, and Corydon with himself. See, however, the doubts of F. R. Hamblin, *The Development of Allegory in the Classical Pastoral* (Chicago, n.d.), p. 81: the convention of *Schluesselnamen* did not become important till after Virgil.

56. See especially L. Herrmann, *Les masques et les visages dans les Bucoliques de Virgile* (Brussels 1930); and articles by J. J. H. Savage, "The Art of the Third Eclogue of Vergil," *TAPA*, 89 (1958), 142–158; "The Cyclops, the Sibyl, and the Poet," *TAPA*, 93 (1962), 410–442; and "The Art of the Seventh Eclogue of Vergil," *TAPA*, 94 (1963), 248–267. For a more moderate approach, see L. P. Wilkinson, "Virgil and the Evictions," *Hermes*, 94 (1966), 320–324: "It must be accepted that these *Eclogues* are not straight allegories; they are Theocritean pastorals with occasional outcrops of reality."

57. For a witty summary of this type of interpretation, see G. Funaioli, "Allegorie vergiliane," *Rassegna Italiana*, 2 (1920), 167 ff.

58. R. Reitzenstein, *Epigramm und Skolion* (Giessen 1893), pp. 228 ff.

59. Carolus Wendel, *De nominibus bucolicis* (Leipzig 1900), chapter 1.

60. We should probably distinguish between *noms à clef*, on the one hand, and nicknames-of-the-moment, on the other. For the popularity of the latter in the third century BC, cf. Diogenes Laertius 10.8: Epicurus called Heraclitus *Kyketes*, Democritus *Lerocritus*, and Antidorus *Sannidorus*. I should think that Simichidas and Lycidas are likely to be epicoristics of this kind—humorous, and easily identified.

61. D. C. Allen, *Image and Meaning* (Baltimore 1960), p. 92.

62. Unfortunately Allen adds: "The nymph has brooded so much over losing her lover that she has enlarged the token of love into a life symbol." Why symbol? And in what sense? Cf. the warning of Tayler, *Nature and Art*, p. 148: "We are not dealing with one-to-one allegory but a technique of allusion almost random in nature."

63. A. S. P. Woodhouse, "Milton's Pastoral Monodies," *Studies Norwood* (Toronto 1952), p. 262.

64. R. Tuve, *Images and Themes in Five Poems by Milton* (Harvard 1957), pp. 109–110. I accept Miss Tuve's term, without being at all certain that I am doing justice to what she intends by it.

65. C. W. Truesdale, "English Pastoral Verse from Spenser to Marvell" (unpublished Ph.D. dissertation, University of Washington, 1956), p. 223, citing Empson. The latter, in *Some Versions of Pastoral* (Norfolk 1950), p. 12, makes things too simple for himself when he argues that this kind of incongruity "no doubt makes the characters unreal but not the feelings expressed or even the situation described." It is difficult to think of unreal characters with real feelings, even on the analogy of gardens and toads.

66. Cf. W. W. Greg, *Pastoral Poetry and Pastoral Drama* (London 1906), p. 18: Vergilius abscondit sub cortice nonnullos sensus.

67. Cf. Servius on *Eclogue* 9.23: Theocriti sunt versus, verbum ad verbum translati, sed tamen Vergilii negotium continentes: nam allegoricos imperat. . . .

68. To avoid misunderstanding, I hasten to disassociate myself from the conjectures of the Cambridge ritualists and their successors. A fair specimen is that of H. H. O. Chalk, "Eros and the Lesbian Pastorals of Longos," *JHS*, 80 (1960), 32–51. For a vigorous attack on the foundations of the thinking of the Cambridge school, see now J. Fontenrose, "The Ritual Theory of Myth," *Folklore Studies*, 18 (Berkeley 1966).

Index

The index does not include material cited in the Notes. Italicized page references indicate quotations from the poets.

Libanius: 196
Livy: 236
locus amoenus: *see* pleasance
locus inclusus: 202
locus uberrimus: 190–1
Lodge, Thomas: *69*, 251, 267
Longinus: 5, 52
Longus, *Daphnis and Chloe*: 8, 9, 40, 47, 135, 241
love: 77–85, 128–9, 146, 151, 160–1, 185, 201–3
Lovejoy, Arthur O.: 45, 54
Lucian: 89
Lucretius: 32, 44, 54, *81*, 148, 185, *217–18*, 220, 225, 243
Lycophron: 39, *234*, 276
Lycophronides: 39
Lynen, John F.: 250–1
lyric: 60–62, 95
Lysias: 50

Mallarmé, Stéphane: 12, *90–1*
Manilius: 5
Mantuan (Baptista Spagnuoli): 26, 165, 207, 211, 253, 273; *Ecl. One*: 27; *Ecl. Two*: 275; *Ecl. Five*: 27, *177*; *Ecl. Six*: 25; *Ecl. Eight*: 25, 127, 165; *Ecl. Nine*: 274; *Ecl. Ten*: 6
Marino, Giovanni Battista: 13
Marlowe, Christopher: 9, *96–7*
Marot, Clément: 18, 93, 111, 113, 171, 184, 197, 244, 271, 275
Marvell, Andrew: 17, 25, 136, 228, 278, 281; "Clorinda and Damon": *78*, *244*; "The Garden": *92*, 143–4, 196, 205; "The Mower Against Gardens": *196*; "The Nymph Complaining for the Death of her Faun": 139, 277; "Upon Appleton House": 23, 207
maxims: *see* proverbs
Medici, Lorenzo de': 18
melancholy: 224–31

Meleager of Gadara: 134, 193, 197, 200
Menander: 68, 105, 106, 239
messages cut into trees: 202–3
metaphors: 247–51
Miles, Josephine: 205
Milton, John: 205, 278; "Arcades": 145; "Comus": 180; "Epitaphium Damonis": 118, 133, 199, 277; "Il Penseroso": *227–8*; "L'Allegro": 227–8; "Lycidas": 15, 51, 56, 59, 62–3, 64, 93, 107, 111, 113, *116–17*, 117–18, 119, *150*, 179, 205, 211, 248, 266, *267–8*, *269*, 272, 277; *Paradise Lost*: 9, 125, 131, *145*, 180, 190, *224*
Minturno, Antonio Sebastiano: 4, 5
Mnasalcas: 77
Mnaseas: 233
Modoin of Autun: 123, 268
Montaigne, Michel Eyquem de: 223
Montemayor, Jorge de: 158, 184, 231, 273
Monteverdi, Claudio: 231
mood: 14–15
moral argument: 108–9, 144; *see also* anatomy
More, Paul Elmer: 179
Moschus: *114–15*, *132*, 248, 263
music: 84–5, *132–5*, 145–67, 185–6, 242–3
mystification: 274–5
mythology: 263

naiveté: 54–60, and *passim*.
names, unintroduced: 107
nature: 18–20, 46, 119–20, 179–86, 249, 262
Nemesianus: 83, 123, 136, 149, 186, 233
noon hour: 76–7, 88–9, 91
nouveau roman: 45–6, 247–8

old age vs. youth: 57–59
Old Comedy: 208–9, 240, 262